Death is

LIGHTER THAN A FEATHER

Also by David Westheimer:

- *Summer on the Water*
- *The Magic Fallacy*
- *Watching Out for Dulie*
- *This Time Next Year*
- *Von Ryan's Express*
- *My Sweet Charlie*
- *Song of the Young Sentry*
- *Over the Edge*
- *Going Public*
- *The Olmec Head*
- *The Avila Gold*
- *Von Ryan's Return*
- *Rider on the Wind*
- *Sitting It Out*

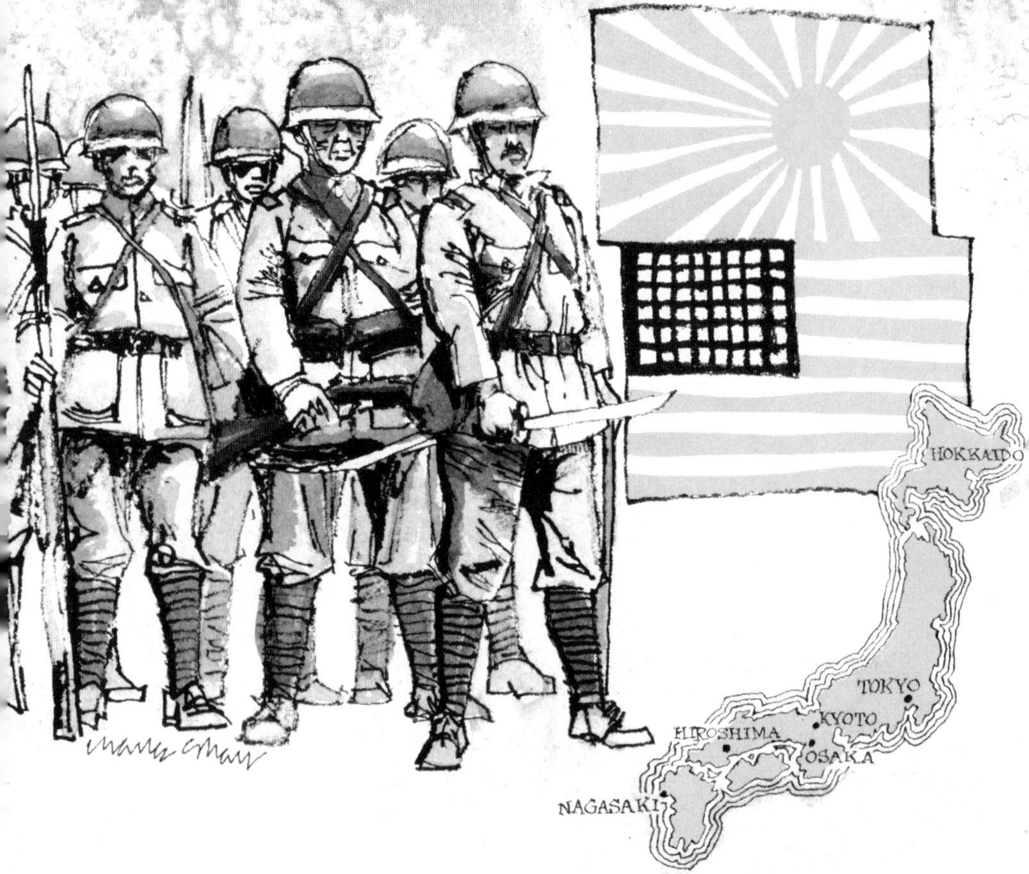

Death is LIGHTER than a FEATHER

David Westheimer
Author of Von Ryan's Express

Afterword by John Ray Skates

University of North Texas Press

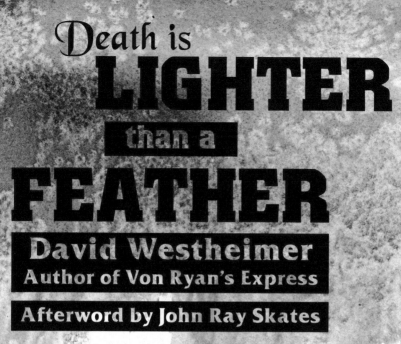

First published in 1971

Printed in the United States of America

94 95 96 97 98 99 6 5 4 3 2 1

Permissions:
University of North Texas Press
P. O. Box 13856
Denton, Texas 76203

The paper in this book meets the minimum requirements of the American National Standard for Permanence of paper for Printed Library Materials, Z39.48.1984.

Library of Congress
Cataloging-in-Publication Data

Westheimer, David.
[Lighter than a feather]
Death is lighter than a feather : a novel / by David Westheimer; afterword by John Ray Skates.
p. cm.
Originally published: Lighter than a feather. Boston : Little, Brown, [1971]
ISBN 0-929398-90-4
1. World War, 1939–1945—Fiction. I. Title.
PS3573.E88L54 1994
813'.54—dc20 94-43781
CIP

For
Kameo Abe
Abraham Rothberg
Marvin Jack Teitelbaum

". . . be resolved that duty is heavier than a mountain,
while death is lighter than a feather."

First Precept of the Imperial Rescript
to Soldiers and Sailors

Author's Note

The characters and incidents of *Death Is Lighter than a Feather* are fictional. Operation Olympic, the planned invasion of Japan, and Ketsu-Go, the planned Japanese defense, are not. The events described in the Prologue are historically accurate until August 6, after which, with the elimination of the atom bomb, the Prologue becomes a projection of then-existing American and Japanese plans.

Prologue

On May 25, 1945, while American and Japanese forces on Okinawa were locked in one of the Pacific war's most bitter struggles, the U.S. Joint Chiefs of Staff in Washington sent out plans for an amphibious invasion dwarfing this encounter. It was but a preliminary to another and greater assault in a master plan: "The Strategic Plan for Operations in the Japanese Archipelago."

Code name: Downfall.

Downfall would end the war and subjugate Japan with two invasions of the enemy's homeland. The first, Operation Olympic, would seize the tip of Kyushu, southernmost of the four main islands of Japan, as a base from which to mount the second, Operation Coronet. The armies of Coronet, including divisions to be brought from conquered Europe and British Commonwealth as well as American troops, would strike directly against the heart of the nation, the Tokyo area of Honshu island.

Target date for Olympic was November 1, 1945; for Coronet, March 1, 1946.

Downfall was the controversial outgrowth of the sometimes opportunistic landings which had at last brought the Allies within fighter range of the Japanese homeland. U.S. troops were already closing in on Manila in the Philippines when the Allied Combined Chiefs of Staff first developed the plan at the Argonaut Conference on Malta in the early days of February, 1945. It was not until April 3, when the invasion of Okinawa had already begun, that General of the Army Douglas MacArthur, Fleet Admiral Chester W. Nimitz and the Army Air Forces' General Henry H. Arnold were instructed to make ready for the campaign against Japan itself.

Late in the war there were still differences of opinion at high levels about the conduct and direction of the final thrust. Many Navy strategists wished to isolate Japan from the Asiatic mainland before launching an invasion, and contemplated preliminary landings on Formosa, Korea or the east coast of China. Most Army strategists advocated attacking the home islands as quickly as possible without wasting time and resources on intermediate objectives. There was also support for a third strategy: not to invade at all but to complete the encirclement of Japan and force capitulation through blockade and bombardment.

There were two chief arguments for preliminary landings in China and elsewhere. They would provide new bases from which to bomb the home islands, reducing Japan's ability to resist invasion, and they would block the movement of reinforcements and supplies from the mainland. General MacArthur opposed this course on the grounds it would send the weight of the Allied advance off on a tangent and so spread Allied strength over a vast expanse of the Pacific that no attack on Japan could be mounted without troops from Europe. Further, he believed the Allies could become so enmeshed in China that even more prohibitive delays might result.

The idea of battering Japan into submission from the sea and air was especially attractive because it offered hope of victory without direct and costly confrontation with the enemy's still powerful ground armies. MacArthur opposed this course as well. He was not convinced airpower alone could defeat Japan. In any case, to rely solely on blockade and bombardment would deny the Allies full use of their enormous military resources and might prolong the war indefinitely.

MacArthur advanced strong arguments for moving expeditiously against the home islands, and in two separate operations. To do so would give the Allies use of their ground forces as well as naval and airpower while denying the enemy time to strengthen homeland defenses. With Tokyo as the prime target, a foothold on Kyushu would place enormous airpower close to the final objective and "would place maximum pressure of our combined forces against the enemy, which might well force a surrender earlier than anticipated."

The final argument may have been the persuasive one. In most minds, the specter of staggering losses overshadowed other considerations. The final decision to invade or not to invade rested upon President Harry S. Truman and the price concerned him gravely. As late as the final week in July, with Japan already reeling, U.S. Army Chief of Staff George C. Marshall told the President at Potsdam that Downfall would cost a minimum of a quarter-million casualties and possibly a million. General of the Army Dwight D. Eisenhower, Chief of Naval Operations Ernest J. King and Admiral William D. Leahy, the President's personal representative on the Joint Chiefs of Staff, who were present, agreed. The forecasts for Olympic alone, however, were less forbidding. A May staff study had estimated 49,000 casualties. In June, the War Department had concluded that casualties for the first thirty days on Kyushu, presumably the critical period, would be no more than 31,000.

Though Operation Olympic had wide support and was approved by President Truman and the Joint Chiefs of Staff, there were those who remained unconvinced that victory would be achieved only by invasion. Among them were Admiral Leahy, who believed casualties would be much higher than projected, Secretary of War Henry L. Stimson, and acting Secretary of State Joseph C. Grew, the former U.S. ambassador to Japan. They believed that Japan might be induced to capitulate through a combination of military, political and psychological moves and that use of military force alone might serve to unify a possibly divided people and goad the enemy to a higher level of resistance.

Operation Olympic evolved uninfluenced by an immense program which, if successful, might have rendered invasion unnecessary. Vast resources were being expended on the Manhattan Project, an attempt to fashion a weapon employing the devastating force of nuclear reaction in uranium. Despite its scope, the project was cloaked in such secrecy that many top military and government leaders, including the Pacific commanders who planned Olympic, were unaware of its purpose. Even had General MacArthur and those who shared his convictions been aware of the attempt to construct an atom bomb it probably would not have altered materially the decision to invade. There was as yet no assurance the project would be successful and the device would not even be ready for testing before the summer of 1946. The possibility of having so awesome a weapon in the arsenal would not remove a basic objection to the conquest of Japan by bombing alone: that such a strategy might prolong the war indefinitely.

Soviet assistance was not considered important to the success of Downfall although in earlier years Russian participation in the Pacific war had been considered vital to the eventual subjugation of Japan. U.S. intelligence estimated Japanese ground strength in Korea, China and Manchuria at two million men, including the million-man Kwantung Army, considered the enemy's best. And Japan relied heavily upon Manchurian factories, natural resources and agriculture. A Soviet invasion of Manchuria was believed essential to prevent the transfer of strong ground forces to the homeland and to choke off the flow of supplies upon which the Japanese economy and war machine depended in considerable measure. As the war continued, however, the value of Soviet intervention diminished. Although Japan's mainland forces continued in being, the destruction of her naval and air forces and Allied mastery of sea and air isolated them from the home islands. By the summer of 1945, with Japan in a state of siege, most American leaders would have preferred that the Soviet Union did not enter the Pacific war. Nevertheless, at the July conference in Potsdam, confidently code-named Terminal, the Allies persisted in encouraging Soviet intervention. Since Stalin could wait until his allies had defeated Japan and still seize what he wished, it was desirable that the Soviet Union commit its armies sooner rather than later. It was also possible that the psychological effect of a Soviet onslaught combined with an invasion of Kyushu would hasten Japan's collapse.

While the United States was planning the invasion of Kyushu and arranging the disposition of Japanese territory with its allies, the Japanese Imperial General Staff was feverishly planning the defense of the homeland. The basic defense plan, Army Directive Number 2438, "Outline of the Preparations for the Ketsu-Go Operation," was sent to commanders on April 8, only five days after U.S. commanders were instructed to begin preparing Operation Olympic.

"Ketsu" derived from "kessen," meaning "a decisive battle." "Go" means "number." Ketsu-Go divided the homeland and Korea into seven military districts and the forces defending them into two general armies. First General Army, with headquarters in Tokyo, was to defend eastern Japan. Second General Army, headquartered in Hiroshima, would defend western Japan, including Kyushu. To defend the home islands, the forces already on hand were to be augmented by divisions from the Kwantung Army and numerous new units mobilized from the population. Mobilization, deployment and the construction of defensive works was to begin immediately.

Soviet intentions were of graver concern to the Japanese than to the Allies. As Soviet intervention grew progressively less significant to the Allies, it loomed ever larger to the Japanese. The Japanese staff knew, as the Americans did not, that the Kwantung Army could no longer be relied upon to blunt a Soviet thrust into Manchuria. Its best divisions had been fed into the Pacific island campaigns and had been replaced by poorly trained and equipped recruits.

Before the invasion of Okinawa, the Allied strategy most feared by many Japanese leaders was that of prolonged siege. Japan might then be ingloriously starved, battered, and burned into submission without an opportunity to employ its sizable army. After the fall of Okinawa in June, the same planners feared the Americans might move immediately against Kyushu and win a foothold with comparative ease before its defenses were established.

During much of early 1945 the Japanese high command played a desperate guessing game with the relentless enemy. Lacking the forces to guard all approaches, the Imperial General Staff altered and shifted its defenses in anticipation of Allied moves as estimates of enemy intentions changed, and great pains were taken not to provoke the Soviet Union into invading Manchuria even though it meant enduring a series of local incursions.

A vast underground headquarters was dug a hundred miles northwest of Tokyo at Matsushiro in an area known as the Japanese Alps, and plans were made to set up a provisional imperial palace at Nagano City, a few miles away, if a last-ditch stand proved necessary. And by midsummer the momentous decision had been reached to stake everything on the defense of Kyushu, Ketsu-Go Area Number 6, at the expense of all others except Ketsu-Go Area Number 3, which contained Tokyo.

About the same time as the military was issuing its plan for an all-out defense of the homeland, a new cabinet was being formed which many observers believed to be a peace cabinet. On April 7, the day before the Ketsu-Go plan went out, Admiral Baron Kantaro Suzuki, a distinguished old warrior of seventy-seven, became prime minister of Japan. Among his supporters was Marquis Koichi Kido, Lord Keeper of the Privy Seal. Lord Kido, who was anxious to bring the war to an end, had the ear and the confidence of Emperor Hirohito.

Admiral Suzuki chose for his foreign minister Shigenori Togo, former ambassador to both Germany and Russia. Togo shared the Privy Seal's conviction that Japan must make peace as best it could and as quickly as possible. Suzuki inherited another peace-minded minister, Admiral Mitsumasa Yonai, from his predecessor. Yonai, the Navy minister, had thought Japan's position hopeless from the outset of the Pacific war and as far back as September, 1944, had directed a subordinate to make a secret study of ways to end it.

The premier and the two ministers were members of the government's most powerful organ, the Saiko Senso Shido Kaigi, the Supreme Council for the Direction of the War. The Supreme Council had three other members, the war minister and the Chiefs of Staff of the Army and Navy. In the Suzuki cabinet these were General Korechika Anami, General Yoshijiro Umezu and Admiral Soemu Toyoda, all dedicated to continued prosecution of the war.

Despite the stance of such men as Lord Kido, Togo and Yonai, and the unspoken sympathies of the Emperor himself, there were few Japanese even in the highest circles who dared speak openly of surrender. The Army, symbol of uncompromising resistance, was still the most powerful force in Japan's internal affairs. In its military police corps, the Kempei Tai, the Army had the means to enforce its views at all levels. Only a few days after the formation of the new cabinet, a former ambassador to England was among hundreds arrested by the military police on suspicion of favoring ending the war. There was also within the Army an unpredictable suppressive force lacking the quasi-legality of the Kempei Tai but nonetheless to be feared. Since the Army's ascendancy in the early thirties, hotheaded junior officers had compiled a bloody history of intimidation and assassination, sometimes with the tacit consent of their superiors and more often than not going unpunished. Despite the notoriously harsh discipline of the Army in military situations, in matters of policy and political action young officers had inordinate latitude and influence. There was even a name for this: "gekokujo," rule by juniors. Admiral Suzuki himself had been wounded by such officers in an attempt on his life in February, 1936.

The week of Suzuki's appointment to the premiership was filled with portents of disaster. On April 1 the Americans invaded Okinawa, the last bastion of Japan's inner defensive ring. Six days later the super-battleship *Yamato* was sunk attempting to close with the invasion fleet, writing an end to the Japanese Navy. Between those two events was another with chilling implications. On April 5 the Soviet Union announced it would not renew its neutrality pact with Japan when the five-year agreement expired in 1946.

Despite that ominous development, the Suzuki government in May began making secret overtures to the Soviet Union to enlist its aid in peace negotiations with the United States. In Tokyo, Koki Hirota, a former premier, was instructed to sound out the Russian ambassador, Jacob Malik, while the Japanese ambassador to Moscow, Naotake Sato, explored other channels in the Soviet Union. This was the first official move toward peace but it was not the first time concerned Japanese had attempted to extricate their country from its hopeless situation. Among the most active had been Prince Fumimaro Konoye, an ex-premier who in 1942 had been prepared to meet with President Franklin D. Roosevelt in the Pacific to attempt to avert hostilities. In September, 1944, the managing director of the newspaper *Asahi* came to the Swedish minister to Japan with a proposal from Prince Konoye that Great Britain be approached through Swedish channels.

While the Japanese government was attempting to approach the United States through the Soviet Union, two groups acting independently and unofficially were trying to make direct contact through the U.S. Office of Strategic Services in Switzerland. One group was headed by Commander Yoshiro Fujimura, Japanese naval attaché in Berne, the other by the Japanese military attaché in Basel, Lieutenant General Seigo Okamoto. Fujimura made his first contact in April, General Okamoto somewhat later. The Fujimura group acted through Dr. Friedrich Hack, a German with strong Japanese ties, and the Okamoto group through a Swedish adviser to the Bank of International Settlements in Basel. The latter had a meeting with Allen Dulles, OSS director, in Wiesbaden, Germany. The OSS dealt cautiously with both cliques since neither had official status.

All unofficial peace proposals were doomed to fail because they did not have the weight of the Japanese government behind them. And even the official overtures faced an insurmountable barrier. The Japanese refused to consider unconditional surrender as the price of peace and the Allies were pledged to accept nothing less. The United States was not unaware that powerful elements in Japan wanted peace and might be helpful in achieving it if given assurance that unconditional surrender did not mean the end of imperial rule or Japan's extinction as a nation. Out of this awareness came Operation I-45, designed to accomplish through persuasion what the planners of Downfall intended to achieve by force.

The instrument of the operation was Navy Captain Ellis M. Zacharias, an intelligence officer who had been assigned to prolonged shore duty in Japan before the war to study its language and people. Captain Zacharias set I-45 in motion on May 8 with a broadcast of President Truman's announcement of Germany's capitulation. As an official spokesman of the U.S. government he addressed himself to "responsible and thinking Japanese" and particularly to old friends, including Premier Suzuki, Navy Minister Yonai and Prince Takamatsu, brother to the Emperor. This and subsequent broadcasts elicited cautious, encouraging response, but not enough to alter materially the rush of events.

The Japanese government and military were taking stock. Soon after taking office, Premier Suzuki directed a thorough study of the nation's resources and capabilities. At the same time, the Army was drafting a "Basic General Outline on Future War Direction Policy" to guide Imperial General Headquarters and the government. Both surveys proved bleak in outlook. The government study indicated that Japan could not continue the war because of battle losses, limited production capacity and shortages of food and material. The Army's War Direction Policy limited the war objectives to preservation of the homeland and the national polity but declared that Japan must fight to the end for these two minimum objectives.

The War Direction Policy was adopted but the government report on the national posture was modified by including the statement: ". . . strong measures must be taken to fully arouse the fighting spirit of the people, especially their traditional spirit of loyalty, and build up at least a minimum fighting power necessary for the prosecution of the war. . . ." The War Direction Policy and the modified report were presented to the Emperor at an Imperial Conference on June 8. They were presented for his information, not his decision. Decisions were made by the government. Traditionally the government did not approach the throne with any matter until it had already been decided by unanimous agreement. The Emperor then had two choices. He could give his approval or he could remain silent. On June 8 the Emperor remained silent.

Thus, though Emperor Hirohito wished peace, as did his foreign minister and Navy minister, and perhaps his premier, the Imperial Conference of June 8 appeared to indicate that the throne, the government and the military were unanimously in agreement to "build up at least the minimum fighting power necessary for the prosecution of the war."

Two weeks later the Emperor took more positive but certainly not definitive action. He called the Supreme Council to an Imperial Conference and urged its members to consider alternatives to continuing the war. The Supreme Council responded by agreeing unanimously to redouble efforts to obtain a negotiated peace through the good offices of the Soviet Union.

Japan knew the Potsdam Conference was in the offing and it was deemed imperative to enlist Soviet aid before Stalin met with President Truman and Prime Minister Winston Churchill. When no progress was made through the existing channels it became obvious that a more direct and candid approach must be made without delay. Hirohito himself decided to send Prince Konoye to Moscow as a special envoy bearing the Emperor's personal message. Despite the most strenuous efforts, Japan's ambassador to Moscow could not obtain Soviet agreement to receive Konoye, and the Potsdam Conference began July 16 with nothing having been accomplished.

President Truman issued the Potsdam Proclamation from Berlin the night of July 26. The Allies had at last directed themselves to the people and government of Japan in a formal statement of demands and intentions.

The proclamation was an ultimatum warning Japan to surrender or suffer a fate worse than Germany's. Although it stated: "We do not intend that the Japanese be enslaved as a race or destroyed as a nation," it demanded Allied occupation of Japan and made no mention of the Emperor or the system of imperial rule. The thirteen-point document concluded: "We call upon the government of Japan to proclaim now the unconditional surrender of all Japanese armed forces. . . . The alternative for Japan is prompt and utter destruction."

On its face, the Potsdam Proclamation appeared to provide Japan's leaders with the answer to the question they had been debating so urgently: how to bring the war to an end. Far from providing them with a common base for a decision, however, it served rather to polarize their differences. They disagreed not only over its exact meaning but also over how to reply to it, if at all, and how much of the text, if any, should be released to the public. And in failing to mention the Emperor specifically, the proclamation provided ammunition for both peace and war factions. Those advocating surrender interpreted the omission as an indication the Emperor's status would be preserved. Those wanting to fight on thought it an implied threat to imperial rule and to the very existence of the Japanese nation. In the Supreme Council, Foreign Minister Togo stood at one extreme and War Minister Anami at the other. Togo believed the ultimatum hinted at terms short of absolute unconditional surrender and that it should not be rejected out of hand. General Anami advocated a vigorous negative reply. Premier Suzuki, who often in the past had been swayed by opposing views to the despair of almost everyone, this time leaned in the foreign minister's direction.

Meetings of the Supreme Council and the full cabinet the day after the proclamation produced an uneasy compromise largely influenced by Togo. For the moment the government would make no reply, continue its overtures to the Soviet Union, and permit the publication of a carefully expurgated version of the proclamation without editorial comment and no statement of the government's position. Premier Suzuki made a catastrophic choice of words in announcing the decision to withhold reply. The venerable admiral said the government would "mokusatsu" the proclamation. Mokusatsu had several meanings, one of which was "remain in a wise and masterly inactivity." But it also meant "treat it with silent contempt." Disastrously for Japan and costly for its enemies, it was the meaning implying intransigence which was pounced upon by next morning's Japanese newspapers.

Even this possibly erroneous interpretation was not strong enough for War Minister Anami and the Army and Navy Chiefs of Staff. They demanded an even more positive denunciation of the ultimatum. Of the military leaders on the Supreme Council, only Navy Minister Yonai, as always, spoke out for moderation.

The prime minister gave Anami almost exactly what he wanted at a July 28 press conference called to discuss the Potsdam Proclamation. With characteristic inconsistency he "clarified" the situation by explaining, "The government does not regard it as a thing of any great value. The government will just mokusatsu it. We will press forward resolutely to carry the war to a successful conclusion."

So, even as Ambassador Sato in Moscow was trying desperately, and in his own opinion hopelessly, to obtain Soviet acceptance of a peace envoy, his countrymen were being informed the nation would fight on. And while Stalin was telling the Allies of increasingly explicit Japanese peace feelers at the still continuing Potsdam Conference, U.S. radio monitors were reporting Japan's contemptuous rebuttal to their ultimatum. Both Japanese and American moderates had been dealt a stunning blow.

The Potsdam Conference ended August 2 with no apparent change in Japan's determination to keep fighting. In Moscow, Ambassador Sato waited without hope for a crumb of encouragement from the Soviet Union. In Tokyo, Japan's leaders awaited word from Sato or some hint from the Allies that unconditional surrender did not really mean unconditional and that the throne would remain inviolate.

In the first days of August the Japanese government seemed almost to cease functioning. The cabinet, the Supreme Council and the Imperial Household waited with diminishing hopes for Soviet response to the Japanese ambassador's urgent suit. The Supreme Council seemed more a debating society than the nation's top policy-maker. Its members wrangled endlessly in a three-to-three deadlock, with the premier, the foreign minister and the Navy minister arguing for peace, the war minister and the Army and Navy chiefs for war. From his influential position at the imperial elbow, Lord Kido urged an end to Japan's agony. The Emperor also wanted peace, but though he was titular leader of the nation and his word was divine command, he was a prisoner of tradition. The Emperor did not make state decisions.

Though it appeared that even now an Allied clarification of the Emperor's status after surrender would make peace negotiations possible, clarification never came. Most American leaders believed, and with some justification, that any direct encouraging reference to the Emperor's future would be considered a sign of weakness by the Japanese. Even if this were not so, the temper of the American public could not be ignored. For more than three years the American people had been promised total victory and U.S. propaganda had made no distinction between Hirohito and the militarists responsible for Pearl Harbor and the Bataan Death March. To accept anything less than unconditional surrender might be interpreted as defaulting on a solemn pledge, if not as outright betrayal. Instead of guaranteeing the Emperor's status, the Allies responded to Tokyo's enigmatic silence with increased military and psychological pressure. Prowling task forces shelled the coasts and swarms of planes attacked cities throughout the nation. Leaflets giving the complete text of the Potsdam Proclamation were dropped by the thousands to counter the Japanese government's expurgated published version. From Manila and Okinawa the air was filled with broadcasts informing the Japanese populace of the enormity of the defeat which had been concealed from it and urging the people to assert and save themselves.

The Japanese military did not share the government's inactivity. Defense plans were refined and set in motion. Work continued on the fortification of Kyushu and vulnerable areas of the mainland. If, despite ominous reports from Manchuria and Soviet evasiveness in Moscow, the government still entertained hopes of Russian intercession, the Imperial General Staff had no such illusions.

For months observers had been reporting continuous and increasing movement of troops and material toward Manchuria on the Trans-Siberian railroad. By the first days of August the Soviet Union had massed a force of a million and half men, 5,500 tanks and self-propelled guns, 27,000 cannon and mortars and 5,000 combat aircraft on the borders of Manchuria. The Japanese estimate of the buildup was painfully accurate, as was the assumption that this mighty host had not been assembled for self-defense. In Manchuria, as in the homeland, Japanese strategists augmented their armies with fresh manpower levies and shuffled units about in hopes of concentrating the greatest strength in the most likely areas of attack. To strengthen the debilitated Kwantung Army, divisions were transferred from China and a quarter-million Japanese residents of Manchuria were called up for combat duty. Many of the existing units were ill-equipped. The new levies often lacked even such minimal needs as rifles and uniforms. Imperial General Headquarters called this "root-and-all" mobilization. The recruits, many of whom had previously been considered unfit for service, had their own name for the new units. "Gisei-butai"—victim units.

There was little hope the Japanese armies could withstand for long the Soviet offensive expected in late summer or early fall by Imperial General Headquarters. Plans were therefore prepared to fight delaying actions and withdraw into a redoubt area between southeastern Manchuria and northern Korea where the terrain lent itself to guerrilla tactics. In anticipation of this, a command post was constructed secretly in the heart of the redoubt.

While Japanese soldiers were digging in for a last-ditch defense against Soviet and American invaders and the government engaged in endless and vain debates, the Japanese people were enduring ever increasing hardships. By August more than a quarter-million civilians had died in air raids. Almost half of them had died in a single raid, Operation Meetinghouse, the March 9–10 low-level incendiary attack on Tokyo by General Curtis LeMay's B-29 bombers. Meetinghouse killed 100,000 and destroyed fifteen square miles of the city. Another half-million were injured and eight million left homeless by this and other air attacks. Twenty-five million Japanese were evacuated from target areas, disrupting not only their own lives but also the lives of those among whom they were crowded. The refugees bore witness to the terrors of bombing for those who had never endured an attack. Many who had not been bombed looked for solace in naive, hopeful rumors. It was widely believed, for example, that Kyoto would remain inviolate because General MacArthur's mother was said to be buried there. The more ignorant or superstitious, or perhaps the more desperate, had their own remedies for personal safety. Though Western attire was unpopular, wearing it protected one from air attack, as did rubbing an onion on one's head.

Though aerial bombardment was widespread and fearfully destructive, there existed a less dramatic but greater threat to the population. Japan was running out of food. In July the daily ration of rice, which made up the bulk of Japanese diet, had to be reduced to two hundred ninety-four grams, about one and a half cupfuls. In the cities few Japanese received the full allowance and even then it was usually mixed with less palatable grain, sometimes even with an edible weed used in better times as chicken feed. Some rice was available on the black market but at prices a hundred times greater than before the war. The supply of fish, by far the most important animal food product, was half that of prewar years.

The future promised graver and disastrous shortages. The rice crop was expected to be the worst in forty-six years. By November 1, which by coincidence was the beginning of the 1946 rice year as well as X-Day for Operation Olympic, existing stocks would provide only four days' issue of the stringent July ration. With the Allies controlling Japanese waters there would be less fish. Loss of producing areas and the Allied blockade had already reduced to a trickle the food imports on which the nation depended so greatly, and could be expected to shut them off entirely.

In August there was as yet no actual starvation, but hunger as much as bombing rent the fabric of everyday life and competition for food threatened the solidarity of the people. The housewife's day centered on getting enough food for the day's needs. City dwellers almost without exception were steadily losing weight while thus far the rural population was in general better off physically than before the war. Townspeople made furtive trips to the country to bargain illegally for food with farmers who often would not accept the depreciating yen and demanded clothing or other valuables.

Food was the most pressing but not the only shortage. The military had stocks of drugs and medical supplies but those available to civilians had diminished by half. There was so little fuel, city dwellers stole out by night to fell ornamental trees and dismantle wooden structures. Cloth and paper almost vanished from the civilian economy. Soap was so scarce it brought two hundred times the official price on the black market.

For the millions in the cities, life was drab, tedious and usually exhausting. The urban population suffered from a general low-level malnutrition and from physical and mental fatigue brought on by the food shortage, long hours of work, lack of sleep and recreation, the large and small harassments of daily living, anxiety and the disruption of life patterns. The medical name for the condition was war edema. It was more commonly known as war sickness.

The plight of the citizenry moved the nation's leaders to positive action no more than the increasing weight of American attacks and the mounting tension in Manchuria. The government continued to await word from Moscow.

The waiting ended on August 22 while a typhoon lashed Tokyo. At 5 P.M. Moscow time, 11 P.M. Tokyo time, Ambassador Sato was at last granted the interview with Soviet Foreign Minister V. M. Molotov he had been so urgently pursuing, and Japan had at last a positive reply to its peace gestures. Molotov read aloud the Soviet Union's declaration of war. At almost the same time, a minute after midnight in Tokyo, the Soviet armies poised along the border swept into Manchuria from the Transbaikal front in the west, the First Far Eastern Front in the east and the Second Far Eastern Front in the north.

The Soviet attack awakened Japan's leaders from their trancelike inactivity. For Lord Kido, Foreign Minister Togo, Navy Minister Yonai and other realists, there could be but one response to this latest calamity. Japan must bow to the ultimatum laid down at Potsdam, asking only for an interpretation of "unconditional" surrender which would leave some hope of preserving the Emperor. Though the Soviet onslaught confirmed the hopelessness of Japan's situation, it failed to daunt War Minister Anami and others who infinitely preferred an honorable death in the samurai tradition to the unthinkable disgrace of surrender. To warriors of Anami's mettle, and to fantasists who still dreamed of victory, the new blow was not so much a disaster as a call to display "Yamato Damashii," the spirit of the Divine Race.

Amid confusing but ominous reports from the new battlefront, the Supreme Council met on the morning of August 23 to chart a course of action. The foreign minister and the Navy minister, supported for the moment by the premier, urged that representations be made immediately to Switzerland and Sweden as a preliminary to direct peace negotiations with the Allies. Japan would request but one concession, that the Allies make a positive statement on the Emperor's future. General Anami, supported by the Army and Navy chiefs, demanded three additional concessions be included in the minimum acceptable terms. Japan must be allowed to disarm its own troops and try its own war criminals, and must not be occupied. Anami refused to alter his stand despite Togo's blunt reminder that Japan was in no position to demand anything. The Supreme Council was still deadlocked when the full cabinet met next day. Though the Supreme Council wielded the greater power, the cabinet alone had constitutional authority to approve a surrender. The cabinet moved the government no closer to compromise. Four ministers supported Togo's proposal, four Anami's and six ranged themselves between the two extremes.

The peace and war factions continued to argue the nation's fate while Soviet forces made deep penetrations into Manchuria, crossed into Japanese Sakhalin and landed on the coast of northern Korea. While the government wrangled in official session there was intense activity behind the scenes. The foreign minister met privately with the Privy Seal, seeking a means of bringing to bear the potentially decisive influence of the throne. The Emperor wished to accept the Allied ultimatum even without assurance of his personal safety and an expression of the imperial will might be all that was needed to end the war. But ancient and honored tradition created procedural problems which must be overcome. Moreover, it was necessary to move with utmost circumspection to avoid provoking the militarists into bloody counteraction.

The caution of the peace advocates was well advised. While they intrigued for surrender, others were plotting to suppress all opposition to continued resistance. Unknown even to General Anami, a group of young officers had weeks earlier begun discussing ways of preserving Japan from the traitors and defeatists bent on delivering the nation into the hands of the enemy. None was of high rank but some had positions of importance on the Army staff. All preferred death to surrender. They were scattered throughout key sections of the cavernous War Ministry on Tokyo's Ichigaya Heights and included General Anami's brother-in-law, Lieutenant Colonel Masahiko Takeshita, and a high-strung, desperate young major, Tatsuya Senda. By the time the Soviet attack prompted the foreign minister and Lord Kido to press for surrender negotiations and it appeared the peace faction might prevail, they had begun meeting secretly in a War Ministry air raid shelter. The plotters counted on Colonel Takeshita to enlist the war minister's support. Takeshita, though no less determined than the fanatical Major Senda, envisioned an orderly and possibly bloodless take-over by the military. General Anami was the key. The war minister had only to resign from the cabinet to demolish the apparatus of surrender.

The cabinet could not itself appoint a new war minister, nor could the Emperor. The war minister had to be a general on the active list and, more importantly, must be approved by Army Headquarters. By withholding approval the Army could bring down the government and prevent the formation of a cabinet not to its liking. Without a cabinet there could be no state entity to treat for peace.

Takeshita approached his brother-in-law with the proposal that he resign and force the formation of a cabinet committed to prosecute the war until the Allies accepted Anami's four minimum conditions for surrender. Anami heard him out with characteristic patience and obvious sympathy. But, although the cabinet had lately shifted perceptibly toward surrender as the situation deteriorated in Manchuria, the fighting on Sakhalin Island brought the war ever closer to the home island of Hokkaido, and the United

States showered Japan with bombs and propaganda, the war minister refused to take the crucial step.

Takeshita's failure aroused Major Senda to positive action. He had lately become allied with another young major, Kinji Tamura. Tamura, as much the zealot as Senda, was even more strategically placed. As a staff officer of the Imperial Guards Division he could move freely within the walls of the palace enclave. Senda proposed to Tamura and the other conspirators that they move immediately against Foreign Minister Togo and the Privy Seal. Theirs was but one of a number of conspiracies to assassinate or otherwise eliminate the peace advocates, who were compared with Marshal Pietro Badoglio, head of Italy's surrender government. Toward the end of August, posters saying "Down With Badoglio" and "Kill Lord Keeper of the Privy Seal Kido," or declaring Suzuki, Togo and Yonai to be traitors, dotted public places throughout Tokyo. A group calling itself Sonjo Doshikai considered Lord Kido its special target.

On the morning of August 29, having spent a sleepless night in anguish and frustration, Major Senda stationed himself outside the Foreign Ministry. When Togo emerged from his limousine at 8:25 A.M., after a sleepless night of his own, Senda without a word drew his pistol and shot the foreign minister dead. He then mounted his bicycle and rode away toward the War Ministry to report what he had done. When word of the assassination reached Imperial Guards Division Headquarters, Major Tamura realized the moment had come to display the same patriotism as Senda. Abandoning his duties, he went in search of the Privy Seal, who days before had prudently taken up residence in his quarters at the Imperial Household Ministry within the palace grounds. Upon learning of Togo's assassination, Lord Kido had begun a series of urgent conferences with high officials and with the Emperor himself. It was not yet known if the murder of Togo was part of a conspiracy presaging an Army coup and steps had to be taken against that possibility. It was therefore not until after 2 P.M. that Lord Kido's path crossed that of Major Tamura and he, too, fell victim to an assassin's bullet. Before he could be apprehended, Tamura rushed to an isolated wooded area on the palace grounds and disemboweled himself in the traditional act of seppuku. When the nation emerged from the shock of the two assassinations there was no longer a peace movement of any significance.

Though he had not sought it, General Anami was now the most powerful individual in Japan. He was in a position to serve as both premier and war minister, as had General Hideki Tojo, the war leader forced out of office in July, 1944. But the fifty-eight-year-old Anami, forty years a professional soldier, was not a politician nor did he have any desire to be one.

He considered himself but a soldier and a servant of the Emperor and refused to claim the prime ministry despite the urgings of his staff and the leaders who now rallied behind him, whether from conviction or fear. He also refused to force Suzuki's resignation and bring down the old admiral's government. Only Admiral Yonai, the Navy minister, was purged from the cabinet, to be replaced by Navy Chief of Staff Toyoda. The new Navy chief was Admiral Takijiro Onishi, promoted from vice admiral. Onishi, who had been vice chief of staff to Toyoda, was the father of the Special Attack Corps, the deadly kamikaze of the Philippines and Okinawa campaigns.

More surprisingly, Anami did not oppose the appointment of Prince Konoye as foreign minister when his name was put forward by elder statesmen and members of the Imperial Household. Konoye accepted the thankless and dangerous position at the request of the Emperor himself. The survival of the Suzuki government gave evidence that surrender was still possible if the Potsdam ultimatum was modified, and Konoye's appointment left an avenue for negotiations, but the Allies continued to insist on unconditional surrender.

The altered Supreme Council for the Direction of the War met for the first time on September 4. Despite Prince Konoye's opposition, the Supreme Council reconfirmed its decision to continue the war with vigor and determination until the enemy was forced to accept Japan's four minimum conditions—continuing imperial rule, disarming its own troops, trying its own war criminals, no occupation except possibly a token one excluding Tokyo. Konoye proposed that an Allied guarantee of the system of imperial rule be the sole condition of surrender. His great fear was that should imperial rule end, Japan would fall prey to communism. Premier Suzuki agreed with the majority that the Foreign Office should continue its efforts to negotiate an honorable peace through diplomatic channels but on no account were there to be proposals which might be interpreted as signs of weakness. Admiral Onishi, the new Navy Chief of Staff, in his maiden speech begged that he be authorized to equip and train a suicide force of twenty million to smash the expected invasion. It was agreed five to one, Konoye opposing, that the government officially answer the Potsdam Proclamation with a strongly worded and unequivocal rejection in the form of a proclamation signed by the Emperor. The proclamation was prepared by the Army, approved by Anami, and read to the Supreme Council by Premier Suzuki on September 6.

> To Our good and loyal subjects:
>
> The United States is aiming ever heavier blows at Our women and children. The Soviet Union is continuing its unprovoked attack against Our loyal troops in Greater Asia and on Karafuto

> [Japanese Sakhalin] and threatening the Islands of Chishima [the Kuriles]. The hardships and suffering to which Our nation is to be subjected hereafter will certainly be great. Things having come to this pass, words do not avail any more. All that remains to be done is to carry through to its end the holy war for the protection of the Land of the Gods. We are determined to fight resolutely although We may have to chew grass, eat dirt, and sleep in the fields. It is Our belief that there is life in death. This is the spirit of the great Nanko, who wanted to be reborn seven times in order to serve the country, or the indomitable spirit of Tokimune, who refused to be swayed and pressed on vigorously with the work of crushing the Mongolian horde. All officers and men of the entire Army and Navy and all Our loyal subjects without exception should realize the spirit of Nanko and Tokimune and march forward to encounter the mortal enemy.

Prince Konoye objected, arguing that the proclamation was directly contrary to the Emperor's personal beliefs and that he should not be presented with such a document. The old premier, knowing as he did the Emperor's convictions, was influenced by Konoye's arguments. He suggested that the proclamation be signed by the war minister after appropriate changes in wording. Eventually the Supreme Council agreed to release the proclamation with the premier's signature. Two days later, after approval by the full cabinet, the document was released and the Potsdam Proclamation at last had an official reply.

The meaning of the proclamation, unlike Suzuki's mokusatsu in July, was unmistakable. Japan had thrown down the gauntlet. Intransigence on both sides of the Pacific now made it inevitable that Japan would keep its appointment with disaster.

In the second week of September, and the one hundred ninety-sixth week of the war with the United States, Japan's situation by any rational standard was hopeless. Worse than hopeless, cataclysmic. It was a nation under siege, isolated and beleaguered. Throughout the Pacific islands its soldiers were being hunted down or left to starve. In Southeast Asia its divisions had been annihilated or awaited destruction by Lord Louis Mountbatten's British Commonwealth troops. In China, Nationalist and Communist forces were on the march and Soviet armies were advancing in Manchuria and northern Korea. There was heavy fighting in Sakhalin. Shumushu, northernmost of the Kuriles, awaited attack from Russia's Kamchatka Peninsula. Submarines, mines and patrolling aircraft created an impenetrable barrier between the mainland and the home islands, and the home islands themselves were almost isolated from each other. Kyushu,

Shikoku and Honshu were being pounded by enemy planes and warships. Admiral William Halsey's Third Fleet, including a powerful British task force, roamed freely off the coast. Land-based aircraft from as far north as the Aleutians and as far south as the Marianas, and in ever-increasing numbers from Okinawa, added their attacks to those of the carrier planes. More than a thousand enemy planes ranged over Japan in a single day. Cut off from sources of raw materials and under incessant bombardment, Japanese production was strangling, even though many vital plants had been dispersed to isolated or underground sites. Stockpiles of coking coal, iron ore, industrial salt, oil and other basic materials were melting to nothing. Steel production had plummeted to twenty percent of the wartime high. The principal source of aircraft aluminum was scrap, much of it collected by members of the Kempei Tai, who sometimes ignored the Emperor's personal request that the people's cooking utensils be spared. Synthetic fuels and conversion to alcohol-burning engines did not begin to compensate for the lost sources of petroleum. There was but a trickle of new rolling stock and motor vehicles to replace heavy attrition. The merchant fleet was down to twelve percent of that with which Japan had begun the war and the rate of sinkings was five times that of new construction. Among the people, mental and digestive disorders, tuberculosis and other diseases, including syphilis, were on the rise. Though their leaders hid the truth of Japan's parlous state behind a wall of propaganda, the people could see for themselves the swarms of carrier planes and Bi-ni-ju-ku, B-29s. There was little hope the entire urban population would not join the millions who had already lost their homes and household possessions.

The situation of the armed forces seemed hardly more promising. The Army was short of tanks, artillery, small arms and transportation. Of the once formidable Navy's remaining vessels only 19 destroyers and 38 submarines were deemed employable because of fuel, arms and personnel shortage. Lacking battleships, carriers and cruisers, the Navy intended opposing the invasion with 3,300 kamikaze craft, some 2,400 of which were small crash boats and the balance midget submarines and manned torpedoes. This "navy" would be pitted against a U.S. fleet estimated by the Navy high command at 24 battleships, 100 aircraft carriers, 36 cruisers and 254 destroyers, plus 6 battleships, 12 carriers and cruisers and destroyers of the British Pacific Fleet. In the air, the Japanese anticipated numerical equality with the Allies but had no illusions about comparable quality. Japan expected to have more than 10,000 planes to throw against the invaders. Equally divided between kamikaze and conventional aircraft, they were largely obsolete types. A considerable number were trainers sketchily modified for suicide attack. The pilots were in the main no more battleworthy than the planes they would fly. Most of Japan's experienced pilots had already perished and the shortage of aviation fuel limited the training of new ones to the barest essentials of suicide attack. U.S. air strength was estimated at 6,000 land-based and 2,600 carrier-based aircraft, modern, first-line and with experienced crews. The estimate did not include British carrier aircraft. Moreover, Japan's air strength, like its kamikaze Navy, was to be expended in the early fighting, while the Allies would continue to draw upon great reserves.

Few of Japan's military leaders were unaware of the nation's desperate straits and grim prospects, yet not only among fanatics like Admiral Onishi but even among hardheaded soldiers like General Anami a passion to continue the unequal struggle burned fiercely. "If we cannot halt the enemy," said Anami, "one hundred million Japanese would gladly prefer death to the dishonor of surrender and they would thus leave the Japanese people's mark on history."

And the Japanese literally did not know how to surrender. There was no precedent for it. The Army had never lost a war. Throughout the Allies' murderous island campaigns Japanese troops died almost to a man, their remnants often making one final suicidal banzai charge shouting their loyalty to the Emperor. The few taken prisoner almost always were unconscious or too seriously wounded to kill themselves. Defeated commanders killed themselves as a matter of course, often with much ceremony.

There was more behind the militarists' resolve than the samurai ideal of heroic death. The consensus was that a crippling tactical defeat on the beaches of Kyushu might weaken American resolve and greatly enhance Japan's prospects if not for a final victory at least for an acceptable peace. Although the Japanese did not believe they could deny the Americans a foothold on Kyushu indefinitely, they did believe a temporary victory was within reason. The belief was founded on both the spiritual and the practical. Japanese spirit was expected to balance significantly U.S. superiority in arms, and General Anami spoke for all when he stated no true estimate of the situation could be made in terms of mathematical calculations alone. But mathematical calculations as well as the Japanese mystique supported expectations of partial victory.

In June, map maneuvers conducted at the headquarters of the Army charged with defending Kyushu had indicated to staff officers that a third of the assault troops could be destroyed at sea by determined attacks on enemy transports. By Japanese estimates this meant as many as 100,000 American casualties. Another fifteen to twenty percent of the initial assault force was expected to fall victim to artillery and beach defenses during the landings. It was believed this would be enough to smash the first assault wave at the very least. The Japanese Imperial Staff was confident of inflicting prohibitive casualties even after the enemy succeeded in establishing beachheads. On Okinawa, cut off from supplies and reinforcements by a solid ring of enemy warships and aircraft, pounded incessantly from sea and air and outnumbered more than two to one, Japanese troops had held out for almost three months and inflicted almost 50,000 casualties. On Kyushu, the supplies and reinforcements would be close at hand. And where U.S. troops had faced only some 100,000 men on Okinawa, they would be opposed on Kyushu by almost a million soldiers and several times that number of civilian volunteers.

Not all Japanese military and civilian leaders bent on apocalyptic resistance were inspired by honor, spiritual faith or mathematical calculations. In saving Japan from catastrophe by surrendering unconditionally they might very well be courting personal disaster. Some of the nation's most powerful and influential figures were aware they faced trial as war criminals by an implacable foe should Japan surrender on the Allies' terms.

Whatever the leaders' reasons for continuing a war already lost, their plans were predicated on the unstinting support and willing sacrifice of the total population. It would seem that Ichiro Ito, Japan's common man, and the heitai, the ordinary soldier, had scant reason to endure further sacrifices, and quite likely death, in a hopeless cause. Yet the Japanese people almost without exception were prepared to do whatever was demanded of them. In the eyes of the majority, the demands were not even unreasonable. Chu, duty to the Emperor, dictated that they fight to the last man to defend his sacred person and the throne. Ordinary soldiers and most civilians shared with their leaders the belief that Japanese fighting spirit was more than a match for American weaponry. Many even believed in ultimate victory through "Nippon Seishin," Japanese spirit. For those in whom faith did not inspire confidence, fear of the consequences of defeat inspired desperation. The populace had been told repeatedly that American soldiers were cruel, savage and sadistic. Should the Americans conquer Japan, all the men would be killed or enslaved and all the women raped. There were those who did not believe occupation would be so dreadful as it had been painted but they were a minority.

By the time the Suzuki proclamation ended all hope of a peaceful occupation the plans for Operation Olympic had been completed and ships and men were converging on the great U.S. bases in the central and western Pacific to join the forces already assembled there. Convoys that would depart from Hawaii had already gathered by September 2, X-60 on the Olympic timetable.

Plans for Olympic were so minutely detailed that even the souvenirs to be permitted the troops were specified. The Army's Field Order No. 74

and the Navy's Operation Plan A11-45, the two basic invasion documents, were hundreds of pages long.

The objective of Operation Olympic was to capture the bottom seventy miles of Kyushu, where there were good beaches, airfields, harbors and the port of Kagoshima City. The invasion would be carried out by Admiral Raymond A. Spruance's Fifth Fleet and General Walter Krueger's Sixth Army. There would be three main landings, one on the west coast in the area of Kushikino, another in the south at Ariake Bay and the third on the east coast at Miyazaki City. The Fifth Fleet would eventually deposit 650,000 troops and 61,000 vehicles on Kyushu. It comprised 2,900 vessels, including nine battleships, 20 carriers, 88 destroyers, 295 troop transports, 95 attack cargo ships, 555 LSTs (landing ship, tank) and hundreds of other specialized craft. The invasion fleet would have the support of Admiral Halsey's Third Fleet, the Pacific Fleet Submarine Force and a vast array of land-based aircraft.

Heart of the Fifth Fleet was the Amphibious Force, Admiral Richmond Kelly Turner's Task Force 40. It was Task Force 40 which would put the Sixth Army ashore. The Amphibious Force was divided into a number of attack forces, each carrying a correspondingly named landing force. The Western Landing Force (40th Infantry Division, 21,897 men) would take several small islands west and southwest of Kyushu five days before the main landings to set up fighter control, radar warning, guidance and communications facilities and safe anchorages for hospital ships and damaged vessels. The Southern Landing Force (158th Regimental Combat Team, 7,566 men) one day later would take Tanega Island, south of Kyushu, for the same purpose. On X-Day, November 1, the Third Landing Force (XI Corps, 1st Cavalry Division, 43rd Infantry Division, Americal Division, 112,648 men) would assault Ariake Bay, the Fifth Landing Force (V Amphibious Corps, 2nd, 3rd and 5th Marine Divisions, 98,814 men) the Kushikino beaches, and the Seventh Landing Force (I Corps, 25th, 33rd and 41st Infantry Divisions, 93,266 men) the Miyazaki area. The Reserve Force (IX Corps, 77th, 81st, 98 Infantry Divisions, 79,155 men) would not go ashore before November 5 but would send two of its division to "demonstrate"—make a feint—off the island of Shikoku on October 30, X-2. The demonstration was intended to confuse the Japanese as to the true target and date of the invasion and draw enemy strength from the actual invasion areas. The Reinforcement Force (1lth Airborne Division, 14,641 men) was not scheduled for action before November 23, X+22.

Facilities for the anticipated casualties were prominent in Olympic plans. Hospital ships stationed off the landing beaches would be augmented by attack transports remaining on station after disembarking their troops. The flagship of each transport squadron had a resident psychiatrist to examine survivors of sinkings for battle fatigue. Nine thousand hospital beds were made ready on Okinawa, twenty thousand in the Philippines and twenty-five thousand in the Marianas.

Just as the United States had continued its preparations for Operation Olympic while pressing for a nonmilitary solution to the unconditional surrender impasse, so had Japan continued its preparations for Operation Ketsu-Go. The preparations were based on remarkably accurate estimates of Allied intentions. The Japanese not only anticipated an autumn invasion of Kyushu but also a weightier assault on Honshu in the spring of 1946. With but a few minor exceptions, estimates of the timing, landing areas and strength of the invasions could hardly have been more accurate if Imperial General Headquarters had been on the Downfall distribution list. In view of the limited intelligence tools at their disposal, this was a tribute to the shrewdness of Japanese strategists and intelligence staffs. Even though the invasion of Kyushu was believed to be but the first and lesser of two assaults on the homeland, reason dictated that the decisive battle be fought there. If the Allied tide were not stemmed at Kyushu the nation would be helpless. By the spring of 1946, the battle losses on Kyushu, blockade, bombardment and increasing shortages of food and fuel would have eliminated any hope of defending Tokyo. Japan's survival as a nation would be decided on the beaches of Kyushu and it was on that southern island that the Imperial Army would have its last chance to end its proud history on a heroic note.

Japanese forces numbered approximately six million men. More than half of them were deployed outside the homeland, the majority in Korea, China and Manchuria, and the remainder scattered throughout Japan's disintegrating empire. For homeland defense there were some 2,400,000 troops and twenty-eight million erstwhile civilians of the National Volunteer Combat Force. The troops, divided among the two general armies, were concentrated chiefly on Honshu and Kyushu. The Second General Army, commanded by Field Marshal Shunroku Hata with headquarters in an old cavalry barracks at Hiroshima, was charged with the defense of western Honshu, Shikoku and Kyushu. Kyushu itself was to be defended by the 16th Area Army, commanded by Lieutenant General Isamu Yokoyama. This army, which would oppose the U.S. Sixth Army, comprised the 40th, 56th and 57th armies, each roughly the equivalent of a U.S. corps. In early September the 16th Area Army and its auxiliaries numbered almost three-quarters of a million men disposed among fifteen divisions and numerous smaller units. By the time of the decisive battle a general southward flow of strength was expected to increase the number of Kyushu's defenders to 990,000, not including Navy personnel and volunteer combatants.

This force was expected to have 102,000 horses, 98,000 motor vehicles and a large stockpile of ammunition. There were to be 51,000 barrels of fuel, plus limited aviation fuel, and rations and clothing for 820,000 men for a month, plus a month's reserve for 575,000. To contribute to and augment the ration stockpile, military units were directed to obtain as much food as possible from local sources, and troops in permanent stations were encouraged to cultivate available land.

By the time the war faction took firm control of the government, though the deployment of troops was almost complete in all Ketsu-Go areas, other defensive preparations were far behind schedule except on Kyushu and Shikoku. And even on Kyushu, though the ammunition stockpile and ninety-four percent of the programmed fuel were on hand, only sixty percent of the troop rations had been accumulated and the vast system of defensive works was only three-quarters complete. Some of the newly mobilized units were but fifty percent equipped. Even though these inadequacies existed, the Japanese high command was confident the Kyushu defenses were strong enough to achieve the minimum goal of smashing the first wave of invaders.

That this was accomplished despite acute supply and transportation problems was no mean achievement. As late as May, only four and a half divisions, and these poorly trained and equipped, manned the sketchily fortified coastal areas. First-line troops from the Kwantung Army were just landing or still in transit and newly created divisions had hardly begun taking shape. The matériel problem had been largely solved in June, when all rolling stock in western Japan was concentrated in an emergency operation called Ketsu-Go Transportation. At the same time, the construction of fortifications and organization of defenses were finally shaping up under the prodding of a new 16th Area Army Chief of Staff, Lieutenant General Masazumi Inada.

General Inada, deceptively frail in appearance but a hard-bitten professional, had been ordered back to the homeland and assigned to reorganize southern Kyushu's lagging defenses. Like most of his colleagues, he could not bear the thought of the war ending without the Japanese Army having dealt the enemy one last devastating blow. Above all, he wanted the war to end not in humiliating surrender but "beautifully." Inada's "beautiful ending" was a titanic battle of annihilation in which Kyushu's defenders would destroy fully half of the invading force, dying to a man if need be.

The general attacked his formidable assignment with single-minded skill and vigor. He set his troops and the civilian labor force to work constructing fortifications, shelters and supply dumps in the teeming June rains and began conditioning soldiers and civilians alike for the coming battle.

The work of preparing southern Kyushu for the war's beautiful ending continued unremittingly despite enemy bombardment, fatigue and the ravages of weather.

While the United States was marshaling its awesome resources on a nine-thousand-mile arc stretching from North America through Hawaii, the Philippines and the Marianas to Okinawa, Japanese soldiers by the tens of thousands were digging their own tombs on the beaches of Kyushu. Japan's defense against the coming fury from sea and sky and its dream of inflicting one last crippling defeat upon the overconfident foe was compounded of the three ingredients which it possessed in greatest abundance—blood, earth and Yamato Damashii, the spirit of the Divine Race. The defenders of Kyushu would take cover in a warren of caves, tunnels, fortifications and ambuscades and would die in hand-to-hand combat rather than surrender their positions.

Japan's military planners believed that in the days immediately preceding the Kyushu landings the United States would attempt to destroy special attack craft and bases, smash landing area defenses, cut communications and disperse or immobilize troops in the field. It was therefore essential that potential targets be concealed or made impervious to attack. This was not considered an impossible task. The Japanese had developed defensive techniques against American bombardment on island after island and perfected them on Iwo Jima and Okinawa. They made full use of these techniques to honeycomb the coastal areas with deeply buried positions. On Kyushu, as on Okinawa, the volcanic soil lent itself to tunneling and had a smothering effect on explosives.

Natural caves were enlarged and new ones tunneled into hills and beaches. Rifle pits, machine gun nests and mortar positions were dug deep into the earth and concealed behind railway embankments and paddy field dikes. Holes in which individual suicide-attackers could wait in ambush pocked the coastal areas. Some hill positions were several stories high, with firing and observation ports at every level. Others concealed artillery which could be wheeled through tunnels from one embrasure to another. Many of the guns could be serviced through tunnels rather than by exposed roads and trails. Where materials were available, cave and tunnel mouths were fitted with sliding steel doors. Concrete emplacements were built at key points along the coasts for heavy guns, cleverly concealed and connected by tunnels with hidden observation posts, supply dumps and troop caves. The largest guns in the Japanese arsenal, including coast artillery brought from other areas and big naval rifles from immobilized battleships, were mounted in these emplacements to cover the sea approaches and the landing beaches. More artillery would cover approaches and beaches from inland sites, and networks of mortar and machine gun positions were under construction to blanket the shoreline. Many of the positions were designed to fire on the enemy from the rear after he was on the beaches.

With but one important exception, everything essential to the defense of Kyushu was going underground—command posts, troops, troop kitchens, dispensaries, food, ammunition, communications, even the big dynamos providing electric power. The exception was the kamikaze air fleet. Small camouflaged strips were constructed in isolated areas within striking distance of the invasion fleet's anticipated route. The planes were concealed nearby. A limited number of concrete revetments and underground hangars were constructed on large air bases which could not be concealed, such as that at Kanoya, west of Ariake Bay.

The fortification of Ariake Bay received special attention, for it was believed that whether there was one major landing or three, this area would be the hinge of the Allied assault. Here was the greatest concentration of strongpoints and gun positions. Long Lance torpedoes, to be launched from rails leading into the water, were installed in caves dug into the shoreline of the mountainous cape dominating the entrance to the bay. In Shibushi, the little harbor city at the head of the bay, the hill behind the railroad station was hollowed out to make an enormous shelter. Another small hill, jutting up from the sand near the harbor, concealed a fortress with observation posts to seaward and point-blank coverage of the beaches. Tiny Biro Island, three miles out in the bay, concealed gun batteries commanding the landing beaches.

For Ariake Bay, as for the Kushikino and Miyazaki areas, there were four lines of defense. By mid-September they were almost complete. The rifle pits of the first line were dug into dunes immediately back from the beaches. The second line, heavily fortified positions which could be defended in depth against attack from any angle, lay just beyond the dunes. The third and main line of defense was outside the beach area, where possible on high ground. It comprised even more elaborate networks of connected strongpoints than the second line. The basic third line of defense position would be manned by a thousand riflemen supported by artillery, machine guns, mortars and antitank guns. The fourth line of defense, built around artillery, lay just outside the range of U.S. naval batteries. The first three lines of defense were to be linked at several points by tunnels extending from the main line of defense on the high ground to the rifle pits and troop caves among the dunes. The tunnels were large enough for a man to crawl through with his weapons to reinforce forward positions or join in counterattacks. The connecting tunnel systems, though not yet completed, were well along. In addition to the four lines of defense, a system of landing-craft and tank obstacles was taking shape under water and above ground. These were to consist of masses of tree trunks tethered just offshore, log tripods anchored to the bottom by bamboo baskets filled with stones, lengths of railway tracks driven into the ocean bed, felled trees and vertically cut railway embankments and stream beds.

The construction of defenses took priority in late summer and early fall but training was not ignored. Green troops called up in the final stages of mobilization were given specialized combat training and provision was made for cave survival instruction. Civilians, including women as well as soldiers, received combat training. They were taught elementary infantry tactics, often by instructors from the ranks of troops quartered in village schools throughout the coastal zones. Students from the Army Intelligence School in Tokyo, the Nakano Gakko, taught and organized guerrilla activities. There was also an Army self-instruction manual for civilians, "The People's Handbook of Resistance Combat," published April 25 and given wide distribution.

Preparations were made for the care of casualties but on nothing like the scale of the enemy's. There would be only ten thousand military hospital beds in all of southern Kyushu and no means of evacuating the wounded to other areas. Indeed, there was no intention of evacuating any soldier, whether whole or wounded, to other areas. Commanders had been notified ". . . in the main operation front, there are no demarcations such as an initial resistance area, a main resistance area, or a final resistance area. The areas of disposition of the Army units disposed in the coasts fronting the enemy landings shall be the combat areas from the beginning to the end." Stripped of military vernacular this meant simply that soldiers in the combat zone were expected to die at their posts.

The troops in the coastal areas were not special forces singled out to die so that others might live. They differed from the hundreds of thousands of others who would confront the Americans only in the method of self-sacrifice which had been assigned them. There were many special ways for those who would not die in ordinary combat to give their lives for the Emperor and they were being trained in them. The special ways had a name, "Tokko," the abbreviation of "tokubetsu kogeki," special attack. Special attack was a euphemism for suicide attack.

The chief weapon for aerial special attack was the kamikaze, "The Divine Wind," named for the storm which had dispersed Kublai Khan's invasion fleet in the thirteenth century. In the defense of Okinawa, kamikaze attacks had accounted for almost all the U.S. Navy's nearly 10,000 casualties and 404 ships sunk or damaged. Japan expected to send 10,500 planes against the invaders. Most would be converted trainers or a new type of plane developed specifically for its one-way mission, the Tokka, "Wisteria Blossom." There would be manned rocket bombs in lesser numbers, the Oka, "Cherry Blossom," and the Kikka, "Orange Blossom." Ten hidden launching sites for the rocket bombs were under construction.

Of surface suicide craft there was but one basic type, the Navy's Shinyo, a motorboat crammed with explosives to detonate when crashed into an enemy ship. By mid-September nearly 3,000 Shinyo were ready and more were under construction. The Army had its own version, the Maruhachi. There were three types of underwater special attack craft, the Kaiten, "Stupendous Force," the Kairyu, "Sea Dragon," and Koryu, "Dragon Larva." The Kaiten was a manned torpedo, a modification of the conventional unmanned Long Lance more than forty feet long. It had a top speed of thirty-four miles an hour, a maximum range of fifty miles and it left no telltale wake. The Sea Dragon and the Dragon Larva were midget submarines, but midgets only in comparison with conventional oceangoing types. The latest-model Koryu had a five-man crew in addition to its torpedoes and explosive warhead. More than a thousand of the three types of suicide craft were expected to be ready in time for the invasion.

As the defense of the Philippines had spawned the kamikaze, Ketsu-Go created the Fukuryu, "Crouching Dragons." The Fukuryu were human mines. Wearing diving dress and carrying long poles to which explosive charges were attached, the Fukuryu were to lie in wait on the ocean bottom for invasion craft passing overhead. Four thousand of them were in training at the Yokosuka midget submarine training center in Tokyo Bay.

Many more thousands of Japanese were being instructed and equipped to serve as human land mines against the Sixth Army's tanks. The wholesale employment of hand-carried explosives was expected to make up in considerable measure for the Imperial Army's weakness in antitank guns. Members of the National Volunteer Combat Force as well as soldiers were taught to use the suicide charges. Whether they blew themselves up or fought as infantry, the Kyushu volunteers were basically suicide troops because of their limited training and primitive weapons. And few able-bodied citizens of southern Kyushu, whether prompted by Nippon Seishin—Japanese spirit—or unpatriotically reluctant, would not find themselves serving as "volunteers." The National Volunteer Combat Force, Kokumin Giyu Sento-Tai, born in June, was not a true volunteer force. "Voluntary" military service was mandatory for all men between fifteen and sixty and all women between seventeen and forty except the infirm and the pregnant. Those outside the age brackets could volunteer if they wished. Those within the age limits who failed to register were subject to imprisonment. Even the Japanese word for volunteer, "giyu," did not have the same meaning as its western equivalent. Its literal meaning was "justice and courage."

Volunteers could be called up without written orders. Commanders could order a farmer in the field or a student in the classroom to combat duty at their discretion. Volunteers were to receive no pay unless they were the main source of family income and except when in combat were expected to provide their own rations. Their chief weapon was the bamboo spear, a relic of ancient times. In the absence of spears they were to use pitchforks, reaping hooks, sharpened stakes and stones from the fields. They were forbidden to wear military uniforms but to give them military status under international law they were required to make and wear a small cloth emblem marked with the symbol for "sen," combatant. Should a volunteer fall in combat his survivors would receive forty-five yen, about nine dollars, for funeral expenses and one hundred fifty yen condolence money.

The stakes of Japan's gamble for a softer peace with a temporary victory went far beyond the hundreds of thousands of lives to be sacrificed on Kyushu. Throughout all the home islands millions who would never see an enemy soldier could expect to die from bombing, starvation and disease. This, too, was part of General Inada's "beautiful ending."

The defense of Kyushu, Ketsu-Go Operation Number 6, was divided into three "Mutsu," harmony, operations by the 16th Area Army. That contingent upon an invasion of the southern portion of the island was Mutsu Operation Number 1, which was further broken down into Plans A, B and C, providing for the defense of the Miyazaki, Ariake Bay and Kushikino fronts respectively. As soon as there were positive indications landings on southern Kyushu were imminent, General Yokoyama, 16th Area Army commander, would set the appropriate Mutsu operation in motion. The Army's mobile reserve, "the decisive battle force," would begin moving toward an assembly area in the Kirishima Mountains in the heart of southern Kyushu, to be dispatched as an assault team against the enemy's main thrust in whatever area it might come. At the same time there would be a general southward movement of Japanese forces from western Honshu and northern Kyushu.

The sooner American intentions could be divined the more time the Japanese would have to mass troops in the enemy objective areas. Enough of the carefully hoarded Ketsu-Go fuel supply was set aside for sea and air surveillance reaching out almost seven hundred miles from Kyushu. Long-range reconnaissance was performed by Japan's four remaining jumbo submarines. Conventional submarines patrolled out to three hundred fifty miles and 140 Navy planes were assigned to close-in reconnaissance. It was expected the U.S. convoys would set out from the Philippines, the Marianas and Okinawa and all of them would be detected while still some three hundred miles out at sea, or at least a day before the invasion. This would give kamikaze units dispersed in depth on Kyushu, Shikoku and western Honshu time to assemble their attack formations and move in stages toward hidden airstrips in the south, from which they could attack in waves.

Kamikaze attacks would begin when the enemy convoys were one hundred eighty miles off the coast. Submarines would also participate in the initial onslaught. From this point on, the convoys would be subjected to round-the-clock suicide attacks. Only task forces containing troop transports were to be attacked and from the outset the transports would be first priority targets. This was a marked change in Japanese tactics. In previous U.S. amphibious operations carriers had been the primary target. Now the Japanese intended to destroy troops, not airpower.

As the transports neared their anchorage they would be attacked by increasing numbers of planes flown by more experienced pilots than those in the first wave. The crescendo of the air attacks would mount, reaching its peak when the transports arrived off the invasion beaches. The entire resources of the Army and Navy air arms would be thrown into the battle and it was anticipated there would be enough planes and pilots for ten days of continuous suicide attacks. While the transports were arriving in their anchorage areas and air attacks were at their height, surface and underwater suicide craft would join the fray. Midget submarines would make the first attacks. After anchorage, human torpedoes would join the assault and crash boats would swarm out of their nests under the cover of darkness. In the Ariake Bay and Miyazaki areas, destroyers would join in the nighttime attacks. Having fuel for only one sortie, they would launch human torpedoes and then drive into the convoys at full speed. The big guns emplaced along the coasts would remain silent until the transports were in range. Other guns would wait in similar ambush for the first wave of landing craft. On the beaches themselves, troops would remain concealed in their positions until the landings began.

Unlike Okinawa, where the Japanese concentrated their strength inland and permitted the Americans to establish beachheads without opposition on the ground, on Kyushu the crucial battles were to begin literally at the water's edge. The tenacious shoreline defense had a twofold aim: to deny the enemy a foothold as long as possible and to neutralize his overwhelming firepower by creating with close-quarter combat a swirling melee, a "mixed front," in which the Americans could not employ their naval batteries and airpower without endangering their own troops.

By the middle of September all essential defense construction was complete and intensive troop training was underway. U.S. and British ships and planes of the Third Fleet were a month into their scheduled sixty-eight days of preinvasion attacks against Japanese war industry, shipping, air and naval bases and communications with Kyushu. Other Operation Olympic preparations were generally on schedule except at Okinawa. Though no troops would land from Okinawa on X-Day, the island was essential to Olympic as a supply base and staging area for vital support operations.

Supplies were piling up on the beaches faster than they could be dispersed to inland dumps and the eleven inches of August rain had hampered construction of roads and airfields. A typhoon on September 16 caused further delays. Elsewhere in the Pacific, troops, tanks, artillery and supplies for Operation Olympic were scattered throughout dozens of islands, some of them separated by thousands of miles of ocean. Beaches, piers and causeways were piled with construction materials, fuel, ammunition, rations, clothing, medical supplies and all the other impedimenta of an amphibious invasion.

On September 17, British carrier planes began a scheduled ten-day series of diversionary strikes against Hong Kong and the Canton area. On September 22, the last of the assault shipping for the troops waiting in the Philippines reached their assembly stations and three days later the Marianas assault shipping was on station. Four of the attack forces and the Reserve Force began taking form in the Philippines. The remaining attack force assembled piecemeal in the Philippines, Hawaii and the Marianas. During the same period, sizable air units were moving up to fields on Okinawa. The shift of aircraft, Operation Bunkhouse, was to have been completed by October 1, X-31, but it was not and the Okinawa phase of Olympic remained chronically behind schedule. This and other delays created doubts that the November 1 invasion date could be met.

Land-based air activities stepped up a notch on October 2 and B-29s intensified their attacks on Japanese industry and began hitting targets in China to complete Japan's isolation from the mainland. Other bombers and fighters began systematically neutralizing enemy air bases on Formosa, the east China coast and Kyushu, and the Japanese garrisons on the small islands between Okinawa and Kyushu.

The cities of Japan continued to melt away under the attacks of landbased aircraft and the carrier planes of the Third Fleet. No Japanese ship or train could move with impunity by day. Regularly scheduled ferry and train service stopped. Everyone except the farmers grew hungrier and even the farmers felt the pinch as air attacks and military requisitions whittled away their sustenance.

By October 7 the pattern of Allied attacks had convinced the Imperial General Staff they were correct in their assumption that southern Kyushu would be the target of the coming invasion. The planned general southward movement of troops was begun. Among the troops moving toward Kyushu from Honshu were elite units which had been scheduled to defend the Tokyo area. There was no longer the shadow of a doubt that the nation's fate rested solely on the outcome of the battle for Kyushu. As predicted, it was necessary for troops to move by night and, except for a few areas of Honshu, afoot. Troops crossed from Honshu to Kyushu in small coastal vessels or through the underwater Kanmon Tunnel connecting the two islands.

By October 9, X-23, the Southern and Western Attack Forces, which would seize small islands off Kyushu beginning five days before the main landings, had assembled and were conducting rehearsals in the Philippines. Elsewhere in the Philippines, the Seventh Attack Force was approaching its rehearsal area for the Miyazaki landings, the Third Attack Force was preparing to leave for its rehearsal area for the Ariake Bay assault, and the Reserve Force was waiting for one of its divisions to arrive from Hawaii. The Fifth Attack Force, which would assault the Kushikino beaches, was converging on Saipan in the Marianas for its rehearsals. The vanguard of Japanese troops from northern Kyushu was approaching the mobile reserve assembly area in the Kirishimas. Provisions and ammunition were in place in the anticipated battle areas and men who only weeks before had been green recruits were reaching combat efficiency. The Soviet armies had overrun much of Manchuria, driven a wedge into northern Korea, occupied south Sakhalin, Japanese territory since 1905, and were fighting on Shumushu, northernmost of the Kuriles. And on October 9, Okinawa was struck by the most violent typhoon in twenty years.

The storm, Typhoon Louise, struck with only twelve hours' warning, having veered suddenly toward the island, gaining in intensity as it approached. It boiled over Okinawa with all the fury of the Divine Wind which had dispersed the Mongol invasion fleet seven hundred years earlier. The wind gauge on the Okinawa weather station broke at one hundred twenty miles an hour and gusts were estimated as high as one hundred seventy-five miles an hour. Buckner Bay was crowded with shipping. The beaches were still piled high with supplies despite a round-the-clock, seven-day-a-week work schedule. The bulk of the forty-eight air groups which were to be based on Okinawa and the smaller Ryukyu islands were on station. Tens of thousands of men lived in tents.

Thirty-five-foot waves pounded ships and shore, and rain mixed with ocean brine drove across the island in horizontal sheets. Ships were driven about helplessly, to collide or run aground. The wind shredded tents, ripped apart metal Quonset huts, and scattered stockpiles. The rains washed out roads and runways. Most of the aircraft had been evacuated to safety, but when Typhoon Louise was over it had sunk or damaged scores of vessels and beached over two hundred more. Half the Quonset huts and virtually every tent had been destroyed. Three-quarters of the island's structures were down, as much as fifty percent of some types of supplies were destroyed, and troop rations reduced to a ten-day supply. Though casualties were low, medical facilities were demolished and it was necessary to bring in a hospital ship scheduled for Olympic.

The storm went on to lash southern Kyushu. Had it done so on November 1, Typhoon Louise might have been the Divine Wind for which so many Japanese were praying. It would have dispersed the troop transports and neutralized the Americans' overwhelming air strength. Conversely, had it been possible to launch Olympic on the heels of the storm, Louise would have been a Divine Wind for the attackers. Elaborate tunnel systems were flooded, fortifications washed out, and communications disrupted. Typhoon Louise was relatively more damaging to Japanese defenses than to American invasion preparations. Although the havoc wrought by the storm was a setback to Operation Olympic, it was not a disastrous one. After the September 16 typhoon it had been decided to maintain reserves of food and tentage, and stocks were already en route when Louise struck. Within a week after the storm much of the damage to facilities had been repaired and air strikes were resumed. Damaged vessels were being made seaworthy or had been replaced. Stockpiles were mounting again, with some of the less bulky supplies such as radio parts and blood plasma being flown in.

Nonetheless, Typhoon Louise was used to advantage by Japanese propagandists. In Tokyo, the controlled press and radio ignored the destruction on Kyushu and greatly exaggerated that on Okinawa. Louise was hailed as a mighty blow to the Yankees. It gave a short-lived but sorely needed boost to the morale of a population which until now, homeless, hungry and in constant fear of air attack, had little to nourish its cherished national spirit.

The effects of the typhoon, other delays and an unfavorable long-range weather forecast for November 1 tipped the scales in favor of postponing the invasion. X-Day was set back to November 12. Postponement of the invasion, with the subsequent prolongation of air attacks throughout the home islands, increased the agony of the Japanese civilian population. After Japan's sixty-six largest cities, excluding Kyoto, were so badly gutted they were no longer profitable targets, the planes began attacking the smaller towns. Tokyo, which in 1944 had a population of six and a half million, was eighty-five percent destroyed and its population fell to slightly over a million. Those who had not fled to presumably safer areas lived in subways and bomb shelters. Thousands built shanties outside the walls of the palace grounds when it became obvious the Americans did not intend bombing the Emperor's residence. As word of Kyoto's immunity spread throughout Honshu, refugees made their way to the sacred city in growing numbers. The city's population soared from one million to three. Hunger and disease took increasing toll and the struggle for survival brought Kyoto close to anarchy.

On October 29, X-14, the Third Fleet shifted its attacks from general targets to concentrate on aircraft, air installations and shipping to prevent further reinforcements of Kyushu. Two thousand Ryukyu fighters and bombers added their striking power to that of the fleet. Heavy diversionary attacks were made on Shikoku. Meanwhile, the Amphibious Attack Forces, which by now had been consolidated in final assembly areas, were completing invasion rehearsals. An Advance Force comprising battleships, carriers, cruisers, destroyers, gunboats and hundreds of specialized craft for minesweeping, underwater demolition, hydrographic survey and radar detection of suicide attackers was already steaming toward the invasion beaches.

The Western and Southern Attack Forces, both part of the Advance Force, set out from the Philippines on November 1. Next day the Reserve Force also sailed from the Philippines and the minesweepers and underwater demolition flotilla of the Advance Force departed Okinawa. Simultaneously, the tempo of the Allied air offensive increased substantially. Planes from carriers and Okinawa concentrated on cutting communications between northern Kyushu and the assault areas. This marked the beginning of an all-out ten-day air offensive intended to eliminate Kyushu's suicide planes, isolate the landing areas, smash coastal defenses, and cover minesweeping and other prelanding operations.

While still hundreds of miles from Kyushu, the Advance Force was provided with constant air cover from the Ryukyus and its own escort carriers. On the afternoon of November 3, a Nakajima Saiun, "Cloudscape," reconnaissance plane managed to elude the air screen and spotted the vanguard of the Advance Force. Based on experience gained at Okinawa, Imperial General Headquarters expected naval bombardment of the assault beaches to begin the next day. Throughout southern Kyushu, local commanders began setting their defenses and sealing beach positions from sea and air bombardment.

The Advance Force reached its objective areas off the small outer islands and the main assault beaches on November 4, X-8, and the opening phase of the invasion of Kyushu began. The ships and planes of the Advance Force were joined by aircraft from the Fast Carrier Force and island bases as far away as the Marianas. The B-29s of General James H. Doolittle's Okinawa-based Eighth Air Force alone were scheduled to drop a thousand tons of bombs on every landing beach by the time assault troops hit them. Battleships, carriers, cruisers, destroyers and gunboats moved in behind the minesweepers to plaster beach defenses with shells, bombs and rockets. U.S. Underwater Demolition Teams began clearing the offshore island beach approaches under cover of smokescreens and intense sea and air bombardment.

On November 6 the Reserve Force arrived at Okinawa and the Southern Attack Force left the island for its November 8 assault on Tanega-shima, the little island fifteen miles south of Kyushu. The Fifth Attack Force left the Marianas for the Kushikino beaches. Next day the Seventh Attack Force sailed from the Philippines for the eastern Kyushu beaches, the Reserve Force left Okinawa in a wide sweep toward Shikoku, and the Western Landing Force hit the Koshiki island chain thirty miles west of Kyushu. On the following morning the Southern Landing Force stormed Tanega-shima. While the Western and Southern Attack Forces were being bloodied on the offshore islands, the Third Attack Force left the Philippines for the Ariake beaches, and Underwater Demolition Teams were clearing the seaward defenses of the three Kyushu assault areas, including Biro Island out in Ariake Bay, and the Shikoku beaches to be threatened in the Reserve Force's feint two days later. Though fighting continued on the offshore islands, combat troops, engineers and swarms of Army and Navy specialists were already at work putting in protected anchorages, emergency repair facilities, radar warning sites and navigational aids. A hospital ship, tankers and ammunition ships were on their way to the Koshiki islands in anticipation of X-Day needs.

On November 9, X-3, sea and air forces softening up the assault areas reached peak strength. Battleships and cruisers of the Fast Carrier Force added their batteries to those which had been shelling the Japanese for five days. Fighters and bombers ranged over southern Kyushu on a twenty-four-hour schedule. By night, flares and star shells illuminated key target areas and smaller vessels took over the incessant bombardment from the battleships and cruisers, which retired to sea during the hours of darkness. Underwater Demolition Teams worked ever closer to the shoreline, blasting underwater obstacles and masses of floating tree trunks. The Japanese did not retaliate. Except for scattered mortar and small arms fire from soldiers disobeying strict orders not to disclose their positions, and furtive nighttime activity detected in the light of flares and star shells, southern Kyushu appeared deserted.

Just before dusk on November 9, a patrolling Japanese submarine, the I-402, detected the Reserve Force on its course for Shikoku. At this point the Japanese were not certain whether the task force would continue to Shikoku or alter course for Kyushu. The defenses of both islands were put on full alert and night reconnaissance planes were sent out to shadow the enemy fleet. When the Reserve Force began what appeared to be a preinvasion bombardment of Shikoku in the early hours of November 10 the Japanese suspected a feint but nevertheless prepared to resist full-scale landings. The major landings were still expected at Kushikino, Ariake Bay and Miyazaki and no shift of ground forces toward Shikoku was begun. Only sea and air units were committed in the Shikoku sector. A hundred and twenty-five Shinyo crash boats were sent against the invasion fleet during the remaining hours of darkness, followed at dawn by 250 kamikaze planes. Most of the crash boats were intercepted and destroyed by "flycatcher" patrols—gunboats, destroyers and a few cruisers equipped with powerful searchlights. A few Shinyo got through the screen to attack the transports, one of which was left sinking, but the others, finding it impossible to penetrate the protective screen, attacked the screening vessels and rammed a destroyer and a dozen gunboats and small patrol craft. Less than 30 kamikaze planes evaded the Combat Air Patrol and antiaircraft fire the first day to score hits, but they did considerable damage. In all, two days of sea and air suicide attacks sank two transports and damaged five more. Of other vessels, 22 were sunk, mostly smaller craft, and three times that number damaged. The ratio of sinkings to hits was greater than at Okinawa because the Shikoku kamikaze carried heavier bombs. The Japanese lost 200 crash boats, 15 midget subs and more than 400 aircraft, including kamikaze escorts.

Although U.S. losses were small in proportion to those of the Japanese, the feint had failed in its primary purpose. No Japanese ground strength was shifted out of the intended landing areas and the bulk of the enemy's suicide craft remained uncommitted.

Meanwhile, the three main Attack Forces were approaching southern Kyushu. Though they had not yet been detected, the Japanese were positive their arrival was imminent. At first light on November 11, a Japanese patrol plane sighted the Third Attack Force two hundred and fifty miles at sea, steaming for Ariake Bay. In what was left of Tokyo, Imperial General Headquarters greeted the news with relief and fierce satisfaction. The bulk of Kyushu's defensive works and soldiery, protected by earth, concrete and terrain, was intact and almost two-thirds of Japan's sea and air suicide craft had survived the attacks on their bases. It appeared Japanese forces were deployed in the best possible position to deal the Americans the one last smashing blow, which all except such fanatics as Admiral Onishi realized would be the only consolation for utter defeat.

By eleven in the morning of November 11, X-1, Japanese submarines and reconnaissance planes had located all three Attack Forces and estimated their strength and objectives. Throughout western and southern Japan the first waves of suicide planes were alerted to intercept the approaching convoys that afternoon and all of the Imperial Navy's remaining submarines and destroyers prepared to sortie out under cover of darkness. Some 1,500 crashboats and hundreds of midget submarines and human torpedoes were made ready to attack when the convoys drew within range. Twenty-five hundred Fukuryu, "Crouching Dragons," 500 on the west coast, 1,200 at Ariake Bay and 800 on the east coast, prepared to enter the sea just before dawn.

The American juggernaut bore down on the beaches of Kyushu. In nests along the coast and at concealed airfields, thousands of suicide boats, midget submarines, human torpedoes and kamikaze aircraft awaited the signal to attack. In the coastal cliffs and in the hills, hidden guns awaited targets. On the beaches, behind the dikes of paddy fields, in the forests and on every commanding slope, Japanese soldiers waited quietly in tunnels, caves, pits and burrows. Southern Kyushu braced itself for the impending holocaust, not in dread but with an eagerness both savage and spiritual.

1

[Lieutenant Minoru Hasegawa/Gunner's Mate Second Class Perry Hurst/ Captain Alfred "Red" Millikin]

Outside the cave it was still full darkness when the bugle awakened Lieutenant Minoru Hasegawa at 5 A.M. He went instantly from deep slumber to full awareness. Before opening his eyes he cleaned his lids of the fine grit that had sifted down from the cave roof during the night.

He swung his feet over the side of his cot and groped for his flying boots. When he pulled them on he stood up and shook out the square cloth he wore tied around his head to keep the grit out of his hair. Inoue called it his hachimaki, the white cloth kamikaze wound around their heads before a mission, and made the same jokes every night. Had he written his will and would he care to leave a strand of hair or some nail clippings as a memento for his family? The others slept with their blankets pulled over their heads but Hasegawa did not like anything over his face. On Iwo Jima he had been buried for almost an hour in an American bombing and if his face was covered he sometimes dreamed of it.

He could hear Inoue and Watanabe hawking and muttering half serious curses. Kuwahara, as usual, continued to snore. It took more than a bugle to rouse him. He always had to be shaken awake. Hasegawa pushed aside the straw mat covering the cave entrance and stepped outside. Too many stars were visible. That meant no clouds and another fine day.

Hasegawa had not thought he would live to see a time when good flying weather displeased him. An overcast would hamper the American reconnaissance planes that flew over at regular intervals. The enemy had not yet detected the hidden Kobayashi airfield but one could not tell when an American photo interpreter might discover some flaw in the camouflage. If that happened they could be sure of a deadly pounding. They had already been forced to abandon the big air base at Kanoya, leaving only ground forces to destroy the paratroops the Americans were almost certain to drop on the heels of amphibious landings.

And this might be the day the transports were sighted. The Americans had been bombarding the Miyazaki coast for a week now and should have attempted landings there two days ago. Perhaps they had learned their lesson at Shikoku, where their invasion fleet had been kept from landing yesterday. No, despite that bloody defeat, the Americans would come to Miyazaki. And if they came today, cloud formations would be better protection against the convoys' air cover than a whole squadron of Shiden fighters.

The air outside the fetid cave was bracing. Hasegawa looked toward Miyazaki City, thirty miles to the east, and listened to the low mutter of the nightly bombardment. Though sound traveled better at night, it was always louder during the day, when the battleships returned to join in the bombardment and the B-29s bombed the beaches. Though the uplands were cool at this hour of the morning, Hasegawa removed his upper clothing and washed his face, hands, neck and armpits in the wooden water pail. He longed for a proper bath, with buckets of hot water and a long soaking in a deep steaming tub. But it was unlikely he would get one before his final bath in the chilly sea. He dressed quickly and went back inside the cave.

Inoue was shaking Kuwahara and shouting, "Wake up, Kuma-san, Mr. Bear. The winter is finished."

Clown, thought Hasegawa. Inoue was not serious enough for the task facing the Kobayashi Squadron when the American troop transports drew within range. But Inoue flew well enough and kept everyone in high spirits. In the weeks of helpless idleness while the enemy had been ranging freely over the land the squadron had needed a clown.

"Ah, Hasegawa," Inoue cried in the darkness, sensing the lieutenant's presence. "Just getting in? Have you been visiting your sweetheart in Kobayashi again?"

Hasegawa's Kobayashi sweetheart was a fiction enjoyed by the entire squadron, for of all the officer pilots except an ensign long impotent from a groin wound, he was considered the one most unlikely to have a woman. Hasegawa, they said, loved only his plane. This, too, was a fiction. To Hasegawa his plane was a weapon and he felt for it as a samurai might have felt for his sword. He had revealed to no one there was a girl in Fukushima, his native city, to whom he would have long since been betrothed had a Navy fighter pilot's prospects of survival been brighter. Nor did anyone know why, even in less desperate times, he had never visited a brothel as so many of his companions did and only rarely had been seen in a bar. Bars and brothels took money and all he kept from the insignificant pay of a lieutenant was enough pocket money for necessities. The rest went to his family in Fukushima. With inflation and the black market his father's pay as a minor prefectural official was not enough to feed and clothe his mother and two sisters properly. For many months his contribution had meant little. Food was scarce at any price and there was hunger everywhere, even starvation.

"Ossan," Inoue went on, persisting. "You didn't answer. You must be very tired after a sleepless night. If we sortie today how will you stay awake?"

All the kamikaze escort pilots in the Kobayashi Squadron called Hasegawa Ossan, "uncle." Only the squadron commander was older than he and except at the controls of his Shiden "Lightning" fighter Hasegawa was as solemn and deliberate in his judgments as a village elder. Age alone had not won Uncle Minoru his nickname. It was also an oblique expression of respect for his prowess. In more than a hundred air battles from Rabaul to Okinawa and in defense of the naval base at Kure he had destroyed eleven American fighters and a B-29. The kamikaze for whom he was to fly cover had not even seen American planes except from the ground.

There had been a time when Hasegawa laughed often, spoke freely, and made friends easily. But all his friends, and there had been a long succession of them, were dead now; so many of them over the years that except for the rawest young kamikaze there was not a pilot in the squadron who did not remind him in one way or another of some comrade lost in action. Hasegawa was solemn and taciturn beyond his years because he was weary to the bone after five years of uninterrupted combat and prey to disturbing thoughts. He tried to think only of the coming days, in which the Americans would be dealt such a bloody defeat that they would welcome an honorable peace, as the admiral had explained in his inspection visit. But he could not blot out thoughts of what his family was enduring if they were still alive. He had had no word of them for two months, nor had anyone else at Kobayashi airfield had recent news of their families.

He was assured a fine death and desired nothing more for himself, but for his parents and sisters there could be only greater hardships in the days ahead. Fukushima, in northern Honshu, was larger than Kobayashi and therefore could not have escaped a similar fate. Kobayashi was little more than ashes and every day hundreds of its citizens seeking food and medical attention had been turned away from the airfield. In the faces of these homeless, starving and often maimed refugees he saw the faces of his parents and sisters.

"You are unusually silent," said Inoue, also a joke because Hasegawa was known for his silence. "You absolutely will fall asleep if we sortie today."

Only Inoue habitually spoke to Hasegawa in this fashion. The others held him in too great respect. Hasegawa wished he were spiritual enough not to dislike Inoue. Men who flew together should be closer than brothers and in the past this had always been so. He scarcely knew Inoue. They had not met until Inoue was assigned as his wingman at Kobayashi. It was not Inoue's overfamiliarity alone that offended Hasegawa. Of all the firebrands vociferously eager to die in combat, Inoue was the most strident. The first precept of the Imperial Rescript to Soldiers and Sailors said, "Be resolved that duty is heavier than a mountain, while death is lighter than a feather." Nevertheless, no man of any worth should go about proclaiming how he desired a glorious death above all else and boasting of the deeds he intended to perform. It was understood that any man who wore the insignia of a Navy pilot was always prepared to meet death. And one did not speak of deeds. Deeds spoke for one.

Kuwahara was at last awake and on his feet, groaning and complaining that Inoue had been too rough. Hasegawa led them all outside for fifteen minutes of calisthenics and deep-breathing exercises. Cave living was enervating and special attention must be paid to keeping fit. Though it was still dark Hasegawa could see that Kuwahara was only going through the motions and he rebuked him for it. A harsh word from Hasegawa was as effective as a blow from someone else.

It was after six and the morning was tinged with light when they went to breakfast. As usual there was no fish, only a little bean-paste soup, a scant bowl of rice and millet, and a few pickles. At that, the pilots ate better than the troops. And as usual, Inoue grumbled, asking how one was expected to shoot down Grummans on such rations. There were millions who were having no breakfast at all, Hasegawa thought gloomily, perhaps even his own mother, but he said nothing. Inoue quickly regained his abrasive high spirits after breakfast. He belched politely, as if acknowledging a repast, and pretended to pick his teeth.

"Today is the day we sortie," he said. "I feel it in my stomach. So I'll treat myself to a cigarette in celebration."

Inoue had said the same thing every morning for weeks. Cigarettes were scarce, even for escort pilots, and everyone rationed theirs stingily.

Hasegawa walked through the trees to the revetment where his plane was hidden. His mechanic was wiping the morning dew from the big four-bladed propeller. The man turned at the sound of Hasegawa's approach and saluted.

"Sir?" he said eagerly, "is there any news?"

"No," said Hasegawa.

A good man, Kato, he thought. One always found him fussing around the plane, even though during the long stand-down it had required little more than protective maintenance.

Kato looked downcast.

"One of the men from signals said there was much activity last night," he said. "I thought maybe . . . but they will come soon, won't they, sir?"

"Yes," Hasegawa said.

"Well, then," Kato said, brightening.

Without being told, he came around the wing and gave Hasegawa a leg up as he had done every day for a number of weeks. Hasegawa slid back the canopy and climbed into the cockpit. It had been wiped dry and the instruments gleamed. Kato had already been at work there. Hasegawa fastened his seat belt and adjusted the straps of his parachute. Escort pilots had been ordered to wear chutes. If an escort plane was hopelessly damaged within range of enemy vessels, the pilot was to make a crash dive. Otherwise they were to get back over friendly territory and bail out. There was a grave shortage of experienced pilots. Inoue had at first declared he would not wear a parachute. It hampered one in the air and indicated a lack of spirit, he said. Hasegawa had given him a direct order and for once had bothered to give an explanation, though it was also a reprimand.

"Our duty is to remain alive and protect the kamikaze until our own time comes to make a special attack," he said bitingly.

Kato pulled the camouflage netting clear of the propeller. Hasegawa started the engine and ran it up. He kept the canopy open. He did not want the thunderous roar filling the revetment to be diminished even by a fragile shield of Plexiglas. His spirits soared with the sound. After two minutes he reluctantly reduced power and shut off the engine. Fuel was more precious than blood. He remained in the cockpit, unwilling to leave his plane even though earthbound. From the dispersal areas came the sound of other engines getting their daily run-up. He could distinguish the type of plane by the noise of the engine, from the full-throated roar of the Shiden to the tinny beat of the old trainers which many of the kamikaze would fly into battle. In the background the constant rumbling at the Miyazaki coast was broken frequently by distant but heavy explosions. The American battleships were back from their night retirement. It seemed that today, as the two days previous, the volume of large-caliber fire had increased. He hoped it meant the Americans would soon attempt their landings.

Hasegawa stood up in the cockpit, his head pressing against the camouflage netting stretched across the revetment. By standing on tiptoe he could see over the mounds of packed earth sheltering the plane. Hinamori Peak rose five miles to the southwest and beyond it the many-humped spine of the Kirishima Range. Mile-high Karakuni, tallest of the Kirishimas, loomed almost directly beyond Hinamori. To Hasegawa's left, eight miles from where he stood, were the twin peaks of Takachiho, where legend said the grandson of Amaterasu the Sun Goddess had come to earth to found Japan, and where the grandson's grandson, Jimmu Tenno, remote ancestor of Emperor Hirohito, was born and became Japan's first emperor six hundred and sixty years before the Christian Jesus lived. Directly ahead of Hasegawa, beyond the trees which helped conceal the presence of the airfield, was a paddy field, dry now after the fall rice harvest and dotted with cylindrical stacks of rice straw. Two farmers were laboriously moving a small, highsided two-wheeled cart across the field, one of them between the shafts like a horse, the other pushing from behind. They would be either women or old men, he knew. All the young and middle-aged men had been conscripted. Some of the local men had been detailed to dig shelters and do other labor. He had seen them. Mostly a sullen lot who did not appear grateful for the honor bestowed on them, a chance to die for the Emperor. Yet he could not fully blame them. What did they know of war except privation and destruction? It was different with him. From his first days in the Navy, Hagakure, the code of Bushido, had been hammered into him constantly. "A samurai lives in such a way that he is always prepared to die." And when he died it would not be without having taken his toll of the enemy. Few conscripts, with their limited training and pitiful weapons, would have that satisfaction.

The cart stopped at one of the cylindrical stacks and the farmers began filling it with straw. They could be either men or women. It was impossible to tell at this distance. They dressed the same. From the south came the familiar sound of aircraft. After a moment one of the farmers appeared to have heard it, too, for he plucked the other by the sleeve and then began running across the field. The sound grew in volume.

"Sir, please come down," Kato said anxiously.

Hasegawa said nothing.

Soon a flight of three planes appeared, flying low in careless formation. They flashed across his line of vision, Grumman Hellcats, huge and silver, painted with the detestable American star. Their course would take them directly over the cart. The plane at the right of the vee dipped a few feet below the other two. Hasegawa saw lights winking on the leading edge of the wing and tracers diving into the cart before he heard the sound of the Hellcat's guns. The cart disintegrated and the farmer who had been loading straw was flung to one side. He lay motionless. The three planes disappeared to the north, the right wingman rising to rejoin the formation. The other farmer kept running across the field and did not stop until the sound of engines had faded in the distance. He turned and looked toward the smoking cart. Hasegawa heard a woman's voice shouting. So the one who had run was a woman. She ran back to the cart. It was burning now.

Hasegawa clenched his teeth and shook his fist at the departed planes. Beast, he thought in helpless rage. Murderer. If only someday he could meet that unspeakable coward in the air. The strawstack as well as the cart was burning now. The woman had dropped to her knees beside the other farmer and was striking the ground with her head.

Hasegawa climbed down from the cockpit, trembling with anger.

"Sir, what happened?" Kato asked.

"They killed a farmer."

"Oh," said Kato, looking relieved. "Is that all?"

Hasegawa's fury turned from the American pilot to his mechanic. He hit Kato hard in the face. Kato staggered, his expression one of astonishment, not pain, then quickly regained his balance and stood at attention. Hasegawa hit him again and again, venting his anger and frustration. Kato reeled against the side of the revetment and slumped to a sitting position, dazed. Hasegawa looked down at him, panting and empty. In a little while Kato got to his feet and came to attention again, as if awaiting more blows. When none came he spoke through bruised lips.

"I apologize for whatever I have done wrong, sir," he said.

Hasegawa did not exactly regret beating Kato, for it had eased him and enlisted men were accustomed to beatings, though it was the first time he had struck his mechanic. It was established practice to discipline subordinates with blows and as a cadet pilot he had himself been beaten many times, and not merely with fists but with bats and straps as well. Yet Kato had not deserved this beating. He did his work well and was not the one who had killed the farmer. Hasegawa felt a craving for a cigarette but he could not smoke near the aircraft. Also, when he indulged himself it reminded him unpleasantly of Inoue.

"Go tend to your face," he said matter-of-factly, indicating the incident was to be forgotten.

Kato smiled, obviously relieved that all was well again. He saluted and as he turned to leave, Hasegawa stopped him and gave Kato the cigarette he had wanted to smoke himself.

"Thank you, sir," Kato said, beaming.

Hasegawa regretted the action almost immediately. Kato might regard the gesture as an apology. He would be severe with Kato tomorrow so there would be no misunderstanding. With that he dismissed Kato from his thoughts.

He set out for the operations bunker to see if there was any news. The signals bunker was actually the place for that, but so many pilots had made a habit of congregating there it had been placed off limits to all but on-duty code and signals personnel and the officers who lived there. Before he reached the bunker he was intercepted by a breathless messenger who told him all pilots were to report to operations at once and raced off before Hasegawa could question him. Hasegawa began running. Other pilots were converging on the operations bunker, some wearing their heavy flying suits as if expecting a scramble. Hasegawa knew it could not be that. They were not allowed to attack enemy formations even when the Americans hit 25th Infantry Division positions in the area. They could only cower in their burrows like hares. But it could be news of a sighting. If it were, he prayed it was not another false alarm.

The pilots, only a sprinkling of whom were officers, crowded into the access tunnel without regard to rank, pushing, shoving, and shouting questions. What had happened to discipline, he wondered, not to mention ordinary courtesy. The tunnel was lined with men standing on either side with their backs against the bunks of operations personnel. Naked light bulbs provided dim illumination. The operations bunker was one of the few places with electricity. The power came from a generator deep within a hill several hundred yards from the airfield. Hasegawa saw Inoue and Watanabe and joined them.

"Where is Kuwahara?" he demanded.

"He couldn't locate his boots so we came without him," Watanabe said nervously.

Hasegawa was on the verge of sending him to fetch Kuwahara when the missing pilot ducked into the entrance wearing a sheepish expression. He joined his comrades, avoiding Hasegawa's gaze. Hasegawa would have wondered how such a man could be assigned to escort duty had he not known Kuwahara was one of the few fully-trained pilots in the squadron, with two victories to his credit.

The tunnel buzzed with suppressed excitement and the air grew thick with the exhalations of many men. Hasegawa studied the faces of the assembled pilots. It was a depressing sight. So many of them were little more than schoolboys and, despite their uniforms, looked it. All except the handful of seasoned pilots were kamikaze. Hasegawa did not know any of the kamikaze and of the lot only two had made any impression on him. One was a youngster of perhaps seventeen with long coarse hair always hanging down over his forehead. The few times Hasegawa had seen him he had the same uncertain look he wore now. Of the other youths in the tunnel, some displayed feigned bravado and the eyes of others glittered with a fanatical light. The second kamikaze was older, older even than Hasegawa.

He stood out from the others because of his appearance as well as his age. His face was smug, self-confident and impassive and he bore himself like a soldier. It was said he had been a hancho at Tsuchiura Naval Air Station, a petty officer assigned to the military training and discipline of cadet pilots. And that his nickname there had been Yaju, "The Beast." Although down to bone and muscle like everyone else, he was still a powerfully built man. He went about carrying a small bat as if it were an officer's sword. It was said it was the same bat with which he had beaten the student pilots in his charge and it had a name of its own, Yamato Damashii Chunyubo, "Bat for Instilling Japanese Spirit." Recalling his own beatings, from which he still bore a chipped front tooth and a scar on one buttock, Hasegawa disliked the man intensely though he wished more of the kamikaze were like The Beast and not frightened or wild-eyed boys.

The squadron commander arrived at last. Everyone fell silent and came to attention, all but the shortest having to duck their heads because of the low roof. Hasegawa, who at five inches over five feet was taller than average, was one of those who could not stand fully erect and he did not feel properly at attention. The squadron commander surveyed the two rows of silent men and, though he appeared bursting with news, let half a minute go by before speaking. From the operations room at the far end of the tunnel came the sound of much activity.

"The enemy fleet off Shikoku has been prevented from landing for the second morning," he said at last.

There was only mild response. The news, though good, was not what they had wanted to hear. The Kobayashi Squadron had not been sent into action against the fleet threatening Shikoku, denying the unit a part in Japan's first great victory in many months. But if the Americans made their anticipated assault on the Miyazaki beaches the Kobayashi Squadron would be assured a principal role.

The squadron commander paused before continuing. He had a fine and sometimes annoying sense of the dramatic.

"An even larger American convoy has been detected on course for the Miyazaki front," he said. "The enemy is sailing directly into our trap."

The pilots cheered wildly, Hasegawa for once as demonstrative as any. No longer would he have to hide himself in the ground while American planes bombed and strafed unhindered and American warships stood in close to shore, shelling Japanese soil without retaliation. Kuwahara in his excitement hit his head against the roof, showering himself and those beside him with dirt. They took no heed of it. The squadron commander, smiling indulgently, waited for the shouting to abate before continuing

"Other enemy convoys have been sighted sailing toward our impregnable defenses on the Ariake and Kushikino fronts."

There was more wild cheering. Hasegawa, having quickly regained his composure, did not participate. He saw no reason to cheer. Those who did were either fools or pretenders. How could they hope to beat off three invasion fleets as great or greater than that which despite its heavy losses continued to threaten Shikoku? For the first time a thought surfaced which he had kept so deeply buried he had not been fully aware of its existence. Japan's cause was so hopeless that no temporary success could materially affect the outcome. Every life lost would be lost uselessly. Though he had never allied himself with the fanatics who desired nothing more than a glorious death, he had felt only contempt for those who questioned the value of dying in a hopeless cause. Now he realized some of them might not be cowards and traitors and that their sense of honor might be no less than the zealots'. He understood for the first time he would die willingly only because it was his duty to die. He would not die joyously even though he could not bear the thought of living to see Japan defeated.

"We have been given the honor of providing twelve special attack units for the first strike," the squadron commander said. "The following pilots have been chosen for the privilege of being the first members of the Kobayashi Squadron to strike a mortal blow against the enemy."

He read twelve names from a list and as he did so each man stepped forward one pace. Among them were the petty officer called The Beast and the schoolboy with the unruly hair. Those whose names had not been called shouted protests. The squadron commander held up his hand for silence.

"Escorts will be Lieutenant Hasegawa, Ensign Inoue and Ensign Kuwahara," he said.

Watanabe burst into tears and rushed up to the squadron commander demanding to know why he alone of Hasegawa's flight had not been chosen. The squadron commander sent him back to his place without a reprimand for his outburst.

"For those of you who must wait, I promise there will be opportunities to display your courage and your devotion to our Emperor," he said.

Orderlies came in with sake and a bag of cups and everyone toasted the pilots selected for the first mission. Those who were to make the attack were given a cup though in normal times a Navy pilot was forbidden to drink even the night before a mission. The twelve kamikaze and three escort pilots went into the operations room and the others were dismissed.

The operations room was a fairly well-lit and spacious rectangular chamber containing a desk, a filing cabinet, two large tables, several chairs, radio equipment and a field telephone. Maps were fastened to the dirt walls with wooden pegs. One corner of the room was screened off. The operations officer slept there.

The depression Hasegawa had felt earlier vanished, to be replaced by mounting excitement. He felt elated, as if the report of the three convoys had indeed been good news, and instead of useless deaths and hopeless causes he thought only of the action to come. Whether he returned or not was of little importance if the kamikaze did their work well.

The squadron commander and the operations officer briefed them on the mission, the operations officer pointing out the approach route and the anticipated position of the American transports and their screening vessels with a slender bamboo wand. The kamikaze were due over the target at 2 P.M. At that time it was expected the transports would be within one hundred seventy-five miles of the Miyazaki coast, almost due east of the airfield. The formation would not fly a direct course but would fly out to sea on a northeasterly heading to conceal its point of departure and to avoid the heavy concentration of enemy warships bombarding the coast. The kamikaze would not form over the field but would do so en route to reduce the chance of detection by American air patrols and long-range radar. The slowest planes would take off first and the speediest last, to overtake them on course.

"You will maintain an altitude of no more than fifteen meters until you have sighted the troop transports," the squadron commander said. "Each pilot will select his target and make his attack from an altitude of five hundred meters. Do not forget your aiming point is midway between the bridge and the center of the vessel. Escorts will remain in the area only long enough to observe results."

Hasegawa did not believe this was the proper tactic. True, a low-level approach avoided much of the antiaircraft fire and lessened the chance of early detection, but it required a degree of flying skill beyond that of the kamikaze pilots. A high-level approach would make it easier for the kamikaze to identify their targets and begin their dives. If there were clouds out to sea they might provide protection for a higher approach.

"Sir," he said, "do you know if we'll have cloud cover in the target area?"

"None," the squadron commander said, smiling for the first time since the briefing began. "The Americans provide us with excellent uncoded weather reports." His face grew stern. "In any case a low-level attack has been decided on for the Kobayashi Squadron. Less capable squadrons will be attacking simultaneously from higher altitude."

Obviously the squadron commander understood the motive behind Hasegawa's question. Hasegawa was glad he had not asked more directly. It could have led to a reprimand which he would have richly deserved.

The kamikaze would fly in four elements of three planes each. There were only two navigation charts. The operations officer gave one to Hasegawa and the other to the ranking kamikaze, an untried ensign. Of the remaining element leaders, two were naval air pilots second class and the other an NAP first class. They appeared competent to Hasegawa but the other kamikaze, except for the hard-faced petty officer, looked as if they belonged in a schoolroom or paddy field. Despite this, they all showed the proper spirit, clustering eagerly around the table where the ensign was plotting the course on the chart, excited and happy as if they were going on a holiday outing. Hasegawa looked among them for the youth he had noticed on other occasions. The boy was not animated like his comrades. He listened with intense concentration while the ensign repeated the briefing instructions. Something broke his concentration and he looked up to find Hasegawa's eyes on him. He gave a guilty start, as if he had been caught in some breach of discipline. He looked away quickly. His reaction puzzled Hasegawa but the young kamikaze was quickly forgotten in the press of more important matters.

Watanabe was waiting outside the operations bunker.

"Hasegawa," he said, "would you ask the squadron commander . . ?"

"Three escorts is the number assigned," Hasegawa said curtly as they walked toward their cave for flying gear.

Watanabe's spirit was to be admired but he should not question the decisions of his superiors. Hasegawa had quite forgotten his own disguised criticism of the method of attack.

"Why were the others chosen and not me?" Watanabe burst out.

Before Hasegawa could reprimand him Inoue clapped him on the back and said, "Don't you know they're saving the best pilots for the big battle tomorrow? We'll all sortie together in the morning."

Hasegawa could not be angry with him for interfering. It was a good thing Inoue had done, offering comfort to a disappointed comrade.

"Look," said Watanabe, "if . . . if any of you don't get back will you wait for me at the gate of Yasukuni Shrine so we can all go in together?"

"I don't intend being a dead hero so soon," said Inoue. "And anyhow we'll have to wait for Kuwahara. He's never anywhere on time."

To his surprise, Hasegawa found himself laughing with the others. Inoue was a clever fellow after all. Perhaps he had misjudged him all along. Hasegawa could picture their spirits hovering impatiently outside the great shrine in Tokyo, waiting for Kuwahara to find his boots before they could join all those who had died in battle.

At 1 P.M. the U.S.S. *Sonoma,* third ship in line in its task unit, cruised at a steady fifteen knots among the other attack transports of its squadron. The transport squadron was fifteen hours away from its anchorage off

Kyushu north of Miyazaki Harbor. Aboard the *Sonoma* was a 1400-man Battalion Landing Team of the 33rd Infantry Division. Shortly after dawn the next morning the BLT would begin storming ashore on Beach Chrysler Blue One in the center of the division's twenty-eight-hundred-yard front.

The *Sonoma's* deck and sides were festooned with the landing craft which would carry the battalion to the beach. In its cargo holds were ammunition, fuel, rations, tanks, artillery and a number of crates which, by a combination of errors, had been loaded aboard the *Sonoma* instead of the attack cargo ship of the floating reserve for which they were intended. The crates contained uniform lengths of white-painted board which, when fitted together, would serve as markers for graves in a temporary cemetery for which a site had already been designated.

The air washing over the sunlit deck was cool and damp. Gunner's Mate Second Class Perry Hurst squatted on his haunches out of the breeze in the tub of his twin 40-mm. gun mount, his back against the metal shield. Hurst was gun captain of the *Sonoma's* starboard forward twin 40s. The chest harness of his telephone mouthpiece was in place but the headset was draped around his neck, the earphones turned in against his life vest so they would not pick up stray sounds and reveal he was not wearing them. The scuttle-shaped helmet which fit over the earphones, and which he was also supposed to be wearing, was between his feet. Gunner's Mate Hurst hungered for a smoke but there was no telling when the gunnery officer, the nosy bastard, a Texan naturally, might come poking around. Hurst was an Oklahoman. He said being so close to Texas gave his state a bad name. The watch still had three hours to go, three hours before he could have a cigarette without the gunnery officer breathing down his neck.

"Hey, Jew," he said. "Let me know if you see the Weasel nosin' around. I want to grab a smoke."

Jew was the nickname he had given Boatswain's Mate Third Class Barber, his gun pointer. Barber, like Hurst, was a Methodist, but he had a big nose and curly hair. Seaman First Class Shore, the gun trainer, was Jewish but was big, blond and gray-eyed. Hurst called him Heinie. Neither Barber nor Shore liked the names but they liked Hurst and took no offense when he used them.

"I'm supposed to be looking out for Japs, not the Weasel," Barber said.

"Lookie," said Hurst, taking a sack of Bull Durham from his sock, "which is worst, a Jap or a Texan?"

Hurst preferred ready-mades but the sack of tobacco had been a long cherished trademark of his. He rolled a firm, evenly packed cigarette, eyed it appreciatively, and lit up. He had spent many secret hours trying to learn rolling a cigarette with one hand but had not mastered the art.

"You guys want a smoke, I'll stand lookout," he said.

"Hurst, you know goddam well my mouth's too dry," Barber said.

"How come you're always scared before and not durin'?" Hurst demanded.

"I'm scared then, too," Barber replied. "Only you're always too scared yourself to notice."

"Like hell," Shore put in. "He's too dumb to be scared. Remember that time we had the stoppage and he threw a shell case at that kamikaze?"

"If I could of hit his prop I'd of had me a Jap," Hurst said.

"You keep squatting like that, you're gonna get yourself a case of piles," Shore said.

"When I was ranchin' I'd go weeks without ever sittin' in a chair," Hurst said.

Ranching was one of several careers to which Hurst professed when the mood seized him. He had been in the Navy eleven years, having enlisted at seventeen with his parents' grudging consent, a year short of finishing high school in Frederick, Oklahoma.

"I've been trying to figure out how old you've got to be," said Barber solemnly. "Counting your fifteen years in the Navy—"

"Sixteen," Hurst interrupted.

"—and your four years at the University of Oklahoma as star fullback—"

"Left half," Hurst said.

"Last time you told it, it was fullback. Ain't that right, Shore?"

Shore nodded.

Hurst grinned, unabashed.

"I was so good they played me every position on the team, one time or another," he said. "Even coached a little. Girls' volleyball."

"You never mentioned girls' volleyball before, did he, Barber?" Shore said.

"I'll tell you about it next liberty," Hurst said. "If I told you now it'd make you too horny and nothin' you could do about it."

"There ain't no liberty where we're heading," Shore replied.

"I wonder if it's true what they say about Jap women?" Hurst said.

He punched out the end of his cigarette and put the butt and the ashes cupped in his hand into a pocket.

"It's Chinese women supposed to be built that way," Shore said.

"I been adding it up and I make you about forty-seven," Barber said.

"Looks older than that to me," said Shore.

"That's because I was left a orphan at five and led such a . . ."

The general quarters alarm sounded, cutting Hurst off. He put on the headset and grabbed his helmet. By the time he was erect, headset and helmet were in place.

"Where?" Barber yelled. "Where?"

The boatswain's mate's pipe shrilled over the public address system.

"All hands man your battle stations!"

Barber and Shore were already in their seats at the left and right of the twin 40s and the two loaders were poised at the breech, ammunition clips in hand. Hurst spoke into the phone, unexcited and with hardly a trace of his conversational drawl. He had been frightened many times but never in anticipation of danger, only in its presence.

"Mount Number Four One, manned and ready," he reported.

The public address system sounded again.

"Now hear this. This is the captain speaking. Screen reports many bogeys approaching from the north and northwest. Strong kamikaze formations are expected in our area no later than fourteen hundred."

"Okay, Slugger," Hurst said, "now tell us about hittin'."

"All you gun crews, I want to stress the importance of hitting early and continuing to hit. Do not take time out to cheer when you hit. This is not a football game. Do not stop hitting if a plane is burning or loses a wing. Keep hitting until you splash it."

"The Old Man always says that so nice," Hurst said. "They must give elocution at the academy."

"Don't you ever shut up!" Barber said.

Fear always made him short-tempered.

"Where the hell are they?" he demanded. "Anybody see 'em yet?"

"Don't worry, Jew," Hurst said without rancor. "If they're anywheres out there they'll find us."

Captain Alfred "Red" Millikin lounged on the crew bench with his hands in his pockets and his ankles crossed. He was aircraft commander of an Okinawa-based B-29, the *Seattle Stomper II.* His flight jacket was worn and his cap soiled and misshapen from long hours of wear under a headset. It was against uniform regulations to wear the cap indoors but he would not remove it until the commanding officer entered the Quonset hut. It was his lucky cap. There was a patch on the left side near the front where a piece of flak had pierced it months ago over this same island.

The Quonset hut was at Bolo Field on Zampa Point. Red Millikin was awaiting a mission briefing to which six crews had been summoned hastily a few minutes earlier. He had not always waited so nonchalantly for a mission plan to unfold. On Saipan the first *Seattle Stomper* had been known to the rest of his squadron, including the resentful members of his own crew, as Sitting Bull. He had been notorious for aborting on missions for which the intelligence officer announced strong flak or fighter opposition could be expected. Twice he had failed to take off when the propellers were sluggish going into feathered position on the circuit check. On other occasions he had failed to get off the ground or aborted before reaching the target area for minor malfunctions which his fellow pilots would have disregarded.

It had caused little except squadron gossip and near mutiny by his crew until the big low-level fire raid on Tokyo in March. The squadron commander summoned him privately to his quarters the morning before the mission.

"Millikin," he said without preamble, "the rumor is we've got a rough one tonight. The *Seattle Stomper* better get off if you have to lift her with your bare hands."

"Major, it's not my—" Millikin protested.

"I'm doing the talking," the squadron commander snapped, cutting him off. "Don't give me any excuses now or tonight. I don't want any props not feathering, no mags going out, no cylinder head temperatures running too hot. You got that? And when you get back, I don't want any bombs in the bays. And don't kill any fish with 'em. They better be on the target."

"But, Major—"

"Lieutenant, everybody from group on down is on to you. What in God's name goes through your head when you hear the guys making jokes about Sitting Bull? I know you haven't got any guts but haven't you got any pride, either?"

"You can't talk to me like that," Millikin said stiffly.

"Like hell I can't! And if you don't get over the target tonight it'll be more than talk. Dismissed."

Millikin returned to his quarters angry and humiliated. The major would be careful, too, if he had a wife and a ten-month-old baby. And you weren't supposed to take unnecessary chances with a B-29 and endanger the lives of your crew when there was a malfunction. Sure, some guys had come dragging back on three engines but how many others had gone in because they hadn't paid attention to the little things?

But he knew he was a coward and only making excuses. And Major Jarman had sensed correctly how he cringed inside when they called his plane Sitting Bull. He was going to get over the target tonight if it killed him. The thought shook him. That was just what it might do.

Two hundred miles out of Saipan the Number Two engine had begun vibrating. In the dim lights of the instrument panel Millikin could see his co-pilot looking at him in contemptuous anticipation. Millikin got the flight engineer on interphone.

"Fazio," he said with feigned nonchalance, "what's the problem?"

"I'm checking, sir."

"Let's hope it's something you can handle," Millikin said.

"Pilot from navigator," the interphone called. "Shall I figure a heading for base?"

"No," Millikin said.

The co-pilot's face began to show signs of surprise.

In a few minutes the engine was vibrating so badly it threatened to shake itself out of the wing.

"Flight engineer from pilot," Millikin said. "Feather Number Two."

"I'll get on the radio and tell the tower we're coming back," the co-pilot said.

"Like hell you will," said Millikin. "Fazio, can we make it to the target on three?"

The co-pilot's mouth hung open in disbelief.

"Yes, sir," the flight engineer replied.

Half an hour later Number Four had to be feathered. They jettisoned the bomb load and turned back. Millikin was close to tears. Though it was obvious the abort was justified, Millikin did not get another chance to vindicate himself. Three days later the group commander, at the suggestion of Major Jarman, took advantage of a request for an instructor pilot to get rid of him. At first Millikin thought the abrupt reassignment unfair and humiliating but when he reached the States and his wife was able to join him at the new station he came to regard the incident more favorably. For a time he was troubled by the possibility that someone from his own squadron might be assigned to the same combat crew training field. When that did not occur, the disquieting memories of his Pacific Theater tour of duty faded. He had been promoted to captain and was looking forward to sitting out the rest of the war as an instructor when he was assigned to the 8th Air Force on Okinawa. His wife was pregnant with their second child.

Millikin had been frightened on his first mission out of Bolo Field. In the safety of a noncombat assignment he had lost the courage gained after his confrontation with the squadron commander on Saipan. But the B-29s had encountered no opposition. Millikin got compulsively drunk that night at the officers' club. He joked boisterously and sang obscene parodies of popular songs with everyone willing to join him. It was a celebration which none but Millikin knew was a celebration. He began seeking missions, volunteering to go in place of temporarily grounded pilots. He acquired a reputation for reckless courage after losing an engine shortly after takeoff and completing the entire mission on three.

"What the hell," he told his protesting co-pilot while the rest of the crew listened in on interphone, "it's only six hundred miles and I could glide her that far on two if I had to."

Millikin feared enemy action but not the complex, temperamental B-29. He was a superb flyer and knew it. His skill had never been questioned, only his courage. He got a Distinguished Flying Cross for the mission, which was what he was after. When he discovered on his first mission there was little flak and no fighters he had set out to fatten his combat hours and add a DFC to the Air Medal previously acquired on Saipan for more routine performance. Now he entertained hopes of a Silver Star. Even Major Jarman at Saipan had not had that. With the DFC and Silver Star ribbons on his chest, if he ever encountered Major Jarman again he could look his former squadron commander in the eye.

Now he lounged in the briefing room, commander of one of six crews chosen for their bombing accuracy. He had made a quick survey of the crew benches and, noting he was the senior aircraft commander present, knew he would almost certainly lead the formation. Because of the haste with which the mission had been organized he knew it must be an important target. And because Intelligence said the Japanese were conserving their strength for the imminent invasion he knew, regardless of the importance of the target, it was unlikely they would encounter serious opposition. This might be his Silver Star mission. He had only to keep his bombardier on the ball.

They rose when the commanding officer entered and sat down again when he took his place on the stage at the end of the hut. The briefing was short, unlike the involved, nerve-racking sessions on Saipan when the missions were long and perilous. A hidden kamikaze strip had been located that morning north of Miyakonojo in the same general area where two others had been neutralized by fighter and dive bombers. The newly discovered strip was to be knocked out in one massive strike before more kamikaze could stage through it to hit the approaching invasion forces. That meant B-29s with their great bomb loads.

"For most of you," the intelligence officer said gravely, "this could be the toughest mission since you hit this theater. Except Red Millikin, there, who's on his second tour."

Millikin felt trapped. He was leading the formation, as he had anticipated, and he had a reputation for completing any mission he began.

The intelligence officer grinned.

"What you have to worry about," he said, "is friendly forces. As usual, no Jap fighter opposition is expected. They're saving everything for our Navy, God bless its little blue bell-bottoms."

Millikin breathed easily again. The intelligence officer was only having his little joke. The Navy was notoriously trigger-happy but nobody was likely to mistake a B-29 for a kamikaze.

"You'll be flying roughly between the Third and Fifth Attack Force operating areas and may not fly over any of ours. But just in case, flash a big smile out of both sides of the big bird so those battleships and cruisers can see how friendly you are."

The other briefing officers took over in turn. Each plane would carry the maximum bomb load, forty five-hundred-pounders with a five-second delay to insure heavy cratering. The planes would make their bombing runs in trail at seventy-five hundred feet, since no flak was expected.

"You will take Route Claude to Point Emerald," the group navigator said, touching the wall map with a long pointer as he spoke. "From Point Emerald you will proceed to Point Schlitz via Route Claude 4. Course to the target from Point Schlitz, three-three-zero. Note this heading will take you almost directly over the middle of Ariake Wan. Intelligence has asked me to tell you to be on the lookout for any unusual activity. It may be very busy there tomorrow."

As they left the Quonset hut Millikin motioned for his bombardier to join him.

"You better lay 'em right in there or it's your ass," he said.

"You know I never miss," the bombardier said. "This looks like a good one, don't it, Red."

Millikin shrugged and settled his battered cap on his head.

"You should have been out here nine, ten months ago," he said. "That's when we had some good ones."

"That's when you got that flak hole in your hat, wasn't it?"

Millikin nodded casually, as if it were a matter of little importance.

Lieutenant Minoru Hasegawa taxied toward the grass runway. The kamikaze were already converging on it from their dispersal areas and lining up for takeoff. The squadron commander and his staff were at attention by the runway, saluting them. Hasegawa's was the first of the three Shiden flying escort for the twelve kamikaze. Inoue taxied behind him. Then came Kuwahara, who would be the last to take off. Hasegawa knew had it not been for radio silence Inoue would be on the air making a joke about that. A bulbous-nosed Shiragiku "White Chrysanthemum" advanced trainer labored down the runway. It lifted off uncertainly, wobbling a bit as if the pilot were fighting the controls. The five-hundred-pound bomb suspended from its belly brushed the treetops well beyond the end of the runway. The plane steadied and flew off toward the northeast. The next plane, another Shiragiku, was already climbing at the end of the strip. It banked to follow the first plane. The wing dipped lower and lower. Hasegawa watched helplessly, wanting to shout instructions. The plane made a long arc and disappeared behind a pine grove. A plume of smoke and flame rose above the trees, followed by the sound of an explosion. They must get off quickly now, Hasegawa thought. The fire might attract enemy fighters.

A Zero was airborne, followed by another, and then in quick succession four Tokka, sleek new planes built for special attacks and carrying eleven-hundred pound bombs. They were flown by the element leaders. Hasegawa was next. Men standing in the concealment of trees and shadows lined the strip, waving their hats and small banners. Hasegawa had flown escort for many kamikaze missions, going all the way back to the early ones from Mabalacat in the Philippines. Of them all, this one had been mounted with the least ceremony. He allowed himself one quick look at the countryside before devoting his attention to the skies and the kamikaze up ahead. Kobayashi smoldered, a black smudge amid the green of grass and woods and the brown of dormant paddy fields on rolling ground and terraced hills.

Inoue and Kuwahara were tight on either wing. He could see them both plainly. Inoue was grinning, an earflap of his helmet tucked up in the manner of brash young Navy pilots of better days. Kuwahara was serious but alert, totally different from the Kuwahara who had to be shaken awake. For a moment Hasegawa knew the old predatory joy of being airborne and on the way to attack, himself and his aircraft of one piece and undefeatable. The escorts quickly overtook the kamikaze, strung out over the landscape like bits of paper floating aimlessly on a pond. It was not until they reached the seacoast well north of Miyazaki that there was any semblance of a formation. The four Tokka, four Shiragiku trainers, two Zeros and one peeling Suisei dive bomber straggled over a dangerously wide area. Though the escorts' assigned position was to one side of the kamikaze, Hasegawa circled them, herding the kamikaze into tighter formation. At times he flew close enough to see the pilots, their heads bound in hachimaki. The Beast was in a Zero, flying tolerable formation; the boy he had watched at briefing in a trainer and unable to maintain a constant distance from his element leader. When Hasegawa had the kamikaze in as close as he thought safe considering their limited training in formation flying, he returned to his station a little behind and off to the right. Throughout his maneuvers, Inoue and Kuwahara had not varied their positions off his wings by more than a few feet.

They flew low over an empty sea beneath an empty sky. Hasegawa was not lulled into a sense of false security. At any moment enemy fighters might appear. Hasegawa interrupted his sweeping search of the sky to look at his watch and the chart on his knee. They would soon reach the point at which they were to make a ninety-degree turn for the target area. One of the trainers fell behind until it was abreast of the escorts. Hasegawa signaled the pilot to increase power. The trainer's propeller slowed and then stopped completely. The plane went into a short, steep glide and hit the water. There was no explosion. In seconds the wreckage was far behind. Two planes lost before they had even seen the enemy, Hasegawa thought angrily.

The lead kamikaze dipped its wings in a signal and the formation banked to the right, spreading out sloppily. Hasegawa glimpsed a cluster of planes high above them. He motioned to his wingmen but they had already sighted the formation. He watched the gnatlike cluster intently, waiting for planes to peel off in an attack. The swarm continued to move deliberately on the same course as the Kobayashi formation. The planes must be Japanese. Hasegawa had not seen Americans fly so sloppy a formation since the war's early years. Though the planes were too far off for positive identification something about their outlines suggested they were Army, and a mixed lot like the formation he was escorting.

Suddenly other planes darted into the swarm above and the Army formation scattered. Enemy fighters at last. Hasegawa searched quickly in all directions. Nothing. Perhaps the Army formation would draw off all the enemy fighters in the area and his low-level formation would go undetected until it reached the American picket ships. For once he thought highly of the Army. Off to the left of the Kobayashi formation a plane plummeted down, on fire and trailing smoke. It was an Army Hayabusa 2. The Kobayashi formation most certainly would be detected now. The American pilots would be watching the Hayabusa's descent, perhaps following it down to be sure of the kill. Farther off to the left the sky rained burning planes and debris. An Army primary trainer, an Akatombo "Red Dragonfly," afire from engine to tail, came floating down, weightless as a leaf. Instinct made Hasegawa wrest his attention from the dismal sight. High and fifteen hundred yards to the right three Grumman Hellcats were boring in toward the escorts. It was an unfavorable angle for the attackers. Because of the formation's minimum altitude the Hellcats would be able to make only one quick firing pass before maneuvering for position again. The American fighters opened fire, their tracers falling away at a safe distance but moving in as the Grummans closed. Had it not been his primary duty to protect the kamikaze Hasegawa was confident a climb and sharp turn in the speedier Shiden would have put him behind the Hellcats. Instead he delayed reacting until the Hellcats were obviously committed to his element of three. He pushed the throttle forward and broke sharply to his right. Kuwahara and Inoue clung to their positions as if they had read his mind.

The Hellcats pulled up to avoid crashing into the sea and climbed swiftly for another pass. Hasegawa racked his Shiden hard to the left to interpose his element between the kamikaze and the enemy. Out of the corner of his eye he saw a fourth Hellcat beginning a long shallow dive toward the rear of the kamikaze formation. A hand signal detached Inoue to face the new threat. The other three enemy planes were completing their turn and returning to the attack. The Hellcat pilots were obviously experienced and Hasegawa did not think he could safely repeat his earlier maneuver. He turned directly into the Hellcats and fired a short burst to convince the Americans he was making a head-on attack. The Hellcats' guns flashed in answer as the opponents closed at great speed. The Hellcats made a climbing turn to avoid a collision and Hasegawa climbed with them only long enough to get off one burst. He thought he saw hits on one of the Hellcats. The precise formation of the American planes in their turn won his grudging admiration.

He turned back toward the kamikaze, unable to follow his advantage. The fourth Hellcat had hit one of the Tokka and was now trying to shake Inoue off his tail. Hasegawa did not dare leave the kamikaze to assist Inoue. The burning Tokka veered out of formation. One wing tip touched the sea and the plane cartwheeled, making two full turns and catapulting its bomb fifty yards before breaking up. The fourth Hellcat, smoking from hits from Inoue's 20-mm. cannon, made a desperate turn, taking it toward the kamikaze formation. Hasegawa watched in helpless frustration, hoping Inoue could knock it down before it reached the sluggish planes. But Inoue, anticipating a climb by the Hellcat because of its low altitude, had been fooled by the enemy's maneuver and was hopelessly out of position. Hasegawa saw the Hellcat's tracers rip into one of the Zeros, The Beast's, he thought. The Zero started burning but did not falter. Only a few bullets must have found their mark, for the obsolescent Zero was fragile. The Hellcat, though smoking heavily, pressed its attack recklessly, boring in at an angle. The Zero snapped to the right, climbed and rammed the Hellcat in a brilliantly executed tai-atari, "body-crashing," maneuver. The planes exploded on impact, spewing fragments from a core of flame. Hasegawa's respect for The Beast's surprising skill was mingled with anger. He had robbed Inoue, a true pilot, of a kill.

Inoue resumed his position off Hasegawa's wing. The other Hellcats had vanished mysteriously. As if in explanation, puffs of black smoke blossomed around the formation, followed by tracers coming in on a flat trajectory. A destroyer materialized directly ahead, broadside to the formation, all guns firing. The Hellcats had climbed to avoid the barrage. On Hasegawa's right, Inoue strafed the deck. Fool, Hasegawa thought. They would need every shell to protect the kamikaze and, if they were lucky, to fight their way back to Kobayashi airfield. The formation climbed a few feet and swept directly over the destroyer. Hasegawa saw upturned faces and more than one fist shaken defiantly. It was fortunate they had come upon the screening vessel unexpectedly. One of the kamikaze might have ignored instructions and wasted his life attacking it. He counted the kamikaze. Eight remained. And the target would not be far away now.

The destroyer's guns followed them. They were picked up by other ships in the screen. Five planes orbited overhead. Before Hasegawa could identify them they tilted one after the other and came slicing down. Up ahead, many ships bridged the horizon. The lead kamikaze slid back his canopy, rocked his wings and began climbing to attack altitude, followed raggedly by the remaining seven. All the canopies were open. The white of the kamikaze's hachimaki was clearly visible. Hasegawa motioned his wingmen to deploy around the kamikaze, Kuwahara to the left side and Inoue to the right. Hasegawa covered the rear. They climbed with the kamikaze but at higher altitude, hoping to draw off the enemy fighters long enough for the kamikaze to make their attacks. From the higher altitude Hasegawa could see transports spread out to the limits of his vision, a host beyond his imaginings. Here and there a fire burned. The transports were not helpless targets. They sent up heavy fire, pocking the air with shell bursts and streaking the sky with tracer.

The five Hellcats reassembled to orbit above the kamikaze formation and avoid the antiaircraft fire. When the kamikaze began leveling off at fifteen hundred feet to select targets, two of the Hellcats detached themselves from formation and swooped toward Inoue's quadrant through the fire of their own ships. One of the three remaining Shiragiku exploded from an antiaircraft hit. Inoue slid over to intercept the enemy fighters. Hasegawa applied full power and raced to assist him. The well disciplined Hellcats ignored the challenge and pressed their attack on the bomb-laden kamikaze. A burst from one of them ripped a wing from the tattered Suisei and the dive bomber fell toward the ocean in an accelerating spiral. Only six of the kamikaze remained. They spread out to select targets. They had nothing to fear from the Hellcats now, Hasegawa thought, for surely the Americans would not follow them down into the intense fire from the troopships and escorting vessels. A glance assured him his wingmen were unhit. In minutes the kamikaze would have made their attacks and the three of them would be low over the water on the return flight to Kobayashi. He could picture the expression on Watanabe's simple face when Inoue described the mission to him.

A realization that the two Hellcats were no longer in sight brought an abrupt end to his brief lapse in vigilance. Even as he turned to search the sky, tracers flickered past the canopy and a blow across the knuckles numbed an arm to the elbow. He looked down. His fingers and the control they had gripped were gone. The cockpit erupted in noise and glare. He felt himself flung backwards. So this was how it was, he thought. He had sometimes wondered. Now he knew. In three months and eleven days Lieutenant Minoru Hasegawa, called Uncle by his fellow pilots, would have been twenty-five.

2

[Cadet Hiroshi Arai/Gunner's Mate Second Class Perry Hurst/Captain Alfred "Red" Millikin]

Cadet Hiroshi Arai, sweatily flying his Shiragiku trainer into a cauldron of metal shards, averted his face for a moment's respite from the terrifying spectacle just in time to see the lieutenant's plane explode. He was shamed and revolted by his reaction. For Hiroshi's initial emotion had been deep relief. The few times he had been in the officer's presence, whenever he had dared look up he had found the lieutenant watching him severely, the lieutenant's cold, knowing eyes looking as if they could see into his very heart. That look had been most disconcerting at the briefing, when Hiroshi believed he had successfully masked his true feelings. But the lieutenant had not been deceived. Of all the people in the world, excepting himself, the lieutenant was the only one who knew Hiroshi Arai was a creature utterly without courage or honor. And doubtlessly loathed him for it.

Hiroshi had expected the lieutenant to demand that he be replaced by someone more worthy of dying for the Emperor. He had been grateful when the lieutenant did not do so even though it meant there would be no reprieve from the destiny that had shadowed every thought since his assignment to Kobayashi base. Hiroshi was afraid of dying and even more afraid of being found out. He was also afraid of failure and hoped he was not a coward but lacked true spirit only because he had not learned his duties well enough to do what was required of him. He envied, almost as much as he venerated, the lieutenant's somber courage and the confidence which came from complete mastery of all flying skills. It was said that the lieutenant had destroyed more than fifty Yankee planes in combat, six in a single day. If he were certain of a successful attack perhaps he, too, might be as brave as the lieutenant.

Hiroshi was seventeen. When he was fifteen his middle school class at Yamaguchi City was assigned to work in an aircraft engine factory. After it was bombed out of existence he had applied for flying training. Though most formal pilot training had already been suspended, his principal at middle school and his superior at the engine factory spoke for him and he was accepted as a Class A Preparatory Flying Student in the Navy's Yokaren program. Hiroshi's father celebrated the occasion by taking him to dinner at a country inn a few miles from Yamaguchi City. Food of every sort was scarce and required ration cards but many out of the way establishments were not as strict in observing regulations as restaurants in the city. His father's closest friend and his dead mother's elder brother were also in the little party and many toasts were drunk. Hiroshi got tipsy on sake for the first and only time.

The party had been very expensive and for a long time afterward Hiroshi had wondered where his father had got the money for it. He had probably sold a valuable piece from his collection of Chinese porcelain, Hiroshi imagined, feeling guilty for his father's sacrifice. His father had been an importer of Chinese wares, which he sold in his own large shop, and before the war had been well-to-do. In the early days of the war he had grown even more prosperous but by the end of 1944 the war had ruined him.

At Tsuchiura, Hiroshi had at first been appalled by the brutality of the petty officers, and the rigorous military training taxed him to the limits of his endurance. Two things sustained him during the weeks which broke three boys in his barracks physically and drove a fourth to suicide. If he failed in any way it would disgrace his father and sully the memory of the elder brother killed in the Philippines. And if he did not fail he would one day be a Navy fighter pilot who would help sweep the skies of the American planes ravaging the homeland. But, although he came through ground training with an excellent record, he was not given the opportunity to fulfill his ambition. By that time Japan was no longer producing fully-trained pilots. Instead he was sent to Atsugi, southwest of Tokyo, to be trained as a kamikaze. He was to pass through Tokyo on his way from Tsuchiura and his father was to meet him there for a few minutes. Train travel had been so disrupted by bombings that they never saw each other. Hiroshi was dismayed by what he saw from the window of his packed car. Tokyo lay in ruins. He wanted nothing more than to give his life in reprisal.

The feeling persisted throughout his meager training. He received a few hour's instruction in takeoffs and practiced diving on the control tower from various altitudes. He and his classmates practiced flying formations on bicycles. And suddenly his training was announced completed. It was then he had his first doubts. He felt as if he had scarcely begun training, yet it was over. How could he be expected to succeed when he knew so little?

Hiroshi was sent first to Kanoya and had not yet been assigned to a mission when the base became untenable and its pilots were sent to less vulnerable fields. At Kanoya he began thinking of the realities of dying. He slept poorly even when there were no air raids and envied the kamikaze who begged to be sent out on missions. Not all the kamikaze seemed so eager to die. There were some who were melancholy or haunted. Hiroshi avoided them, hoping that if all his companions were brave he might capture their spirit.

Kobayashi was even more trying than Kanoya, for at Kobayashi there was nothing to do but wait. And the waiting would only end in death. Many of the kamikaze, Hiroshi among them, spent much of their idle time writing and rewriting their last letters home. Hiroshi worked at his until he was sure it expressed the thoughts expected of a true son of Japan. It was not genuine but it would bring comfort and honor to his father. He was determined his actions would not tarnish the false image it created.

"Dear Father," he wrote. "When you receive this I will already have joined my noble elder brother at Yasukuni Shrine. When I was a boy I never dared hope for so much honor. I look forward eagerly to the moment when I will dive with my brave companions against the enemy and drive him from our shores. I do this for our Emperor, but also for you, my revered father. I hope to make you as proud of me as you are of Natsuo. We will wait together joyously for your next visit to Yasukuni. Thank you for all you have done for me."

When he finished the letter he had looked up to find Petty Officer Tsutsumi reading it over his shoulder. He had been apprehensive lest Tsutsumi ridicule him for his boastfulness but Tsutsumi had nodded approval and said, "It is good to have a parent to write to. I have no one. No one at all."

Though Hiroshi had not known Petty Officer Tsutsumi at Tsuchiura, he knew Tsutsumi had been a barracks chief there. The younger kamikaze had feared Tsutsumi at first because of his brutal face and his nickname, "The Beast." When they found he meant them no harm they forgot he represented a particularly difficult period in their lives. Other noncommissioned officers did not fraternize with cadets but Tsutsumi sought them out. It was as if they were a substitute for family.

"When I was at Tsuchiura I was very stern," he said more than once. "But it was only to make real gunjin out of young men like yourselves. I am not really an unkind person."

Because of the lieutenant, Hiroshi had felt a special bond with Petty officer Tsutsumi. The lieutenant had stared at Tsutsumi as often as he had at Hiroshi and had not tried to conceal his dislike. Hiroshi thought it strange and most unfair that the lieutenant should understand him so well and not understand Tsutsumi at all.

Sometimes when Tsutsumi visited them he would sing, beating time on the dirt floor with his bat. He sang badly and in a sentimental manner not at all in keeping with his appearance. It was always the same song, the traditional "When Going Away to Sea."

If I go away to sea,
I shall return a corpse awash.
If duty calls me to the mountain,
A verdant sward will be my pall.
Thus for the sake of the Emperor,
I will not die peacefully at home.

Hiroshi wondered if Tsutsumi sang to inspire the young kamikaze or simply because he liked the song. It did help stiffen Hiroshi's resolve to die bravely because it reminded him that he, a simple schoolboy, was being permitted to join the ranks of heroic warriors stretching back to antiquity.

Tsutsumi had gone out of his way to speak to him as they were walking to the plane for their final sortie. His bat tucked under his arm, his intimidating face almost benign, he said, "Cadet Arai, today you will make your father proud of you. If possible I will hold my own attack until I have seen you strike home."

Tsutsumi had flown the other wing of the three-plane formation to which Hiroshi was assigned. Though it had required all of Hiroshi's attention to maintain a position within yards of the proper place off the flight leader's wing, he had occasionally stolen time to look over at the petty officer. Each time Tsutsumi had waved encouragement. The gesture evoked a cruel mixture of shame and gratitude. Hiroshi was proud that such a man as Tsutsumi would take an interest in him but the older man's friendship was undeserved.

Hiroshi remembered all these things when Petty Officer Tsutsumi flew his Zero into the Grumman. Tears filled his eyes, not because Tsutsumi had died but because Tsutsumi was denied what he wanted most, to die on the shattered deck of an American transport. Tsutsumi's death strengthened Hiroshi's resolve to conquer his fear and to die well at great cost to the enemy. When he sank a transport it would be for Tsutsumi as well as for his father. And it would show the lieutenant that Cadet Hiroshi Arai was worthy of respect. When the Grumman knocked down the lieutenant's Shiden, Hiroshi did not in the first rush of emotion regret he could not now give the lieutenant proof of his mettle. It was more important that there was now no one to bear testimony that his courage had faltered. Hiroshi quickly put down so ignoble a thought. The lieutenant had died protecting him and his fellow kamikaze. He could repay the lieutenant only by giving meaning to that sacrifice. If he did not score a hit he would not merit a place at Yasukuni.

From his altitude of fifteen hundred feet the transports seemed far apart and unending. Planes dived toward them or fell into the water between them in quickly extinguished billows of smoke and flame. The sea twinkled with muzzle flashes and tracers swarmed upward like luminous insects to curve away leisurely toward the surface again, fading away in mid-arc. He was approaching the transports at right angles to their course, favorable for a hit on the side or superstructure but not on the deck. He kicked left rudder and approached them head-on. He flew through teeming fire, selected a target and pushed the stick forward. Some of the fire hemming him in might be coming from above but he did not take his eyes from the ship. Even if Grummans were on his tail he knew he could do nothing to elude them.

The circle of visibility narrowed as he plummeted down at a steep angle until there was only the target, spewing projectiles. Despite his resolve and his silent vow to avenge the lieutenant he was frightened. The fear was concentrated in his belly. His stomach muscles ached from fighting it. Strangely, he had not been hit though streams of tracer converged on his clumsy Shiragiku from the length of the transport. In a remote corner of his mind was a memory of fireflies in his father's garden. That he could recall so peaceful a scene at such a time gave him a higher opinion of himself. He rode the tracers down as if they were lighting a path for him. Holes appeared in the windscreen. Something hot burned his cheek and punched into his right shoulder. The rudder controls shuddered beneath his feet. Hiroshi fought to keep the plane on a steady course, forgetting his fears, forgetting the lieutenant, Tsutsumi, his father, thinking only of the steadily growing target and the spot into which he must plunge. With that one act he would be cleansed of all past dishonor.

There was fierce pain in his right eye. He could no longer see from it. The trainer bucked savagely. It took all his strength to keep it from flipping into a spin. He was lined up perfectly on the bow of the transport, heading directly for a thicket of booms and masts. Those fools at Atsugi. They had not told him such obstacles would block his way to the target area. The ship rushed up at him, carrying a burden of landing craft nested on the deck and slung alongside. He could see figures in the guntubs, some standing at their posts and continuing to fire, others diving for cover. He could no longer see the entire ship, only the thicket of booms growing until it rose higher than his plane, and the bridge. There were men on the bridge wings, the faces of some eerily veiled beneath their helmets.

He plunged toward the thicket. On the port bridge wing an unveiled mouth opened in a shout Hiroshi could not hear above the roar of his engine and the wind. The bridge vanished and his world was a lattice of stays and yardarms and a landing craft resting crosswise on the deck. The right wing of the Shiragiku struck the mast fifteen feet above the deck, jerking the plane around to the right, nose up. The last thing Hiroshi glimpsed was the sky, streaked with fire. His last emotion was terror.

The approach of the kamikaze formations was heralded by messages from the attack force's flagship, the Amphibious Force Command Ship *Ancon,* over the Talk Between Ships system and by the U.S.S. *Sonoma's* own radar. The *Sonoma,* however, was not aware of the Kobayashi Squadron's low-level formation until the visual sighting by the destroyer in the northern screen. Gunner's Mate Hurst and his 40-mm. gun crew, as all the ship's company, were kept informed by the public address system. The *Sonoma's* captain came on to warn the gun crews to be especially alert for the low-flying formation, which was still too low to be picked up by the ship's radar. He repeated his familiar admonition to keep hitting. This time Hurst made no comment. His attention was riveted on the arc of northern sky in which the suicide planes were expected to appear at any moment. His mind automatically filtered out any phrases not pertinent to his immediate function.

The twin 40s moved restlessly in a continuous sweep of the as yet empty danger area. The movement was not a reflection of the nervousness of Hurst's gun pointer, Boatswain's Mate Barber. It was standard practice when attack was imminent. Both Barber and Seaman First Class Shore, the gun trainer, kept their eyes fixed on the wires of their sights. The movement of the gun mount enabled them to maintain surveillance of a wide expanse of sky.

"I see 'em, I see 'em!" Barber yelled.

Hurst did not bother to ask where. Barber always saw suiciders before anyone on the foredeck and it was always a false alarm. The bridge lookouts, because of their binoculars and elevated positions, usually were the first to spot enemy planes. Hurst was invariably the first of the gun crew to see them. He said it was because his eyes moved faster than ordinary men's and his peripheral vision was greater, both of which had been factors in his phenomenal success as a broken field runner at the University of Oklahoma. The first evidence that the kamikaze were drawing close was a blossoming of antiaircraft bursts far to the north.

"Company's comin'," said Hurst. "Let's have somethin' hot for 'em."

A bright, soundless flash lit the distant sky.

"That's one not comin'," Shore said.

"Means that much more for his little bitty buddies," Hurst answered.

Barber did not complain, as he had done earlier, that his gun captain talked too much. The greater his fear the more silent Barber became, leading to his reputation for being cool under fire. But fear had never slowed Barber's reflexes. Hurst said that Barber was the best gun pointer in Transron 18. During the October invasion rehearsals in the Philippines Hurst had tried to cash in on his conviction by proposing a squadron-wide gunnery competition for attack transports and cargo ships. He had intended backing his crew with his considerable gambling winnings. He had acquired his skill as a gambler, Hurst claimed, by studying the odds in craps and blackjack while working as a dealer in the back room of the Sui Jen Club in Galveston, Texas. Hurst's proposal had gotten no farther than the *Sonoma's* gunnery office, adding to Hurst's list of grievances against him.

The public address system announced the positions of two formations approaching from the north. Hurst found one and then the other. Though they were far out of range of the 40s, the guns began tracking them.

"Don't forget the bunch s'posed to be comin' in low," Hurst called out.

The five-inch gun on the afterdeck began firing, shaking the *Sonoma* along its full length. The PA system boomed the same message Hurst was receiving on his telephone.

"All guns, air action starboard, air action starboard!"

"There they are!" Hurst cried. "Oh-eight-oh and low."

A small cluster of black specks was driving toward the column of transports at sea level. The *Sonoma's* 40s opened fire, Hurst's mount a fraction before the others. Separate vibrations shook portions of the *Sonoma* within the heavier jarring of the five-inch gun. Five Hellcats which had been orbiting a bit to the north dived one by one toward the approaching Japanese planes. They pulled up when the kamikaze began climbing into the thickest part of the barrage. Every gun in the column which could be brought to bear poured fire into the kamikaze formation but the enemy planes continued to bore in, miraculously unhit, and leveled off at fifteen hundred feet.

Two of the Hellcats came diving down into the barrage toward them. Crazy bastards, Hurst thought admiringly. He did not make irrelevant remarks aloud when his crew was in action. A kamikaze erupted into a shower of flaming wreckage from a direct five-inch shell hit. Cheers rose from the *Sonoma*. The Old Man ain't goin' to like that, Hurst thought. He licked his lips. If Barber thought he was the only one in the gun crew whose mouth got dry he was crazy. Three Japanese planes had arranged themselves at a higher altitude around seven others in the loose formation. The Hellcats evaded them and knocked the wing off a Judy dive-bomber. The kamikaze spiraled toward the water to the accompaniment of more cheers from the *Sonoma*. The enemy planes were close enough for Hurst to see the three at higher altitude had no bombs slung beneath them.

"Go for the low ones!" he shouted. "Forget them Georges."

The Hellcats came in for another pass. Though Hurst's eyes were on the six bomb-laden planes, at the upper limits of his field of vision he saw the Hellcats closing in on one of the Georges. Their tracers plowed into it and a few moments later it exploded. There were no cheers now. Too many kamikaze were too close. The kamikaze had split up for their target runs. One of them, burning, began a long, smoking glide toward the first ship in the *Sonoma's* column. It flew into a cone of converging tracers and fell into the sea short of its target. Two more were hit. One blew up and the other continued its dive toward the *Sonoma*.

"Get him, get him, get him!" Shore yelled.

Shore had told Hurst he never knew what he said during an attack, or even that he cried out at all.

"I wouldn't believe any of the stuff you say I yell if my throat wasn't so sore. Like after a Bruin-Leaf game."

The plane veered off one hundred fifty yards from the *Sonoma* and slipped sideways into the sea. Hurst relaxed. Only three left and none heading for the *Sonoma*.

"All guns, air action forward, air action forward!"

Hurst's gun slewed around until it pointed directly over the *Sonoma's* bow. A thousand yards ahead of the *Sonoma* a suicide plane was passing over the first ship in the column on a head-on course.

"Watch out!" Shore yelled. "He's coming in!"

The *Sonoma's* fire overlapped that of the two transports ahead of it but the Japanese plane kept coming, shedding pieces of its wings and fuselage. It was an ungainly plane with swollen cowl flaps like an inflated inner tube.

"What's that funny-looking . . ." Shore cried.

The kamikaze jerked this way and that, buffeted by gunfire.

"He's after the *Bend!*" Hurst shouted.

The *Fort Bend* was the second ship in the column, just ahead of the

Sonoma. As the kamikaze plunged toward the *Fort Bend* the *Sonoma's* fire threatened the other ship's superstructure.

"Cease fire, cease fire!" the PA system ordered.

When the kamikaze crashed the *Fort Bend's* deck forward of the bridge the *Sonoma's* guns were already sweeping the skies for new targets. At the moment there were none within range of the 40s and 20s. Only the five-inch gun continued firing in support of a column five thousand yards distant. The two George fighters escorting the low-level attackers and the last two kamikaze had vanished. Apparently the *Fort Bend* was the only ship hit in the *Sonoma's* task unit. Leaping sheets of flame were visible above its superstructure.

Hurst lifted his earphones one after the other and jiggled a little finger in each numbed ear.

"That was a trainer, Heinie," he said.

He had to shout. The headset muffled the noise of the 40s for Hurst but the others in the crew had no such protection and their hearing was deadened.

"What are you talking about?" Shore demanded.

"That just hit the *Bend.* You said what was that funny-lookin' plane."

"The hell I did."

It was more a question than a denial.

"I wonder how bad she's hit," said Barber.

"Let's just worry about the *Sonoma,*" Hurst said. "Get back on that goddam sight."

As if confirming Hurst's order, the captain's voice came over the PA system.

"Now hear this. This is the captain speaking. The *Fort Bend* has been hit. There is nothing we can do about it from here. Our job is to hit and keep hitting. All hands give one hundred and ten percent of their attention to their own duties. There are no spectators on this ship. We are all in the game."

The *Fort Bend* slowed and fell out of formation to avoid being overrun by the column of ships. A destroyer came driving to her assistance at flank speed, great curls of white-crested water cleaving back from its prow. Landing craft began dropping from the transport's davits, and combat-laden troops swarmed down nets and ladders hanging over its sides.

"They're abandoning ship," Hurst said incredulously. "She don't look hurt that bad."

Other landing craft, empty, were heading for the *Fort Bend* from the last transport in the column.

"Naw," Hurst said. "They're just transferring troops."

Then he was too busy to continue his running account. New suicide formations arrived and, as Hurst had anticipated, began attacking the *Fort Bend* and ships in her vicinity. The destroyer stood in close to the *Fort Bend*, throwing up a great umbrella of protective fire. The surviving kamikaze transferred their attention to other ships, including the *Sonoma*. Another transport was hit but again the *Sonoma* escaped, unharmed. There was a lull in the action. Hurst's loaders started clearing out the litter of shell cases in the guntub. A single Japanese plane, new and shiny, with an enormous bomb slung beneath it, burst into view only a few feet above the water. It was heading for the *Fort Bend*, protected from the guns of the destroyer by the burning transport's own bulk.

"Watch out!" Hurst yelled.

The kamikaze hit the *Fort Bend* at the waterline a hundred feet from the stern. The flash of the explosion momentarily obscured the entire after section of the ship. As the sound of the explosion came rolling back to envelop the *Sonoma* the stern section reappeared, revealing a black, cavernous hole in the ship's side. Seconds later a gush of flame spewed out of the hole and a smaller jet leaped from the deck above it. The *Fort Bend* stopped dead in the water.

"Jesus," said Shore. "What was she carrying?"

"Whatever it was, I hope we ain't got none aboard," said Hurst.

The boatswain's pipe sounded.

"All hands. Set Condition Two."

Hurst slid down to his haunches, his back against the side of the guntub. He put his helmet between his feet and draped the headset around his neck.

"Hey, Jew," he said wearily, "keep an eye out for the Weasel. I got to grab a smoke."

Before rolling a cigarette he folded his arms across his knees and rested his forehead on them. Things were sure to get worse before they got better.

Despite its twenty-thousand-pound bomb load, the *Seattle Stomper II* lifted off easily from the Bolo Field runway. The run to the hidden kamikaze strip north of Miyakonojo was much shorter than the distances for which the B-29 had been designed and the aircraft was not carrying a full fuel load. The six B-29s of Red Millikin's formation flew in two three-plane elements. Millikin surveyed the formation with a proprietary eye. It was the first time he had led a mission of such importance. The carpet bombing runs on the beaches were nothing compared to this one. It was damned white of the squadron CO to let him take it instead of grabbing it for himself. The squadron CO had been partial to him from the first, not resenting at all the fact that he had more left-seat time in B-29s. Or maybe the group CO had picked him to lead the mission. If the colonel had picked him personally, that meant group had its eye on him and the idea of a Silver Star was not so farfetched. He might even be in line for a promotion and a squadron of his own.

"Hey, Platt," he said to his co-pilot. "I never saw such a sloppy formation. Let's get those jokers in tight."

"You expect fighters?" the co-pilot asked.

"You never know," Millikin replied casually, though he did not. "But it's not that. I never could stand sloppy flying."

He got on the radio and called the planes in closer.

"Let's look good for the Navy," he said.

When the planes were positioned to his liking he lit a long Manila cigar and sat back with his hands behind his head.

"Take it, Platt," he said. "Get yourself a little formation practice. If I ever get a squadron you're gonna be an aircraft commander."

He meant it. Millikin liked his co-pilot. Platt was a little afraid of him, which was flattering, and was always trying to win his approval. When there were newcomers sooner or later Platt would start talking about the mission they had completed on three engines so that Millikin never had to mention it himself.

The airstrips on the smaller Ryukyu islands north of Okinawa were busy, with Marine fighters and fighter bombers landing and taking off. Beyond the Ryukyus Millikin looked in vain for surface craft. Though he knew he was flying between two great invasion fleets, the sea below was empty. At Point Emerald, a Strike Group Orbit Point well south of Kyushu, the formation turned northeast. In a quarter of an hour the northern end of Tanega-shima, the offshore island on which the 156th Regimental Combat Team had landed three days earlier, came into view. There were ships offshore with traffic plying between them and the island. A few minutes later the bombers reached Approach Point Schlitz and altered course for the target area.

"Hey, Red!" the co-pilot said urgently. "Are those Jap fighters?"

Millikin's hands were suddenly clammy.

"Where?" he asked, struggling to keep his voice normal.

"Twelve o'clock."

Millikin saw them even before Platt answered. Three silvery planes were weaving lazily up ahead a hundred feet higher than the bombers. The planes, fighters, either had not seen the formation or were uninterested.

"F6Fs," Millikin said, hiding his relief. "Don't you know a Hellcat when you see one?"

"Oh, yeah. I can see now."

The Navy fighters turned toward the formation, dropped off to the left, passed under, and reappeared above the bombers in inverted position, tucked in tightly.

"Show-offs," said Millikin.

He rocked his wings to acknowledge their presence. The fighters responded in the same manner and flew off to resume their station. The bomber formation flew between the headlands enclosing Ariake Bay. Flashes lit the surface and billows of black smoke drifted over the water. The Fire Support Group was pounding the beaches and suspected defense positions. Two miles off the beaches a line of battleships and cruisers fired deliberately spaced salvos. From a thousand yards closer in, a line of destroyers added their fire. Even closer, and moving slowly to follow the curve of the coastline, a swarm of LCIs and LSMs, landing craft types, plastered the beaches with rockets and mortars. Masses of logs floated offshore and littered the beaches. The land was pocked with craters from the water's edge to the high ground thousands of yards inland. Showers of earth and debris shot into the air from hits. There was no return fire. The slashed and ravaged dunes, fields, woods and hillsides were silent and empty. The site of Shibushi, the little harbor town at the head of the bay, was a smoldering waste.

"Man," Platt said, "would you look how chewed up everything is? Those GIs are gonna walk in like they were going to church."

"You really think so, maybe I can get you on detached service so you can walk in with them," Millikin said.

"The Japs don't have any church of my denomination. I'm a devout coward."

They were flying now over forests, fields and hills. Occasionally there would be a single dwelling or a small huddle of them, visible from seventy-five hundred feet but from that altitude revealing no sign of occupancy. Millikin and his navigator searched for the checkpoints given in the briefing.

"There's the river," Millikin said over the interphone.

"Miyakonojo ought to be off the right wing," the navigator said. "You see it yet?"

"If it looks like the Portland dump I do," Millikin replied.

"I don't know what the dump looks like in Portland," the navigator said.

"If you get your butt up here and look out Platt's window at Miyakonojo you will."

The navigator laughed.

They reached their initial point and adjusted course for the kamikaze strip, going from vee formation into trail. The other five B-29s were strung out behind the *Seattle Stomper II* in a long line. In the nose of the plane the bombardier picked up the target and assumed control of the aircraft. The bomb bay doors opened. Millikin could dimly make out the shape of a landing strip. If he had not been told exactly where and what to look for he would not have known anything lay below but innocent countryside.

"Pilot from tail gunner," the interphone said. "Jap fighter at five o'clock, on the deck."

"You sure it's a Jap?" Millikin demanded.

"Yes, sir. A Tony. Looks like it's goin' in for a landing."

"Good. Maybe he'll get there just when we drop a load."

Millikin looked over at his co-pilot.

"The old *Stomper* got three when I was flying out of Saipan," he said. "It's about time we got one in my new bird."

The tail guns and remote control bottom turrets started firing.

"What the hell?" Millikin cried.

"He's makin' a pass!" someone shouted on the interphone.

Millikin grabbed control of the aircraft and began evasive action.

"Call him in, God damn it!" he yelled. "Call him in."

"Fighter at six o'clock, one thousand yards and closing," the interphone reported.

Millikin squirmed around in his seat trying to locate the fighter. He could not.

"Where is he now?" he shouted, his voice close to a scream. "Keep calling him in!"

"Six o'clock, closing."

Millikin racked the big plane around trying to find the Tony. Tracers flew past the nose of the *Seattle Stomper*.

"Get him!" he screamed. "Get him!"

"He's gonna ram!" a voice shrilled over the interphone.

"Oh, God," Millikin whispered.

To the Japanese crouched in the burrows on the ground, in the moment before the planes exploded it appeared as if the Army Hien had disappeared into the bomb bay of the Bi-ni-ju-ku.

3

[Petty Officer Naoto Shiizaki/Storekeeper Second Class Frank Diefenbach]

Along the east coast of Kyushu and at Ariake Bay the Kaiten made ready to attack the approaching transports. Some had already been for days aboard the mother-ship destroyers of the 31st Torpedo Attack Unit or on itto yusokan, the specially built six-Kaiten transports. At Hososhima, north of Miyazaki City, Petty Officer Naoto Shiizaki's Kaiten rested on the deck of a kaibotei coast defense boat. The forty-five-foot torpedo was the sole cargo of the wooden vessel. Petty Officer Shiizaki was disappointed that he would not be going into battle with the comrades with whom he had shared the cruel frustration of two aborted submarine-borne missions earlier in the year. After the second they had prepared a written testament, signed with their own blood, swearing they would not fail to die together at the next opportunity.

Shiizaki would not be completely alone when he sortied against the Americans. With him he would take the ashes of Petty Officer Shoda, his dearest friend since the first days of training. Shoda had died in a practice mission off the Otsujima Island Kaiten base when his unmanageable torpedo had stuck fast in the muddy bottom. They had promised each other that should one survive the other in training he would see that his comrade was not denied a combat sortie. On Shiizaki's first sortie, the mother submarine had returned with four of its six Kaiten unlaunched. Shiizaki had apologized to the ashes of his friend. The second time he returned alive after a solemn departure ceremony, Shiizaki's humiliation had been too great to permit him to do anything but creep back to the barracks and lie there for twenty sleepless hours without food or water.

Until today the memory of his two returns had never for long been out of his thoughts. Now, at last, he had ceased regretting previous failures. He had been spared for something more important than the random sinking of enemy ships far out in the sea lanes. Tonight he would prevent a thousand Yankee soldiers from reaching Japanese soil. Shoda would share with him an even greater victory than had been promised. All afternoon Shiizaki checked his Kaiten, unperturbed by the familiar explosions shaking the earth above the boat pens dug into the shore. He was assisted by a technician from the maintenance crew who would remain aboard the boat when it slipped out of its pen after dark. The Kaiten were balky. Controls and instruments which performed flawlessly in shore checks sometimes malfunctioned at launching time. Though Kaiten pilots were trained in maintenance as well as operations a good mechanic was indispensable.

Shiizaki was five-feet one-inch tall, like many good Kaiten men, short but exceptionally strong and deft. The technician, older than Shiizaki's twenty years but no larger than the petty officer, climbed into the pilot's compartment first and carefully wiped away all traces of lubricants. Some maintenance men were overzealous in their use of oil and grease, making the controls slippery and difficult to operate. Shiizaki wiped the controls a second time before testing them repeatedly. When he climbed out of his weapon he found three of the boat's crewmen struggling to bring aboard a two-hundred-fifty-pound aerial bomb they had found somewhere.

"What are you doing with this?" he asked.

"We'll fit it to the bow," one of them said. "After we've launched you we'll get a Yankee transport of our own."

"Stupid!" Shiizaki cried angrily. "Who will return to report the results of my attack? Get rid of it or I'll tell the lieutenant."

The crewmen hung their heads sheepishly and shuffled off with the bomb. Shiizaki was sorry he had called them stupid. It was natural they should want to hit the enemy, and no official order had been issued that kaibotei crews were to return to report the success of their Kaiten. It was only his own vanity that had prompted his outburst. When he smashed a transport his old friend Shoda would know and that was enough. He was friendly with the boat crew. One of the seamen was a local man and had shared the rice brought back to the base surreptitiously from his mother's farm. He apologized when they returned and told them if they wished they could bring the bomb on board again. The seamen talked it over and decided they would prefer to return with news of his victory. If they were lucky they might be given a second Kaiten and sink another enemy ship.

"Where did you get it, anyhow?" Shiizaki asked. "I have never seen such a bomb before."

The seaman who shared rice grinned mischievously. He had a goodnatured, pimply face.

"Oh, yes you have, Petty Officer," he said. "A whole skyful of them. It's one from a Yankee Corsair that didn't explode. A friend of mine in ordnance fixed it up for us."

"Wonderful!" Shiizaki exclaimed. "You've got to take it with you when you go out again and give the Americans their bomb back."

They all laughed together.

Late in the afternoon the Kaiten men ate together. With the rice were sun-dried local fish and pickled plums. Afterward there was sake for a toast. As was the custom before a sortie, the Kaiten pilots toasted the coming victory in plain water. Back aboard the kaibotei Shiizaki had a second and better meal. One of the crewmen had found a good-sized sea bream which had floated ashore after being stunned by an underwater explosion. They cut it into thin slices and ate it raw with rice. It was the first sashimi Shiizaki had tasted since a visit home to Kurume in 1944. This was fresher and there was more of it. He hoped it was not ungrateful of him to think so. His father had bicycled eight miles to the coast to buy half a kilo from a fisherman who had been a classmate in primary school many years before Naoto was born, and his mother had pretended she was not hungry so there would be more for Naoto and his three younger brothers.

Shiizaki had been fortunate enough to see his family again for the last time in June. Only his seventeen-year-old brother, next in age to him, had not been there. He was in the Army, stationed somewhere on the west coast below Kushikino on the other side of Kyushu. There had been no raw fish then and his mother appeared to have aged greatly. She had asked him to tell his twelve-year-old brother not to be in such a hurry to join the newly announced National Volunteer Combat Force.

"Your father has been no help at all," she had said, looking down uncomfortably because it was not her habit to criticize anything the elder Shiizaki did. "He has already been promised an appointment to staff and can't wait to be called up himself."

"I'll be a better soldier than these young ninnies they're taking nowadays," his father had said.

In September, his mother had written him that his father and his fifteen-year-old brother were in the Volunteer Combat Force. His father's unit had been assigned to road repairs and when not working at that received instruction in spear fighting and tank ambush methods. The brother had been sent south to work in the ordnance depot at Hitoyoshi. His little brother was still at home. His father had ordered the boy to remain there and help his mother. Shiizaki chuckled when he read that part of the letter. Unless his father was firmly set against something his mother usually managed to have her way.

Aboard the kaibotei the unexpected banquet made everyone jolly and they behaved as if it were a drinking party. The local man began singing "Country Wrestling," a mildly risqué farmer's song. Soon all were clapping their hands in time with the song. An officer came around then and ordered them to be silent, not leaving until he assured himself they had not been drinking.

"You'd think it was a crime for an ordinary sailor to have a good time," someone grumbled.

"This is my lucky day," said the irrepressible local man. "I had a bottle of shochu and was going to bring it aboard but something told me not to."

He began humming "Country Wrestling" in a low voice and soon everyone was in good spirits again. Shiizaki was pleased such fine fellows were taking him into battle.

The morning reconnaissance photos of the Fifth Landing Force assault areas had revealed evidence of unusual nocturnal activity at the shoreline five miles south of Kushikino. Furrows in the sand at Beach Studebaker Red One indicated that several heavy objects had been dragged out into the water and left there, presumably anchored on the bottom during the 6:25 P.M. low tide the night before, when the water was shallowest. A special reconnaissance mission failed to detect the objects. Concentrated bombardment by vessels of the Fifth Fire Support Group failed to cause explosions or dislodge whatever had been planted by the enemy across the route to be taken next morning by a Battalion Landing Team of the 2nd Marine Division. Aboard the U.S.S. *Hollis,* the high-speed transport fitted out as an amphibious force command ship and serving as flagship of the Underwater Demolition Flotilla, the flotilla commander decided the situation was important enough to send in swimmers at the next low tide. The suspected obstacles were located in the operating area of the Fifth Underwater Demolition Group. The *Hollis* was accompanying the Third Underwater Demolition Group south of Kyushu. The flotilla commander's decision was therefore dispatched to the commander of the Fifth UD Group, who in turn called in one of his Underwater Demolition Team commanders for a personal conference to work out details of the operation. Out of this conference came a decision to send in three swimmers to locate the objects and remove or destroy them. Due to the nature of the assignment and the continuous strain under which all the teams had been working in more than a week of reconnaissance and demolitions, the swimmers would be volunteers.

Thus it was that Storekeeper Second Class Frank Diefenbach had another and unexpected chance to keep a promise he had made to himself. Diefenbach was determined to be the first man in all the Amphibious Task Force to set foot on Japanese soil. It had begun as a joke among members of his platoon. There was an intense rivalry among the four platoons of the Underwater Demolition Team, as there was among the teams of the UD squadron. Diefenbach's platoon had argued that as the best platoon of the best team of Underwater Demolition Squadron 1, it would no doubt be called upon for the more important assignments. This the platoon would welcome, even if it meant reconnoitering the beaches as far back as the enemy's guns. The argument eventually took a more realistic turn and bets were made on which platoon would get a man closest to the beach. As the UDT worked its way toward the beaches charting natural hazards and eliminating obstacles emplaced by the Japanese, the swimmers left secret markers at the farthest point of advance. The winner would be determined when the first assault waves went in the morning of November 12. UDT men accompanying the first waves as boat guides were excluded from the competition. A man had to swim in to be eligible. The plan was kept from the team's officers. Every swimmer on a mission had a specific and arduous assignment. It was not expected that anyone in a position of authority would be kindly disposed toward a scheme involving extracurricular activities.

Within the platoons men made individual bets on themselves. Storekeeper Second Diefenbach abstained.

"I don't mind taking those other guys, but not my own buddies," he said. "Everybody knows old Dief is first and fearless. He's not taking your dough on a sure thing."

"What's such a sure thing?" Quartermaster Third Class Vasquez had asked. "Sposin' our platoon don't have to blow anything close in? You might not get a hundred yards from a beach."

"Want to bet?" Diefenbach demanded.

"That's what I'm getting at, for Christ's sake," Vasquez said triumphantly.

But Diefenbach had not risen to the challenge, though he was confident as he professed to be. Somehow he was going to get closer to the Japs than anyone else. More than that. He was going to get all the way in. The first man to set foot on Japanese soil would have a place in the history books. Not that he was particularly anxious for a place in history. It was simply that Diefenbach was proud and intensely competitive. He made light of the Purple Heart from Peleliu and the Bronze Star won at Okinawa.

They were all in the day's work and any demolition man could have had them and many did. To be outstanding among demolition men would be something special and to be special you had to do something special. And the thought of being the first of all the hundreds of thousands who had fought in the Pacific to leave his own personal mark on Japanese soil was tempting.

By X-l he had not even come close to achieving his goal. Vasquez had been right. Their platoon's last assignment had been a reconnaissance of the bottom no closer than eighty yards off Beach Studebaker Green One. He had finished charting the sector assigned him and begun swimming toward the tidal flats below Akasaki when an ensign saw him and ordered him back. His ship, the U.S.S. *Herman T. Sperling,* a highspeed transport converted from a destroyer escort, now lay to nine miles offshore in Operating Area Bean. The shore was not even visible at that distance. All he could see of Japan was the outline of hilltops. Normally a man who ate prodigiously, he had little appetite for the special Sunday dinner the *Sperling's* captain had ordered prepared to celebrate the team's successful completion of its scheduled demolitions. He hardly touched the baked ham and candied sweet potatoes and finished only half the lemon pie, his favorite dessert.

He hunched over his mess tray drinking cups of sugared black coffee and wondering why everyone was so cheerful when none of them had done anything particularly worth mentioning. During cold-water training at Morro Bay in California they had been told the next amphibious operation would be the roughest yet. It had proved the least dangerous. The water had been even colder than at Okinawa but they were prepared for it this time. They had worked to exhaustion clearing the beach approaches of obstacles and mines but scarcely a shot had come their way. Some of the less experienced men thought it was because the unremitting shelling and bombing had knocked out the Japanese defense positions. Diefenbach knew better. The Japs were there, all right, just laying low until they had better targets than a few men in rubber suits. That was one thing that made his failure so hard to take. If Mr. Hamill hadn't ordered him back to the LCP he might have crawled ashore in broad daylight without being shot at. He didn't blame the ensign. Mr. Hamill was a good officer even if the most salt water he'd seen up until a couple of years ago was just enough to gargle for a sore throat. It was his own fault for not explaining to the officer what it was all about. Mr. Hamill might have gone for it. He had a reputation among the men for being willing to take chances. To get a reputation like that in an outfit where everybody had to be half fish and half crazy, a man couldn't be very particular about sticking to the book. But it was too late now.

No one had paid much attention when the team commander shoved off in one of the ship's LCPs with no one else aboard except the landing craft's four-man boat crew. Even the fact that the boat was running at its full souped-up eighteen knots caused little comment. The rumors started only after a *Sperling* radioman told a UDT man that the team's commander had been summoned to an urgent conference with the Underwater Demolition Group commander. Such a summons could only mean that the team had fouled up or that a special mission was in the wind. It could not be the former because when the last swimmer was aboard from the morning's demolitions the team commander announced they had received a "well done" from the *Auburn,* the Fifth Attack Force flagship. By the time the lieutenant commander returned, two-thirds of the team was lined up along the *Sperling's* railing waiting for him. Diefenbach wedged his way to the front. He wanted the skipper to see him. That way the team commander would have him in mind when he started picking swimmers. Diefenbach knew from experience the way to get picked was to catch the skipper's eye and let him know you were aboard. Conversely, if you wanted to dodge the duty you kept out of sight. This was information which Diefenbach and other discerning veterans did not share with the less observant.

He tried to read the results of the excursion in the team commander's expression but very little of the skipper's boyish face was visible. The CO wore a baseball cap pulled down low and a nonregulation Navy flying jacket with the collar turned up to his ears. He stood rooted to the pitching deck of the landing craft, feet wide apart and hands thrust into his jacket, looking up quizzically at the row of faces staring down at him.

"Man overboard?" he asked drily. "Somebody drop me a line. I'm getting too old for all this climbing up and down cargo nets."

The team commander was twenty-eight, one of the youngest UDT men of his rank.

Diefenbach snatched a rope out of the hand of the man next to him, made a loop secured with a swiftly tied bowline knot, and dropped the line over the side a fraction ahead of several others. The skipper looked up at him and slipped the loop under his armpits. With Diefenbach heaving at the other end of the line, the team commander came up the *Sperling's* side in a walking motion. He wriggled out of the loop and handed it to Diefenbach.

"You striking for chief, Diefenbach?" he asked before disappearing in the direction of the chartroom.

Diefenbach, smiling, watched him walk away. There was no doubt the skipper knew he was aboard.

Within the hour the Underwater Demolition Team assembled in the crew mess. Only one member of the one-hundred-and-five-man team was absent. He had contracted bronchitis after a week's regular immersion in cold water and was now resting comfortably in sick bay with a medicinal hot toddy prescribed by the ship's doctor.

"The smoking lamp is lit," the team commander said. "There will be a brief pause while Vasquez bums a cigarette."

Diefenbach was encouraged by the fact that the CO had gone out of his way to mention Vasquez by name. Vasquez, who was notoriously always out of cigarettes, was his partner in the UDT's two-man buddy system. That meant the skipper was thinking about them.

"I need three volunteers for a special job," the team commander said.

Instantly every hand shot up, some of the men shouting for attention.

"Knock off the noise!" the team commander ordered.

He waited for silence.

"Doesn't anybody want to hear the details first?"

"No, sir," Diefenbach said.

"Maybe you ought to," the team commander said. "It gets a mite airish out there after dark. A man could catch himself a bad cold."

The men laughed. They all knew, as did their commanding officer, that the fact their only casualty had been one case of bronchitis was no guarantee they would get off so easily another time. The team commander looked at the assembled men. He had anticipated they would all volunteer and had already decided whom he wanted. He knew the names of every man in the team and the background of most of them. Even among the sturdily built demolition men Storekeeper Second Diefenbach stood out physically. There were a few taller than his six-feet one-inch, or more powerfully muscled, but none gave quite the same impression of poise and instantly available strength. He was one of the early Seabee volunteers from Fort Pierce combat demolition training days, at thirty older than most of the newer men. He could swim four minutes underwater, load a line of obstacles by sense of touch alone and under fire was neither excitable nor reckless.

"Okay," the team commander said. "Diefenbach, Vasquez and Wrong Smith. You're elected."

Carpenter's Mate Third Class Smith was one of the team's four Smiths. He got his nickname because of his habit of never listening for initials and answering for other Smiths at muster. There were those who maintained that his Silver Star was really intended for one of the other Smiths.

The three volunteers met with the team commander in the cramped quarters he shared with a ship's officer. There was scarcely room for the four of them to crowd around the chart spread out on his bunk. Vasquez was almost as large as Diefenbach, and Smith, though short, was broader than either.

"Next time I'll be smart enough to pick skinny swimmers," the team commander said. "How do you stay so fat on the chow they dish out? You must eat a hell of a lot better than the officers."

"It's those packages from home, sir," said Diefenbach.

It was a common complaint among members of the team, officers included, that their mail and parcels never seemed to catch up with them.

The team commander went over the details of the mission carefully, not omitting the background information given him by the group commander.

"You're to reach your objective at dead low tide," he said. "That means 1905 and not one minute later. Sunset's at 1721 and there's not much moon so you'll be working in the dark. You'll have exactly thirty minutes to locate whatever the Japs planted, load it, and get the hell out. That's all gunfire support will give us. At 1935 they're going to start plastering the beach again whether they hear from us or not."

"Any idea what we're looking for, sir?" Diefenbach asked.

The team commander shook his head.

"When you find it we'll all know," he said. "Intelligence says the Japs may have suicide swimmers out to meet the landing force tomorrow. They shouldn't be out tonight but keep your eyes open for little strangers. Just don't go killing each other by mistake."

"How about supper?" Vasquez asked. "Do we eat it or not?"

"You'll be in the water too soon after evening chow," the team commander replied. "Better have a snack now."

He joined them in the deserted mess and had a cup of coffee while they ate. He pulled his head back distastefully when Diefenbach offered him a thick Spam sandwich.

"How can you eat a chunk that size?" he said. "How can you eat any size chunk of Spam?"

"Keeps us from floating too high in the water, sir," Diefenbach said.

"Smith, you better take another one, then," the commander said. "That big butt of yours sticks up like a channel buoy. You ever been hit there?"

"Only by my old man, Commander. With a hairbrush."

"The Japs won't be using hairbrushes tonight," said Vasquez.

"Quit your bitching, Cisco," Diefenbach said. "It all counts toward your twenty years."

Vasquez's first name was Edward but they called each other Cisco and Pancho after a radio show they both liked.

"You a career man?" the commander demanded.

"Yes, sir," said Vasquez.

The commander laughed.

"You sure picked yourself one hell of a career, Vasquez," he said.

After eating, Diefenbach, Vasquez and Smith went down to the powder magazine assigned to the Underwater Demolition Team. Wearing their long woolen underwear, they began preparing the demolition charges specified by the team commander.

"Cisco," said Diefenbach, "we're a cinch to win the pool now. Nobody's been in that far that I know of."

"Don't spend the money yet, Pancho," Vasquez said. "Low tide's a long way out. Don't forget there's more than a three-foot drop between high and low tide."

"I haven't forgotten," said Diefenbach.

He did not tell Vasquez he intended going all the way in to the highwater mark. That would win all bets. And it would place him unquestionably on Japanese soil.

It was believed that the Japanese had planted mines of some sort off the beach rather than heavy obstacles, since such obstacles would have been emplaced much earlier in their defensive preparations. Consequently the swimmers would take only one Hagensen pack, a waterproof canvas pouch filled with C-2 explosive, and a number of smaller charges. The smaller charges were two-and-a-half-pound blocks of tetrytol, wound around with instantaneously burning Primacord so they might be tied to a connecting line, and with malleable iron wire for fastening the charges to the obstacles. The charges were made up into Schantz packs for easy carrying, a tetrytol block in each of the four pockets. When this was done the three swimmers made a quantity of waterproof fuses. Diefenbach also lettered a small sign, fastened at each end to a stick, which he would not let the others see.

While they squirmed into their tight rubber suits and received a final briefing from the team commander, the *Sperling* moved through the night to within three miles of the beach. There it lowered one of its landing craft, personnel (ramp). The swimmers dropped their packs into the waiting hands of the LCP(R) crew and prepared to climb down the cargo net. The team commander shook hands with all three.

"You men are going to one hell of a lot of trouble just to get a shot of brandy," he said.

"Sir," said Diefenbach, "since this is above and beyond, can I have mine with soda?"

"The coxswain will take your order when they pick you up," the commander replied. "Good luck."

The landing craft headed toward the shore, which was marked by steady explosions from the line of gunboats working over the beaches.

"Find a steady yellow light and steer toward it," Diefenbach told the coxswain.

"You don't have to tell me," the coxswain snapped. "I know."

A rocket-launching landing craft was holding yards off the swimmers' objective to mark it for them. A yellow light to seaward, invisible to the shore defenses, was the prescribed signal.

"There it is now," the coxswain said.

Diefenbach, Vasquez and Smith threw their charges into the inflated rubber boat lashed alongside the landing craft, donned swim fins and goggles, and rolled over the side into the boat. Each wore a waterproof watch on one wrist and a waterproof compass on the other, and a belt from which dangled a slate for recording information, pliers, a knife and other implements. In addition, Diefenbach had a coil of light line draped over a shoulder and the Schantz pack into which he had thrust his sign. The landing craft moved past the gunboat, which stopped firing on the beach. Diefenbach looked at his watch. Eighteen twenty.

"Right on time," he said.

The demolition gear was attached to flotation bladders with lines leading from them. The three swimmers tied the lines to their wrists.

"I got two fifteen-foot lengths of line," Diefenbach said. "When we get in close you guys take an end apiece. I'll be in the middle. That way we can cover a ten-yard stretch."

"What if whatever the Japs laid down is contact-fused?" Vasquez asked.

"We'll save the U.S. Navy some high-priced tetrytol," Diefenbach replied.

"And three slugs of cheap brandy," Smith added.

The gunboat had gone to single-battery fire, lobbing in deliberately spaced strings of rockets. It was another aid to the swimmers, marking a path toward the suspected obstacles. Three hundred yards off the beach the landing craft turned sharply to parallel the shoreline and the three swimmers rolled out of the rubber boat one after the other. Though not unexpectedly, the water was shockingly cold on Diefenbach's face. It had been much worse at Okinawa where the water had not been as cold but where the swimmers had worn only trunks and silvery axle grease.

By 6:48 P.M., swimming against the outgoing tide, they were in water shallow enough to drag Diefenbach's two lines across the bottom. Two minutes later the rope between Diefenbach and Vasquez snagged on something. Two tugs on the other rope advised Smith of the find and the three of them groped their way toward the obstacle. It was a rock of no great size. It had not been noticed in earlier reconnaissance missions.

"Mark it down, Cisco," Diefenbach whispered.

Vasquez grunted and jotted the position on his slate.

They spread out again and resumed their careful progress. The line between Diefenbach and Vasquez snagged again. This time there were three objects set in a ten-foot triangle. Diefenbach ran his numbed fingers over them gingerly. Two were cylindrical with smooth tapered ends.

"I think they're Jap bombs," he whispered. "Watch out for contact fuses topside."

The other was a sphere with protruding knobs.

"Careful," he whispered. "This one's mine."

He groped at his belt for a flashlight fitted with an amber lens and, shielding it with his body and a cupped hand, signaled to seaward that the objects had been located.

"You and Smith load 'em," he whispered. "I'll be back in a few minutes."

"Where the hell you think you're going?" Vasquez demanded.

"There may be more further in."

"The skipper said not to expect but two or three," Vasquez protested.

"Don't hurt to be sure," said Diefenbach, "long as we're here anyway."

He looked at his watch. A minute after 1900. Plenty of time to crawl in and back, pull the fuses, and swim out for pickup. He took his sign from the Schantz pack and began snaking toward the beach. To his left and right explosions raddled the shore. Ahead, all was blackness and silence. The sliver of a moon cast little light. He was tempted to stand up and walk in but caution prevailed. His elbows began aching from dragging his body over the wet sand. By now he must be in beyond any previous swimmer. But by the time the first assault wave went in the area might be under water. He continued to press forward. The sand was dry to his touch but he could not be certain he was beyond the high-water mark. This stretch of sand could have been exposed long enough to dry. He inched forward several more yards and dug his fingers into the sand. It was dry and loose. Now. He unfurled his sign and planted the sticks. He wished there was light enough to read it. "Dief was here," it said. "Pay up." The previous day the team had left a larger sign farther out. It said, "Welcome U.S. Marines. Turn left for geisha girls. Courtesy UDT."

Diefenbach looked at his watch. Twelve minutes after 1900. Plenty of time to get back before the stuff started flying again. He turned to crawl back toward Vasquez and Smith. They were probably sore as hell at him. He stopped crawling. He had promised himself he would be the first to set foot on Japanese soil. He hadn't really set foot on it. He had only crawled over it on his belly. There was no indication of life ashore. He rose cautiously to a squatting position. Nothing happened. He rose to his full height and planted a foot firmly in the sand, working it back and forth to make a deep print. He thought he heard a scraping sound from the nearby darkness. Or was it only the squeak of sand under his own foot? It didn't matter. He had to get back before the stuff started coming in. Vasquez and Smith must be wetting their crotches by now.

As he dropped back down to the sand a single shot, hardly audible in the crash of exploding shells and rockets a hundred yards on either side, came out of the darkness. Frank Diefenbach, storekeeper second class, was the first man of Operation Olympic's hundreds of thousands to die on Japanese soil.

4

[Petty Officer Naoto Shiizaki/Gunner's Mate Second Class Perry Hurst]

The coast defense boat bearing Petty Officer Naoto Shiizaki's manned torpedo slipped out of its pen at midnight. If all went as intended it would intercept the American transports approaching their anchorage off the Miyazaki front at approximately 3 A.M. Shiizaki climbed through the top hatch of his Kaiten while the kaibotei was still in the shelter of the pen. Though it might be several hours before he was launched against a target he had to be prepared to be lifted off immediately if the mother boat was detected. Shiizaki left the hatch open. There were no telephone communications as there had been on the two fruitless sorties on submarines. He had practiced closing and securing the top hatch until he could do so in five seconds. A flashlight and a stopwatch hung on strings from his neck. A chartboard was strapped to his left thigh. If the kaibotei managed to get within sight of a troopship undetected, its skipper would give him course and distance to the target. With stopwatch, chart and compass to aid him, Shiizaki would be able to make his run with minimal use of the telltale periscope.

He did not spend his time idly during the long approach. He checked his instruments and controls repeatedly and in his mind rehearsed a variety of target runs taking into account every conceivable contingency. There was so much to be done during an attack it would be necessary to make every move instinctively.

At midnight the attack transport *Sonoma,* second in line in its task unit since the sinking of the *Fort Bend,* was four hours away from its anchorage off Beach Chrysler. Until two hours earlier the *Sonoma's* squadron had been under almost constant kamikaze attack since early afternoon. Gunner's Mate Second Class Perry Hurst and the crew of the starboard forward twin 40-mm. guns were sleeping fully clothed in their bunks, exhausted. In another two hours, if they did not have to man their guns before that, they would be awakened for an early breakfast.

Aboard the kaibotei, the local sailor stuck his head in the hatch and asked Shiizaki if he would like some hot tea to warm him. Shiizaki, sweating from his constant exertions in the cramped pilot's compartment, refused irritably. Didn't the fool know a Kaiten pilot was too busy to be interrupted needlessly. It was a mystery how such a bumpkin had found his way into the Imperial Navy.

The boat crept along at well below its fourteen-mile-an-hour top speed in order to move as quietly as possible. When a distant vessel turned on searchlights and fired star shells to illuminate the sea the kaibotei shut off its two engines and wallowed in the swell. Shiizaki closed his hatch and the hoisting cables holding the Kaiten were drawn taut. If they were detected he would be launched against the enemy ship, presumably a destroyer. Though the Kaiten had enough range to reach the transport area under its own power, locating a target from it in the darkness would be extremely difficult. When the enemy ship moved off in another direction the kaibotei continued on its way. A rapping on the hull of the Kaiten signaled Shiizaki all was clear and he opened his hatch. He was glad he had not been obliged to expend his weapon on a destroyer. A troopship was a far more important target and the chance of hitting one was greater. A destroyer was not only much more maneuverable than a transport, it could also exceed the Kaiten's thirty-knot top speed.

Many times during the night, flashes and explosions bore witness to engagements being fought in the distance. Destroyers, special Kaiten mother ships, and midget submarines, as well as kaibotei, were moving toward the enemy transports. Once aircraft were heard in the distance and flares were dropped ahead of Shiizaki's kaibotei. The boat slowed to a standstill and

Shiizaki again secured his top hatch as the enemy patrol attacked a target not visible from the kaibotei. Soon after, the sky was lit by an explosion which could only have come from the three-thousand-pound warhead of a Kaiten. One of the crewmen described it to Shiizaki when he reopened his hatch. What a waste, Shiizaki thought. Perhaps he should request that his Kaiten be launched and proceed the rest of the way submerged. But then he might miss the transports entirely in the darkness. He wished he might have sortied by day. A Kaiten left no wake and he was confident he could stalk a troopship with only an occasional elevation of his periscope. If they had waited until morning, however, the transports might already have loaded out their assault troops.

By 2:15 A.M. Gunner's Mate Hurst, Boatswain's Mate Third Class Barber and Seaman First Class Shore were at breakfast with the rest of the *Sonoma's* crew and the combat troops were being fed in their own mess. Hurst and Shore ate their way methodically through cornflakes, grilled sausages and French toast with maple syrup. Barber was too tense to eat and had only a glass of milk and a cigarette.

"I know you ain't supposed to eat pork sausages, Jew, but what's wrong with the French toast?" Hurst demanded of Barber, who did not reply.

"He could eat pork if he wanted to," Shore said. He often joined Hurst in pretending Barber was Jewish and had long ago given up trying to convince his gun captain that many Jews, like himself, did not keep kosher. "We all got a dispensation from the Jewish pope. Like Catholics can eat meat on Friday. There's this war on."

"Is that what's goin' on?" Hurst said, his mouth full of sausage and French toast. "I thought all them planes was just buzzin' us yesterday to give us a thrill."

"Why don't you two dumb bastards shut up!" Barber demanded.

The captain's voice sounded from the public address speakers.

"Now hear this. This is the captain speaking. Numerous small surface craft and midget submarines have been detected approaching our anchorage area. From now on we may be subject to attack from both sea and air."

"Let's see if the Old Man's changed his pep talk any," Hurst said.

"All lookouts keep a sharp watch. All you gun crews, I want to stress the importance of hitting early and continuing to hit."

He continued with the same instructions he had given the day before, adding, "and the same applies to surface craft."

"Some," Hurst said. "He changed it some."

"Yesterday the five-inch 38 went into action before the order to commence firing," the captain continued. "That will not happen again. No itchy gunner is making my ship an illuminated target for Japs."

At 2:45 A.M., with all hands at battle stations after reports of midget submarines within the area and surface craft approaching, the *Sonoma's* transport squadron reached a point twenty miles off the Japanese coast, the outer limit of Operating Area Potato. Potato, on the northern flank of the Attack Force, was bounded by an arc drawn from Point Tosaki, a cape eight miles south of Miyazaki City and code-named Point Brooklyn. And by this time it was obvious to the men aboard Petty Officer Shiizaki's Kaiten carrier that the kaibotei was nearing its target area. Enemy destroyers and smaller patrol craft wove their search patterns in increasing numbers. Star shells and air-dropped flares burned holes in the darkness across the horizon. Now was the time for an air attack on the enemy transports, Shiizaki thought, to force the Americans to reveal their whereabouts to the Kaiten. Running footsteps and muffled anxious cries on the deck on the kaibotei reached him. Something was happening. Had they been detected by the enemy? Why didn't the fools keep him informed? He thrust his head out of the Kaiten's top hatch.

A five-man, eighty-foot-long Koryu submarine had broached the surface not a hundred yards from the kaibotei and the nervous crew had almost opened fire on it, thinking it an enemy vessel. It was now attempting to free its stuck diving planes and resubmerge. Meanwhile it was continuing on the surface. Shiizaki was tempted to climb out of his weapon for a closer look but he did not do so. He hoped some of the midget submarines would attack troopship columns in the center of the Yankee formations. American defensive fire would silhouette troopships on the flank for the Kaiten.

A swarm of planes passed over the kaibotei at two or three thousand feet before anyone was aware of their presence. As Shiizaki dropped down into his seat the sound of their engines told his practiced ears they were Japanese. His fear turned to joy. Good. Now the troopships would be forced to reveal themselves to him. If he were lucky that would happen before the kaibotei was detected. He asked the kaibotei commander's permission to be launched as soon as the Americans opened fire on the kamikaze and to begin his run-in without instructions from the deck. The commander agreed to do so. The sky to the south erupted with tracer and exploding shells. The kaibotei commander shouted orders.

The steel cables rasped across the Kaiten's hull as the crane lifted it off the deck and lowered it into the sea. Shiizaki saluted the mother ship and as he slammed the hatch shut thought he heard the local sailor's voice cry out, "Good luck, Petty Officer." He reached back and hit the starting lever as the cables fell away. The oxygen-driven engine surged with power. With his left hand he cranked the diving plane control. When the depth gauge indicated six meters he was already correcting to the proper five meters. At fifteen feet the periscope would just skim the surface and the Kaiten would be at the ideal depth below the waterline of its target. On Shiizaki's first training mission the Kaiten had plunged eighty feet before he could reverse the stiff control crank and then had shot almost a third its length above the surface as he overcorrected. Now everything was going perfectly, as he knew it would. He cranked up the periscope with his right hand. A slight forward movement brought his face to the eyepiece. He waited for the swell blocking his vision to subside, found the distant flashes, noted his compass heading, and cranked the periscope down again. He would use it only sparingly until he found a target. He reached up to his right and increased speed to twenty knots. Until he was closer to the transports he would conserve fuel by cruising at an intermediate speed. The flashes grew closer and brighter as he raised the periscope at irregular intervals.

His gaze moved restlessly from one instrument to another, checking depth, speed, course and fuel consumption, and his hands reached instinctively for the controls to make minor adjustments. As the Kaiten consumed its oxygen fuel he let an even flow of sea water into the ballast tanks to compensate for the loss of weight and maintain his weapon at a constant depth of fifteen feet. His exertions and the closeness of the pilot's compartment made him sweat. He wiped his hands repeatedly on his coveralls until they were as wet as his skin. I'm sweating like an American, he thought. He had heard water poured out of them as if they were squeezed sponges. Soon he would be giving them a squeeze they would never forget.

Shiizaki's competence and the Kaiten's uncharacteristically smooth responses filled him with euphoria. He thought not of death but of how perfectly the mission was going. Underwater detonations some distance away nudged the Kaiten, reminding him that no matter how well his weapon performed he still must evade the enemy destroyers protecting the transports with their sound gear and depth charges. And he realized with a touch of shame he had not once thought of his family or even his friend, Shoda, whose ashes rested in his lap, since seeing the gunfire of the American convoy. No matter. He would apologize to Shoda at Yasukuni Shrine.

On the *Sonoma,* Gunner's Mate Hurst and his 40-mm. crew had known no respite since entering Operating Area Potato. Suicide planes dove from the star-shell illuminated sky and the PA speakers crackled with warnings of underwater and surface craft. Destroyers and destroyer escorts raced among the transports chasing underwater sounds and dropping depth charges. A two-man Kairyu rose to the surface off the *Sonoma's* starboard bow, forced there by a depth charge exploding below it. It lay broadside to the *Sonoma,* sleek as a shark. But it was a wounded shark and sluggish as it turned to bring its torpedo tubes to bear.

"Get, get, get the bastard!" Shore yelled.

All the *Sonoma's* guns that could be brought to bear at so depressed an angle opened fire simultaneously. Gobbets of fire pelted the submarine. Hurst was certain he saw the twin streams of his gun's tracers in the core of the *Sonoma's* fire. The Kairyu blew up with a violence that drove the ship sideways and sent Hurst crashing against the side of the guntub, snapping the lead-in to his headset. The concussion sprang the *Sonoma's* plates in a ten-frame area near the bow and knocked Hurst's gun mount askew but did no major structural damage. Hurst struggled to his feet in the tilted guntub.

"Somebody get me a headset!" he yelled to his ammunition passers.

Without his headset he had no communication with gunfire control and would be dependent upon his own sightings and the PA system, now flooded with instructions to damage control parties.

"Periscope!" Barber cried. "I see a periscope!"

"Where, damn it!" Hurst yelled. "Sing out!"

"No, it ain't!" Barber cried.

"You son of a bitch," said Hurst.

Someone, he did not know who, handed a headset into the guntub. He snatched off his helmet and flung the old useless earphones from him. The midget submarine was quickly forgotten in the heat of a new kamikaze attack. An Oscar fighter plane blew up almost immediately over the *Sonoma,* showering the upper deck with hot fragments. One of them ripped the back of Hurst's hand. There was blood but no immediate pain and he could still move all his fingers. A cheap Purple Heart, he thought. I could of done without it.

The sea in which Shiizaki's Kaiten swam was alive with sounds. Though he did not think his weapon was itself under attack, depth charges were exploding close enough to shake him in his pilot's compartment like a pea in a dried pod. He cranked up his periscope just in time to see a great flash light the sky directly ahead of him. The shock waves rolling back through the water drove the Kaiten toward the surface but he responded so quickly he had it under control at a depth gauge reading of two meters and back down to five within half a minute. He must find a target and attack quickly now. At two meters' depth it was possible part of the Kaiten had been visible above the surface. He increased the flow of oxygen to the engine until the Kaiten streaked through the water at thirty knots. He raised the periscope again and kept it elevated. He could waste no more time in finding a target. He must depend upon speed alone to elude the destroyers.

Gun flashes lit the darkness around the Kaiten but the periscope was so low above the surface he could not see the ships making them. Gently he brought the Kaiten half a meter closer to the surface. The periscope would make an unmistakable feather now but he must risk it. Five hundred yards ahead and only thirty degrees to port a burst of light clearly outlined an American transport, a big one. Shiizaki had spent many hours studying models and silhouettes of American ships. This one appeared to be of the Bayfield class. A true prize. He altered course until he was heading directly for it, at the same time easing the Kaiten down to proper attack depth. It was time to crank down the periscope, for at this distance and this speed the target could not possibly evade him with a change of course. He chose to leave it up.

The dark bulk of the ship grew darker and bigger. His ears sang as if he heard a thousand crickets. A not unpleasant tightness gathered from his belly to his throat. In his loins was a sensation he had felt before only when he touched a woman.

"Periscope, periscope!" Barber screamed.

"Where, you dumb bastard!" Hurst cried angrily.

The explosion of the Kaiten's three-thousand-pound warhead tore out the *Sonoma's* bow, killing every man on the starboard side from the Number One hold to the upper deck and from the jack staff to the foremast, twenty-five feet aft of the forward 40-mm. guns.

5

[Private John Robert MacCauley/Corporal Podjalak/ Superior Private Hikozo Maeda/Jiro Matsuyama]

By 4 A.M. all the vessels of the Third Attack Force which were to participate in the X-Day assault on Ariake Bay had entered Operating Area Lettuce and reached their assigned positions in Station Wagon Beach Zone. The transports and cargo vessels bearing XI Corps' 1st Cavalry and 43rd Infantry divisions stretched seaward in orderly rows from a line seven miles off beaches Essex and Ford. For sixteen hours the Third Attack Force had undergone continuous suicide attacks from sea and air. Ships had been hit and men lost, more than in the approach to any previous amphibious landing, but no major assault unit had been critically weakened. Now, while attacks from the air had temporarily slackened, those from the sea intensified as swarms of Shinyo crash boats crept out of their pens to join the Kaiten human torpedoes and Koryu and Kairyu midget submarines. It was a battle more heard than seen by the men aboard the transports. Screening vessels lay smoke around the transport area to conceal the troopships from the suicide craft. The transports could see little of the furious action beyond the smoke except for flashes lighting up the pall like lightning within a storm cloud. The transports generated no smoke of their own, maintaining visibility in their immediate area so they might see and engage suicide craft evading the screening vessels. Some smoke drifted in among the transports. It had a foul smell and could be tasted.

The area outside the smoke was illuminated by star shells, aerial flares and the searchlights of the flycatcher patrols. The destroyers and gunboats of the patrols were clearly visible targets, but no shore-based fire fell among them. The Japanese batteries were still concealing their positions. The patrol vessels rove unceasingly outside the transport area, flooding sonar-located underwater craft with depth charges and attacking the Shinyo with machine gun and cannon fire. The Shinyo used the same tactic as the Kaiten-carrying kaibotei, coming in as quietly as possible at low speed hoping to elude the screen long enough to sight a transport before roaring in to collide at full tilt. Few of the suicide craft managed to elude the screening vessels. When discovered and taken under fire, they attacked the patrol ships, exacting a considerable toll. Some kamikaze, either unable to find the transports in the darkness or demoralized by the intensity of the defensive fire, also attacked the screening vessels and several dived on the flaming wreckage of their own Shinyo.

By the time the transports reached their stations the troops aboard them had been up for two hours. John Robert MacCauley, a private in the 1st Cavalry Division Battalion Landing Team assigned to make the assault on Beach Essex Yellow Two, had been awakened at 2 A.M. when the lights came on in his troop compartment and a noncom strode through shouting the men awake as if the duty gave him great pleasure.

MacCauley groaned and huddled in the nest of blankets on the narrow canvas shelf which was his bunk. He felt as if he had just fallen asleep. Gunfire and thoughts of what faced him in the morning had kept him awake for hours the night before. Everyone else, it seemed, had fallen asleep immediately and he had wondered peevishly if he were the only one who was scared. Men cursed and hawked a few inches above and below him and feet hit the steel deck as the troops rolled out of their closely tiered bunks. He tried to go back to sleep. Breakfast was never ready until an hour after reveille and he was not hungry, anyway. Maybe he would feel better and get an appetite with another half-hour's sleep. Beach Essex. He could not go back to sleep for thinking about it. It was just his luck to draw a beach called Essex. It was bad enough to be on what they said would be the roughest landing in the whole war, worse than Tarawa, even, without drawing Essex to boot. Until that happened he had thought that no matter how bad things got he had a good chance of getting through it. He had always been lucky. But drawing Essex was a sign.

When he was just a kid his pop had bought a '36 Essex, a blue one, that turned out to be a lemon. Nothing but trouble. The very first trip in it, to Harrisburg to see the capitol and have a picnic in the park on the Susquehanna River, they'd had a flat on the way there and burned out a bearing on the way back because of an oil leak. His pop had finally managed to unload it on his uncle, a brother of his mother. His mother had nagged his pop about that for years afterward. "I told you that Essex was a lemon," his pop would say. "Here I ain't even got it no more and it's still giving me trouble." MacCauley smiled at the memory of that and for a moment forgot his forebodings. If he did come out of the war okay his pop would get a large charge when he told him the name of the beach he'd hit. And it could be worse. They could be hitting Essex Blue instead of Essex Yellow. That would have cinched it. Same car and same color.

Corporal Podjalak, the assistant squad leader, came through the compartment on the way back from the head and shook MacCauley.

"Hey, Choc," he said, "ain't you goin' to chow? It may be a while before you get anything else hot to eat but lead."

The men in MacCauley's squad called him Choc for Chocolate because he was from Hershey, Pennsylvania, and his father worked in the factory there making candy.

MacCauley slid off his bunk and rubbed his eyes.

"Okay," he said. "You don't have to shake my teeth loose."

He ought to eat whether he was hungry or not. The old-timers said never miss a chance to move your bowels, take a drink of water, or eat a hot meal. You never knew how long it would be before you got another one. Podjalak had saved him a place in the chow line but MacCauley did not squeeze in. Everybody complained when someone tried to crash a line and he did not blame them. He was one of six children and had been taught to wait his turn. Podjalak said he would save him a place at the table. That was all right. Everybody saved seats for their friends. There were pork chops for breakfast. Everyone made the usual jokes about the condemned men being fed a hearty meal. The jokes were new to MacCauley. The assault on Beach Essex Yellow Two would be his first combat. He forced down one bite and pushed the meat aside to breakfast on pineapple juice, milk and cornflakes.

"If you don't eat 'em you're gonna kick yourself," Podjalak said. "After you been crawling in the sand on cold Ks for a few days you'll be dreaming about pork chops."

"They're supposed to make you seasick," MacCauley said. "Greasy."

"You'll get seasick faster on them liquids you're pouring down," said Podjalak. "Sloshing around in your gut. You don't want 'em, I'll eat 'em."

He speared a chop off MacCauley's mess tray and studied MacCauley's chin.

"You didn't shave," he said. "You can't go ashore looking like that."

MacCauley showed him an extended middle finger. Though he was nineteen his beard was fair and sparse and he shaved only occasionally. Podjalak's whiskers were so black and luxuriant he appeared lightly tattooed. They had a cigarette before carrying their mess trays to the stacks. MacCauley had only been smoking eleven months, since he joined the Army. He had promised his mother he would not smoke until he was nineteen but had felt that being an Army man entitled him to start a few months sooner.

"Let's go upstairs and see what's going on," Podjalak said.

He had never accepted Navy terminology and still called topside upstairs, a bulkhead a wall, and a ladder steps. MacCauley wished he could be like that. Navy language was awkward for him but he was afraid if he did not use it the others would think it was because he did not know any better. Everybody knew Podjalak knew better. Podjalak had more time between islands than some guys had time.

It was cool on deck and there was a bad smell in the air. MacCauley was sensitive to smells. Hershey, Pennsylvania had always smelled of chocolate. He had only to hold a chocolate bar to his nose to be reminded of home.

"Smoke screen," Podjalak said. "Hope they lay smoke for us on the beach today."

"If they can't see us they can't hit us," MacCauley said wisely.

"Choc, ole boy," Podjalak said, "them Jap mortars can smell you."

"You know something, Poge," MacCauley said. "They say when you're really scared it makes a smell."

"Yeah," Podjalak replied, "right in the seat of your pants. Don't forget to take some spare drawers."

The sound of gunfire and explosions rolled over the water, from the heavy crump of big shells to the drumming of machine guns. The ship's PA system kept pouring out instructions and reports of enemy activity but the guns of the transport remained silent. In the distance ships were being attacked but the sight and sound of the battle seemed too remote to spell danger for their ship.

"'Bout time they left us alone," Podjalak said. "We caught our share yesterday."

It was cool on deck in the predawn breeze and they went back below. For the half-dozenth time MacCauley spread out everything he was taking with him on his bunk. It did not seem like very much to fight a war with, although Podjalak had assured him that after a few hours of wearing it he would find it more than enough. Other than the OD uniform and combat jacket he was wearing there were his rifle, cartridge belt full of clips, grenades, helmet, ditty cap, leather-palmed gloves, canteen, mess kit, first aid pouch, gas mask, extra long johns, a change of socks, two handkerchiefs, bayonet, sheath knife, entrenching tool, poncho, half a roll of toilet paper as suggested by Podjalak, two packs of cigarettes, one of the new assault lunches, a can of C ration, a D-bar and matches.

The D-bar had the texture and appearance of chocolate that had been allowed to freeze. D-bars were intended as emergency rations and their taste was disappointing. It was a joke in MacCauley's platoon that what his father made in the factory at Hershey was D-bars for the troops and if that was the best he could do MacCauley better put the old man straight when he got back home. If he got back. The matches were in a condom to protect them from seawater. MacCauley had carried the contraceptive in his wallet for almost ten months. At basic training the first sergeant always made sure you had one before letting you out on pass, the town was so full of VD. MacCauley was still a virgin, though he would deny it furiously.

When he went ashore everything on the bunk would either be worn or stowed in the upper part of his field pack. Everything else, blanket, extra clothing and the like, would be left behind stowed in the bottom part, the cargo pack, tagged with his name and unit, to be brought ashore later.

"Do you think we'll ever see our stuff again?" he asked Podjalak.

"You got one chance outta four," Podjalak replied. "You'll get to the beach and your pack'll get to the beach. Or you'll get to the beach and it won't, it'll get to the beach but you won't, or neither one'll get to the beach."

At 5:03 A.M. the Third Attack Force flagship, the U.S.S. *Mount Olympus*, signaled "Land the landing force." H-Hour was 7:30 A.M. except for a Battalion Landing Team of the 40th Infantry Division, the division that had attacked the offshore islands five days earlier. At sunrise, 6:45 A.M., the BLT would hit Beach Model T on Biro Island, an islet three miles out in the bay. The hilly islet dominated a broad stretch of Ariake beaches and the BLT was to silence any enemy guns which might be dug in there and establish a fire base to support the main invasion. A few moments after the signal from the *Mount Olympus,* officers and noncoms came through the troop compartments telling the men to get into their gear and await orders to go to boat stations. MacCauley's mouth went dry. This is it, he thought. Podjalak helped him into his gear, adjusting his rolled poncho and straightening the straps of his belt suspenders. The assistant squad leader had been looking out for him ever since rehearsals at Lagonoy Gulf in the Philippines.

"You're the most helpless twerp I ever saw," he had said. "If I don't show you the ropes now you could get me killed some day."

MacCauley did not think that was the reason. He thought it was because he was the youngest man in the squad and Podjalak was the oldest, twenty-six. Because of that Podjalak treated him like a baby sometimes and it made him mad. But mostly, like now, it was good to have somebody experienced and steady to give you a hand. If they both made it through the war they would keep in touch forever after. He had promised Podjalak he would come visit him and meet his wife. He had never been to North Dakota, where Podjalak lived and worked in a feed store. Until the Army, he had never been much of anywhere.

A shattering roar penetrated the troop compartment, like thunder but sharper.

"Battleships," someone said. "They're starting the prelanding bombardment."

MacCauley noticed Podjalak was peering at him. It was not the first time the corporal had done so since they were told to stand by for orders. It irritated him.

"What the hell's wrong?" he demanded.

"Nothing," Podjalak replied with a mysterious grin.

Minutes passed. The pack grew heavier on MacCauley's shoulders. Podjalak shrugged out of his pack and put it on his bunk.

"Take off your pack and let's sneak upstairs and see what's going on," he said.

"They said to wait down here," MacCauley protested.

"Screw that," said Podjalak.

MacCauley put his pack next to Podjalak's and they climbed up to the deck. It was still dark. Ship's crewmen were moving around busily but other than that nothing much was happening. The boatswain's pipe sounded over the PA speakers at 6:05 A.M. MacCauley disliked the sound. Not as bad as the whistle the barracks chief had used to wake them at basic, but bad enough. What he liked was a bugle. Even when one woke him up for five o'clock reveille he didn't mind the sound.

"Away all boats, away," the PA system boomed.

"This is it," MacCauley said, noticing Podjalak was staring at him in the same irritating manner as before.

Podjalak laughed. It was a nervous laugh but nonetheless genuine.

"I been waiting for you to say that," he said.

If it had been anyone else kidding him like that MacCauley would have given him a punch on the arm. But somehow, as much as he liked Podjalak, he could never get that familiar with him. It would be almost the same as getting familiar with his pop.

At "away all boats" the sailors went immediately into action. Landing craft dropped alongside the ship from davits, their four-man crews scrambling aboard over the rail, or were hoisted from the deck on long swinging booms. MacCauley envied the sailors' noisy efficiency. They shouted, swore, and joked as they went about their tasks, unlike the troops below decks who for the moment had nothing to do and were for the most part silent. Sailors could joke and holler, MacCauley thought. They were sitting miles offshore and weren't going right in the Japs' front yard in little boats that would hardly stop a rifle bullet. Except for the boat crews. They had to go right in with the GIs. But even the boat crews would head back after they'd left the troops on the beach. And they knew exactly what they had to do and had done it a lot of times before. With the sailors it was always the same whether it was a rehearsal or the real thing. But with the troops it was different. Sure they had plenty of practice climbing down cargo nets and running down ramps on the Lagonoy beaches, but on this beach the real thing started being different from rehearsals. No telling what the Japs would be throwing at them on the way in or what they had waiting for them when they got there. What if the boat got hit on the way in, or when they hit the beach Japs were all over the place? He did not really feel ready to do what he was supposed to because things might not be the way he had been told they would be, and he wouldn't even know what it was he was supposed to do. If he had just done the real thing once before maybe he wouldn't be so scared and unsure of himself. He would stay near Poge and do whatever Poge told him to do. He just hoped two things. The main one was that he wouldn't get killed and the other was he wouldn't be too scared to do whatever Poge said.

"We better go back down," Podjalak said. "The VPs'll be circling back to load up."

They went below and put on their packs. And waited. The order came to report to boat loading stations. It was awkward climbing the slippery, narrow ladders with full gear. Someone stepped on MacCauley's hand and he cursed the man irritably, using phrases he had learned from Podjalak. Sometimes he wondered what his mother would say if she knew he was using that kind of language. When he was a kid she had washed his mouth out with Octagon soap just for saying hell. His pop never cursed around her, either, but could sound off pretty good when she wasn't there. Not as good as Podjalak though. Podjalak used dirtier words and more different ones. The troops waiting to climb down stood jammed together, shuffling their numbing feet on the unyielding deck plates.

"The Navy ain't no different from the Army," said Podjalak. "Hurry up and wait. You doin' okay, Choc?"

"Yeah," said MacCauley.

He wanted to say more, one of the flippant remarks he had been hearing from some of the men waiting to climb down into the boats, but he did not trust his voice. Most of the remarks sounded forced, anyway.

"You just stick near me when we hit the beach," Podjalak said. "You'll be okay."

Irregular blotches of fire the shape of inkblots covered the shoreline in the thinning darkness, mixed with scattered sharp flashes like the light of a pinball machine. Two sounds mingled overhead, a sizzling and a deep, almost inaudible sough.

"We're getting shelled," Podjalak said.

The Japanese batteries had at last broken their silence. White columns of water rose into the air among the transports. The ship's five-inch guns began firing, shaking the deck beneath MacCauley's feet.

"Kamikazes!" someone shouted.

MacCauley looked up into the sky but could see no planes, only the lazy falling away of tracers and the short-lived bloom of exploding shells. He knew from yesterday the suicide planes could come diving in at any minute. He forgot his envy of the sailors and was anxious to leave the false safety of the ship. Better to be on a small target than a big one. Podjalak gave him a shove. The men in his squad were climbing over the side.

The boat crew was holding the landing craft against the ship's side with engines and muscle. The topside of the landing craft was painted yellow, the beach color code, and it was marked with a large black 4-3. MacCauley was in the third LCVP of the fourth wave. The boat and the transport were heaving in the swell. MacCauley held desperately to the net, feeling as if the equipment which burdened him was alive and conspiring to pull him loose. If he should fall at a moment when the landing craft bobbed a foot or two away from the side he would drown or be crushed. At the bottom of his descent he groped with one foot for the heaving side of the landing craft. Touching it, he released his hold on the net and dropped to the bottom. He timed the drop wrong, landing just as the craft rose. The bottom hit flat against his soles, driving his legs up, bent at the knees, as if he had dropped from a great height instead of only a few feet. His head snapped forward and his chin knocked against a kneecap. He tasted blood from his bitten tongue. For a moment he thought wildly he had bitten it off. Someone grabbed his shoulder, jerked him erect and pulled him away from the net down which other men were climbing. He squatted on the bottom with his back against the side. He swallowed the blood in his mouth and felt his tongue gingerly. Not bitten off, just bitten.

"What's the matter, Choc?" Podjalak asked.

"Bit my tongue."

"Say it was a Jap did it and you get the Purple Heart."

"It ain't funny," said MacCauley.

"If it keeps bleeding, spit the blood out," Podjalak said. "You swallow blood, it makes you sick to your stomach."

MacCauley was already feeling sick from nervousness and the motion of the boat.

The landing craft was loaded now and moving out after Boat 4-2. The wave guide led the boats toward the line of departure, from which they would move toward their assault beach in a long line abreast. The noise of the boat's engine drowned out all but the loudest explosions. MacCauley was glad of that. He wished he could look over the side and see how close the shells were landing but he knew he must keep his head down. He sat with his legs drawn up and his back against the side.

"Be sure you got something between you and the side of the boat," Podjalak said.

"I got about a thousand pounds of stuff between me and the side of the boat," MacCauley said.

"I was in a VP once," said Podjalak, "a shell hit close and busted a soldier's spleen sitting jammed up against the side. Concussion."

"What does that do to you, a busted spleen?"

"How the hell should I know? I ain't no medic."

Podjalak looked around to see if the squad leader was watching, saw he was not, ducked down and lit a cigarette. MacCauley envied him the nonchalance to do a thing like that. Podjalak took a long drag and slipped the cigarette to MacCauley, hiding it with his body. MacCauley felt too squeamish to smoke but took a drag anyhow before handing it back. Podjalak let out air with the next drag, half sigh, half gasp.

"This is it," he said.

"I've been waiting for you to say that," MacCauley said.

Superior Private Hikozo Maeda of the 187th Regiment of the 86th Infantry Division knew it was not so, yet he could not rid himself of the notion that of all the millions awaiting the attack he was the one waiting in the very forefront. It was true there were many other positions all along the curving beach embracing Ariake Bay, but none was any closer to the water's edge as far as he knew. And, since his position was almost precisely in the center of the arc of tempting beaches at the head of the bay, he was sure the enemy would try to land here whether their main attack was against Shibushi to the east or the approaches to Kanoya on the west. The honorable platoon leader had said as much months before when Second Squad was assigned to dig the position with the help of civilian laborers.

"It fills us with trepidation that the Emperor is pleased to permit our platoon to stand at the head of his loyal troops," the honorable platoon leader had said.

Private Second Class Tamura, one of the elderly conscripts, had been so overcome with emotion that he became very pale and close to fainting.

Though forty-seven, he was from a small, backward village and knew nothing of the world or the Army. Superior Private Maeda had thought it necessary to take him aside and explain it was not the Emperor himself who had assigned the platoon its positions. It was only the honorable platoon leader's manner of speaking.

The honorable platoon leader had received the order from the honorable company commander, who had received the order for the company's disposition from the honorable battalion commander, who in turn had received orders from someone even higher in authority. It was true that if one wished one could trace the authority for any order back to the Emperor, for every superior officer represented the will of the Emperor to his subordinates, but all the same Maeda thought it presumptuous and even disrespectful for the honorable platoon leader to attribute to the Emperor himself a decision of the honorable company commander. If the honorable company commander ever learned of the frivolous manner in which the honorable platoon leader habitually made use of the Emperor's name, the honorable lieutenant would be harshly reprimanded. For himself, Maeda hoped this would never happen. If it did, the honorable lieutenant would berate the honorable squad leader and, as always, there would be beatings for privates.

Superior Private Hikozo Maeda knew a good deal about the manner in which the Army operated. Conscripted at twenty from Okayama in westem Honshu, he had served two and a half years in China before being discharged in 1939. Like other conscripts, he had been obliged to remain in the reserves, subject to call-up at any time. During his service in China he had seen many reservists who had already completed one tour of duty and been called up again for the mainland campaigns, and he knew it might as easily happen to him. He had detested Army life, as did many of his fellow conscripts, and did not want to return to China. There were two ways to avoid the risk of a second call-up. One was to take a job in Manchuria and the other was to be a skilled worker in a war industry in the homeland. With the memory of the North China winter still fresh in his mind he did not want to take his new bride to Manchuria. And his father had not wanted his grandchildren that far from home. Maeda had found himself a good job in a munitions plant in Osaka. The work was hard but the pay was more than he could earn in an ordinary job. By the early spring of 1944 he had two children and life was getting more like the Army every day. He was living in Army-style barracks with other specialists and worked twelve hours a day with two holidays a month. He had sent his wife and children to stay with his parents outside of Okayama to escape the bombing and so did not even have the consolation of being with his family.

Later in the spring the plant was so damaged by bombing that there was not work enough in Maeda's specialty and he was called into the Army again. He was sent to Kyushu, where experienced soldiers were wanted as cadres for the new infantry divisions then being formed. Maeda had not minded being back in the Army as much as he had expected. Though there was no break in the training and labor, he did not find the life of a superior private in Kyushu as distasteful as that of a first year soldier in China, which had turned him against the Army in the beginning. And in China he had marched and countermarched against an elusive foe for reasons he never fully understood. Now he was defending his homeland.

Nothing lay between Maeda's position in the dunes and the enemy but two hundred yards of sand and a thousand yards of sea, while behind it all the men, guns and tanks of the Imperial Army were deployed. Though there were two other men in the dugout with him, old Tamura and that clumsy farm boy, Iwagami, he felt that he stood alone between two mighty hosts. Before him, beginning with the slowly cruising gunboats which day and night sent shells and rockets crashing on the shore from a thousand yards out at sea, was a bridge of warships and troop-crowded transports reaching all the way to America. Behind him, stretching all the way to Tokyo itself, were divisions of infantry, battalions of tanks, batteries of heavy artillery and untold millions of volunteers. Maeda thought constantly of that, often with apprehension but more often with pride, feeling sometimes small and insignificant and sometimes very important. He did not wish to die. Who truly wished to die, no matter how many times the honorable platoon leader told them nothing was more glorious than to give one's life for the Emperor? But die he must, whether stationed here in the screen of infantry or farther back in a more elaborate position. And if die he must, where better than here, face to face with the very first enemies who dared set foot on the sacred soil of Japan?

He had actually seen the enemy already, not merely their ships and planes but living men. Every day they had come swimming in, clad all in black like ninja, practitioners of the ancient art of invisibility, to fasten demolition charges among the underwater obstacles and the floating trunks of trees. Warships and planes had covered their activities with showers of projectiles and when the wind was right other planes had come low over the beach streaming great billows of noxious smoke to hide them. He had remained at the rifle port with his binoculars and watched them. More than once they had come within range of his rifle and though he had stared at them across the sights he had not fired. His orders had been most strict on that score. No rifleman was to fire until the landings had begun and then only at close enough range to assure hits. Though he knew the order must be part of a wise strategy which a private could not be expected to understand, it was nonetheless galling.

Maeda hated Americans. Not for the way they for so long tried to keep Japan from its rightful place among nations as the leaders had explained even before this war had begun, or for their lack of culture or the many barbarities of which he had heard, but because of the insufferably insolent manner in which every day and every night they shelled and bombed so unceasingly. Let them fight with rifle and bayonet, man against man, and they would learn that one Japanese soldier was worth ten Americans. Oh, their insolence made his blood boil in his veins!

The dugout occupied by Maeda and his two-man detail was dug into a low dune with the rifle port facing the sea. Some of the other advance positions faced away from the sea to take the enemy from the rear when he attempted to move inland. Maeda was glad he had not been placed in one of the reverse fire positions. He wanted to see the enemy come ashore and be the first rifleman to kill one. Unlike many of the soldiers in his platoon, he was an expert marksman. The rifle port was narrow and so well concealed it was invisible from more than a few feet away. Thanks to Tamura it was invulnerable to anything but a direct artillery hit. The old man was from a hamlet on the Kuma River outside of Hitoyoshi and had worked as a logger. Working slowly but without wasted motion he had cut a five-foot length from one of the big trees dragged down from the mountains to be anchored offshore and had split it neatly in half with wedges. The two halves had been installed horizontally a few inches apart, the flat sides facing away from each other, to form a rude casement. Maeda's binoculars and flashlight hung on thongs from the bottom half. The binoculars were his own, brought with him from Osaka. It had taken much luck and ingenuity to prevent their appropriation by a long succession of superiors.

Some of the stronger beach positions were connected with intermediate positions by long cramped tunnels so that should they survive the early fighting they could be reinforced from the rear and harass the enemy within the enemy's own perimeter. Maeda's dugout, however, was part of a position that could be entered only from the land side of the dune itself. The dugout was one of two rifle positions flanking a Model 99 light machine gun position and connected with it by tunnels. The entrance was now blocked, and had been for three days, with a large rock covered with sand.

"Hard work!" the honorable platoon leader had said by way of farewell when the rock was rolled into the entrance of Second Squad's position.

No sooner was the rock in place when Iwagami announced timidly he had to do the big-service.

"Stupid!" Maeda had cried, wanting to cuff him but not wishing to waste the energy. "You should have moved your bowels before we were sealed in. We will smother in your dung before the Americans come to us."

This was not true, for there was a deep latrine in a small alcove, but the position would be stench-filled soon enough without Iwagami's premature contribution. Both Iwagami and Tamura had had diarrhea for several days before the position was sealed. Tamura had brought his under control by eating only half of his scanty ration but Iwagami continued to eat everything he could lay hands on, including the remains of Tamura's meals, until Maeda forbade him to do so. At least now Iwagami would have to curb his appetite, Maeda thought spitefully, even if the inactivity of dugout life did not do it for him. The five-day ration with which they had been sealed in did not include the midnight snack and special allowance for troops doing night labor. Maeda intended making it last longer than five days on the chance they could hold out for some time after the initial assault.

They had hard biscuits, rice boiled with barley, shredded dried radish and a few tins of whale meat and fish. Water would be a greater problem than food though they would not lose any through sweating as they had when doing heavy labor. The honorable platoon leader, a college graduate, had a theory one would require less water if he held his urine within himself as long as possible. He had not attributed this theory to the Emperor but had taken full credit for it himself. Maeda had instructed Tamura and Iwagami to do so. It would be difficult for Iwagami, Maeda thought with pleasure. The lout urinated like a horse, filling the air with the smell of ammonia. Iwagami must surely be the village simpleton, without enough wit to tell a weed from a rice plant. Perhaps he had been used as a horse, although he was not all that strong, either. He did have patience, however, and never complained, which were great assets when one was sealed in a position. There would at least be no problems such as the one the day before the entrance was closed. A near miss had blocked the dugout's line of fire and Maeda sent Private Second Grade Iwagami out after dark to clear the sand away from the rifle port. Despite Maeda's specific instructions, Iwagami had forgotten to sweep away his tracks behind him when he reentered the dugout and Maeda went out into the barrage himself to make sure it was done properly.

When the last sounds of the party sealing the position died away, Tamura had muttered, "We are buried alive. It is one thing to die but it's another to be treated as dead while the breath is still in you."

Tamura worried, too, because after the attack his body would remain buried in the sand. There would be no one to wash it or light candles to the six Jizo guarding the way to heaven or to drop the paper flags inscribed with sutras into his grave.

"Don't worry, Tamura," Maeda said reassuringly, "you won't need any of that. You'll die a soldier and your soul will fly straight to Yasukuni without all that nonsense."

But Tamura had not been reassured for he did not feel like a soldier despite his uniform and rifle and the Emperor's rice he ate. Maeda thought it strange that an old man with most of his life behind him would be so concerned with death while a boy like Iwagami with most of his life ahead of him did not seem to think about death at all. It must be because Iwagami was stupid and had no imagination, he decided.

The day after the squad position was sealed a lucky hit from a delayed-action aerial bomb knocked out the machine gun and its crew and collapsed part of the tunnel connecting the gun position with Maeda's dugout. Tamura was more convinced than ever that they were buried alive. The dugout was on its own and Maeda was in sole command.

The fourth night since the sealing of the dugout was now almost over. Everything was covered with sand despite the straw mats and the wooden shoring overhead. Shells exploding nearby started new trickles regularly and Maeda had long since stopped brushing the sand from his uniform. His only concem was that it might foul his rifle. He tied a handkerchief over the bolt and had Tamura and Iwagami do the same. He had grown accustomed to the smell of the latrine and no longer noticed it. Iwagami had never been bothered by the odor at all, having spent all his life among paddy fields fertilized with human excrement.

Maeda was stiff despite the simple exercises they performed at regular intervals, and the constant noise and concussion wore at his nerves. Tamura flinched and muttered prayers every time a shell exploded nearby. Maeda thought that after a while the old man would become accustomed to it, but if anything he had grown worse. Tamura had been frightened since the position was sealed and had eaten almost nothing. That had fit in nicely with Maeda's plan to conserve rations and had permitted him the added pleasure of denying Iwagami Tamura's uneaten food.

Though they had been instructed to sleep as much as possible, only Iwagami had been able to enjoy unbroken slumber in the intervals between turns on watch at the rifle port. He irritated Maeda even when sleeping, for he snored. Maeda did not know which was more annoying, Iwagami's snores, Tamura's praying or the Yankee shelling.

Before dawn there came a marked increase in the number and size of incoming shells. The dugout shook and Maeda could hear sand falling all about outside as if dropped from a hundred shovels. Tamura moved close to him, trembling. Iwagami snored on.

"Will they come today, Honorable Superior Private?" Tamura whispered shakily

"Speak up, old man!" Maeda cried. "How often must I tell you?"

The constant shelling had dulled their hearing yet Tamura persisted in whispering, as if afraid the Americans might be hiding just outside the position, listening. Tamura repeated the question in a louder voice. Maeda stopped him in the middle of it.

"Quiet!" he ordered.

He was listening.

There was a change in the sounds outside the dugout, a greater variety in the shells and rockets passing overhead and a different timbre to some of the explosions to the rear and on the flanks.

"Yes, Private Tamura," Maeda said. "The Americans will come today."

The guns dug into the cliffs and mountains, so long voiceless, were speaking out.

The western entrance to Ariake Bay was guarded by Ko-saki, a rugged, precipitous cape rising twenty-seven hundred feet to a mountain called Kunimi. Near its base the steep, densely wooded slopes were strewn with boulders. Higher up, the woods were broken by fields terraced for tea and rice. The hills of Ko-saki were gashed and burned by the shells, bombs and napalm of the enemy. Farmers had once lived among the terraced fields and a few fishermen had dwelt in little houses tucked away in indentations farther down. The farmers and fishermen and their families were gone now, either conscripted or sent away by the Army and Navy, which had dug fortifications in the mountainside and rock-walled torpedo pens along the shoreline. Their houses had been destroyed by the guns of battleships and cruisers probing the hills for concealed emplacements. Even now, in the predawn darkness, projectiles continued to fall among the shattered trees.

Near the ashes of a house a few hundred feet above the shore lay a tiny untended garden of sato imo, a kind of taro, sweet potato, and the giant radish called daikon. A bamboo pipe thrust between two half-buried boulders dripped spring water into a container fashioned from a single joint of bamboo five inches in diameter. Among other boulders imbedded in the hillside was a small opening. Within, in a nest of grass and twigs, a man lay sleeping despite the violence being done the surrounding hillside.

He was Jiro Matsuyama, sixty-one, a little deaf, and blind in one eye. The garden was his and the ashes had once been the home he shared with his son, his daughter-in-law and four grandchildren. In August their one-sail fishing boat had been sunk with its nets by a patrolling carrier plane and his club-footed son killed. An older son had been killed at Aitape in 1944. Six weeks after the loss of the fishing boat a sergeant in the Army had come with an official-looking document and told them they must leave.

The area was important to the defense of the nation and only soldiers were permitted to remain on the seacoast. It was as much for their own safety as anything, the sergeant had explained when Matsuyama protested it was his home and had been his father's before him. In a few weeks, six or seven at most, there would be heavy fighting here and everyone on the mountain would die. Toshi, his daughter-in-law who had been properly reared, said nothing but it was obvious to Matsuyama that she was anxious to take the children to a safer place. Since one could not ignore an official document anyhow, Matsuyama agreed to leave. The sergeant regretted the Army could spare no transport to move Matsuyama's family and belongings out of the coast defense zone.

He advised them to go as far back from the coast as possible, preferably into the mountains. If they went into the mountains they vould be dependent on what food they took with them and they had very little. Matsuyama, who was of a more independent turn of mind than most inhabitants of the area, suggested that since he was only leaving to please the Army he would be obliged if the Army would provide them with food. The sergeant regretted the Army had no food to spare, in fact he was wondering if Matsuyama might have a little dried fish or seaweed he cared to sell. Matsuyama did not, but he did give the sergeant a drink of shochu and a bit of takuan, daikon pickle, and told him to feel free to forage in the garden when the potatoes ripened. The sergeant was, after all, an exceptional man. Matsuyama had heard more than one tale of how soldiers had come into peasant homes and taken what they wanted with no offer of payment.

Toshi humbly suggested that they go to the farm of her sister, five miles from the coast on the other side of Mount Kunimi near the lakeside hamlet of Nagano. Her sister had had no word from her soldier husband since the Americans invaded Luzon and was all alone. It was time to harvest the rice in her small field and she would welcome their help. Matsuyama permitted himself the rare luxury of a smoke in his kiseru, a three-puff thimble of pipe, before agreeing. It would please neither of them if he accepted her suggestion without appearing to have studied it carefully. They left the next morning with their possessions piled on a wooden-wheeled barrow and the daughter-in-law carrying the smallest child slung across her back. Toshi had been very helpful since his son's death, doing the work of a man. Matsuyama hoped his own daughters gave their fathers-in-law the same respect Toshi gave him. There had been no news of either of them in several months and it was possible they might also be widows. Both their husbands had been conscripted. What little of their possessions they could not carry in the barrow or on their backs Matsuyama hid in a hole among the rocks. He would return for them after the Americans were driven back into the sea.

Although Nagano was only five miles away from the bay there was no road leading over the mountain to it. They would be obliged to go five miles along the coast to the Kimotsuki River, four miles inland to Koyama Village and another three miles south to Nagano. A narrow dirt road hugged the shoulder of the mountain a few hundred feet above Matsuyama's house. Set back from it in the hillside almost directly above the house was the concrete emplacement the soldiers and local people had toiled for so long to construct for the 15-cm. gun pointing out into the bay. The casement was three feet thick and stretched nine feet back from its lip to the cannon hidden inside. Matsuyama marveled at how well the mass of concrete was concealed by earth, trees and underbrush. He had helped in the digging and had hoped he would be permitted to witness the cannon firing on the Americans if they dared sail into the bay. Near the crest of the hill above the emplacement, barely visible among the trees from the road, was the gun's observation post, a cylinder of thick concrete almost completely buried, with a narrow slit overlooking the bay. Farther along the road was a similar post and underground powder magazine. They were all connected by tunnels which Matsuyama had helped to dig. He wondered if the sergeant had not been exaggerating about everyone dying on the mountain. Surely there could be nothing more safe than the deep caves and the concrete. It would have been better if they had been permitted to wait inside the tunnels until the Americans were driven away.

Soldiers stripped to the waist and wearing sweatbands around their foreheads were working in the concealment of the trees along the road. Some of them paused to shout good-natured ribaldries at Toshi or call "Hard work!" to Matsuyama. Toshi looked modestly at the ground but Matsuyama believed she was flattered by the attention paid her. One of the soldiers dashed out of the trees to pat the children on their heads.

"I have two of my own at home," he said.

Matsuyama watched him closely out of the corner of his eye. The man was walking very close to the barrow and soldiers could be lightfingered. When they had passed and the soldier remained in the road to wave at them Matsuyama was ashamed of his suspicious nature.

It took all day to reach Nagano. There were other evacuees on the narrow road and they were obliged to stop frequently to permit the passage of horse-drawn Army wagons and an occasional truck. A flight of Grummans flew over the road before they reached the river and everyone scrambled pell-mell into the trees. The planes did not open fire but shortly after they passed, the sound of their guns could be heard farther back attacking a truck that had gone by some minutes before.

The children were excited by the outing and ranged the sides of the road looking for fuki, marsh rhubarb, to be boiled and eaten that night.

Matsuyama watched them with great pride. His son had given him all male grandchildren. It was the first time his family had been so blessed in three generations.

"Toshi," he said in an embarrassing burst of affection, "do you wish to rest?"

"Thank you, Father, but I am not tired. If you like we will stop and I will make you tea."

"No need for that," Matsuyama said gruffly. "We've hardly started out yet."

They reached the farm of Toshi's sister before nightfall. It was a small farm with only about two acres, less than one cho, of paddy land and a few square feet of garden on the hillside. It was obvious from the disrepair of the farmhouse and barn there was no man around. There were no animals. The Army had taken the sister's most valuable possession, a horse bought with all their savings when her husband went into the service, and left a slip of paper in return. The few chickens had disappeared mysteriously. The sister welcomed them but looked apprehensively at all the children. They were too many mouths to feed even in the best of times and the Army had already given notice most of the rice harvest would be requisitioned. She cheered up when she saw they had brought a little dried fish and seaweed and Matsuyama began speaking immediately of the rice harvest and the repairs he intended making on the farm buildings.

Matsuyama's daughter-in-law heated water from the well and gave him a vigorous bath in the little bathhouse in the yard. An old widower with no living son could want nothing better in life than such a devoted daughter-in-law, he thought. After a supper of barley, dried fish, pickle and the fuki gathered by the children, Matsuyama went to bed. It made him sad to be sleeping in a strange house in his old age. Toshi and her sister gossiped far into the night. Although they lived only a dozen miles apart they saw each other rarely.

Matsuyama remained on the farm three weeks, helping harvest the rice and lay the straw on poles for drying, repairing the two farm buildings, and putting the garden in order. At the end of that time he walked to Koyama and tried to enlist in the local Volunteer Combat Unit. His offer was refused with amusement. A one-eyed old man would only get in the way when the Yankees came.

"Go home and hide in the privy, old man," he was told. "You will be safe there."

He returned to the farm fuming. A few days later, despite the respectful though dogged protests of his daughter-in-law, he left to return to his own house.

"Father," she had pleaded, "who will look after you?"

"You're as bad as those impudent fools in Koyama," he said. "I'm still not too old to look after myself."

He took nothing with him but a little rice, planning to fish at night and dig whatever might be left in his garden. There would be other abandoned gardens where the soldiers might not know to look and he needed little to sustain him. And he had left a bottle of shochu hidden in the hole among the rocks. At his age shochu was more sustaining than food.

He found the house burned to the ground when he crept down the hill after dark and was more moved than he had believed possible. His children had been born in the house, and himself before them. His wife had died there. With his sons dead and his house gone he felt that his own life had ended. The sergeant had said that everyone remaining on the mountain would die. He would remain here and die with the soldiers. If the Americans came ashore he would fight shoulder to shoulder with the troops. He would make a better job of it than those fools in Koyama. The Yankees would learn he was not too old to fight. He enlarged the hole among the rocks and gathered twigs and long grasses for his bed. By day he remained hidden inside so the soldiers would not find him and send him away again. At night he slipped down to the shore to fish with a hand line and grope for small sea creatures among the rocks.

American warships began sailing boldly into the bay by day and night. During the day smoke rose in the distance all along the head of the bay and at night the shoreline was marked with explosions and fires. When the ships bombarded Ko-saki he remained in his hole among the boulders. It puzzled him that the 15-cm. gun on the hillside above him did not shoot back at the warships and sink them or drive them away. It also made him angry. If the gun had driven the Americans away when they first came, perhaps his house might not have been burned. He considered asking a soldier why the gun remained so strangely silent, but did not. The soldier might report his presence to someone in authority and there would be questions. Matsuyama was displeased with the soldiers. They never showed themselves in the daylight, as if they were afraid of the Yankees. If he did not hear them moving about at night he would think they had all gone away and left him alone on the mountain. But sometimes at night they were very busy on the road above his hole. He could hear men's voices and the sound of trucks and wagons. After his first night back, when the sun rose to reveal a deserted hillside, he thought the sounds had been of their departure. Now he knew they had merely been working. For the past few days there had been no activity even at night, only occasional sounds from the positions above and the caves in the shoreline below.

Matsuyama slept a great deal. Sometimes he felt as if he were already dead and the hole was his tomb. He wished now he had told his daughter-in-law to come for his body when the battle was over and see it received a proper burial. But she would come without being told.

He was sleeping now, undisturbed by a scattering of shells falling along the face of the hill. Farther north, from the Kimotsuki River all the way along the coast to Shibushi across the bay, the bombardment was heavier than it had ever been before. Had Matsuyama known it he would have been outside his hole, watching. He was awakened by a thunderous clap of sound which sent reverberations rolling down the hillside and into the narrow opening of his cave. The ground moved under him. In the first moment of awakening he thought he was out in his boat and had been overtaken by a thunderstorm. He rubbed his good eye and thrust his head outside. Thunder shook the earth again and a red glowing blur darted out over the bay. The 15-cm. gun was shooting.

He crawled out of his hole and stood erect among the taro plants in his garden, cheering. Shell after shell roared from the hillside above him. The Yankee warships were too far out in the bay for him to see them but he could imagine the shells falling on them and sending them to the bottom. He went back into his hole for the bottle of shochu he always kept at his side and brought it out. He poured a cup and, facing the hillside above him, raised it high in a toast to the gun. He sat on a rock with the bottle of shochu between his feet, shivering in the morning damp and drinking. The face of the sea grew lighter but he could not see the ships at which the gun was firing. He shook his fist.

"Cowards," he cried, "show your faces."

Though he could not see the ships they made their presence known over the whole surface of the bay with fiery flashes and puffs of smoke. The sky as well as the sea was filled with them and he could see the far-off glint of planes in a great melee. From beyond the river the sound of the Yankees' shells falling on the beach made a steady thunder. Below, men shouted as they launched their torpedoes from the rocky pens. He rose to his feet and toasted them as he had the gun. The sergeant who sent him away had been a big fool. It was the Yankees who would die, not those on the mountain. Perhaps even now they were turning tail, pursued by shells, torpedoes and the little boats which had lain hidden along the shore. When they were gone he would build a new house to replace the one they had burned. All the families would return and they would help one another rebuild all the houses. He drank a toast to the ashes of his home.

A salvo of incoming shells blustered overhead and crashed into the hillside. A wall of air knocked Matsuyama flat. He lay on his belly with his arms cradling his head while clods and stones pattered around him and mounds of earth tumbled down the hill toward the sea. He was furious. The Yankees had killed his gun. The gun began firing again. He got to his feet again, staggering as much from the shochu as from the concussion, and shouted triumphantly. He drank another toast to his gun. A second salvo knocked him down again and while he was trying to get back on his feet airplanes came out of nowhere to drop fire and explosives on the hill. The heat of the fires came down in waves. He heard the trees burning. There was an ache over his blind eye. He touched the spot and brought his hand away covered with blood. There was a roaring in his ears. He did not know if the sound came from within or without. The gun kept firing. He reached for the shochu to drink another toast to the brave gun but the bottle was broken.

Matsuyama shrugged and sat down on a mossy boulder overlooking his garden, the ashes of his home and the disputed sea. As long as the gun continued firing, nothing else mattered. More shells and more planes came. Matsuyama sat quietly, watching.

6

[Private John Robert MacCauley/Corporal Podjalak/ Superior Private Hikozo Maeda]

The Third Attack Force filled Ariake Bay, stretching from a line of gunboats a few hundred yards off the beaches to the outer limits of the transport anchorage twelve miles offshore. The gunboats, fifty of them, poured cannon, mortar and rocket fire on meticulously plotted sectors of the three miles of beaches where two of XI Corps' three divisions would make the opening assault. Farther out eight battleships, ten cruisers and nineteen destroyers added the weight of their batteries to the cascade of metal and explosives falling on Japanese positions from beachfront rifle pits and obstacles to the guns dug into the hills. Under this umbrella 150 transports, freighters and large landing ships would disgorge their troops, tanks, artillery and tons of equipment and supplies on beaches Essex and Ford. Fighters from carriers, Okinawa and the smaller islands of the Ryukyu chain gave protection to the armada and joined sea and land-based bombers in massive strikes against the deeply buried enemy.

The long silent coast erupted to meet the challenge. The Japanese fought back against the still seaborne invaders with swarms of suicide planes, midget submarines, Shinyo, shore-launched torpedoes and Kaiten, land-based Oka manned rocket planes, Fukuryu "Crouching Dragons" and skillfully dug-in artillery.

Hundreds of individual battles swirled in the air and on the sea, littering sky and surface with wreckage. Despite the fury of the Japanese onslaught and the losses in men and ships, the Landing Force disposed itself in the complex patterns laid down months earlier in the calm security of planning rooms. The gunboats went first to saturate the beaches from close in. Four thousand yards offshore, control ships flying the colors of the assault beaches marked the line of departure and the routes of Landing Teams assembling in landing craft among the transports. Other control craft flying beach colors marshaled amphibian tanks and the landing craft into waves and shepherded them toward the line of departure.

Amphibian tanks, LVT(A)s, formed the first wave. They wallowed toward the beaches behind the gunboats at four knots in a line three miles wide. Behind the tanks at carefully timed intervals came waves of troop-carrying landing craft, LVT amphibious tractors and LCVPs. The second and third waves bore chiefly riflemen. In the fourth wave were more infantry, with mortars, machine guns and flame throwers, and the key men of the shore and beach assault parties. The shore and beach parties, comprising Navy and Army men, would set up aid stations, communications posts and supply points. Other waves followed with troops, matériel, supporting units and command staffs. Amphibian tractors, tank lighters and DUKW amphibian trucks made ready to bring in artillery, tanks, heavy equipment, ammunition and supplies when the infantry had wrested from the enemy a beachhead on which to land them.

When the waves of amphibian tanks neared the beaches the gunboats turned aside to let them through. The barrage from the sea stopped abruptly and formations of planes swept low over the beaches with machine guns and napalm. When the planes finished, the tanks laid down point-blank fire with their 75-mm. howitzers and 20-mm. cannon. The warships shifted their barrage farther inland. The amphibians turned away when the second wave, the LCVPs loaded with infantry, neared the shore. Mortar shells began dropping among the landing craft from emplacements behind the dune line and on the reverse slopes of hills which had escaped the barrage intended to neutralize them. Crouching Dragons thrust their explosive charges at landing craft passing over them or writhed on the surface from the concussion of their own mortars, to be picked off by riflemen and the LCVPs' machine guns.

Private John Robert MacCauley was in the fourth wave, twelve minutes behind the amphibians. There were twenty infantrymen in the boat, MacCauley's fourteen-man reinforced rifle squad and a six-man heavy machine gun squad with its weapon and ammunition. The riflemen sat with their heads down, rifles held upright between their knees. MacCauley's stomach churned in harmony with the rolling of the boat. He imagined he could feel the milk and pineapple juice from breakfast sloshing from side to side within him in a motion like the sea's. He swallowed air to keep from vomiting. He was glad he had not taken Corporal Podjalak's advice and eaten the pork chops. Nausea, fear and the morning cold chilled him, making his thighs jerk uncontrollably. He hoped if anyone noticed they would understand it was not because he was so scared but because he was sick and cold. He did not see how he could possibly do any of the things he was supposed to do on the beach. He should be in bed under blankets until he was over his chill. But it was better to be here than back on the ship. The ships were getting it from every angle. As far as he could tell nobody was shooting at the LCVP. Yet. He tried not to think about what waited on Essex Yellow Two. He wondered if somewhere someone was still driving Pop's old blue Essex. His uncle had finally managed to unload it after his pop stuck him with it. The car would be nine years old now, almost half as old as he was.

Suddenly MacCauley was taken with a shattering conviction that his own fate was inextricably bound with that of the car. Why else was he on his way to a beach called Essex and, in the middle of such danger, should he be thinking about an old car that had passed out of his life when he was a child? He hoped desperately that the car was still running, that someone owned it now who had cured its breakdowns and understood its cranky ways. He saw it somewhere on a junkpile, wheels gone and doors hanging loose. He shivered.

"Okay, Choc?" Podjalak asked beside him.

MacCauley nodded, his helmet knocking against his rifle barrel. It was stupid to think the old car could have anything to do with what happened today. But at least it had taken his mind off his seasickness. He still felt queasy but not as if he had to vomit.

The coxswain, bent over the wheel in the after part of the landing craft, kept up a running commentary for the soldiers crouching behind the ramp.

"First wave's on the beach," he said. "Oh, Christ, they're catching it!"

MacCauley heaved himself up to look, using his rifle as a support. Podjalak grabbed his arm and pulled him back down.

"Dumb twerp!" the corporal cried angrily. "What you think the armor plate's on this baby for?"

"Straighten it, straighten it!" the coxswain shouted meaninglessly to a boat in the wave ahead. "You want to swamp her?"

The port machine gun began firing. Half the troops raised up to see what the sternman was shooting at.

"Keep down!" the squad leader yelled.

MacCauley was proud of himself. He was not one of those who had tried to look.

"I think we got ourselves one of our own frogmen," someone said.

"Frogman, hell," the squad leader replied. "That was a friggin' Jap. You see that pole charge in his hand?"

"Sarge," said Podjalak. "You looked."

"Up yours," said the squad leader. "I get paid to look."

"Another thousand yards," the coxswain said. "Three minutes."

"Everybody get set," the squad leader called.

The bowman left the starboard machine gun and plowed through the troops to his station at the ramp latch. The weapons squad gathered up its machine gun, tripod and ammunition boxes. The riflemen checked their pieces and readjusted their packs and dangling equipment.

"You guys by the Browning ammo grab a box and carry it off," the squad leader said.

"When I joined the Army the recruiting sergeant told me I wouldn't never have to carry nothing heavier'n a rifle," a soldier said.

MacCauley wished he could think of something funny to say, too. He laughed though he did not feel like laughing. Everyone was very quiet, then someone said, "I'm thirsty. Pizzo, gimme a drink of water."

"You got your own goddam canteen," the soldier named Pizzo replied, irritable with tension.

"Can't get to it."

"Think I can get to mine, you dumb bastard?"

The squad leader peeked over the ramp.

"Two minutes," he said.

There was a whispering in the air. The sides of the landing craft quivered and water spattered on the crouching men.

"We're getting mortared," Podjalak said.

The coxswain opened the throttle. The wave of landing craft would hit the beach at full speed.

"Get set," the squad leader ordered.

"Poge," MacCauley whispered urgently, "what's the oldest car you ever heard of? Still running, I mean?"

Podjalak looked incredulous.

"What did you say?" he demanded.

"Bowman, stand by to release ramp latch," the coxswain shouted.

"When that ramp drops don't stop to pick no daisies," Podjalak said. "Get your ass up that beach and find a hole. I'll be right with you."

"Okay," said MacCauley.

He wished Podjalak did not sound so nervous. He was counting on

Poge to steady him. The surf picked the boat up. MacCauley's queasiness returned abruptly. It was like being in a fast elevator.

"Grab ahold!" the coxswain yelled.

The boat dropped with a lurch.

"Ramp going down!" the coxswain yelled.

The ramp dropped in a shower of spray as the landing craft hit bottom with a bone-jarring thump, nosing aside a shattered LCVP wallowing broadside in the surf. In the moment before he went sprawling with the others in a tangle of limbs and equipment, MacCauley had his first brief glimpse of Beach Essex Yellow Two, sharp and detailed as a photograph.

In the foreground, a body bobbing jerkily in a boil of water; cratered sand spurting puffs of smoke and earth; lengths of sawn trees scattered like giant kitchen matches spilled haphazardly, the fresh wood showing vividly where steel had torn it; men huddling among the logs, some moving, some not; motionless dark shapeless objects which might have been ammunition boxes, abandoned packs or pieces of bodies, though displaying nowhere the red of blood. In the background, thickly sewn geysers of fire, smoke and dirt; tangles of broken-limbed trees felled whole, some burning; behind them a smoky pine woods and in the distance hills abloom with explosions. Overlaying all, sounds, as if the dropping of the ramp had opened his ears. A roar of boat engines, a sighing, coughing and rattling in the air, explosions, the crack of small arms and chatter of automatic weapons, shouts, screams.

And nowhere a visible enemy.

"Move!" the squad leader cried.

The men closest to the bow pulled themselves free of the tangle and stumbled down the cleated ramp into knee-deep water. Some of them went down and MacCauley thought they were hit until he saw they all had managed to keep their rifles out of the water, raising them above their heads as they fell.

"It's cold!" someone gasped, outraged.

MacCauley laughed harshly, without mirth. What a hell of a thing to complain about at a time like this. Podjalak pulled him to his feet and started him toward the ramp. MacCauley scrambled forward, bent low, tripped as he reached the ramp and went rolling into the water. His arm shot up instinctively, lifting his rifle clear. The shock of immersion drove the breath from his lungs but he had no distinct impression of cold, only wetness. He felt like a fool. A hand wound itself into his belt suspenders and dragged him erect. Poge's angry voice grated in his ear.

"Left-footed son of a bitch!"

"I couldn't help it," MacCauley said, gasping.

"Shut up."

Podjalak shoved him toward the beach. A man in front stumbled and went down. MacCauley paused to help him up as Podjalak had helped him The man did not cooperate. He lay face down on the sand, his feet in the water. He was dead. MacCauley pulled his hand back quickly from the inert shoulder. He had seen only one other dead man so close up, his grandfather in a coffin, and had never touched one before. Someone bumped him from behind and swore at him. It wasn't Podjalak. Where was Poge? Poge had gone off and left him. He was filled with rage. Podjalak had bawled him out for something that wasn't his fault and now he'd gone off and left him. He lumbered across the sand, slowed and oppressed by the intolerable weight of his equipment, shouting, "Poge! Podjalak!"

"This way!" Podjalak shouted.

He was only a few paces ahead. MacCauley followed him a hundred yards to the shelter of two thick logs laying at an angle. Two men were already there, one from MacCauley's squad, the other a stranger. The latter was shaking violently. Finkel, the man from MacCauley's squad, was smoking a cigarette.

"Rough, huh?" he said conversationally.

He jerked his head toward the shaking man.

"Came in with the first wave," he said. "Hasn't moved an inch since."

The man smiled weakly, showing chattering teeth.

"Stopped us cold," he said.

He did not sound as frightened as MacCauley expected he would. Although the air was not cold, MacCauley's own teeth began chattering when the breeze played over his soaked uniform.

"Cold," he muttered defensively.

"Wish I had a picture of you rolling down that ramp," said Podjalak. "Where the hell's the rest of the squad?"

"I saw two guys jump in a hole over there," Finkel said, waving a hand toward the left. "Haven't seen anyone else."

"Somebody got it in the water," MacCauley volunteered, feeling useful for the first time.

"Who?" said Podjalak.

MacCauley shrugged.

"Not Noble, I hope," said Podjalak, worried.

Sergeant Noble was the squad leader.

"Naw," MacCauley said.

Noble was a big man. The dead soldier was his own size.

"What you think we ought to do?" Finkel asked.

Podjalak raised himself on one elbow, keeping his head below the level of the two logs.

"Noble!" he shouted. "Sarge. You okay?"

"Over here," a voice answered on the left. "How many with you?"

"Two more," Podjalak called back. "And a guy from First Platoon. Finkel, is Noble where you saw the two guys?"

"No."

"Couple more by you if they ain't dead," Podjalak called.

"We ain't dead, you dumb bohunk," a strained voice called out. "Just restin.' Pizzo and Jones are in the next hole."

"I got three with me," Noble shouted. "Anybody else from Second Squad?"

"Williamson," a new voice called off to the right. "I thought I was the only one made it."

"We're doing better than I thought," Noble called. "I'm gonna see if I can find the lieutenant. Everybody stay down till I get back. Poge, take over."

"Take over what?" Podjalak muttered. "Okay," he yelled. "Start digging," he said to his companions. "These logs ain't helping us none with the stuff dropping behind us."

Mortar shells were still dropping on the area. When a shell hit among the logs strewing the beach, it sent slivers of wood flying like darts. MacCauley felt an itching in his calf and reached down to scratch it. He found that a splinter the size of a toothpick had pierced his trousers and dug itself into his leg. He wondered if he should pull his pants leg up and put something on the scratch but decided it was too much trouble. And Poge and the others might wonder what kind of sissy he was if he made a fuss over a little scratch.

They scraped a shallow hole in the sand and lay in it. A man came running from the water's edge and threw himself among them.

"Watch it!" MacCauley cried irritably.

A second man tumbled into the hole behind the first.

"We're too bunched up," Podjalak said. "You guys find another hole."

"In a minute," said one of the newcomers, breathing heavily.

"Now!" Podjalak snapped.

They crawled away meekly, hugging the sand, rifles cradled in the crooks of their arms. MacCauley watched them go, glad that he could stay where he was and that he was with Podjalak.

For the first time he looked about. The shoreline was cluttered with landing craft. Some were just coming in, others were backing out to sea empty. Derelicts lay shattered on the sand or bumped broadside in the surf. The incoming waves had to push through the abandoned craft or skirt around them to find open beach. Boxes, packs, clothing, equipment and bodies littered the water's edge. The bodies tossing in the surf looked alive and trying to swim clear. The surf worried at those on shore, as if trying to drag them out to sea. None of it looked exactly real to MacCauley. He tried to locate the body of the man who had been hit in front of him. He was not sure but he thought he picked it out. He was glad he did not know who it was and that it was not him or Podjalak out there with his face in the sand. A yellow cloth beach marker erected by the first wave ashore stretched between two poles, a ragged hole almost exactly in the center. MacCauley wondered why the Japs didn't try to shoot it down. Maybe they didn't know boats coming in were guiding on it. The beachmaster was running up and down unmindful of the mortar fire, bellowing orders through a bullhorn. Beach and shore parties worked feverishly, clearing away debris and supplies clogging the shore or huddled around marker pennants operating radios, stacking ammunition, and tending to wounded. The machine gun squad with which he had come ashore had dragged logs around a shell crater and set up their weapon in the improvised position. They had not fired it yet. MacCauley realized that neither he nor the others in the hole with him had fired yet, either. There was nothing to shoot at. He had not expected it to be this way. He had expected to see Japs swarming all over the beach and maybe having to fight them with his bayonet. He did not know which was worse, being mortared by somebody you couldn't see or having to fight them hand to hand. The Japs were used to fighting with swords and knives and he wasn't. To tell the truth, he wasn't used to fighting with anything.

Somewhere a robust voice, a baritone almost professional in quality, began singing.

Oh, what a beautiful morning,
Oh, what a beautiful day,
I've got a terrible feeling,
Everything's coming my way.

"That crazy Polichino from Able Company," Finkel said. "He auditioned for Jimmy Dorsey once."

MacCauley wished he could sing like that, and had the guts to. Next to being off Essex Yellow Two, he wished that the most.

"Where the hell's Noble?" Podjalak demanded. "We can't sit here all day. Choc, your piece is full of crud. Brush it off."

MacCauley got out his cleaning brush and brushed the sand off his rifle. He took out the clip and checked the action, feeling professional and glad to have something to do. He only wished he had done it without Podjalak having to remind him. A shell came in with a swish and a whoomp, covering everyone with sand and tossing a log into the air to come crashing down a few feet away.

"Short round," Podjalak said. "Hope them bastards out there adjust."

More shells fell along the beach, louder than the mortars and earthshaking.

"What's the matter with those bastards?" Finkel cried. "Don't they know we're here?"

"I don't think they're ours," Podjalak said nervously. "The Japs got us enfiladed. Where's that goddam Noble?"

An officer came zigzagging along the beach, running bent over. His right hand clutched his left wrist, holding his useless left arm across his body. He kept shouting monotonously.

"Move in, get off the beach, move in!"

"Lieutenant," Podjalak shouted, "Noble went looking for you. You see him?"

"Noble's dead," the lieutenant said, breaking stride. "Get off the beach. They're cutting us to pieces. Everything's piling up."

He began running again and shouting, "Move in, get off the beach, move in!"

"That friggin' Noble," Podjalak said. "Leaving me in a spot like this."

MacCauley was shocked. He thought Podjalak and the squad leader were buddies. You didn't talk that way about somebody who got killed.

The amphibian tanks had come ashore and were now ranged along the beach just behind the troops, firing over their heads. MacCauley felt the muzzle blasts wash over his back and thought he heard the 75-mm. shells whizzing just above his head. The machine gun a few holes away was also firing now, as was a nearby mortar, at what MacCauley had no idea. At intervals the naval guns firing inland would pause and planes would come in with bombs, machine guns, rockets and napalm. Enemy fire seemed to MacCauley to have diminished somewhat, though he thought it might merely be that the sound of the enemy's projectiles were being blotted out by the tank guns.

Bulldozers landed from fifty-foot LCMs were working all around, shunting aside wrecked landing craft, dragging wooden pallets piled with fuel, ammunition and medical supplies to the colored pennants marking supply dumps, and clearing away the logs obstructing the beach. As the tide moved in and more men and matériel came ashore, the narrow beachhead grew increasingly crowded.

"We don't haul ass like the lieutenant said, we're gonna get run over," Podjalak said.

He raised his head cautiously above the logs protecting their refuge and studied the terrain.

"See any Japs?" MacCauley asked.

"No. They must be dug in good."

Podjalak dropped back down, took out a cigarette and then put it back in the pack.

"Hey," he shouted, "you two resting guys. Abbott, you still okay?"

"If you call this okay, we are," was the answer.

"Pizzo, Jones. How about you?"

"I'm still here. Jones got hit and crawled back looking for a medic."

"Bad?"

"Naw. I've been hurt worse in a fist fight. He was just looking for a ticket off the beach."

"How about Noble's three?"

"Yo," a voice called.

"You hear what the lieutenant said about Noble?"

"Yeah. Wonder was he messed up much?"

"Williamson, you still there?"

There was no answer.

"Williamson," Podjalak called again. "You okay?"

This time he got an answer, a chilling sound between a gurgle and a moan.

"Hit bad, sounds like," Podjalak said. "Crap."

He looked indecisively from Finkel to MacCauley.

"I'll go," Finkel said.

MacCauley felt as if he had let Podjalak down by not volunteering. But he wouldn't know what to do if Williamson was badly wounded. That was a medic's job. Podajalak did not look disappointed with him. If anything, he looked relieved.

"Fix him up if you can and try to get a medic over there," he said. "Don't take all day, either."

Finkel straightened his equipment and crawled off, leaving his rifle. You weren't ever supposed to do that, MacCauley thought. But Podjalak didn't say anything so it must be okay.

"Abbott," Podjalak yelled. "There's a hole with a bush in front of it about thirty, thirty-five yards in. A little to your left. When I say move, take Primeaux with you. Pizzo, you and Jones move out with Abbott. Knight, you guys stay put till I tell you."

The man from First Platoon, who had stopped trembling, cleared his throat.

"Maybe I ought to try and find my platoon," he said.

"Suit yourself," said Podjalak.

The man from First Platoon took a deep breath and trotted off at a crouch, his canteen bouncing on his hip.

"He ain't looking for no First Platoon," Podjalak said disgustedly. "He's looking for another hole for himself. You doin' okay, Choc?"

"Yeah."

"You quit shakin.' Got hot enough for you, huh?"

"Yeah," MacCauley said again.

He had forgotten about being cold and wet. It was warm in the sun.

"I'm gonna move the squad up in a couple minutes. There's a kinda' hump straight ahead. Maybe thirty-five yards. We'll head for that. Zigzag and keep low."

MacCauley's chest tightened. He thought about the old blue Essex rusting on a junkpile somewhere. The beach behind him looked like a junkpile, come to think about it. The sand rustled and Finkel's head came poking around the logs.

"Dead," he said. "Got it in the throat."

"Four gone outta the squad and we ain't even seen a Jap," Podjalak said. "My mother told me there'd be days like this."

"But she didn't say they'd come in bunches like bananas," said Finkel.

He said it without any particular inflection. It was a ritual.

"There's this little rise about thirty-five yards straight in," Podjalak said. "I'm moving Abbott and his bunch out and then we'll head for it."

"About time," Finkel said. "You looked at the water lately? We're running out of sand."

"Abbott," Podjalak shouted. "You all set?"

"Yeah."

The platoon sergeant trotted up behind the hole, sweaty and out of breath.

"Where's Noble's squad?" he called.

"Noble's dead," Podjalak said.

The platoon sergeant dropped into the hole.

"I know," he said, panting. "Everybody moves up at oh-eight-forty. How many you got left?"

"Nine for sure. Maybe ten. I'm getting ready to move em' up now."

"Nobody moves until oh-eight-forty."

"Why don't the friggin' lieutenant make up his friggin' mind? He said move ten minutes ago."

"This came from battalion," the platoon sergeant said. "The whole line's moving up. They just evacuated Lieutenant Swoboda. Busted arm. The planes are coming in with smoke. Four hundred yards in. Move all the way up to the smoke and dig in."

"Four hundred yards?" Podjalak demanded. "What good's smoke up front with all this crud hittin' us in the ass?"

"Oh-eight-forty," the platoon sergeant said flatly. "Listen for the whistle."

He squared his shoulders and trotted off to find the next squad. Podjalak took a long cautious look over the logs.

"Four hundred yards," he said incredulously. "All the way to the woods. Through the paddy fields. There's Japs in them paddy fields."

"Can you see 'em?" MacCauley demanded, raising up.

Maybe if he could see a Jap it would be more real.

"Naw, you can't see 'em," Podjalak said impatiently. "Get your goddam head down."

He passed along the platoon sergeant's orders to the rest of the squad.

"Try and keep a line but don't bunch up," he said. "Abbott, is Third Squad on your left?"

"How the crap should Ah know?" Abbott shouted. "Ah been right here in this hole the whole time."

"It's supposed to be. Find out. First Squad, you over there?" Podjalak called to his right. "This is Podjalak."

"We know it's Podjalak," a voice answered from a dozen yards away. "You ain't shut up for five seconds."

"Smallwood tell you about moving up at oh-eight-forty?"

"You have to remind us?"

A flight of Hellcats skimmed over the ground along the edge of the woods, trailing dense smoke.

"Right on time," said Podjalak.

Whistles blew and men shouted.

"This is it," said Finkel.

"I was wondering when you were going to say it," MacCauley said.

"Come on!" Podjalak cried. "Move!"

They scrambled over the logs and dashed toward the smoke. MacCauley kept his head down, afraid to look up or to either side. Part of his mind said faster, faster, but another part said careful, you're running into something that can kill you. He heard someone cry that he was hit, and then from another side a startled yelp. Two little spurts of sand kicked up in front of him as if something alive but invisible was digging holes. Small arms fire. There were Japs in the paddy fields, all right. He wondered if he should try to get his bayonet out of its sheath and put it on his rifle. He looked around for Podjalak. Podjalak was a few yards ahead of him, running so low his knees seemed to hit his chin with every stride and cutting from side to side like a broken-field runner. MacCauley, who had been running in a straight line, imitated him. Finkel was a bit to Podjalak's right. He stopped suddenly, as if he had tripped. His knees hit first, then his elbows. His rifle shot forward through the air and landed muzzle first. It remained upright a moment before toppling over. Finkel was on his hands and knees. His head drooped until it was touching the ground and the rest of his body melted into a heap.

Then Podjalak did a curious thing. He ran to a low hillock and thrust his rifle into the sand among scruffy bushes, firing and shouting at the top of his lungs. MacCauley ran to him, unnerved. If Poge had cracked up, what hope was there for him to make it?

"Shoot," Podjalak yelled. "Shoot! Japs!"

It was only then MacCauley saw Podjalak's rifle was thrust into a narrow aperture in the hillock. He stuck his own rifle into the slit and pulled the trigger. The trigger did not move. He had not taken the rifle off safety. Cursing and trembling, he pushed the safety off and pulled the trigger again. The rifle did not fire. What a lousy time for a malfunction. And then he realized he had not slid a cartridge into the chamber when he replaced the clip after brushing the sand away. He worked the operating rod handle. Before he could fire Podjalak jerked at his arm and cried, "Outta my way!"

He had a grenade in his hand. He flipped it into the aperture, gave MacCauley a shove, and cried, "Come on."

"Finkel got hit," MacCauley gasped as they ran.

They jumped a marshy ditch with water in the bottom and went abruptly from sand to stubbly paddy field. Machine gun fire sounded close at hand. MacCauley wondered how the machine gunners had got their weapon up so fast and in firing position. The gun did not sound right. He realized it was not an American machine gun. He flung himself flat and lay there. He did not want to go any farther. The smoke seemed no closer than when he started running and there was no telling what was in it and beyond. The smoke could be full of Japs just waiting for him. Whose damn fool idea was it to lay smoke, anyway? The Japs this side of it could see them and the mortars were zeroed in, smoke or no smoke. All it did was hide the ones waiting beyond the fields. Pillboxes like the one Podjalak had shot up were probably all over the place. He had forgotten all about Podjalak. Panic welled up in him. If he got separated from Poge he'd get killed for sure. That goddam blue Essex.

"Poge!" he shouted. "Poge!"

"I ain't goin' nowhere, you dumb twerp," Podjalak said from only a few feet's distance.

He was lying flat, his rifle across the hollows of his elbows, methodically studying the ground around them. Off to one side the tops of two helmets showed in a shell hole. Other men huddled in small depressions or behind low dikes dividing fields.

"I think I got it spotted," Podjalak said. "See those three bushes over there where two dikes run together?"

MacCauley looked. He could see nothing.

"Yeah," he lied.

"Maybe we can get close enough for grenades," Podjalak said. "Where the hell's First Squad? They're supposed to be over there."

He had no sooner spoken when a figure rose to one knee and lobbed a grenade in a stiff-armed, sweeping motion. It fell in the stubble and exploded.

"Did he get it?" MacCauley cried eagerly.

"Nowhere near," Podjalak said disgustedly. "You can't get a pillbox throwin' at it. You got to work in close and drop one in."

"Oh, yeah," said MacCauley. "Yeah."

"Where are the goddam tanks?" Podjalak demanded. "They never show up until we clean out the Japs for 'em."

"Poge," MacCauley said, trying to spit sand from a mouth in which there was no saliva. "What are we going to do?"

"We ain't staying here, that's for sure. This is worse than where we just come from."

"We going back there?"

Podjalak looked at him over his shoulder, a pained expression on his dirty, sweat-streaked face.

"See that smoke up there?" he said. "That's where we're goin'."

He worried his canteen free and took a swallow of water. He wormed over to MacCauley and handed him the canteen. MacCauley took a long drink. He felt it trickle far down into his body. He had not known how parched he was.

"Thanks," he said.

"You can pay me back in whiskey," Podjalak said.

A geyser of earth flew up a few dozen yards beyond them, then another.

"They spotted it," Podjalak said. "The amphibs spotted it. Come on, Choc."

He started working his way toward the smoke, which was beginning to thin. Behind them a loud cracked voice shouted, "Keep moving, everybody keep moving."

When they had moved perhaps a hundred yards through heavy mortar, machine gun and small arms fire, Podjalak gestured toward a large crater and they threw themselves into it. It was already occupied by three men. Two of them were from MacCauley's squad, one named Knight, the other Primeaux. MacCauley did not know the third man though he remembered having seen him on the transport. He was dead, lying flat on his back without a visible wound. MacCauley thought his leg was blown off until he saw it was only tucked under his thigh at a grotesque angle. Primeaux was on his back, also, the front of his jacket sliced away and his entrails neatly displayed in a gaping cavity. MacCauley tasted something hot and acrid in his throat. He choked it down, thinking, I look just like that inside. Primeaux's eyes were closed. His face was mottled gray where the skin was visible in the grime. Podjalak looked at Knight, who was smoking a cigarette. Knight shrugged.

"He jumped just when it hit," he said. "Came down like that."

"Somebody ought to get a medic," MacCauley said.

"A medic ain't gonna do him no good," said Podjalak.

"I heard that you son of a bitch," Primeaux whispered, not opening his eyes. "I'll be around to piss on your grave."

"Jesus, Primeaux, I'm sorry," Podjalak mumbled. "I thought you was . . ."

"I know what you thought I was."

"Want me to try and find a medic?" MacCauley said.

"Yeah," Podjalak replied. "A medic and a couple litter bearers."

As he spoke he shook his head, indicating MacCauley was to do nothing. His lips silently formed the words, "Ain't no use."

"We'll have a medic here in no time, Primeaux," he said reassuringly. "Okay, you guys, let's go. Hey, Primeaux, take it easy."

"Screw you," Primeaux said.

He had not opened his eyes the entire time they were in the hole.

Progress through the dry paddy fields was slow. Small arms and machine gun fire from the fields themselves was sparse but fire from the woods and heavy, accurate fire from mortars and artillery on the high ground forced the troops to move cautiously and take cover frequently. The Japanese guns were so well concealed and dug in that despite air and ground spotting, bombing and naval gunfire failed to knock them out in appreciable numbers. By the time MacCauley's squad reached the woods' edge the smoke laid by the planes had long since dissipated and no planes had come to lay more. The Japanese had felled trees to make tank barriers. The trees were sawed partly through a few feet above the ground and toppled forward toward the beach. Most of the trees which were not already charred skeletons were burning. MacCauley, Podjalak and two others from the squad had taken refuge in a pocket which offered protection from anything except a mortar shell dropping straight in. MacCauley felt safer now than he had felt at any time since leaving the safety of the hole behind the logs near the beach. Once they were through the dunes, small arms fire had grown heavier, and from all sides, but there had been little shelling. The Japanese gunners were concentrating their fire on the beach, where men and matériel continued to pour in and crowd together.

Embers from burning trees drifted in the wind and fell into the pocket.

They burned holes if not brushed away. MacCauley's uniform as still damp from his soaking. An ember the size of a thumbnail landed on his back and before Podjalak noticed it and knocked it away the pocket was filled with the stench of smoldering damp cloth. One of the men, Abbott, grinned and sniffed the air in an exaggerated manner.

"Y'all hear the one about this sergeant givin' close order drill to these WACs?" he said. "Well, he was drillin' 'em right hard and the wind was blowin' off the post dump and they were burnin' all these old tires. So after awhile this sergeant noticed this here smell, y'all know how rubber smells when it's burnin', an' he stopped 'em an' he said, 'Am Ah marchin' you ladies too fast? "

Everybody laughed. MacCauley thought it was one of the funniest jokes he had ever heard. Like the others, he had relaxed in the temporary safety of the pocket. He had not once thought of the car jinx since reaching it.

MacCauley's tranquillity was shattered when Podjalak said, "Crap, we can't stay here all day. Finish your cigarettes and let's get moving."

"Ah don't hear nobody else movin' up," Abbott protested.

"You couldn't if they was," Podjalak said, "with all that crud flying around."

"It seems like somebody would tell us something once in a while," MacCauley said.

"Yeah," said Podjalak. "I wonder what happened to that friggin' Smallwood? The platoon wouldn't be scattered to hell and gone if the lieutenant hadn't got his arm busted. I don't even know where the line is now. If we got a friggin' line."

He sat a moment, musing, then said, "You guys take it easy. I'm gonna see if I can find out what's going on."

He slung his rifle, settled his helmet, and crawled out of the refuge. MacCauley relaxed again, feeling reprieved. As long as he was safe for the moment he was not overly concerned about what might come later or what was happening elsewhere to other people. And he was pleased with himself. It was almost his idea that Podjalak should try to find out what was going on before they made a move. He started to field strip his cigarette. The incongruity of the action struck him and he poked the butt into the dirt instead. He shrugged off his pack and got out the can of C ration and the assault lunch. He was not especially hungry and put the C ration back in his pack although it was his favorite kind, frankfurters and beans. His mother made them sometimes, but not cut up the way they were in the C ration. He tore open the assault lunch. He put the pack of cigarettes, box of penny matches and chewing gum in his pocket, threw away the water purification and salt tablets and ate his way methodically through the two chocolate bars, caramels, salted peanuts and raisins. The chocolate bars were Hersheys. He held one to his nose and suddenly had an aching sense of home. His pop might have helped make it. He wished there was some way he could let his pop know he was sitting on a beach in Japan eating a Hershey bar his pop had made.

"Hey, Abbott," he said. "You know something? You can't hardly get Hersheys in the States. My mom wrote me."

Abbott was eating cold C ration ham and egg from the end of his sheath knife. He kept the knife razor sharp and MacCauley wondered how he kept from cutting his mouth. His own bitten tongue had not troubled him since the ride in to the beach. Abbott looked up, genuinely interested.

"No crap?" he said. "You can't just go to the store and buy yourself a Hershey bar?"

Then he grinned.

"An' all the time Ah been thinkin' we was winnin' this here war. Ah guess we're pretty durn lucky to be in the Army. Ah mean if you got that big a hard on for Hersheys."

"I wish we had the kind with nuts," MacCauley said wistfully.

Abbott laughed.

"If that's the best you can wish for Ah feel sorry for you, boy," he said.

An object so big and slow-moving it could be briefly seen hurtled overhead and moments later exploded behind them with a shattering roar. The three men occupying the pocket groveled in sudden fright, abruptly conscious their feeling of security had been illusory.

"Oh, God," MacCauley whispered, aware he was taking the Lord's name in vain and hoping it would not count against him, "what was that?"

"Spigot mortar," Abbott replied shakily. "Three-twenty millimeter stuff."

"How big is that?" MacCauley asked. "Three-twenty millimeters? It looked like a truck."

"Too damn big," Abbott said. "On Okie we called 'em flying boxcars."

Abbott had been with the 77th Infantry Division on Ie Shima and Okinawa before coming to the 1st Cavalry Division when the division was beefed up for Kyushu.

"Why do they call them spigot mortars?" MacCauley said.

"How the hell should Ah know!" Abbott snapped.

"You've been acting like you know it all," MacCauley snapped back.

They were both irritable with tension. Normally MacCauley liked Abbott. He was always telling jokes and his Southern accent made them seem even funnier. They fell silent, waiting for another foot-thick mortar shell to fly over. None came and gradually they began breathing more normally.

"Hey, Choc," said Abbott, "that ole spigot mortar scared the whey outta you, didn't it?"

"I wasn't really scared," MacCauley protested. "It just surprised me, was all. I never saw nothing like that before."

"That's what mah girlfriend told me first time she saw me with mah shorts down," Abbott said, grinning. "Ah didn't believe her, neither."

Knight, the other man in the pocket with them, laughed. It was the first noticeable sound he had made except for his stentorian breathing after the spigot mortar hit. His fingernails were bitten down to the quick.

"I'm not all that scared," MacCauley protested. "Look."

He held out a hand to show how steady it was. He was surprised and chagrined at the way his fingers trembled.

"You can be nervous without being scared," he said. "You think I'm scared, let's see your hand."

"Ah ain't nervous," Abbott said. "Ah'm plain old-fashioned scared. You couldn't drive a needle up my ass with a ten-pound hammer. That's the only reason Ah ain't got a drawer-full like ole Knight, here."

Knight looked down at his feet uncomfortably.

"Yeah," Abbott went on. "There's some pucker up and some go loose as a goose. Ole Private Knight, he goes loose."

"Knock it off!" Knight said angrily.

"I've got some toilet paper," MacCauley said.

"You shut up, you little sissy bastard!" Knight spat.

MacCauley was as much hurt as angered. He was only trying to be helpful. Knight wouldn't have talked that way if Podjalak was there. Where was Poge, anyhow? He had been gone fifteen or twenty minutes. That was a long time to be out there with all that stuff flying around. He began to worry. After a while he said, "Abbott, you think anything's happened to Poge?" After he said the words he was sorry he had spoken. It might jinx Podjalak to say something like that out loud.

"Nah," said Abbott. "Probably just stopped off at the PX for a beer."

That was somehow reassuring. If Abbott could joke like that he must not be worried about Podjalak. And Abbott knew the score. MacCauley thought about the blue Essex. He was relieved to find it no longer bothered him to think about it. He had been on Essex Yellow Two for hours now and nothing bad had happened to him. If there really was such a thing as a jinx he would be dead by now. Or maybe he had just transferred the jinx to somebody the way his pop had got rid of the Essex to his uncle. Maybe the guy in front of him when they landed, or Finkel, who'd been in the hole with him. If he'd put his jinx on somebody else he hoped it wasn't Poge. There was a flurry of movement outside the pocket and everyone snatched up their rifles as Podjalak came rolling in among them.

"Am I glad to see you!" MacCauley cried.

"What'd you find out?" Abbott demanded.

"Lemme rest a minute," Podjalak panted. "I'm pooped out."

They waited impatiently for him to catch his breath. He had brought back a knobby sack and an extra canteen, which he held gingerly by the chain on the cap.

"Ah told you he stopped off at the PX," said Abbott.

Podjalak put down the sack and canteen and pulled a folded section of brightly dyed cloth from his combat jacket. He looked from face to face, then handed it to MacCauley.

"MacCauley," he said, "get your butt out there and spread out this front-line panel. Stay on your belly and don't go more than four, five yards."

Podjalak sounded unusually businesslike. MacCauley had not failed to notice Poge had called him by his last name, not his nickname. He reached for his rifle, trying to look impassive.

"Leave it," Podjalak said. "Abbott, you and Knight get up to the lip and cover him."

MacCauley unfolded the panel and crawled up the slight rise dragging it behind him. He felt naked outside the pocket. When he tried to work his way over the ground he found it difficult to do so clutching the end of the panel in one hand. He held the end of the panel between his teeth, letting the panel trail over his body. What a target, he thought, expecting at any moment to feel the smack of a bullet in his flesh. When he thought he had gone five yards he looked back. He had gone scarcely six feet. He went a few more feet and could force himself to go no further. He spread out the panel, smoothing it down neatly and anchoring the ends with handfuls of loose earth. He was proud of himself for thinking of it without Podjalak having to tell him. Before crawling back he took a quick look at the churned earth within the smoking woods. It was empty of visible life. He saw two or three mounds that might have been dugouts or pillboxes but no shots came from them. He crawled back quickly, feeling terribly competent. Podjalak looked relieved when he slid down into the pocket.

"Couple or three suspicious-looking humps off to the left and about a hundred, hundred-twenty yards in," MacCauley said with what he hoped was easy professionalism.

"Thought I told you to keep your head down," Podjalak said, but there was approval in his tone.

He picked up the canteen and held it out.

"Coffee," he said. "Watch it. It's still hot."

The coffee was strong and black and stung the bitten place on MacCauley's tongue. He did not like coffee much even with cream and sugar. He swallowed some now because it was a reward for a job well done and a special treat he did not want to miss and because Podjalak had taken the trouble to bring it back to them. He gave the canteen to Abbott and the canteen passed from hand to hand until it was empty. Podjalak talked while they drank.

"We got us a new company commander," he said. "Lieutenant Thompson. Captain Bondurant caught one in the head. Smallwood's got the platoon. And I'm acting assistant platoon leader. Not bad for a raggedy-ass corporal, huh?"

"What about us, Poge?" MacCauley said. "What are we supposed to do next?"

"I'm getting to that," said Podjalak. "Don't you for Chrissakes want to know what's going on?"

"I got dysentery," Knight said. "Bad. Maybe I ought to go back and get something for it. What you think, Poge?"

"They got guys with their guts hanging out waiting in line for help," Podjalak said. "Stick a cork up your ass. We're five hundred yards through the woods from Hishida," he continued, dismissing Knight. Hishida was the little town they had been told was their initial objective. "Battalion's supposed to take the woods to the railroad just this side of town and set up a line along it before dark."

Now that Podjalak was assistant platoon leader he seemed to have changed, MacCauley thought. He was talking like an officer. MacCauley felt lonely and left out.

"Hey, Poge," he said desperately, "how about that spigot mortar? You hear it?"

"I ain't deaf," Podjalak said impatiently. Seeing MacCauley's crest-fallen expression he added, "For a minute I thought it was an ammo dump going up. How'd you know it was a spigot mortar?"

"Abbott said so."

"Abbott, I'm making you acting squad leader. I meant to tell you before."

"Do Ah get another stripe?" Abbott said. "Mah daddy made corporal in the world's war and Ah got to do at least as good as him. If Ah don't get another stripe you can shove it."

"You know I ain't authorized," Podjalak said.

"You dumb bohunk," Abbott said. "Ah know you ain't authorized to give no stripe. Ah was just . . ."

"Then cut the crap and listen," Podjalak interrupted impatiently. "We got to open up some beachhead so they can bring in the battalion reserve. They been landing artillery and tanks the last half hour."

He looked at his watch.

"Another five minutes they're gonna start plastering the woods between here and the railroad. Ten-minute barrage. Then the planes come in for five minutes. After that they start hitting the Jap big stuff in the hills and we move out with tank support. Knight, what happened to the two guys with you?"

Knight shrugged.

"Abbott, see if you can find 'em. And Pizzo. And anybody else from the platoon. Give 'em the word."

Podjalak emptied the sack onto the ground. It was full of grenades. He counted them and put half back in the sack. He gave the sack to Abbott.

"Any of our platoon you find, give 'em two each long as they last," he said.

"How much am Ah s'posed to get apiece for 'em?" Abbott asked solemnly.

He slung the sack over his shoulder and left.

"Crazy bastard," Podjalak said admiringly when he was gone. "Got more guts than brains."

MacCauley felt a twinge of jealousy. He longed to do something to make Podjalak say the same thing about him. He was glad Knight was there with them. Compared to Knight, he had plenty of guts. It took guts just not to show how scared you really were. The way Abbott joked and kidded, you wouldn't know he was scared at all if he hadn't said so himself.

In a few minutes the barrage began. They huddled at the bottom of the pocket and held their hands over their ears. The ground quivered and miniature avalanches slid down the sides of their refuge. A short round landed a few yards off to the right and men could be heard shouting and swearing. They sounded irate, not wounded. When the barrage ended after ten minutes, a great pall of silence seemed to descend even though Japanese shells were still falling on the beach and tank engines were grinding. The planes came over while Podjalak was dividing the grenades. He and MacCauley could not resist the temptation to climb to the lip and watch. They counted 62 planes. The planes laced the woods with rockets and machine gun fire and dropped high explosives and napalm. Seen at close hand, the napalm was awe inspiring and vivid. The canisters tumbled down and skidded along the ground, spewing sheets of flame and flinging driblets of fire into the air. It set new fires among the trees. MacCauley pointed out the spots he thought might be concealing enemy soldiers. One was scorched and blackened, another proved to be merely earth thrown up by shellfire and a third showed no aperture.

"Could be a reverse fire position," Podjalak said. "With the fire port on the other side. Be careful going around it."

After the planes came a new barrage, and the tanks. The shells landed far inland. MacCauley could not see the points of impact, only the smoke rising from them. The tanks came in loose groups of two and three advancing far apart in a ragged line. They were not the thin-skinned amphibians but hulking mediums, Shermans, with high-velocity 75-mm. cannon thrusting out of their turrets. Their thirty-cylinder engines and churning tracks made a fearsome racket. Waves of infantry skulked among the tanks. A scattering of combat engineers preceded the tanks, some with mine detectors and others probing the ground with bayonets. The tanks would pause while they tested an area, then move forward again when the engineers advanced. The planes and shellfire had already exploded many of the antitank mines. Mortar fire increased in intensity as the Japanese attempted to strip the troops from the armor, and flat trajectory shells from medium artillery employed as antitank guns made barely audible soughing sounds as they passed low overhead. More infantry materialized from holes and craters to join in the attack as the tanks rumbled through the lines. The first tanks clanked abreast of MacCauley's position, their treads dripping showers of earth and charred fragments of the felled trees in the tank barrier.

"Come on!" Podjalak shouted, joining the advance.

MacCauley followed close behind him. Knight stayed in the pocket.

"Knight!" Podjalak shouted. "Get your butt up here."

MacCauley guessed what was delaying the other soldier.

"He's emptying his drawers," he said, for a moment feeling Podjalak's equal.

He ran in close behind a tank, seeking the shelter of its armor. Podjalak motioned him to one side, where he belonged. It was their job to protect the purblind tanks from enemy troops attempting to slip up on them with satchel charges. MacCauley trotted close alongside the nearest tank.

"Stay clear!" Podjalak cried. "They're drawing artillery fire."

Fifty yards ahead of them through the trees a Sherman took a hit with a dull clanging sound. It rolled forward a few feet as if nothing had happened, then stopped dead. While it was still rolling, hatches flew open atop the turret and above the driver, and a man tumbled out of each, hit the ground sprawling, and jumbled to his feet to race for safety. Just as a third man was climbing from the turret he was blown out in a gush of flame. He struck the earth hair and clothing afire, scrambled to his feet, ran a few steps, and fell to the ground again, thrashing and screaming.

"Can't we do something?" MacCauley squeaked in tight-throated horror.

"You can shoot him if you got the guts," Podjalak said.

His stricken expression belied the coldness of his words.

MacCauley tore his eyes from the grisly sight and chased after Podjalak. Ahead of them a tank was passing the mound he had pointed out to Podjalak a few minutes earlier. A grotesque little hunchback popped out of it as if materializing from the ground and ran toward the tank. MacCauley watched, petrified. Podjalak jerked his rifle to his shoulder and shot the creature. The little hunchback disintegrated in a clap of thunder, pieces of his body flying through the air. It was only then that MacCauley realized he had at last seen the enemy and that the hump on the Japanese soldier's back had been a satchel full of explosives. The episode engulfed him in a welter of impressions which for the moment smothered his fear: chagrin at his failure to react when the Japanese popped out of the mound, shock at the suddenness of it all and the grotesque appearance of the explosive-laden figure and its diminutive size, a resolution to respond quickly the next time a Japanese showed himself, a feeling that he was not an active participant in the assault because he had not yet fired his rifle. Together they made him feel inept and useless. He wondered when Podjalak was going to catch on that he wasn't a real soldier at all, just a fake dressed up in a uniform. Dirt kicked up in front of MacCauley and a row of shallow furrows appeared.

"Hit it!" Podjalak yelled.

MacCauley dropped immediately and rolled toward a slight rise which a few hours before he would have thought worthless as protection if he had noticed it at all. He raised his head carefully, as he had seen Podjalak do, and looked for the source of the machine gun fire. He was determined to locate it before Podjalak did and to shoot at it no matter how far away or well dug in it might be. Air stirred around his head and more dirt kicked up near him.

"Behind us," Podjalak called.

He was prone in a shallow crater a few yards away. MacCauley gathered his legs under him and lunged toward it, diving the last few feet through the air. He landed on top of Podjalak. The breath left Podjalak in an angry grunt and he knocked MacCauley away with a vicious sweep of his forearm.

"I'm sorry, Poge," MacCauley gasped.

"It's off over there," Podjalak said calmly, gesturing in the direction from which they had come.

Bullets plucked the air above them.

"They got us spotted," Podjalak said.

"What do we do now?" MacCauley asked.

"Friggin' tanks," said Podjalak. "Ain't never around when you need one."

He drank from his canteen, being careful not to expose any of his body over the rim of the crater. MacCauley waited for Podjalak to hand him the canteen but Podjalak replaced it without looking at him. MacCauley drank from his own canteen, then got out his cleaning brush and dusted off the operating mechanism of his rifle. He felt that the war had narrowed to a personal duel between the machine gun and himself and Podjalak. And it was not an even match.

Podjalak lined up three grenades beside him.

"Take off when I start throwing," he said. "Find a hole you can cover me from. We got to get close enough to do some good."

MacCauley looked around for a promising hole. He saw a prone figure snaking toward the hump concealing the machine gun. The man was approaching from the side, where he could not be seen from the firing aperture.

"Hold it, Poge," he said excitedly. "We got us some help."

The machine gun opened fire again, its fire skimming overhead. The man stopped crawling toward the gun when it began firing, then resumed his stealthy approach. When he got close enough he pulled the pin of a grenade and flipped it into the aperture. The gun stopped firing and the grenade flew back out. The man got up and ran, throwing himself to the ground as the grenade exploded.

"Crap!" said MacCauley.

"Dumb son of a bitch," Podjalak said. "He should have held it longer."

A man with a burden on his back ran at the position from the other side through the charred trees. MacCauley raised his rifle, determined to fire before Podjalak. Podjalak knocked the weapon aside and began shooting at the mound.

"Cover him!" he cried.

The man with the burden on his back was American. Before MacCauley could obey Podjalak's order the soldier pointed a long nozzle and a stream of fire shot toward the hump, splashing first in front of it and then directly into the aperture. The gun stopped firing and MacCauley heard screams. The soldier ran closer and thrust the nozzle into the aperture. Heavy black smoke rolled out of the opening. The soldier slipped out of his tank harness and sprawled with his back against the mound mopping his face with an olive drab handkerchief.

"If there's anybody here beside Nips, how about a butt?" he called.

"Over here," Podjalak cried.

The soldier crawled toward them, dragging his flame thrower behind him. They made room for him in the crater.

"The little bastards got positions pointing every which way," he said. "There's more fighting back toward the beach than there is right here."

"Give the man a butt, Choc," Podjalak said.

MacCauley gave him a cigarette.

"Light?" the man said.

"That's a hell of a little lighter you're carrying," Podjalak said, holding out a match.

"My legs must have got two inches shorter since they stuck that thing on my back," the man said. "How about you guys teaming up with me? I got separated from my squad."

"We got to find our platoon," Podjalak answered. "I'm acting assistant platoon leader. Come on up with us and I'll give you a couple men."

The soldier blew smoke out of his nose.

"I'm gonna hold up here a minute," he said. "Get the kinks outta my back."

He worked his shoulders backward and forward.

"How about one of you guys giving me a whack between the shoulder blades" he said. "It kind of helps."

Podjalak hit him in the middle of the back with the side of his fist. The soldier sighed luxuriously.

"Thanks," he said.

"Take it easy," Podjalak said, getting up.

MacCauley trotted along behind him.

"I wouldn't want to do that," he said.

"What?" Podjalak demanded.

"Use one of them things."

"Ain't no chance of burning yourself if you know what you're doing."

That was not what MacCauley had meant but he thought it better not to say so.

The railway right of way was two hundred yards ahead of them through what was left of the woods. The rails and ties were gone, having been used for obstacles and construction materials. Beyond the right of way were bare fields and beyond the fields high ground. To the right, a pall of smoke identified Hishida. There were tanks and troops scattered all the way to the far edge of the woods. Though there appeared to be little fighting in the area itself, enemy shells fell steadily from artillery ringing the beachhead. MacCauley counted five immobilized tanks, two of them still burning, between himself and the right of way. The other tanks had halted just inside the meager concealment of the woods. They were firing at distant targets off to the left and right. An Army spotter plane circled high above them like a model at the end of a wire, making no attempt to evade the scattered antiaircraft fire coming up at it. Other planes attacked targets beyond the right of way and dropped colored smoke bombs in the areas at which the tanks were firing. Occasionally, a figure would emerge from concealment to scamper forward a few yards, or off to one side or another, or even back from the direction of the advance. To MacCauley the movements looked aimless.

It was like a war movie, but one in which he was a member of the audience instead of an actor. Though he knew the shells falling in the woods were real and could kill him he had no real sense of involvement because he had not yet fired his rifle. And he had seen only one Japanese soldier. He knew enemy soldiers had manned the machine gun that pinned him down and had even heard their screams as they roasted, but because he had not seen them the machine gun, like the mortars and artillery firing from the hills, seemed devoid of human direction. With Podjalak he dodged his way forward, moving from crater to crater. Podjalak no longer found it necessary to tell him when to move, or where, and on occasion it was MacCauley who was first to spy the next temporary refuge and tumble into it with Podjalak following. Often the craters were already occupied by dead or living men, some of the living wounded. The wounded men were real enough to MacCauley, not at all like actors in a war movie. Their blood and entrails and mangled limbs, and their groans, were not only horrifying but also in a strange way embarrassing. It was not from any sense of guilt at being whole but rather because he was intruding on the privacy of their agony. It was somewhat the same as when once, at eleven, he had surprised a couple making love in the back seat of an automobile parked on a back road. He wondered if he would ever learn to behave as Podjalak did with wounded men. Podjalak gave water to those not wounded in the belly, put lighted cigarettes between the lips of those unable to help themselves, performed what first aid he could, and told aid men where they could be found when they encountered medics in their erratic advance through the woods.

At every opportunity Podjalak asked for news of their platoon. No one had any idea where it was. Many of those he questioned had become separated from their own units and were trying to rejoin them. It was already afternoon when they found a rifleman from their own company who said he knew Sergeant Smallwood, the acting platoon leader, and thought he had seen him in the past hour or so. They made their way toward that part of the beachhead where Smallwood had last been seen. The soldier named Pizzo was the first man they encountered from their own squad. He was sitting at the bottom of a shell crater with one boot off, massaging his foot.

"Hi, Poge," he said anxiously, "what the hell's happening?"

"I just got here," Podjalak said. "We got separated from the platoon."

"You and everybody else. This friggin' blister!"

"You seen Smallwood?" Podjalak said.

"Over there with the lieutenant."

"What lieutenant?"

"Some joe from battalion."

"You seen Abbott?" MacCauley asked.

"He's around here somewhere. Him and Knight and a couple other joes."

"Take it easy," Podjalak said. "Come on, Choc."

"Yeah," said Pizzo. "You guys take it easy."

They found Smallwood in a shell hole that had been deepened with shovels, the earth mounded neatly around it. With him were an officer and a soldier, the latter crouched over a portable two-way radio repeating what sounded like gibberish to MacCauley.

"Somebody told me they saw you get hit, Podjalak," Smallwood said by way of greeting.

"We can't have this many men crowding into this hole," the officer said irritably.

"This here's Corporal Podjalak, sir," said Smallwood. "Acting assistant platoon leader."

"Assistant platoon leader should be a sergeant," the officer said.

MacCauley wondered if the officer was always so short-tempered or if it was just because there were too many men in the hole.

"That's fine with me, sir," Podjalak said.

The officer did not smile. He looked at MacCauley and motioned with his thumb like a baseball umpire throwing a player out of the game.

"Find yourself another hole, soldier," he said.

When MacCauley turned reluctantly to climb out, Podjalak put a restraining hand on his arm.

"He's the platoon runner, sir," Podjalak said.

Smallwood opened his mouth, then shut it again without speaking.

"Keep yourself out of the way then," the officer said. "There's too many men in this hole."

"The lieutenant says we got to clean up everything in the battalion rear before dark," said Smallood.

"Right," the officer said. "There's still Japs dug in all the way back to the beach. And we've found some holes in the woods that look as if they might be tunnel exits. We expect the Japs to try infiltrating from the high ground through them tonight."

The way he spoke reminded MacCauley of an English teacher he'd had in high school. He hadn't liked the Engiish teacher, either.

The officer unfolded a map and showed them where the battalion line was to be established the other side of the railroad before dark and where the company would scour the woods for dug-in Japs and tunnels the enemy might use in their anticipated counterattack that night. MacCauley felt a tingle of excitement at getting the picture firsthand. Since the briefings aboard ship, no one outside the platoon had told him anything. Things hadn't gone the way they'd been told aboard ship and most of the day he hadn't even known what was happening to the rest of his squad, let alone the company and battalion. He changed his mind about the officer being a horse's ass. It wasn't every lieutenant who would take time to explain what the whole battalion was doing instead of just telling you to go here and do that.

"We haven't run into their real defenses yet," the officer was saying.

"You mean it's gonna get worse?" Podjalak said.

"You ain't seen nothin' yet," the officer said.

Coming from someone who had been speaking so precisely, the flippant words sounded condescending. MacCauley revised his opinion of the officer again.

"Sergeant," the officer said, "you stay here with me until I find out if they're going to bring up a hot meal for the troops with the ammo. Send your runner out to locate the rest of your platoon. And find out what's happened to the rest of Charlie Company."

"You got that, uh . . ." Smallwood said.

MacCauley's name had escaped him.

"Yo," said MacCauley.

Maybe he really was platoon runner now. He was not sure he liked that, especially if it meant he would be separated from Podjalak. He was more confident now than he had been when he first hit the beach but he did not relish the idea of being on his own.

"I'll go with MacCauley, sir, and round up the platoon," Podjalak said.

"Good idea," said the officer. "There's too many in this hole. How old are you, MacCauley?" he added unexpectedly.

"Sir? Nineteen."

"Really," the officer said, as if he did not believe it.

He turned away and began giving orders to the radio operator.

"Take it easy," said Smallwood.

As soon as they were out of the hole Podjalak sprinted to the nearest crater and dived into it with MacCauley just behind him. He propped his back against the side of the crater and took out a cigarette.

"The lieutenant said locate the rest of the platoon," MacCauley protested.

"Up his," Podjalak said. "You didn't really believe that crap about being platoon runner?"

MacCauley shook his head, not wanting to admit he had.

"We ain't chasing all over the place with all that crud coming in. The platoon's around here somewhere. We'll join up with it when Smallwood moves it out."

They smoked a while in silence, ducking instinctively when a shell landed close enough to throw dirt.

"What the hell were you talking about this morning?" Podjalak said. "About old cars or something?"

MacCauley had forgotten all about the blue Essex.

"My pop had this '36 job," he said. "Then he sold it to my uncle. I just wondered if it was still running."

"That's a dumb thing to think about when you're getting your ass shot off."

"Yeah," said MacCauley. "I guess it is."

He meant it.

Smallwood emerged from the hole and Podjalak whistled him over to join them.

"The lieutenant's pissed off," Smallwood said with a grin. "No hot meal for the troops."

He looked at MacCauley.

"You're supposed to be out hunting my platoon," he said.

"I told him to wait for you," said Podjalak.

"Who's in charge of this friggin' platoon, me or you?" Smallwood demanded.

"Neither one, soon's they get us a lieutenant up here," Podjalak said. "I thought it was going to be him."

He jerked his head toward the officer's dugout.

"We don't need no lieutenant," Smallwood said truculently.

"I'll be damned," said Podjalak. "Sucking for a battlefield commission, ain't you?"

"Shove it," Smallwood said. "Look, the lieutenant give us and First Platoon a crap detail. We gotta work our way from the edge of the woods to just this side of the railroad and check a two-hundred-yard front for Japs and tunnels. He's got this friggin' idea the whole Jap army's gonna come crawlin' out behind us tonight."

"Why don't the engineers do it? That's what they get paid for."

"Cause the lieutenant said for us to. You take your squad and whoever you can find from First Squad. I'll take Third Squad and some men that got separated from First Platoon."

"Fattening up your command, ain't you Smallwood?"

"I'm warnin' you, Poge."

"Ain't you got no sense of humor, for Christ's sake?" Podjalak said. "Let's go round up the squad, Choc. Take it easy, Sarge."

"You, too," said Smallwood.

It took twenty minutes of dodging from hole to hole to find Abbott and the others. Knight, the private who had pleaded dysentery, looked really ill and Podjalak sent him back to the rear. Abbott he sent to find the sergeant in charge of the other squad and pass along Smallwood's instructions. As Abbott was leaving, MacCauley said nonchalantly, "Take it easy."

The three rifle squads of the platoon, which had lost twelve of its forty-two men since landing that morning, inched forward in a straggling two-hundred-yard line. They did not move forward as a unit but in twos and threes, with Smallwood or Podjalak giving the signal to hold up or push forward. They searched among hummocks and the exposed roots of tree stumps for holes which could conceal Japanese soldiers or be the end of tunnels from across the railway. When a soldier found a hole he thrust into it with his bayoneted rifle. If he could not feel the bottom he dropped a grenade into it. MacCauley, who was midway between Podjalak and Abbott, found no hole though he did get a fright when he knocked against what appeared to be a bared Japanese arm thrusting out from the base of a tree. It was only after he shouted an involuntary warning that he saw to his embarrassment it was a root. Shortly after that Abbott shoved his rifle into a hole and then began yelling.

"Somebody's in there!"

The somebody in the hole had hold of the other end of Abbott's rifle. Abbott kept yelling and trying to pull his rifle free.

"Pull the trigger, you dumb bastard!" Podjalak screamed. "Shoot!"

Abbott fired four quick shots in succession, the rifle coming free after the first.

"Ah got me one, Ah got me one!" he cried triumphantly.

He held up his rifle for all to see. There was blood on the bayonet where the Japanese soldier had gripped it. Abbott began poking the bayonet into the ground to clean it.

"Get down, Abbott!" MacCauley yelled. "You want to get your dumb butt shot off?"

He thought that sounded very much like Podjalak. When Abbott hit the dirt immediately MacCauley was pleased. He wished he could find himself a hole with a Jap in it. He still had not fired his rifle. He wondered if Podjalak had noticed that.

They worked their way within shouting distance of the tanks ranged at the far edge of the woods. The tanks were firing only desultorily now. They were running out of ammunition and the amphibian trucks which were to bring up more were still busy unloading artillery and supplies on the beach. The beachhead and offshore waters were still too heavily interdicted by the enemy for LSTs to land the conventional truck battalions. Word passed along from Smallwood that they would advance no farther for a while. The tanks were still the principal target of the enemy artillery and the shelling around them was intense. MacCauley, who was alone behind a stump, crawled to Podjalak's hole.

"What do we do now?" he asked.

"Smallwood oughta know something," Podjalak said. "The way he's been brownnosin' that lieutenant. I'm gonna go see."

"I'll go with you," said MacCauley.

"You buckin' for platoon runner?" Podjalak demanded. "You got any brains, you don't leave no hole you don't have to."

"We'll cover each other. You might run into some Japs."

"Okay, you dumb twerp. It's your funeral."

They began working their way toward Smallwood's hole. By now they were working as a team, coordinating their movements without the need for vocal communications. One would dash forward and find cover, the other would join him. They had leapfrogged thirty or forty yards in this manner when a shell landed close enough to bowl MacCauley over and sting his hands and face with flying dirt. His ears rang as if he had been clubbed. He lay on his face for a few seconds without moving, dazed. He shook his head to clear it.

"That was close, Poge," he said shakily. "Hey, Poge, you okay?"

There was no answer. He shouted Podjalak's name and rose to a sitting position. Podjalak lay half covered with dirt, a severed arm still clad in the sleeve of his combat jacket and his watch still intact on the wrist a few feet away from his headless body. MacCauley leaned slowly forward until his helmet touched the ground between his forearms and began to cry.

7

[Superior Private Hikozo Maeda]

There were times during the early morning bombardment of the beach southwest of Masumaru that Superior Private Hikozo Maeda thought he would not live to see the Americans come ashore despite the many feet of sand protecting his position and the cleverness with which it had been concealed. The shells came so thickly, one explosion could hardly be distinguished from the next. The smoke made one's eyes water and the smell of the explosives was sharp enough to make its presence known even amid the reek of the latrine, which Private Second Class Iwagami had used with great regularity throughout the four nights and three days they had been sealed in the dugout. Then the bombers had come, not visible through the narrow firing port but announcing themselves with a mighty beat of engines and thudding bombs that shook the dugout from floor to low ceiling and made one's ears ring. After the bombers came the fighters, distinguishable by the higher voices of their engines and by the rivulets of liquid fire streaming across the sand in their wake. Some of them flew low enough to be seen from the firing port, streaking past in a flash of silver and vanishing in almost the same instant. Then, with unbearable insolence, the enemy resumed his shelling. If he should die without the opportunity to retaliate Maeda knew that his spirit would mourn at Yasukuni through all eternity. He must live to see the Yankees come ashore and kill as many of them as possible. For a time this thought pushed into the background the knowledge that before the day was over he almost certainly would die and that he would never again see his wife and children, or his mother and father, or drink good sake among friends, singing.

Through it all Tamura, the forty-seven-year-old conscript, prayed constantly, his lower lip trembling and spittle shining on his chin. Iwagami, the country bumpkin, when not squatting in the niche that served as a latrine, stared dumbly at Maeda with his mouth and eyes wide open as a newly caught fish. It was difficult for Maeda to tell if he were frightened out of what little wits he had or was simply bewildered by the bombardment. A fine pair the honorable squad leader gave me, Maeda thought. An old man too frightened to be of any use and a simpleton little more than one great bowel. They were no worse than some of the other conscripts at that, he supposed, and at any rate he would not have to endure their company many hours longer. When they were all dead it would not matter that one could not control his fear and the other his bowels. And at least he was the senior soldier in the dugout. It would be worse if he were sealed in with a corporal he disliked and whose orders he was compelled to obey. Here no one could tell him what to do or make fatuous speeches about the Emperor. He truly pitied anyone who might be occupying a position with the honorable platoon leader, who was vain and, even for an officer, notably self-indulgent. Maeda had never felt so free to think such thoughts, and so shamelessly, as he had during the time since the bomb had destroyed the adjacent machine gun position and isolated the dugout.

Maeda lay on his stomach, propped on his elbows, binoculars fixed on the approaches to the beach before the position. He put the binoculars down only to take a few mouthfuls of rice and barley, a bite of tinned whale meat and a sip of water. It was not necessity that made him so abstemious. They had more food than he now believed they would live to eat. He had rationed the supply even more stringently than ordered in the expectation the first enemy waves would be destroyed at sea and the Yankees would be delayed in overrunning the position. Now the might of the enemy's bombardment made it clear the first waves of invaders would have to be destroyed on the beaches. Maeda ate little because he had lost interest in food. His only concern was killing as many Yankee soldiers as possible and, hopefully, being the first of the defenders to kill one. Tamura ate nothing at all. In the three days they had been sealed within the position he had eaten only when ordered to do so. Iwagami, of course, was always ravenous. How could he be otherwise, Maeda thought, when everything he ate passed through him like water through a drain. This morning he permitted Iwagami to eat as much as he wished, not so much out of kindness as because the sight of Iwagami's open mouth and witless stare irritated him so. It was only when Iwagami was shoveling food into his belly that he was bearable.

From the narrow aperture facing the beach Maeda watched the assault unfold as if from his favorite seat in the Umeda cinema at Osaka. It was, in fact, much like a film, for at the cinema Maeda always became totally involved in the events on the screen. First came the gunboats, ugly as the gaunt cows he had seen during his service in China. What excited him most were those firing rockets. The rockets departed in a belch of smoke and fire to soar out of view trailing tails of flame like so many comets. Some of them fell near the dugout but did no damage. Next came something truly astonishing, tanks riding the water as if they were corks. They wallowed from side to side and bobbed up and down without sinking, firing cannon.

"Tamura," he said. "Iwagami. Come look."

They crept to the aperture and squeezed beside him.

"Oh, my," said Iwagami. "Oh, my. What must we do, Honorable Superior Private?"

"Nothing," Maeda said. "We do nothing until the soldiers come."

He did not know how many times Iwagami had been told that. The simpleton could remember nothing. He hoped Iwagami had not forgotten how to load his rifle and pull the trigger. Tamura made no comment. The only effect the spectacle had on him was to make his prayers come louder and faster. Maeda was uncomfortable squeezed in between the two soldiers and regretted bringing them to the aperture. He ordered them away from the opening, wishing he could be rid of them entirely.

The tanks did not come ashore. Instead they remained in the water, still shooting their cannon. Then they turned away and landing craft appeared, looking empty except for an occasional helmet showing above their armored sides. Water spouts began shooting up among them. Now it was the Yankees' turn to get a taste of Japanese powder. A hole appeared in the side of one of the landing craft. Man threw themselves over the side to flounder in the sea, divesting themselves of packs and helmets. A small, fast boat came in to take them aboard but some had already sunk beneath the surface. Maeda shouted with joy. Iwagami crawled forward to learn the source of Maeda's excitement. Maeda elbowed him away with an angry grunt. A black-clad figure such as he had seen setting charges among the offshore obstacles popped out of the sea to almost its full length before falling back. Maeda adjusted the focus of his binoculars. In the figure's hand was a slender pole ending in a cylindrical object. It was not a Yankee but one of the Japanese divers, a Crouching Dragon.

"What is it now, Honorable Superior Private?" Iwagami asked.

Maeda did not answer. His attention was riveted on the black figure swimming into the path of all approaching landing craft. The Crouching Dragon stopped swimming, turned over on his back, and slowly sank from view. Maeda swore. Landing craft began poking their noses onto the sand. Their fronts dropped down and men poured out laden with equipment. A few fell down and did not move again but the others kept running across the sand to disappear into shell craters and behind the logs which had washed ashore after the Yankee swimmers scattered the floating obstacles. Yankee bodies littered the water's edge and the first few yards of sand. Maeda hoped they had all been killed by mortars and artillery. He did not like to think a rifleman had killed one before he got a chance to do so. If he only had a sniper's rifle with a special sight he could have killed several by now, but he had only an old 1905 Model 38 of the type he had carried in China. He was tempted to take a chance anyhow—he had once killed a Chinese guerrilla at much greater range—but discipline prevailed.

Landing craft which had been disabled before reaching the shore drifted in among those discharging troops and the Yankees appeared to be in disarray. None had yet dared approach his position. If only the soldiers lying in wait at the second line of defense would come up through the assault tunnels they could push the Yankees back into the sea. He looked eagerly for evidence of a counterattack but there was none. The waves of landing craft seemed to come on endlessly, but the soldiers emerging from them did not advance inland. The shells falling among them pinned them down. Maeda began to understand how wise the leaders were not to counterattack yet. It was now the Yankees who were being bombarded with no one to shoot at in return. Now the Yankee riflemen knew how he felt. He was no longer so impatient to open fire. He would wait until he was sure of killing many before revealing his position.

Some of the Yankees were running upright along the beach. With his binoculars Maeda could see that they were shouting. They must be officers ordering their cowardly troops to attack. Maeda felt grudging admiration for their bravery at not taking cover. He longed again for a sniper's rifle. To kill a Yankee officer would be doubly satisfying. He detected movement among the logs and craters. The Yankees were beginning to move out of their narrow strip of beach. He considered summoning Iwagami to the firing aperture. Tamura would be worse than useless. Mumbling away at his elbow, Tamura might spoil his aim. He decided against placing Iwagami in firing position as well. Two rifles were better than one only if both were truly aimed. The fire from the position would be most effective if he manned the aperture alone and had Iwagami load for him. He made Iwagami demonstrate his ability to free the mechanism of sand and insert the five-cartridge slip.

"When I hold out my rifle you will take it and give me back a loaded one," he said.

"When you hold out your rifle I will take it and give you back a loaded one, Honorable Superior Private," Iwagami shouted, repeating the order verbatim as he had been taught.

"Good, Private Second Class Iwagami," Maeda said. "You said that very well. Now, do you know what it means?"

Iwagami nodded. Maeda was satisfied. Even a simpleton like Iwagami should be able to carry out so uncomplicated an order.

In the days and nights of waiting Maeda had pictured the same scene over and over again. He saw Yankee soldiers running from the sea toward him and falling as fast as he could pull the trigger. Tamura and Iwagami were never present in this scene. Now, as Maeda watched the enemy soldiers inch cautiously across the sand, he formulated a new and more realistic plan. The longer the position remained undetected the longer he would survive and the more Yankees he would kill. He would select his targets like a sniper, being careful not to fire when more than one enemy was facing his position and then only when he was confident of a kill. In this way he would avoid disclosing his position until the enemy drew close enough to see the camouflaged aperture.

Had the attack come before the dugout was cut off from the rest of the platoon by the bomb hit on the machine gun position Maeda would have been incapable of reaching such a decision independently. All his training had stressed following orders swiftly and without question. Initiative was rigidly suppressed. Had he remained in the Army continuously from the time of his China service even the three days of complete independence and authority over the two privates with him possibly would not have broken the pattern of absolute obedience to the letter of all orders. As it was, at first he felt uncomfortable rather than pleased with himself at having decided on a course of action not specifically directed by a superior. Why should he be so concerned, Maeda asked himself. Whether his plan was a good one or a bad one he would never have to answer to anyone for it. He hardly imagined he would be obliged to report his actions to the honorable platoon leader at Yasukuni. He turned his head and looked at Iwagami.

"Private Second Class Iwagami," he said.

"Yes, sir, Honorable Superior Private!" Iwagami shouted, thrusting forward a loaded rifle.

"I am not ready!" Maeda snapped. "Only when I give you my empty rifle. And do not shout. Soon the Yankees will be close enough to hear you."

Tamura looked at him with wet, helpless eyes.

"Will we die soon, Honorable Superior Private?" he whispered.

"Soon enough," said Maeda. "But don't be so frightened. They say it is not all that bad."

But he had never heard anyone say that to whom it had actually happened. Dead men did not speak. He tried to remember if he had ever seen a comrade die smiling. He could not recall a single instance. Then Maeda said what had been in his mind when he first turned to Iwagami.

"It fills me with trepidation that the Emperor is pleased with my plan to kill the Yankees so carefully."

Iwagami stared at him as if he had gone mad. Maeda laughed. Iwagami laughed, too, his face empty of understanding. Maeda thought it unfortunate there was no one present to appreciate the fine joke he had made at the expense of the honorable platoon leader, whose habit it was to speak as if he were in the Emperor's confidence. Then he was frightened. Was it possible that the Emperor, in his infinite wisdom, knew the joke he was making? Maeda shook off the notion. He was not an unworldly peasant like Tamura or a simpleton like Iwagami. The Emperor's mind was filled with important matters and spiritual things. Yet still he regretted having spoken so familiarly of the Emperor.

"Tamura," he said, "if you must pray, pray for all of us and not just yourself."

"I was praying for you, Honorable Superior Private," said Tamura. "If you wish I will also pray for Private Second Class Iwagami."

During the exchange with Iwagami and Tamura, Maeda had continued his careful observation of the enemy soldiers. In the past few minutes they had come considerably closer. Some hundred and twenty yards from the dugout two shells landing in the same area had dug a large crater. Maeda had no doubt that very soon one or more of the Yankee soldiers would take shelter within it. The emergence of the first Yankee from the crater would be his signal to open fire unless another came in range from a different angle.

"Private Second Class Iwagami," he said, "what are your orders? And do not shout."

"I will . . ." Iwagami began, stopping in confusion.

"You will give me a loaded rifle when I give you an empty one," Maeda prompted, forcing himself to be patient when what he wanted most was to slap Iwagami soundly.

Iwagami nodded vigorously.

"I will give you a loaded rifle—" he began.

"Enough," said Maeda. "Just do it at the proper time."

He followed the movements of half a dozen soldiers as they dodged from cover to cover in the general direction of the crater he had chosen. Although they kept low and made good use of every bit of cover, he believed he had an excellent chance of killing two or three before they reached it. But he must not permit himself to become impatient. He must wait until there was no possibility of missing. He studied the forward lip of the crater over his rifle sights. When the moment came to squeeze the trigger it would be almost like firing from a fixed stand. As he watched the enemy soldiers working their way toward the crater they began assuming individuality to him and he gave them names. One was the Fox because of the manner in which before leaving one shelter for another he lifted his head and seemed to sniff the air nervously. Another was the Ox because he was large and slow. He was much bigger than Iwagami but Maeda imagined they must be alike. If he had confidence in Iwagami's aim he would let Iwagami kill him. A third, to whom Maeda took an instant dislike when he studied his face through the binoculars, he named Shima, after his foreman at the artillery shell factory in Osaka. Shima affected superior airs and accused him of shirking. He had a withered leg and a boring habit of proclaiming were it not for that he would have long since volunteered for frontline combat duty in the Army as befit a descendant of samurai. Like Shima, the Yankee wore a thin mustache of the sort only a vain person would have. Though the Yankee was a foot taller than Shima it was not difficult for Maeda to picture him ordering one about as Shima had done. The approach of the soldiers became to Maeda sort of a contest which he hoped would be won by Shima.

At times the Ox would be nearest the crater. Although he was slow he was the most reckless. Maeda thought he must be either as stupid as Iwagami or exceptionally brave. If he himself were such a large target he would be much more careful about showing himself. When the Fox changed positions he did not remain exposed as long as the Ox, but covered more ground because he ran swiftly, scurrying from side to side. A piece of equipment hanging down from his pack was like a tail. Shima advanced as one would expect, timidly, sometimes running forward no more than a few feet before throwing himself behind a log, or not running at all, merely crawling with his nose touching the ground. Yet his timidity did not delay his doom. His path toward the crater, though slow, was direct, not erratic like the others. There was a fourth so1dier for whom Maeda did not feel as much hatred as the others. Maeda saw that as he ran he would occasionally reach back with his hand and feel gingerly between his buttocks. He appeared to be suffering from ji, piles. Maeda had himself endured the condition for a number of years though it had been some months since he suffered an acute attack. This soldier he named Bad Luck. Bad Luck, old fellow, he thought, soon your piles will trouble you no longer. Superior Private Maeda of the 187th Regiment of the 86th Infantry Division will see to that.

Maeda noticed that all the Yankees made the same mistake. They would lift their heads for a moment to look about immediately before leaving cover. The direction in which they gazed the longest was invariably that they took. Thus, when they reached his crater, he would be able to anticipate their next move. The Fox was first to reach the crater. Maeda, forewarned by his observation of the Yankees' habits, could have shot him before he dived headlong into it and would have done so were it not for the one he had named Shima. Shima made for the same cover but did not offer so good a target because he crawled on his belly along a small trough. Bad Luck might have joined the two Yankees had not a mortar shell landed almost at his feet. Both of his legs were blown off, one at the knee and the other at the hip. What remained of his lower trunk was a mass of bloody tatters draped in entrails. Maeda could hear his screams. They died away quickly. How do you like our Japanese treatment for Yankee piles, Maeda thought.

The Ox angled off in another direction. Maeda was not particularly disappointed. He had Shima. A helmet emerged cautiously above the lip of the crater until only the eyes, or where they would be if Maeda could see them at that distance, appeared. Maeda could not tell if they belonged to Shima or the Fox. The tilt of the head indicated the Yankee as looking off to the right. Maeda took deliberate aim at a point eighteen inches above the crater. When the Yankee's shoulders rose above the lip he would hit him between them a bit to the left, where the heart lay. The Yankee's upper body popped out of the crater exactly as Maeda had anticipated and he squeezed the trigger. The Yankee continued rising and fell forward half out of the crater. He did not stir. Maeda knew he as dead. It was the Fox. Maeda felt cheated.

The report of the rifle filled the dugout. Tamura gasped and Iwagami leaned forward to look. Maeda caught him in the mouth with an elbow, drawing blood.

"Remain where you are," he ordered.

An object sailed out of the crater to explode in the sand twenty yards away in the direction the Fox had sought to take. How like Shima. Maeda thought, to waste a grenade without first examining his dead comrade's wound to learn from which direction the shot had come. The body began sliding into the crater, drawn from behind. No, perhaps he is getting wiser, Maeda thought. A helmet rose slowly from the crater. Maeda took aim, then relaxed. He knew from the manner in which the helmet slanted it was not on a Yankee head, but at the end of a rifle. Despite Shima's superior airs his intelligence had not been the equal of his own. Everyone in his work unit, even the middle school boys who had replaced most of the men of military age had known that he, not Shima, should have been foreman. The helmet descended. When it rose again Maeda knew it was attempting to locate the position from which the Fox had been shot. The helmet rotated as if Shima were studying the terrain inch by inch. Maeda put down his rifle and picked up the binoculars, confident Shima would not be coming out so soon. He could see the Yankee's eyes. They seemed to be looking into his. Surely Shima had seen the aperture despite its camouflage. But the eyes turned away.

Now a dilemma confronted Maeda. Other Yankees had come within easy range. If he killed them even a fool like Shima would quickly locate his position. And probably remain where he was while others attacked it. Reality asserted itself. The Yankee in the shell crater was not Shima, nor was there any other reason why he should be singled out when Yankees were moving toward the dugout in increasing numbers. Already there were so many he could not hope to remain undetected much longer, no matter how carefully he chose his target. He had been wrong in thinking his wisdom was as great as that of the honorable platoon leader. Maeda made wordless apology. He would atone for it by doing his duty—killing as many Yankees as possible as quickly as possible. And it was Iwagami's privilege as well as his own to do so. Iwagami could load and point a rifle and pull a trigger. That much at least he could do. Maeda would have liked to bring Tamura to the firing port as well. It was not proper that the old man should die without being permitted to engage the enemy. But Tamura was paralyzed with fear and would only be a hindrance. Maeda called Iwagami to his side and ordered him to open fire. Iwagami fired all five rounds so rapidly Maeda knew he could not have taken time to aim. He interrupted his own fire to slap Iwagami's face.

"Take careful aim, imbecile!" he cried. "Don't waste bullets."

Maeda fired quickly but carefully. He hit the Ox, who was off to the right, but the big Yankee kept running, one arm hanging limp. Another Yankee fell and crawled back to the hole from which he had darted. The other two shots did not find targets. Maeda was angry with himself. He must aim more carefully and not rush his fire. He reloaded his rifle quickly. The Yankees around the dugout had taken cover and were throwing grenades. He could see their arms describing arcs above logs and craters. There were no less than five of them attacking the position. Most of the grenades fell short. The few which did not, threw sand into the aperture but did no damage. The Yankee grenades were very strong but the position was well built. Maeda felt grateful to Tamura for the split log protecting the firing port. The sand irritated his eyes. He blinked to get rid of it. Iwagami was rubbing his eyes with both hands and complaining.

"Iwagami," he said. "Soon the Yankees will rush our position. Some of them will try to draw our attention by firing from cover while others run in. Do not shoot at those who stay behind, only at the Yankees coming to us."

A shower of grenades came from all directions and men rose up firing.

Two Yankees ran directly toward the dugout. Maeda fired and heard Iwagami fire beside him. A Yankee fell. Not the one Maeda had fired at. Maeda's ran to one side and disappeared behind a hummock. Maeda swallowed his irritation.

"Good shooting, Iwagami," he said.

He stole a glance at the crater in which Shima, and now two more Yankees, were hiding. A helmet protruded above the far rim. Perhaps they had enough and were retreating. The helmet rose no higher. The Yankee must be looking toward the rear, summoning help. He fired at the helmet and saw a black smear appear on it before it ducked out of sight. Grenades no longer fell around the position. He had guessed correctly. The Yankees were waiting for reinforcements. The Yankee Iwagami had shot was crawling toward the hummock behind which the other Yankee had disappeared. Maeda raised his rifle. Before he could fire, the other Yankee ran out and seized the wounded man's foot and began dragging him toward safety. Maeda shifted his aim but missed. The Yankees began shooting their rifles and hurling grenades again. Maeda believed it a prelude to some sort of new activity. Perhaps they would try rushing the position again. He warned Iwagami to prepare himself. Maeda sensed, more than heard, the passage of a bullet and heard Tamura cry out. He looked around. Tamura was still sitting with his back against the dugout wall but now the old man stared back at Maeda with three eyes. Blood, barely visible in the shadowy dugout, began trickling past Tamura's nose from the middle eye.

"Honorable Superior Private!" Iwagami cried.

Maeda turned back to the aperture. A knot of heavily burdened Yankees was moving toward the crater, stumbling under the weight of a machine gun, its tripod and boxes of ammunition. Maeda and Iwagami emptied their rifles at the machine gun squad. Maeda did not know if they staggered from hits or the weight of their burdens, for all four reached the shelter of the crater. What were the Japanese mortar men thinking about, Maeda thought angrily. His position and the surrounding area were certainly under observation from at least one mortar position. If they knew their business they would have seen the Yankees concentrating in the crater and by now would be shelling so worthwhile a target. A single 81-mm. trench mortar shell would get them all. Shells did begin dropping around the crater, but none fell into it.

"Be alert," Maeda said to Iwagami. "When the gun opens fire it may cover a rush. They may also try to creep up from the side. You will fire at the gun to disturb its aim."

"Yes, Honorable Superior Private Maeda," Iwagami said. "I will fire at the gun to disturb its aim."

He sounded calm and almost intelligent. Perhaps he had the makings of a soldier of the Emperor after all, Maeda thought. And fighting seemed to have strengthened his bowels. Unless he had relieved himself in his trousers. Not once since the battle began had Iwagami asked permission to do the big-service. The blows he had dealt Iwagami had not been wasted.

The nose of the machine gun poked over the edge of the crater, a helmet behind it. Iwagami shot at the helmet without apparent effect, for the gun began firing. Its bullets kicked up dirt in front of the dugout and thudded into the log protecting the firing port. Maeda ducked down instinctively, noting as he did so that Iwagami did not flinch. Only a fool does not try to preserve his life, Maeda thought. Bullets struck the aperture. They did not pass through the sixteen-inch-deep slit, but dug into the wood at the top and bottom and sent splinters flying. Maeda felt them sting his face. Beside him Iwagami screamed. Maeda turned to him. Iwagami's hands were clapped to his face. Maeda pulled them free. A long sliver of wood protruded from Iwagami's left eye. He screamed again when Maeda pulled it out. Maeda shook him frantically.

"Put strength in you, Iwagami," he shouted.

Iwagami stopped groaning immediately.

"Can you see to shoot your rifle?" Maeda demanded.

"Yes, Honorable Superior Private," Iwagami said in a weak voice.

"Then resume firing."

The machine gun stopped firing. The silence was ominous. Nothing moved outside the dugout but the sand flung into the air by exploding shells. Maeda thought he heard faint sounds nearby, outside the line of sight from the aperture. The machine gun ripped off a long burst. Iwagami fired back at it while Maeda held himself ready for the coming attack. Something black and round, like the snout of an inquisitive animal, poked into the aperture. Maeda grabbed for it. Fire gushed from the snout.

The interior of the dugout grew bright as the sun and Maeda was enveloped by excruciating heat. He did not know if the screams he heard were Iwagami's or his own.

8

[Miho Naito/Corporal Yogi Okida/Staff Sergeant Arthur Simmons]

By nightfall, of the 215,000 combat troops in the three U.S. Army corps assigned to the X-Day landings, more than 140,000 were ashore. In the landings and the actions preceding them there had been 11,000 Army and Marine casualties including almost 3,000 dead. The Navy had lost 5,000 killed, wounded or missing. Eighteen thousand combat troops had not yet been committed and remained offshore under continuous attack from kamikaze and, to a lessening degree, surface and underwater suicide craft. There was no fighting room for them in the narrow beachheads. Two complete divisions of the three assault corps, numbering 5,000 combat troops, were still en route from the Philippines. They were not scheduled to arrive for another thirty-six hours. Another 60,000 combat troops were close at hand. These were the three divisions of the Reserve Force, IX Corps, two of which were retiring from the feint at Shikoku and the third waiting at Okinawa.

The invasion beaches were clogged with wrecked landing craft and with equipment and supplies accumulating faster than they could be dispersed, even had the beachheads been large enough to permit dispersal. Transports and freighters were obliged to abandon the invasion plan for discharging cargo with all possible dispatch. Cargo was instead unloaded to fill specific needs and only priority matériel, chiefly artillery, bulldozers, ammunition and medical supplies continued toward the beachheads in an unbroken stream. The bulldozers opened lanes through the beached landing craft while harassed beachmasters struggled to make room for the incoming supplies. Some heavy equipment was landed directly on the beaches by LSTs. Shuttling tank lighters, LCTPs and amphibian trucks brought in other cargo, often being obliged to stand offshore under continuous shelling until places could be made for them to unload. Landing craft removed the wounded to the operating rooms and sick bays of transports whose troops had been brought ashore earlier in the day. The hospital ships originally scheduled to stand off the invasion beaches were being held at sea and in protected anchorages at Koshiki Retto, the group of islands west of Kyushu, until enemy suicide attacks abated.

I Corps' 25th and 33rd Infantry divisions were strung out along the Town Car Beach Zone beachheads north and south of Miyazaki City on the east coast. The corps' third division, the 41st Infantry Division, was to arrive from the Philippines on X+2, November 14. XI Corps' 1st Cavalry and 43rd Infantry divisions clung to its narrow strip of beaches in Station Wagon Beach Zone at the head of Ariake Bay in the south. Its third division, the Americal, was also due to arrive on X+2. On the west coast, south of Kushikino, V Amphibious Corps' 2nd and 3rd Marine divisions and part of its reserve division, the 5th Marine, struggled to expand their cramped beachheads in Roadster Beach Zone.

Nowhere had there been a deep penetration, and no direct assaults had been mounted against the heavily defended Japanese strongpoints lying beyond the screening positions on the beaches. Nowhere, however, did there appear to be imminent danger of any American unit being pushed back into the sea. The first attack waves had been badly mauled but none had been smashed. Enough troops had been put ashore in the first hours of landings to blunt counterattacks on the limited scale which at the moment lay within the capabilities of an enemy engaged in bringing up his mobile reserve.

Three divisions of Japan's 40th and 57th armies took the brunt of the initial attacks, the 156th "Gosei" Infantry Division at Miyazaki City, the 86th "Seki" Infantry Division at Ariake Bay and the 303rd "Takashi" Infantry Division at Kushikino. They were bulwarked by other forces either established in strong defensive positions or poised to counterattack. North of Miyazaki City the 154th and 212th Infantry divisions were deployed in depth along the coast in much the same fashion as the embattled 156th. The Fifth Tank Brigade, with 112 tanks and self-propelled guns, was arrayed immediately behind the 156th Infantry Division. The 98th "Strong Will"

Independent Mixed Brigade was dug in on the 86th Division's right flank, guarding the eastern shore of Kagoshima Bay. South of Kushikino's 303rd Division, the 206th and 146th Infantry divisions and the 125th Independent Mixed Brigade protected the Satsuma Peninsula and the western entrance to Kagoshima Bay. Two more infantry divisions, the 25th and 77th, and the Sixth Tank Brigade were deployed farther inland. More divisions, including two infantry and one tank division of the Tokyo area's crack 36th Army, moved to Kyushu at the beginning of autumn, were on the move from the north.

A modified "Plan Mutsu lB," the defense of southern Kyushu with Ariake Bay as the key, had gone into effect with the American landings. The defenders of the Miyazaki and Kushikino fronts would attempt to hold the enemy penned along the east and west coasts, the former with the three infantry divisions and tank brigade in the area and the two infantry divisions now on the way, and the latter with three infantry divisions and the independent mixed brigade already in place and another two infantry divisions moving down from rear areas. The 77th and 25th Infantry divisions and Sixth Tank Brigade would join the 86th Division in the battle of Ariake Bay and attempt to contain the enemy while three additional infantry divisions and a 36th Army tank division proceeded south by forced night marches to enter the decisive battle for the homeland.

Miho Naito was eighteen. She was the only civilian in the little cluster of farmhouses behind a low cliff at Akasaki, south of Kushikino. Of the other twenty or so persons who had lived in the hamlet, the men of military age had long since gone into the Army, the children and old people had fled inland to the mountains when the Americans began shelling the coast, and the others, men and women alike, had gone off with their Volunteer Combat Platoon. Miho was also a member of the platoon but when the time had come to go to the assembly area she had run away. She had been told many times it as her duty to die if it became necessary and if she must die she wished to do so with Yoji Okido. Yoji was a corporal in the 303rd Infantry Division. He had been very angry with her when he discovered she had remained behind.

"You must leave this place at once," he said sternly, so unlike his usual self. "When the Americans come everyone here will die."

"The headman said it is our duty to die for Japan," she protested. "And even if we do not try to fight them the Americans will kill all the men and all the women will be . . ."

She hesitated. She did not wish to use indelicate words with Yoji. He was very cultured, having graduated from the middle school at Omuta and worked in an office in Tokyo. Had he not been conscripted he might have someday attended the university.

"You know," she finished lamely.

For "you" she used the word "anata" with the inflection used by lovers or married couples.

The endearment did not soften him.

"Raped?" he said harshly. "The Americans won't do that. Only Japanese soldiers do that."

When she had first heard Yoji speak so outrageously she had been aghast. Eventually, though she never believed the terrible things he said about the Army and the nation's leaders, she had grown accustomed to it.

"The headman said the Americans are all savages," she persisted. "He showed us a photograph from a newspaper. An American girl with the skull of a Japanese soldier. Her lover had sent it to her as a souvenir. She was smiling."

"Your soncho is an idiot," said Yoji. "That's the kind of thing the militarists want us to believe so we won't mind dying for them. The Americans kill our soldiers because we're too stupid to surrender. They're kind to civilians. On Okinawa they gave them food and medicine when the battle was over."

"Is that really so?" Miho asked.

She was pleased. Yoji was no longer angry with her but with the soncho, the village headman, and with the militarists in Tokyo.

"Of course it is really so. I heard it on the radio. Look, I have heard many things on the American broadcasts and they are all true. Do you know they give warnings to the people before they drop their bombs? And I believe them when they say they are not fighting the Japanese people. They are fighting the militarists. They believe as I do."

"They'll kill you anyhow," Miho said. "You're a soldier. You won't surrender, will you?"

"I'll not have the chance," Yoji said. "I may even be killed before they set foot on the beach. I wouldn't surrender anyway," he added angrily. "Even though I know it's the sensible thing to do. I've been stuffed with all that nonsense about honor just like all the rest."

He realized he had been diverted from the subject with which the conversation had begun. His voice grew gentle. It was the voice that Miho knew best.

"Really, Miho, you can't stay here. When the Americans come there'll be heavy fighting."

"I'm a soldier now," Miho said. "If I don't fight the Americans here I'll have to fight them somewhere else with my unit."

She pointed to the two-by-three-inch patch of white cloth sewn to her cotton jacket over her right breast. Meticulously drawn on it were the characters for sen, "combatant," and below that her name. She had made it herself as directed by the village headman. At sixty-two the soncho had been two years beyond the age for compulsory volunteer service but had joined the village Giyu Sento Ku-tai, Volunteer Combat Team, anyhow. Miho's mother had said tartly at the time it was probably for the monthly one hundred yen promised a family head to make up for lost family income if he had to fight for more than fifteen days, not to mention the generous one hundred and fifty yen condolence money and forty-five yen burial allowance if he should be killed. Those who were not the main source of family income got no pay at all, only three-quarters of the seven-hundred-and-five-gram military food ration.

"I shouldn't be surprised if old Fukajima manages to get himself killed for the condolence money," she had said. "Everyone in the mura knows he's in debt to the rice broker up to his ears."

"That scrap of cotton doesn't make you a soldier," said Yoji. "A girl with a bamboo spear! And you can't even use it properly."

He laughed when he said the last sentence, like the Yoji Miho knew. The first time he had seen her she had a bamboo spear in her hand. With the other members of the volunteer unit she had come to the village primary school for military training. Yoji, as well as the instructor and other members of the Army unit stationed in the area, was quartered there. Most of the younger girls flirted with the soldiers, many of whom had been conscripted locally. Miho had not flirted, nor had Yoji, who kept his nose in a book. Miho had been attracted by him even then. He had a sensitive, brooding air and his face was handsome in an almost delicate way. He was extraordinarily young for a corporal and his uniform was neat and his boots clean. These things, and his indifference to the bustle around him, made him stand out sharply from the other soldiers, most of whom had been farmers or workmen. The other girls had been either scornful of his manner, attributing it to affectation, or overawed by it. Miho was one of the latter.

During the period of instruction in the martial art of spear fighting she had closed her eyes every time she thrust or parried. Despite the exasperation of the instructor and the laughter of the other volunteers she could not keep them open no matter how hard she tried. Her mother, however, had proved surprisingly adept, letting out a fierce cry as she lunged, like a feudal spearman. Once, in her enthusiasm, she caught Soncho Fukajima in the buttock with the point of her spear, though only strongly enough to draw a shriek instead of blood. Though her mother had apologized in great embarrassment Miho did not believe it to be as much of an accident as her mother pretended.

The laughter at Miho's performance distracted the corporal's attention from his book after a while and he looked toward her just as she flinched and shut her eyes tight. When she opened them she was looking directly at him. There was an amused smile on his face. At first Miho was pleased he had noticed her, then angry with him for laughing at her like the others. When he turned back to his book she found herself wishing he would look at her again even if it were only to smile at her ineptitude.

In the following days she thought often of the solemn young corporal as she helped her mother pickle plums, sow millet, and tend the young cucumbers. At the next instruction period she kept stealing glances at him. As before, he read his book instead of participating in the partylike merriment of the young people but occasionally she found his eyes on her.

Miho's mother did not find it unusual when she began looking forward so eagerly to their regular visits to the primary school. Even in normal times there were few amusements to break the monotony of continuous labor in the hamlet. Young people got a chance to mingle only on festival days. Now they met regularly, and in a noble cause. Though Miho still closed her eyes during spear training she was quick in learning other things: how to take advantage of cover, how to fashion a fire bomb and creep up on an imaginary tank, how to prepare ambushes for troops and tanks, how to use grenades and firearms—without actually doing so—and how to conceal oneself from low-flying aircraft. Now when Miho stole a glance at the young corporal, whose name she had learncd was Yoji Okido, more often than not he was looking at her instead of his book. However, they had yet to exchange a single word. One evening she was disappointed to find him absent. She learned by discreet inquiry that he was off with a labor party constructing a defense position in a narrow cleft in the ridge not two hundred yards from her own home. After the instruction period she moved through the darkness in such haste that her mother, stumbling along behind her, grumbled.

As they brought out the sleeping quilts for the night Miho raised her head as if in surprise and said, "Listen. They're working at the end of the ravine."

"What's so remarkable about that?" her mother demanded, yawning. "The soldiers are always digging somewhere, night and day. But why must they do it under our noses? If they keep being so noisy about it we won't sleep a wink all night. And tomorrow we've got to finish weeding the rice."

Miho went to the fire pit and put straw under the iron kettle hanging from a hook above it.

"What in the world are you doing?" her mother demanded.

"I thought I'd take them some tea," Miho replied. "With all their hard work they must be very tired and thirsty."

"Tea? At this hour of the night? And with tea so dear? Come to bed at once."

"Don't be so hardhearted," Miho replied. "What if it were Masuo out there?"

Masuo was her brother. He had been with the Army on Kwajalein and they had not heard from him in more than a year. They presumed he was dead although they had not received the little white wooden box in which cremated remains were customarily returned. Almost no one in the mura, or village, who had sons or husbands on Pacific islands overrun by the Americans had received such a box. Before the war with America the boxes had come without fail from the fighting in China and brought great honor to the families that got them. Some said it was because the Army no longer bothered with ordinary people and reserved the traditional niceties for the rich and influential. The wiser ones, who suspected it was because the defeats were of such magnitude the Army was unable to carry out its obligations to the families of fallen soldiers, kept it to themselves, for such thoughts were unpatriotic.

It made Miho sad to think about Masuo. They had not seen him for four years, not since he left at nineteen to serve in the Army. Her father had not been conscripted until almost three years later. And he had not been heard from, either, since the invasion of Okinawa that spring. She wondered why she had thought of her brother in connection with Corporal Okido. She was sure it was not simply because it was a means of persuading her mother to let her take tea to the soldiers. That would be too cruel. It must be because Corporal Okido reminded her in some way of Masuo even though Masuo was loud and full of mischief and not at all handsome. But both were soldiers and young and might never see their mothers again or have families of their own.

Miho's mother did not answer immediately. The rice straw was already blazing under the iron teapot when she spoke.

"That conceited young corporal wouldn't be out there, would he?" she said. "I saw the expression on your face tonight when he wasn't at the primary school. You looked as if you had a mouthful of shiso leaves."

It was Miho's first inkling that her mother was aware of her interest in Corporal Okido. She felt herself blushing.

"How can you say such a thing?" she said. "You've said yourself what a hard life soldiers have, working day and night and nothing but slaps and more work for thanks. Worse even than a farmer's life, you said."

With the men of the family off to war and the two of them doing everything that had to be done on the farm, Miho had grown less submissive and sometimes spoke to her mother almost as if her mother were an older sister. And, except when it posed a direct challenge to her authority, her mother seemed to relish it.

"Except for the sergeants and officers," Miho's mother answered. "You'd think they were daimyo from ancient times, ordering one about and taking what they want in exchange for a piece of paper with senseless writing on it."

It had been twenty-nine years since Miho's mother graduated from primary school, and through lack of practice she no longer wrote or read with ease.

"Well," she continued, "there's no point in wasting good straw. And since your mind seems to be made up. No one listens to their parents any more. This war has changed everything for the worse."

Though she pretended to be angry, Miho knew she was not. If she had been truly angry she would have refused Miho permission to go. The water was soon bubbling in the teapot. Miho made the tea and put on her coat.

"You know the plums from last year?" her mother said. "You might take a few with you. Now that we have this season's it wouldn't hurt to get rid of them."

Miho knew then that her mother was thinking of Masuo and how he might have been one of the soldiers working at the end of the ravine had fate been kinder.

"And Miho," her mother said.

"Yes, Mother?"

"Don't let yourself get too interested in that young corporal. If he were back home with his elegant friends he wouldn't give you a second glance."

Miho did not answer. She was afraid her mother was right.

Although it was dark Miho had no trouble picking her way along the path through the grove of bamboos which lay between the house and the cleft in the ridge. She had trod it many times on her way to the beach, which lay but a few yards beyond. The sound of voices, hammering and digging grew louder as she approached. She tried to guess which voice was that of Corporal Okido. She had seen him many times at the primary school but she had never heard him speak.

The work sounds stopped abruptly and a stern voice cried out, "Who's there? Is that you, Private Imamura?"

Someone laughed and said, "It won't be Private Imamura. He's much too sly to get back from company headquarters in time for work detail.

He'll say the honorable sergeant kept him late."

"Quiet!" the stern voice said. "I'm trying to hear who's out there."

"It's only Miho Naito," Miho called out. "From the house just back there."

Now that she was actually here she questioned the wisdom of her action. Corporal Okido would think her terribly forward.

"Miss Naito?" the stern voice said, not so stern now and coming closer, and apparently recognizing the name. "What are you doing out at this hour of the night?"

She was almost giddy with joy and agitation. The stern-voiced soldier must be Corporal Okido and he knew her name. He had taken the trouble to learn.

"I thought the men might like some tea," she said.

"Tea?" he said incredulously.

She heard him running along the path while behind him the soldiers greeted her announcement with coarse but friendly remarks. There was the thud of someone falling and Corporal Okido's voice muttering curses. Miho suppressed a giggle. She reached the spot where Corporal Okido had fallen as he was picking himself up.

"Really," he said, sounding greatly embarrassed, "you shouldn't be about alone this time of night."

His voice sounded exactly as she had expected, or rather hoped, it would, gentle and cultured. Surprisingly it was he, not she, who felt at a disadvantage and she was quick to sense it.

"This isn't Hokkaido," she said mischievously. "There aren't any bears."

"What?" he said. "Bears? Oh. There are many rough soldiers about. A young girl like you."

He took the kettle from her and led her toward the place where the men were working. Miho permitted him to do so with pleasure although she knew it was more sensible for her to lead the way. She knew the path far better than he. There was light enough at the site to see that the men were stripped to the waist and one was clad only in his fundoshi, his loincloth. Corporal Okido, even more embarrassed than he had been after his tumble, angrily ordered the soldier to put on his trousers, using the same stern voice with which he had first challenged Miho in the darkness.

The soldiers emptied their work snack from the metal rice container each carried and Miho, retrieving the kettle from Corporal Okido, poured tea into them. Though military custom dictated Corporal Okido should be served first, he chose to display his civilian manners and elected to be last. The corporal's tea she served in the family's best cup, which she had brought with her for that purpose. After they had drunk the tea with the polite gusto expected of them, she gave each a pickled plum, popping it into their open mouths with the chopsticks she had brought along. She felt an unaccustomed sensual thrill when she gave Corporal Okido his plum. He apparently experienced an unaccustomed sensation as well, for he turned his face away quickly after receiving the fruit.

"Back to work, everyone," he said roughly. "There is still much to be done and the honorable sergeant will be making an inspection in the morning."

The men returned to their digging and hammering.

"Look," he said uncomfortably, "I'd better see that you get home safely."

Miho started to protest that she was perfectly capable of finding her way home alone but thought better of it.

"Thank you, Corporal Okido," she said, blushing when she realized she had let slip the fact she knew his name.

Now he would know that she had made inquiries about him. But Okido already knew that. The other noncommissioned officers had teased him about it and the privates made jokes when they thought he was not listening.

"Hard work," one of the soldiers called after Okido.

The sally was followed by stifled laughter. Corporal Okido stopped and turned around.

"Was that you, Private Watanabe?" he demanded.

"No, Honorable Corporal," Watanabe said.

"Who was it then?"

"I don't know, Honorable Corporal. I've been much too busy digging to take notice."

"It was Private Watanabe, all right," Corporal Okido told Miho as they continued toward her house. "He thinks he can take such liberties because he knows I don't beat my men. He may get a surprise if he isn't careful."

Miho could not imagine Corporal Okido beating Private Watanabe or anyone else.

"We're constructing a heavy machine gun position," Okido went on, as if he feared silence would be too embarrassing. "Very special. We'll be able to move the gun about in the position as we please."

"How very interesting," Miho said with enthusiasm. "They must think very well of you to put you in charge of such important work."

"Not really," Corporal Okido said modestly. "I'm only obliged to see that the men follow the plans carefully."

"Still, I don't think just anyone could do that," Miho said.

She did not know where her self-possession came from or how the right words seemed to come so naturally. It could only be because Corporal Okido was so considerate one could not possibly be intimidated by him. She stopped at the barely discernible track leading through the bamboos from the main path to her house.

"Here we are," he said. "Miss Naito, my men and I have been obliged."

So Corporal Okido not only knew her name but also where she lived. Her house was but one of several in the bamboo grove. She had no doubt whatever that he had been making inquiries about her.

"It was really but a small thing," Miho said. "Thank you very much for bringing me home."

"I am honored," Corporal Okido replied. "Do please give Mrs. Naito my most humble greetings."

"Good night, Corporal Okido," Miho said, taking the teapot from him.

If he should now ask her to call him Yoji she would ask him to call her Miho.

"Good night, Miss Naito. Sleep well."

Miho was not overly disappointed. The excursion had already turned out extraordinarily well. She undressed quietly and lay down beside her mother on the sleeping quilt as carefully as possible lest she awaken her. She lay with her eyes open thinking about Corporal Okido.

"Well?" said her mother.

"What?" Miho said, startled.

"Did the soldiers enjoy the tea?"

"Very much."

"I thought I heard someone with you out there."

"Corporal Okido was kind enough to see that I got home safely."

"Home safely? You couldn't find your way a dozen steps on a path you've walked since I stopped carrying you on my back?"

"He's not at all like I thought," Miho said, as if she were speaking not to her mother but to an older sister. "Not a bit conceited. He's really very shy."

"I daresay," her mother said. "See here, my girl, just because you've been up half the night don't think I'll not get you up as soon as there's light to see by. Serving tea to soldiers doesn't pull any weeds."

"Corporal Okido said to please give you his most humble greetings," Miho said.

"Humph," said her mother. "Go to sleep. The sun will be up before you know it."

She did not sound too displeased.

After that Corporal Okido began seeing Miho and her mother home from the primary school when he did not have night duty. On the nights he supervised construction of the machine gun position Miho would visit him. She did not always bring tea, for it was scarce and they were poor, and she did not always come all the way to the position because of what the other soldiers might say. Instead she remained within the bamboo grove and gave a signal they had agreed upon, the call of a uguisu, a nightingale. One night when there was a stillness in the grove and no moon, and they had been unable to meet for several days, they unexpectedly became lovers. Miho was a virgin. Yoji apologized abjectly for his animalistic nature and asked her to marry him.

"I'll try to get word to my father in Omuta if he's still there and ask his permission," he said. "And you ask your mother."

"Your father wouldn't let you marry an unimportant person like me," said Miho, who was not nearly so upset as Yoji.

She was, in fact, a bit surprised by Yoji's reaction. Apparently virginity was much more prized in Omuta than in her little village.

"Then I'll kill myself," Yoji said fiercely.

Miho came home very late that night. Her mother, who had grown accustomed to her visits with Yoji and was usually sleeping when she returned, was awake.

"What took you so long?" she demanded. "When you didn't come home at the usual time I woke up and couldn't go back to sleep."

"Yoji, Corporal Okido, had been working so hard and was so tired he fell asleep just sitting there. I didn't want to wake him and I didn't think I should go off and leave him. If the sergeant should come and find him sleeping when he was supposed to be on duty . . ."

"I daresay," said her mother.

It was not until almost a week after they became lovers that Yoji admitted he had also been a virgin. If it had been anyone but Yoji making such a claim Miho would not have believed it. After all, he had lived in Tokyo and everyone knew what a wicked city it was. And she doubted if any of the young men in her village had reached Yoji's age of twenty-three without having anything to do with a woman. The girls remained chaste, or so they maintained, but the young men were always slipping off to the nearest town when they got their hands on a few yen and no one believed it was just to drink tea with the geisha. The geisha in the towns weren't like those in the big cities, or so she had heard, who received fortunes for merely being pleasant to men and singing and dancing. Even her brother Masuo had visited a geisha teahouse before he went off into the Army, and it was said he knew that silly Ayako Iatsui much better than he pretended, or why had she cried so and not stopped until her father beat her when Masuo went away? But Miho believed Yoji because he said it not as an excuse for the way he had behaved with her but as if he were ashamed of it, thinking she would think him less a man because at twenty-three he had not known a woman's love.

In the end, Yoji did not write his father for permission to marry Miho. He knew she was right in believing his father would never agree and, of course, if his father did not give his permission there could be no marriage. His father might even order him to stop seeing her.

"I wouldn't live to have a family anyhow," he said bitterly. "That doddering old Suzuki and the militarists in Tokyo have given me my death sentence."

"Suzuki?" said Miho. "Who is Suzuki and what has he to do with you?"

Yoji shook his head sadly. At first Miho thought it was at her ignorance but when he spoke she understood that was not the reason at all.

"That's how it is in our enlightened country," he said. "You don't even know our premier's name and yet he asks you to die for him. Only he says it's for the Emperor."

"Hush, Yoji," said Miho. "It frightens me when you say such terrible things."

"They're true, all the same."

They never looked each other's way again at the primary school after they became lovers. Because of this all the older persons suspected their relationship. None of them remarked on it openly, however, for all of them, even Fukajima the village headman, were mindful of her mother's sharp tongue. Though Miho's mother was only forty-one she was as much respected as any grandmother twenty years older.

Every night when there was no training period at the primary school and occasionally even during the day when Miho could slip away from her chores and Yoji could leave his detail in charge of a trusted private first class, they would meet in the secret place they had fashioned for themselves in the bamboos where they first became lovers. Miho had never been so content, even when Yoji spoke of his impending death. She had never heard anyone speak with such wisdom and eloquence, not even the principal of the primary school or the lecturers sent by the Katakura Spinning Company to address the village silkworm-raising association. Sometimes he spoke of his death angrily and at other times with great sadness.

"Stupid as it is to die without reason, I wouldn't mind it so much if it weren't for you, Miho," he said. "If the militarists have their way there won't be much left to live for in Japan."

They were lying quietly in the hollow they had scooped among screening young bamboos. Yoji's tent sheet was over them. It was only early fall but it had rained most of the day and the air was cool.

"When I was in Tokyo I was ambitious," he went on. "I couldn't wait until my father saved the rest of the money to send me to the university. When I got my degree, if the war was over by then, I was going back to the company and work my way up."

"What was your sweetheart like in Tokyo?" Miho asked, as she had done many times before.

At first it had been in hopes of trapping him into admitting he had been in love before. Later, when she no longer questioned his sincerity, it had been a way of teasing him. But he no longer rose to the bait.

"I didn't know what true happiness was in those days," he said, as if it were a thousand years ago instead of only four. "Now all I want to do is marry you and live to be an old man. It's so beautiful here."

Miho got up on her elbow and looked at him quizzically. He had often spoken of wanting to marry her but she had supposed he also wanted to carry her off to the kind of life he had known before he was sent to the south. And she had never thought of the place where she lived as being beautiful. Miho was not insensitive to beauty. She could stare for minutes at a wild plum in blossom and she loved the look and feel of her one kimono, which she was permitted to wear on festival days. But she had never thought of her valley as beautiful.

"I thought Tokyo was full of beautiful and exciting things," she said. "You've said so yourself. The palace. Shrines. Ginza Street."

"Tokyo's like a field of stubble that's been burned over. But even before the fire-bombings there was more ugliness than beauty. The ugliness was everywhere. You had to go looking for the beauty. But here the beauty is all around you. Even the way the young rice covers the entire bottom of the valley in the summertime. It's like a river. Haven't you noticed how much it's like a wide green river?"

Miho shook her head. A paddy field looked like a paddy field, not a river. And no river was crisscrossed by dikes and hedges like those separating one field from another. But if the valley was like a river to Yoji, she would try to think of it as a river.

"And the susuki grass. Have you observed how when there's a wind it's like old men shaking their beards?"

Miho laughed. She had not, but the notion was amusing.

The American bombings grew fiercer but did not touch the cluster of houses among the bamboos. There were strongly fortified positions just to the north and east of the hamlet and although the Americans suspected their presence and sometimes attacked them, the hamlet itself lay so close to the ridge along the coast that the cliff and the thickly growing bamboo in the ravine offered protection and concealment. The ridge also protected the hamlet from the great typhoon of October, though the storm destroyed many of the Army's caves and tunnels and forced the soldiers to seek shelter in the civilian homes which remained standing. Yoji's machine gun squad, which had been moved from the primary school to its defensive position, was among those washed out by the typhoon and was temporarily billeted in the house of Miho's mother. It was extremely difficult for them to be so close together and to take no overt notice of one another. Among the soldiers was a sergeant, thickset and coarse, and it disturbed Miho to see how he ordered Yoji about as if he were a common soldier and how Yoji was obliged to endure it in silence. It gave Miho her first real insight into Yoji's hatred of the Army.

When news came that the typhoon had proved to be the Divine Wind which all Japan had been praying for, destroying the American invasion fleet at Okinawa, the soldiers were jubilant, and Miho with them. Her mother brought out the last of her father's shochu and several of the soldiers got drunk, including the sergeant. When the sergeant began addressing himself lustfully to Miho she was less afraid for herself than for Yoji. Yoji, who had joined in the celebration only halfheartedly, now looked murderous and she was afraid he was on the verge of doing something terrible. None of this had escaped her mother. When the sergeant reached for Miho as if to draw her to him and Yoji's hand went to the bayonet at his belt, Miho's mother stepped between Miho and the sergeant, put her hands on her hips, and gave him a fierce look.

"See here, Sergeant," she said, "this isn't one of your Army brothels. Behave yourself or I'll see that the authorities learn all about your disgusting manners."

The sergeant answered her sharply and slapped the face of the private named Watanabe, who had been imprudent enough to smile, but did not annoy Miho again. When everyone was asleep Miho and Yoji went outside and stood huddled under his tent sheet in the rain and dying wind.

"If he had touched you I'd have killed him," Yoji said.

"I was so frightened for you," Miho said. "Think how awful it would be if you got in trouble just when there's not going to be an invasion."

"You don't really believe all that nonsense about a Divine Wind?" Yoji said incredulously.

"Of course I do," she said. "So do all the others."

"They're all fools. A typhoon at Okinawa won't save us. The Americans have bases all over the Pacific. Okinawa's just one of them. It may delay the invasion a few days. That's all."

"How can a corporal in the Army know more than our leaders?" Miho demanded, talking to him spitefully in her disappointment.

"They know it," he said. "They know it far better than I do. It's just propaganda so we won't lose heart. I wouldn't be surprised if the storm hasn't done us more harm than it's done the Americans. We've got to start digging all over again. You know, Miho, your mother is a remarkable person."

The change of subject took Miho by surprise. She said nothing.

"She saved Sergeant Hayakawa's life. And no doubt my own. It would have been a pity to lose the few days we have left over such a pig."

"She's very good to me," Miho said. "Everyone says she permits me too many liberties but she tells them to mind their own business."

"I wonder if she would despise me if she knew I was your lover?"

Miho could not believe her ears. She had long since stopped thinking of Yoji as a sophisticated Tokyo libertine, but this was too much. Her mother had known about it from the first time, when she had come home so late. She started to tell Yoji but did not. She feared he would be too embarrassed in her mother's presence if he knew.

"I'm sure she wouldn't," Miho said. "She thinks you are very intelligent for one so young."

Her mother still thought Yoji was very conceited, as well, but Miho did not tell him that.

"It's strange, but there are ways in which she reminds me of my father," said Yoji. "Do you think it unnatural of me to think that?"

"Yes," Miho answered. "How can you say such a thing of your father? That he's like a woman."

"I can't imagine what I see in you," Yoji teased. "You're always getting things turned around backward. What I meant was that in some ways your mother is like a man. I remember the first time I saw her, when she jabbed old what's his name . . ."

"Mr. Fukajima," Miho prompted.

"Old Fukajima in the behind. That's just the sort of thing my father would do to someone he didn't like. Although he would hardly pretend it was an accident."

"You saw that but you wouldn't take your nose out of your book to look at me? Except to make fun of me. Do you think your father would approve of me if he knew how much I loved you?"

Yoji did not answer. Instead, he sighed. Miho wished she had not asked. She knew someone like Yoji's father would not approve of an uneducated farm girl but had hoped Yoji would lie to please her. Yet that was one of the things she loved about Yoji, that he was always honest.

In November the American warships began bombarding the beaches up and down the coast and the higher ground inland. Shells fell in Miho's valley among the fields and on the slopes where troops were concealed in deep caves. Occasionally one would slam into the ridge where Yoji's machine gun was hidden. When that happened, the wind from the explosions would shake the thin walls of Miho's house.

Mr. Fukajima sent a grandson to the hamlet to lead the old people and small children to a safer area back in the hills and to summon members of the Volunteer Combat Platoon to muster in the village center, where the primary school had been before the American planes destroyed it. The platoon, with other Volunteer Combat Units in the area, was to retire to a back area out of the way of the emplaced Army units and prepare to harass the Americans if they succeeded in pushing inland. Miho told her mother she would not leave Yoji. Her mother commanded her to come along to the platoon muster.

"If you stay here you'll certainly be killed," she said. "We'll be safe in the mountains. The Americans will never get that far."

"Yoji said they will," Miho said stubbornly. "And then we'll have to fight their tanks with spears. And we'll all be killed, too. Yoji said when they come we shouldn't fight. To hide ourselves until the battle has moved beyond us and then give ourselves up. Yoji said the Americans will not harm us."

"Yoji said," her mother mocked. "Your corporal thinks he knows everything. Fukajima's an old fool but he's wise enough to know what will happen to us if the Yankees catch us. Do you think they'd miss the chance to enjoy a well-formed young girl like you? Even your young corporal couldn't do that."

"I don't care," Miho wailed. "If you make me go I'll kill myself."

"I daresay," said her mother.

She took the big kitchen knife from the possessions she had assembled to carry with them to the muster and before Miho knew what she was about gathered Miho's long hair in her hand and held the knife poised above it.

"Very well," her mother said. "Give me your hair to take along as a remembrance and I'll let you stay."

Miho began wailing and pleading. How could the mother who had borne her and nursed her and become an older sister as well as a mother be so cruel?

"I thought you were prepared to kill yourself rather than leave your corporal," her mother said dryly. "You won't even part with a few locks of hair for him. Stop your sniveling and come along."

She divided the household goods and personal possessions into two piles and put them into two large baskets. She pushed the lighter of the two toward Miho, took the other on her back, adjusted the headstrap, and started toward the path leading to the village without a backward look at Miho or their home. Crying bitterly, her nose running, Miho picked up the other basket and followed her mother. She had not even had an opportunity to say good-bye to Yoji. But after dark, when the volunteer platoon stopped to rest, she slipped off and ran all the way back to the ravine without stopping. Yoji was kneeling in the abandoned house, his stricken face distorted by the wavering light of a single candle, tears running down his cheeks. With his fountain pen he was writing something on a piece of paper held flat between his knees on the floor. His unsheathed bayonet lay beside him. He was so intent on his writing he did not hear Miho until she burst into the room. His expression was at first startled and incredulous. He explained later that he had thought her an invention of his mind.

They rushed together so precipitously the candle was knocked over. Yoji burned his fingers in his haste to set it upright again before the house was set afire. It was after the first joy of seeing her that Yoji grew angry and scolded Miho for coming back. Then, even after the memory of the first time he had seen her performing so ludicrously with a bamboo spear at the primary school put him in good humor, he persisted in his efforts to persuade her to save herself. For a while she stilled his arguments with caresses, but after they had made love he resumed them. Miho was adamant. In the end she was successful. She had been no match for her mother but Yoji was not so forceful. Yoji remained with her until just before morning light, although if he had been discovered away from his post it could have meant his death. It was the first time they had made love indoors and among soft sleeping quilts. Miho felt as if they were truly married and Yoji confirmed it by saying, "Now you are my wife."

In the following days the bombardment from the sea grew fiercer and American planes flew over at all hours of the day and night. The houses in the grove survived in the shelter of the ridge. Yoji, who took his life in his hands to steal away from the gun position for a few hours each night, said the Americans would be landing any day and before they did the houses and the bamboo grove concealing them would probably be destroyed. They deepened their former trysting place and brought the sleeping quilts from the house. Miho began living there instead of the house. Yoji made her promise that when the Americans came she would not kill herself.

"It will be easier for me to die if I know you'll go on living," he said. "When you hear our gun firing get inside your shelter and stay there until the first Americans pass through the ravine. If you come out while they're still attacking they may kill you. Keep food and water in the shelter with you. You may be there for a time because they'll not dislodge us so easily."

He said the last with a trace of grudging and unwonted pride in Japanese prowess.

"When it sounds as if the battle has ended, hold up a bit of white cloth on the end of a stick before showing yourself. And when you do come out of the shelter be sure your hair is showing so they'll know it's a woman. If they think you're a soldier even the white cloth might not save you."

When they made love just after dark, although they did not know it, it was the last time they would see each other again. Miho did not even have a presentiment when Yoji left her to steal back through the ravine to the troop cave in the ridge. She slept contentedly until after the sun was up. She might not have awakened even then had not a new sound joined that of the shells falling on the beach and slamming into the seaward face of the ridge. The valley reverberated with thunder. The Japanese artillery hidden in the hills enclosing the valley was firing out to sea. It was only then that she knew she would never see Yoji again. He had told her that the firing of the cannon would announce the arrival of the invaders.

Miho thought of joining Yoji at his machine gun and dying there with him but knew he would only send her away and that the memory of Yoji among the other doomed soldiers would blot out the tender memory of him as he was at their last parting. Also, she had given her promise that she would save herself. She huddled in the bottom of her shelter and for the first time thought of her mother as well as Yoji. She hoped her mother had forgiven her for being disobedient and returning home. And she hoped her mother would not try to fight the Americans but would do as Yoji advised and surrender to them. Then they would be together and someday, when the war was over, they would live here again and they could spend the rest of their lives near the place where Yoji had died, two widows sharing their sorrow, for Miho already thought of herself as a widow although no marriage ceremony had been performed and Yoji was still alive.

It was not until sometime after the guns in the hills began firing that Miho heard the machine gun. It clattered fiercely, then stopped. Had the Americans killed them so quickly? It started up again. The gun continued to fire in this manner, rattling off angry bursts, stopping and beginning again. It seemed such a small voice in the maelstrom of other sounds—explosions, a roaring of countless engines from the sea, the quickly swelling and fading thunder of aircraft. No human voice was to be heard. She had expected the shouts of the Americans as they stormed ashore. Perhaps Yoji had been wrong and the others right, and the Americans were being driven back before they could land. The firing and the engines continued all morning and still Miho heard no human voices. She could contain her curiosity no longer. It overcame her fear and the solemnity of her promise to Yoji. She left the shelter and stole through the ravine to where it narrowed into the cleft piercing the ridge. The machine gun sounded much louder and men called urgently to one another. Was it Yoji's voice that shouted commands so authoritatively?

The cleft was dark and dank and smelled of urine. Dangling vines and a few starved bushes festooned its steep raw sides. The cleft widened a bit as it rose but the worn track on its floor was broad enough to accommodate no more than two persons walking closely abreast. Because the cleft was narrow and pierced the ridge in angles Miho could glimpse neither the shallow beach nor the sea beyond it. She crept forward, balancing herself with one hand against the wall of the cleft, until she was almost directly beneath the gun position. Here the floor of the track was piled with empty cartridge cases. Even as she watched, a stream of cases cascaded down from the wall of the ravine to rattle among them. The stutter of the machine gun was deafening in the narrow cleft. In the intervals when it was not firing, Miho could hear the earth-muffled activities of its crew and their voices, Yoji's now distinguishable among them. But she could see nothing. It was as though Yoji had gone an impossible distance from her, and the few feet of earth between them was the boundary between life and death.

She stumbled over the cartridge cases until she caught a glimpse of sand and sunlit water at the end of the cleft, a view restricted by a turn in the narrow passage. The beach was empty of life but the sea was aswarm with open boats shaped like boxes, blind iron monsters belching fire, and behind them larger and more lethargic vessels from which hurtled bright streaks of many-colored flame. They moved as if unaware of or indifferent to the explosions among them. Far out to sea and high above it fireballs kindled and quickly faded again in the sky. Yoji, as always, had been right. The Americans were too many and too strong to be destroyed. She hurried back to the shelter of the bamboos, pausing only long enough to hear Yoji's voice for the last time, shouting orders. She huddled in the damp pit, trembling, frightened by what she had seen and moved by the sound of Yoji's voice, never to be heard again. She longed for her mother's comforting strength, despising herself for being torn between a desire to remain near Yoji and to flee to her mother's side wherever she might be.

No Americans landed that day on the little beach below the ridge. Late in the afternoon, planes came to attack the gun position with rockets and fire but failed to destroy it. The houses in the grove were set afire and burned quickly. Because the green bamboo of the grove was not entirely consumed, Miho survived in her deep shelter but for a time thought she would be suffocated by the heat and smoke. The gun fired intermittently during the night, sometimes awakening Miho from a deep, unnatural sleep troubled by vivid dreams which she could not remember. Previously Miho had almost never dreamed. In the morning the Americans at last came to the little beach on the other side of the ridge.

The ridge concealing the gun position paralleled the sea for several hundred yards before falling away to lower ground at either end. In some places it rose from the water's edge and in others, as at the entrance to the cleft which pierced it, overlooked small, narrow beaches. The coastline north to Toskino Point, beyond which some of the American landings had come, was a series of shallow and sometimes rocky arcs. To the south, where the other landings had been made, the coastline was more regular and the beaches deeper.

Corporal Okido's gun position was so constructed that his single weapon could be shifted to fire either from an opening in the clifflike face of the ridge, traversing the seaward approaches to the south, or from a second opening within the cleft, from which it had a narrower field of fire to the north. Because the machine gun was but one weapon among many, and because no landings were attempted on the beaches around it, it was early afternoon the day of the invasion before the gun's location became known to the Americans. Even then, because other targets had greater priority, no concentrated effort was made to knock it out. An amphibian tank was detached briefly from the fighting on the landing beaches to lob a few shells into the cliff face, and a flight of three planes attacked it with rockets and napalm. Throughout the night the gun continued to harass invasion troops dug in along the coast to the south. In the morning, because of the shallowness of the beachhead and the concentration of artillery fire from inland, the Americans decided to expand the beachhead northward and land supplies and reinforcements in the shelter of the ridge.

The ridge lay just beyond the area designated by the Americans as Beach Studebaker Green Two, the northern extremity of the beaches assigned to the 2nd Marine Division. Early in the morning of the invasion's second day a single plane lay a trail of smoke across the face of the ridge. Screened by the smoke, two squads of Marine riflemen from Studebaker Green Two were landed with a flame thrower, a light machine gun and satchel charges. When the smoke cleared they had established themselves at the foot of the ridge. Corporal Okido's gun could not be depressed enough to fire on them. The Americans, however, were also at a disadvantage. The face of the ridge where the gun lay was sheer. Neither the American machine gun nor the flame thrower could be brought to bear on the fire port without moving out to an exposed position on the beach. At first the Americans tried to lob hand grenades into the aperture from below, but the angled inside walls of the gun position deflected the grenades. Then they fired at the aperture with their rifles to cover a comrade moving back from the cliff face with the flame thrower. A short burst of the machine gun killed him. Another American was killed and two wounded by a grenade dropped among them from the aperture. One of those wounded was the lieutenant commanding the two squads.

Before the officer lost consciousness he sent one of his men to reconnoiter the ridge for another avenue of attack. The Marine discovered the cleft, which was partially obscured by the bushes, young bamboo and susuki grass growing in front of and within it. The lieutenant was by this time unconscious. A sergeant, who was now in command, sent six Marines to the cleft to climb to the top of the ridge and swing satchel charges into the aperture at the end of ropes.

Corporal Okido had anticipated a move of this nature. After the American with the flame thrower was killed he did not think the Americans would attempt another frontal assault immediately. He had the machine gun shifted to the aperture opening on the cleft. Five Marines had entered when the gun opened fire. Three were killed, one wounded and the fifth escaped unharmed. The wounded man rolled behind a bend in the cleft and was helped to safety by the other survivor. Neither had a clear picture of the conformation of the narrow passage or had observed the precise point from which the burst had come. The fifth man, who had just entered the opening when the gun opened fire, believed it might have fired into the cleft from a position on the other side of the ridge. The wounded man, who had been hit in the forearm and was not badly hurt, was sure the gun was inside the cleft. Neither supposed it was the same gun which had been firing on the beach.

The sergeant deduced that the assumed second machine gun was supporting the first and that if it could be eliminated the way would be clear to get at the cliff position. Leaving a few men to keep the aperture under observation, he moved the others to the cleft entrance. They threw grenades inside as if preparatory to an attack and made a good deal of noise in the greenery. An overanxious machine gunner fired at the sounds. The sergeant now knew that the gun was inside the cleft and, from the point of impact of its fire, was on the right side a bit lower than midway from the top. He had the light machine gun set up just outside the entrance and sprayed the interior with several long bursts. Then he crawled into the cleft on his stomach, pushing his helmet ahead of him with a stick. The helmet had just nestled against the body nearest the entrance when the machine gun riddled it. The sergeant backed out quickly, having seen the empty cartridge cases and now aware of the gun's position. He went back along the ridge base and looked thoughtfully at the flame thrower attached to the body of the Marine killed earlier. Then, while his men lobbed hand grenades into the cliffside aperture, he ran out on the beach and dragged the body back to the shelter of the ridge. Not knowing the gun had been shifted, he presumed it had been prevented from firing by the rain of grenades.

He removed the flame thrower from the body of the dead Marine and examined it. It was intact. He strapped it on his back and crawled to the angle within the cleft behind which the man wounded in the first reconnaissance had taken cover. The machine gun set up at the mouth of the cleft opened fire at his signal. Protected by this diversion, he looked around the angle, made a swift but careful survey of the interior, and fixed the position of the aperture in his mind. He thrust the nozzle of the flame thrower around the corner at an angle he judged covered the aperture, loosed a stream of fire, adjusted the angle somewhat, and loosed another. The machine gun fired after the first discharge but not after the second. The sergeant assumed that the crew, if not already incinerated, had been forced to withdraw deeper into its cave. He gave a third and longer burst of flame and, calling to his men to follow him, ran deeper into the cleft, spraying fire directly into the aperture. His men came running behind him. One of them, climbing upon the shoulders of another, pushed a satchel charge into the still-smoking aperture and they all ran out of the cleft. There was a heavy explosion and smoke drifted out of the cleft. The detail left to guard the aperture in the cliff face reported excitedly that smoke and debris, including a human foot, had also shot out of their side of the ridge. For the first time the sergeant knew the two apertures were connected.

Using a tactic he had never seen employed in actual operations but which had remained in his mind from a long-ago and otherwise forgotten training film, he got a man up to the aperture in the cliff face. He had three men stand two feet apart with their backs against the cliff, grasping rifles extended horizontally between them. Two other men balanced on the rifles, cursing him enthusiastically as they did so, and held another rifle between them. A sixth man, smallest and lightest in the squads, then climbed up to the aperture using the rifles as steps and threw a satchel charge into it. The bottom tier broke and ran as soon as the charge was placed, causing the top man to fall a dozen feet to the sand below. He lay there unable to move, the breath knocked from him, and was half buried by dirt when the charge went off. The first man to rush to his aid he hit in the mouth. He would have attacked the rest of the laughing Marines had not someone pinioned his arms from behind.

The assault party's orders had been merely to eliminate the machine gun but the sergeant, encouraged by his success, decided to exploit it. If there were no Japanese dug into the reverse slope of the ridge it might be possible to take up positions beyond the ridge before the enemy reacted. He had his radioman report that shore and beach parties were now free to land and that there were casualties requiring medical attention. He left two men with the wounded and took the others back through the cleft. They moved cautiously through the narrow passage. One of the Marines, who had seen his first action only the day before, filled his pockets with the empty cartridge cases littering the track beneath the blasted aperture. He considered them ideal souvenirs, easy to carry and convenient to mail home to family and friends. What he wanted most for himself was a genuine samurai sword. When they were staging through Saipan, a friend of his had given a Seabee fifty dollars for a samurai sword that turned out to be a fake. The only way to be sure a sword wasn't fake was to take it off a Jap officer's body yourself.

Finding the reverse slope unoccupied, the sergeant set a detail to digging an emplacement for the machine gun and sent a runner back to the beach to await the arrival of an officer who would decide whether to move beyond the ridge in strength. He sent scouts into the ravine with orders to move a short distance into the valley beyond it and, from concealment, scan the area for signs of enemy positions. He went with them to the end of the ravine and looked out into the valley. It was narrow at this point, broadening gently inland and curving between the confining hills. The floor of the valley was patterned with dikes and hedgerows. Nevertheless the sergeant thought it looked much like a river. Despite the sights and sounds of the artillery duel which still continued between the Japanese guns in the hills and American guns in the beachheads and at sea, the scene was almost peaceful. The bamboos among which the sergeant crouched rose nakedly from the cinder-covered earth, leaves and shoots burned away from the less flammable stems. Among the bamboos were several clearings in which lay traces of the houses which had stood there. When a Japanese farmhouse burned, little remained. The sergeant rose and began walking back to the place where his men were digging in.

Miho had heard the fighting in the cleft and voices calling out in a barbaric tongue. When Yoji's machine gun ceased firing and soon after she heard a loud explosion in the cleft, she knew he was dead. She wished she had her mother's kitchen knife with her in the shelter so she could kill herself despite her promise to him. She felt the sharp, firehardened diagonal slash which formed the point of her spear. She had kept it with her despite Yoji's objections. It would be a simple matter to fall upon the spear and join Yoji in death. The thought of it ripping into her body and the hours of pain which might follow terrified her. Instead, she tied the piece of white cloth she had been saving to the end of the spear and lay quietly at the bottom of the shelter, waiting. After a long while she heard men coming out of the cleft speaking the ugly tongue she had heard earlier, though this time softly and with much less urgency. She waited for the sounds to move beyond her, as Yoji had instructed, but instead the Americans remained at the far end of the ravine. She could hear them digging. She tried to summon courage to emerge from her shelter and approach them. Before she managed to do so, steps went past her on the path through the bamboo grove. Miho raised her head cautiously until she could see just over the edge of her shelter. Three enormous men were walking past the ashes of her mother's house, bent low. They were extravagantly uniformed in bulky coats and fine leather boots and hung with belts and straps from which dangled many objects. They must be officers of high rank, she thought, to be so garbed and equipped. She must be prepared to raise her white cloth when the next American came down the path. None did. Instead, after a few minutes one of the three who had gone by returned.

Miho shrank down into the shelter and thrust the spear into the air so that the white cloth tied to it showed a foot above the ground. She remembered at the last minute Yoji's instruction to show her hair and she removed the cloth binding her head before showing herself. When she rose to full height she found herself staring into an eye of startling blueness fixed on her over the sights of a rifle aimed directly at her face. She would die with Yoji after all, she thought in mingled joy and terror. She closed her eyes and prepared to receive the bullet of the blue-eyed American giant.

Staff Sergeant Arthur Simmons was startled but not frightened by the unexpected appearance of a white flag in an area he had thought free of the enemy. He felt a certain professional embarrassment for failing to check the grove adequately. There might be other Japs hiding in it, though why they had not ambushed his men he could not imagine. He put his rifle to his shoulder and waited for the Jap to appear, ready to fire if the Jap came out shooting or holding a grenade, as they often did. His finger tightened on the trigger as the head and shoulders of a Japanese rose slowly out of the ground. His instinct was to fire rather than risk being blown up with the Jap if he was hiding a grenade or, at the very least, to avoid the nuisance of looking after a prisoner until the beach party arrived. But the troops had specific orders to take prisoners if possible. Japanese prisoners were sometimes as valuable as they were rare. Sergeant Simmons hesitated long enough to observe that the Jap soldier he saw over the sights of his rifle had long black hair and, under the grime, a pretty face. By God, he thought, it's a girl. It was the fantasy he had evoked a hundred times made real.

Simmons had a nickname, fairly won. It was Stud. He had been a

Marine for three years. In those three years he had been in many cities in the United States and in foreign lands. In every city, in each foreign country and on every Pacific island with a civilian population he had held a woman and, he boasted truthfully, "I never paid for it once." Almost every young soldier went looking for women at one time or another but most of them also gambled, got drunk, went sightseeing, or hunted for souvenirs. Simmons allowed none of these things to divert him from his quest. In the cities his successes were considered no great thing, but he found women where none were thought to be available and on this his growing reputation was based. It was not merely presentation of this reputation that prompted his diligence. It was a matter of personal need, both physical and psychological. When he settled down at last after the war, and he had no doubt that he would one day settle down, his mementos would not be snapshots, postcards and souvenirs but the memory of women enjoyed. When his companions spoke of samurai swords, he spoke of Japanese women, delicate and exotic. He knew it would be difficult for he had heard how, on Okinawa, women had sometimes been on raiding parties with Japanese soldiers, fighting alongside them with primitive weapons, at least one, it was said, carrying a baby in her free arm. But he knew that somehow, sooner or later, he would find a Japanese woman not fanatically bent on killing him. Stud Simmons always found a willing woman.

All through landing rehearsals at Saipan and in the days and nights at sea on the way to Kyushu, even when the Kamikaze bore in on the troopships, he thought about the many ways in which it could happen. Sometimes it was an older woman, still beautiful, wearing a silk kimono, beckoning to him from an ancient doorway. At other times it was a young girl, frightened at first, who had to be coaxed, or if not coaxed, treated just a little roughly before she responded. In every case but one it echoed something he had done before but now was heightened by the thought the woman would be someone rare and exotic, a Japanese woman. The one exception was rape. Simmons had never taken a woman against her will. That was also a part of his boast. But the fantasy of rape was more stimulating than the other fantasies and without the onus of rape. Everyone knew how Jap soldiers treated women in the cities they captured and it would serve them right if their women were treated the same way. And yet, however exciting the fantasy, Simmons did not believe he could rape a woman, even a Jap woman. Of all crimes that was the most reprehensible to him, and if the woman could not be persuaded, taking her would be meaningless, something an ordinary man could do.

Sergeant Simmons lowered his rifle. The girl did not respond to this cessation of menace because her eyes were tightly shut.

"Hey," he said carefully.

Miho opened her eyes slowly. The American was no longer pointing his rifle at her. He was a strange-looking creature. She had never before seen eyes so round and blue. The large steel helmet he wore was pierced with jagged holes. It puzzled her that he should be alive and unhurt after this had been done to it. He did not look as if he wished to kill her. Poor Yoji. He had known the truth about Americans but he was dead all the same.

Sergeant Simmons motioned for her to raise her hands. She looked like just a kid but with a Jap you couldn't afford to take chances. Miho raised her hands above her head, letting the spear with its white cloth fall. Simmons showed her a grenade hanging from his belt suspender.

"You got any of these hid on you, kid?" he said.

He mimed the question as well, pointing to the grenade, then inside his combat jacket, then at the girl. Miho understood. She shook her head and lowered her hands long enough to open her coat and let him see nothing was concealed beneath it. Because of the loose garment she wore beneath her coat Sergeant Simmons could not tell if she were only a kid or merely flat-chested like Jap women were said to be. Just his luck if she were only a kid, with that face like a doll's. He took a quick look around to see if he could be seen from the position his men were digging. The position was not visible from where he stood nor were the two men he had posted to watch for a counterattack. He jumped down into the hole beside the girl. She was small, hardly five feet, if that. That didn't necessarily mean she was a kid. Japs were little. He leaned his rifle against the side of the hole and indicated with signs that he must search her for weapons. He patted each baggy trouser leg from ankle to crotch. The girl's legs were muscular as a man's. Simmons was disappointed and a little repelled.

Miho stood docilely. She was not frightened by the American, only by the strangeness of the situation. He was not handling her as a man handled a woman and as she had feared before Yoji told her otherwise. The way he felt her legs was impersonal.

Simmons felt under the back of her coat and then under the front. This was no kid. She had breasts. Desire leaped up instantly within him.

"What do you know," he said in a low, thick voice. "You're a big girl, aren't you?"

Miho tried to pull away. The American's touch was no longer impersonal. It was like Yoji's, only not so gentle.

"Don't be afraid," Simmons said coaxingly. "I wouldn't hurt you for the world."

She began struggling more violently as he forced her down to the floor of the shelter. His weight was like a great rock crushing her. His big clumsy hands clutched at her, hurting and unbelievably strong. Yoji, she thought wildly, you should have let me die with you.

This girl's slippery as a snake, Simmons thought as the girl squirmed beneath him. At least she wasn't yelling or anything and attracting attention. Her frantic movements increased his desire and he knew he would have her, willing or not. He hoped he would not have to slap her around to quiet her down but if that's what it took that's what he'd do. He reached for the waistband of her trousers.

When the American's big hands released her, Miho twisted around with all her strength and squirmed from under. She snatched up the bamboo spear with the worthless scrap of white cloth tied to its end and scrambled out of the shelter before the American could stop her.

She backed away a few feet, the spear thrust straight out before her as she had been taught at primary school. The American stood up in the shelter, facing her. There was no anger in his face, only a look such as she had sometimes seen on Yoji's before making love. He spoke words she could not understand in a low, gentle voice. But Miho did not believe the voice. She believed the expression on his face and the way he had handled her in the shelter.

"Come on, baby," Simmons said. "Don't be so scared. Old Art just wants to be nice to you."

She looks like a scared rabbit, he thought. But she still hadn't attracted attention by yelling. She might not be as unwilling as she acted. If he could just get that stick away from her and get her back in the hole. He came out of the hole slowly, not taking his eyes off her, hoping she would not run.

Miho had no thought of running. She knew the American, with his long legs, could catch her easily. And she dare not turn her back on him.

Simmons edged toward her, avoiding any sudden movement, the way he did when making friends with a suspicious dog. He reached out slowly for the bamboo pole.

"You better give me that, baby," he coaxed. "You might hurt yourself."

Miho backed away, the spear still outthrust. The words of the instructor in hakuhei-sen, hand-to-hand combat, echoed in her mind and she remembered the page in the People's Handbook of Resistance Combat which illustrated them. "Neither swing vertically nor horizontally but always thrust tall Yankees in their belly."

Simmons grabbed for the pole. Miho closed her eyes and lunged forward. His outflung arm knocked it upward. Miho felt the spear drive home and heard a clotted, gasping sound. She opened her eyes. The spear was in the American's neck. He held the end of it in both hands preventing it from entering further. Blood spurted out of his throat and dyed his hands red. His mouth was open in a shout for help but only low, choking sounds emerged. Miho clung doggedly to the spear as he tried to wrest it from her. It felt as if her arms were being wrenched from their sockets. Blood spattered his green coat and ran down the spear to drip from her hands. It crept under her coat and she felt its wetness on her forearms. As the American weakened, the struggle became more equal. Miho kept pushing on the spear. The American no longer tried to pull it from her grasp and fought only to prevent its deeper entry. He gave ground to relieve the relentless pressure. He stumbled and fell on his back, still holding the spear in both hands. Miho stood over him and pushed on the spear with all her weight. She felt it go through his neck and into the earth beneath it. His booted heels and his elbows dug into the dirt. His body described half a circle round the spear before its thrashing ceased. His legs jerked a few moments longer, then he was still. His hands still clutched the spear and his round blue eyes stared up into the sky.

Miho's arms ached. She was exhausted and empty of emotion. She sank to her heels beside the body and squatted there. She still had not moved when one of the Marines returned along the path from the valley and shot her.

9

[Corporal Aaron Bibb]

By November 16, X+4, Operation Olympic's three corps had consolidated their beachheads on the west, south and east coasts of Kyushu. There had been 18,000 Army and Marine casualties, of which 4,000 were killed. The Navy had lost 10,000 men, half of them killed or missing in action. Sixty ships had been sunk and nearly 500 damaged, many of them smaller vessels. Aircraft losses were relatively light. The Army, Navy and Marines lost less than 300 planes, a quarter of them on carriers and most of the balance from ground fire.

In the same four days of fighting, the Japanese lost 33,000 dead, including almost every man in the screening positions and some 15,000 in sea and air suicide attacks. Farther inland, where there were many more wounded than killed, the Japanese strength remained basically intact because of the soundness of defense construction. In the air and on the sea the kamikaze force which was to have decimated the U.S. fleet within ten days of unrelenting attacks had ceased to exist, most of its planes shot out of the air or destroyed on the ground, and the Shinyo crash boats, Kaiten human torpedoes and midget submarines which had not been destroyed in the preinvasion bombardment or the subsequent mass attacks on the anchorages had been blasted in their pens. The 2500 Fukuryu "Crouching Dragons" were dead. Japan must now fight its decisive battle entirely on the ground.

Troops streaming to the battle areas from the north failed to reach the fighting in sufficient numbers to launch decisive counterattacks, those on the coastal highways being hampered by losses and the constant disruption of even foot traffic, and those moving inland slowed by the lack of roads. They did, however, reinforce the troops already in place astride the inland approaches.

The deepest American penetration in strength after four days of bitter fighting was on the east coast, where the 33rd Infantry Division succeeded in pushing inland two miles to the northern environs of Miyazaki City. The division's Beach Chrysler landings had been made in an area where the principal Japanese defenses were set in the hills some distance back from the shore and only positions of platoon strength barred the way. The division had, however, been hard hit by shelling and mortar fire and subjected to troublesome long-range fire from 28-cm. artillery. The eleven-inch guns, largest in the Kyushu arsenal, had been brought from coastal batteries guarding the Shimonoseki Strait between Honshu and northern Kyushu. South of Miyazaki City, the 25th Infantry Division took one of its main objectives, the Navy airfield near the coast. The airfield was still too exposed to Japanese artillery to be used as planned for fighter operations.

In the South, XI Corps found the going brutal even after the arrival of its reserve division, the Americal, on November 14th. The right flank of the 1st Cavalry Division, pushing along the coast toward Shibushi from Beach Essex, was stopped short of the objective. The coastal town and its little harbor were defended by deep, powerful positions on either side. The positions east of Shibushi were particularly strong in artillery enfilading the beachhead. A regiment of the Americal Division made a secondary landing east of these positions at Natsui. Although the regiment established a beachhead, it failed to reduce the positions and pierce the eastern defenses of Shibushi.

Elements of the 1st Cavalry Division at one point drove north out of Beach Essex about a mile before running into a skein of fortifications on rising ground. Elsewhere the division was confined to a strip of coastline little more than half a mile deep. The same was true on the 1st Cavalry Division's left flank, where the 43rd Infantry Division carved out a narrow but solid foothold on Beach Ford.

V Amphibious Corps on the west coast likewise failed to pierce the enemy's major defenses even though the two Japanese divisions opposing it, the 303rd and 206th Infantry, were untried, having been organized only that summer. As it happened, the bulk of their strength in V Amphibious Corps objective area was concentrated near the landing beaches in position to offer maximum early resistance. Nevertheless the 3rd Marine Division was able to expand its Beach Winton beachhead a mile and three-quarters along the coast to Kushikino, preparatory to pushing inland toward Sendai. The 2nd Marine Division, to the south, had landed directly into Japanese strength and opened little breathing space out of the Studebaker beaches until reinforced by elements of the 5th Marine Division.

And, on the fourth day after the landings, the U.S. Sixth Army began committing IX Corps, two divisions of which had made the feint against Shikoku on November l0th. The 77th Infantry Division was loaded out of Okinawa for Ariake Bay and the 81st Infantry Division was on its way to the east coast to bolster the forces attacking in the Miyazaki area. The corps' third division, the 98th Infantry, launched a new full-scale amphibious assault at the foot of the Satsuma Peninsula, thirty miles southeast of the Kushikino beachhead and west of the entrance to Kagoshima Bay. The 98th Division's landings on Beach Plymouth in Beach Zone Limousine were made in the teeth of the 125th Independent Mixed Brigade and the 146th Infantry Division, but the division encountered little opposition from sea or air and its losses were not as severe as those of the X-Day landings.

Behind the 220,000 combat and combat auxiliary troops now firmly established on Kyushu, 60,000 of the Sixth Army's more than 120,000 service troops had come ashore. With their help, order slowly began emerging from the disarray of the first days. Field hospitals provided emergency treatment, field kitchens sent hot meals forward, communications lines were laid, headquarters, command posts and cemeteries were established. Construction materials and equipment, vehicles, pierced steel mats for aircraft landing strips, fuel, portable bridges, ammunition, blood plasma, rations and other supplies poured ashore. Some of it was deposited directly on the beaches by landing craft and LSTs, some trucked ashore on pontoon causeways reaching out to sea. Some came from the holds of transports and cargo ships of the invasion fleet, some from Liberty ships which had departed weeks before from ports in the United States. Men and supplies moved inland by amphibian tractor, amphibian truck and conventional trucks. Almost 50,000 vehicles, from Sherman tanks to jeeps, had been landed.

At sea, U.S. and British battleships, cruisers, aircraft carriers and destroyers supported the fighting with their firepower; hospital, barracks, repair and refrigerator ships and tankers lay offshore. In them and in shore parties were almost 300,000 Navy men, and their number was growing toward a scheduled 323,000 by X+6.

By the end of X+4, Phase I of Operation Olympic was over. The three corps beachheads had been seized and consolidated, the enemy had been prevented from moving reinforcements in significant numbers to the battle areas, and construction of air base facilities had begun. Phase II, coordinated attacks out of corps beachheads to seize additional airfield and base areas and open Kagoshima Bay to American shipping, was about to begin.

"Come on, man, shake it up," said Corporal Aaron Bibb, snapping his fingers impatiently. "You holdin' up the whole war."

He stood with his feet crossed at the ankles, an outstretched arm propping him against the side of his DUKW, a six-wheeled amphibious truck. The soldier to whom he spoke had stopped stacking cases of mortar shells in the bed of the Duck to mop his brow, temporarily halting the flow of cases being passed hand to hand from the ammunition dump. A line of other vehicles, most of them conventional two-and-a-half-ton trucks, waited behind Bibb's DUKW.

"Give a nigger wheels, right away he starts showin' off," the soldier said angrily.

He was a shade lighter than Bibb, who was very black.

Bibb looked slyly out of the corner of his eye at the white officer standing off to one side. Lieutenant Lefko, his amphib truck company's maintenance officer, looked pained, as Bibb had anticipated. It distressed the lieutenant to hear the word nigger whether it was used by a black or a white man, but particularly by a Negro. Bibb had observed, and enjoyed, the fact that many things distressed Lieutenant Lefko, including the personal insignia it had cost Bibb half a bottle of whiskey to have painted on his DUKW. What made that all the more a source of secret delight was the fact that the lieutenant had given him the whiskey. Bibb's personal insignia was a playing card. Underneath it was lettered "The Ace of Spades."

"That has derogatory implications," Lieutenant Lefko had said. "You of all people shouldn't perpetuate it."

Lieutenant Lefko was from up East.

"You spend more time stackin' and less time talkin' I wouldn't be standin' around waitin' for one of them big Jap shells to blow my black ass to Glory," Bibb said, unruffled.

Bibb was not really too worried about that possibility. Most of the Japanese artillery that had not been knocked out or overrun was too busy trying to keep the tanks and infantry from pushing inland. He said it because he knew the port battalion men working around the ammo dumps lived in constant fear of a direct hit. Sixteen hundred rounds of 75-mm. had gone up just a couple of days before and everybody in the Beach Cord area south of Miyazaki City was jumpy. Bibb did not start getting edgy until he got close to the fighting, in range of Japanese mortars and smaller, more personal stuff. They still had plenty of that left. For him, coming back for a load of ammunition was a breather marred only by the fact he could not smoke near the dump. He was not supposed to smoke while driving a load of ammunition, either, but he did unless Lieutenant Lefko was making the run with him. That was one of the things Bibb could not understand about the lieutenant.

The lieutenant did not have to go into the front lines, in fact he was not even supposed to. His place was back at the amphibian truck pool keeping the DUKWs running. He had told Bibb the only reason he volunteered for the Army in the first place was to get in the infantry and kill Germans for killing Jews.

"Where I made my mistake was telling the truth about my civilian occupation," he had told Bibb.

Bibb knew a lot about Lieutenant Lefko, much more than the lieutenant knew about him. Lieutenant Lefko was a talker. Bibb was, too, but a good deal of what he told the lieutenant was false. Sometimes he lied to the lieutenant to tell him things he knew the lieutenant wanted to hear and at other times to tell him things he knew the lieutenant did not like to hear, depending on Bibb's mood at the time. Bibb knew that the lieutenant was one of five brothers and two sisters and that four of the brothers worked for a big laundry in Chicago owned by their father. Lieutenant Lefko had run the truck fleet. The lieutenant thought that Bibb was one of thirteen children, all of whom had been raised on tenant cotton farms and labored in the fields from dawn to dusk. Bibb, as a matter of fact, was one of three children. The other two were older sisters, one of whom did housework and one of whom taught in a Negro elementary school in Rosenberg, Texas. The latter did not have much use for her brother, Aaron. Bibb, born and raised in Houston, had never lived on a farm or chopped cotton in his life. He had not had a hoe in his hand since his early teens when he helped his father do yard work for white families in Riverside Terrace. He had, however, done a good deal of heavy manual labor in his later teens and early twenties after marrying at eighteen and fathering a daughter. That was before, as his schoolteacher sister described it, he turned bad.

Just as the lieutenant found himself in an amphibian truck company because he told the truth about his civilian occupation, Bibb was in amphibs because of lying about it. When his engineering unit, which did the kind of work Bibb was accustomed to before he turned bad, was disbanded, Bibb had learned the Army was looking for experienced Negro truck drivers. Not wishing to be sent to another engineering unit for more heavy lifting and digging, he had said he drove a garbage truck in Houston in civilian life. This was only a partial invention. He had worked on a garbage truck during a run of bad luck, but as a loader.

Bibb did not consider it the worst job he had ever had. It was hard work but he had the muscle for it and he got to ride around a lot. It was not like digging foundations on a construction job where the boss gave you a hard look if you stopped to light a cigarette. And on the early morning part of the route he could wake the rich white folks by banging the trash cans around. There was also satisfaction in bending their trash cans against the side of the truck when he emptied them. Occasionally people on the route threw away usable furniture, articles of clothing and metal objects the junkman paid good money for. Bibb never took any of it home, even a good chair or a dress that might fit his wife. Though he had been raised to the contrary like everyone he knew, he did not want anything a white man had thrown away in his house or on his wife.

Neither his parents nor his wife, nor Bibb himself, understood why he felt like that. His schoolteacher sister said it was pride. It was one of the few things about him to which she did not object. Bibb sold or traded his finds at the Dowling Street pawnshops and secondhand stores. What money he got for them he used for gambling. He considered that fair enough. He always brought his pay home intact which, among his acquaintances, was uncommon. Even steady work was uncommon among them. Bibb associated with men who lived by their wits, preying impartially on whites and blacks though more often on blacks because it was less perilous. Bibb did not like conning another Negro unless the stud really asked for it.

When the DUKW was loaded with 60-mm. mortar ammunition Bibb prepared to climb over the side. The lieutenant came over and looked at him speculatively. Bibb knew what Lieutenant Lefko wanted. Lieutenant Lefko wanted to drive. Bibb did not like anyone else driving his Duck. He felt as much the owner of the DUKW as he had of the old Cadillac he had paid down on during a run of luck shooting dice in Houston. When he steered the DUKW around the craters, stumps and potholes behind Beach Cord he always looked from side to side to see who was noticing, just as he had when he drove the dented but well-simonized Cadillac up and down Dowling Street. But if the lieutenant asked, Bibb was going to let him. An officer did not have to ask. All he had to do was say. For all his simpleminded Northern ideas and ways, Lieutenant Lefko wasn't such a bad white man. He never ordered anybody around except in the line of duty. Not that he couldn't be as ironass as anybody when you didn't do right. Except that he was always easier on Negroes than whites. Some of the company's officers, who were all white, disliked him for it and not all of the drivers, who were black, liked him any better because of it.

"Look, Aaron," the lieutenant said when Bibb did not speak out. "Is it okay if I drive this trip?"

He always called Bibb by his first name instead of corporal. That was what Bibb considered one of the lieutenant's simpleminded Northern ways. Back in Houston the whites always called Negroes by their first names. You could work for a man a year and he wouldn't know your last name unless he saw it on the payroll. But Bibb knew the lieutenant called him by his first name to show him how equal he was. Lieutenant Lefko didn't even have enough common sense to know what he really wanted to be called was corporal.

"Yes, sir, Lieutenant," Bibb said. "But mind goin' into third. I think I'm gonna have me some trouble with my transmission they don't get me some new gears."

Lieutenant Lefko had once asked Bibb to call him by his first name, too, when no one was around.

"I'm a civilian and you're a civilian," he had said. "You're a man and I'm a man." He said the last sentence so self-consciously Bibb had wanted to laugh. "So why don't we forget all this rank business? Take a little breather from Army horseshit."

"Yessir," Bibb had said, but he never did.

Officers no more had first names to him than he had a last name to whites back home.

The first part of the run was parallel to the coast, down the main highway leading south out of Miyazaki City. The engineers had put it in good shape, better, some said, than when the Japs had it a week earlier. There was much traffic on the road, directed by MPs with white armbands, and it crawled along from ten to twenty miles an hour. After a mile and a half they turned inland at the charred, abandoned village of Gunjibun and headed due west toward Shimmachi, three miles away where the Kiyotake River angled north. There was still fighting going on around Shimmachi. The Japanese were dug in there in strength. Bulldozers and dump trucks were still working on the dirt road out of Gunjibun. Not far outside the village a spur of high ground thrust down to the road. Here the road-building crews carried carbines slung over their shoulders. There were still some Japanese holdouts tucked away in caves and holes. From that point on there was high ground north of the road all the way to Shimmachi.

"Better give her the gas, Lieutenant," said Bibb, who had made the run before. "They's still Japs up there."

The lieutenant gunned her to forty, jolting over rough spots and slowing down only to go around rocks or creep through deeply rutted stretches. He double-clutched expertly through a bad spot and glanced at Bibb for approval.

"You drive good, Lieutenant," Bibb said. "I wouldn't let jess anybody drive my Duck."

The lieutenant grinned.

Some officers is just like children, Bibb thought. You just got to know how to treat them.

Up ahead, a group of people squatted by the road, guarded by a soldier holding a rifle loosely in the crook of his arm. The lieutenant jammed on the brakes. The heavily loaded amphibian slewed sideways in a cloud of dust, throwing Bibb against the side of the cab.

"What the shit you doin'?" Bibb cried angrily before he could stop himself.

Oh, oh, he thought. I finally did it. Now I'm gonna get it. You didn't talk that way to an officer, not even a damn fool officer, not even a damn fool officer as easy as Lieutenant Lefko.

"Gee, I'm sorry," said the lieutenant. "Are you okay?"

He did not sound mad, just apologetic.

"Yessir," Bibb said.

"Those are civilians," the lieutenant said, excited. "First Japanese civilians I've seen."

"Yessir," Bibb said again.

What the hell was so great about a bunch of ragged Japs, he wondered. The lieutenant was just about the most simpleminded stud he ever saw.

"You got anything to eat in this thing, Aaron?" the lieutenant asked.

"Sir?" Bibb answered more sharply than common sense dictated.

He did not like anyone calling his DUKW a thing.

"They look starved," the lieutenant said.

At that moment Bibb disliked the lieutenant. All his talk about there being no difference between blacks and whites didn't mean a thing if he felt the same way about Japs. It was like saying Aaron Bibb was the same as a raggedy-ass Jap. The lieutenant rummaged around in the cab and found two cans of C-ration meat stew Bibb had been saving for an afternoon snack.

"Okay if I give this to them, Aaron?" the lieutenant said.

Listen to the man, Bibb thought. Like he thinks I'm gonna say no to an officer if I want to say no. If it was important enough he might but this was not important enough.

"If they'll eat it, Lieutenant," he said. "Japs don't eat nothin' but fish heads and rice."

When he said that it made him think of the way his wife fixed snouts and rice. Poor-folks food, but not the way Ernestine fixed it. He hadn't had snouts and rice since he left home. Most places he'd been in the army they had not even heard of it. He wished he was back home right now with his legs under the table and a big plate in front of him. After they'd left Rebecca next door with Mrs. Kennington and had the day in bed.

The lieutenant laughed.

"Fish heads and rice?" he said. "The Japanese cuisine is among the world's greatest. If you ever get up to Chicago I'll take you to a Japanese restaurant you'll never forget."

His voice began losing its enthusiasm toward the end of the sentence and he looked embarrassed. Bibb knew exactly what was going on in the lieutenant's mind. The lieutenant had just realized he was making a promise he couldn't keep even if he really wanted to. But at least it showed the lieutenant hadn't thought about him being black, even if it was only for a half a sentence.

"These here ones don't look like they been eatin' much of that kweezeen," Bibb said, rescuing the lieutenant.

There was an old man, an old woman, a younger woman with a baby slung on her back and three children in the party. They all squatted in identical positions, their expressions stolid and unrevealing. When the DUKW turned off the road toward them one of the children turned around, wide-eyes curious, and started to rise. The young woman reached out and pulled him down again.

The soldier guarding them said, "You come to pick 'em up?"

"No," the lieutenant said. "We're taking a load of ammo up to the line."

He stuck his head out of the cab and tossed the cans of C ration to the Japanese.

"What the hell you think you're doing?" the soldier said angrily.

He had not noticed the lieutenant's insignia nor had it occurred to him that an officer would be driving a load of ammunition.

"I'm Lieutenant Lefko and I'm giving these people food," the lieutenant said curtly. "Got any objections, Private?"

"No, sir," the soldier said quickly, his face changing. "I didn't—"

The lieutenant cut him off.

"And did you ever consider standing at attention when addressing an officer?"

The soldier drew himself erect, his face sullen. Bibb grinned. It did him a world of good to see a white boy chewed out by his ace buddy, Lieutenant Lefko. The lieutenant put the DUKW in gear and gunned it back on the road.

"Poor bastards," he said. "All the spirit knocked right out of them."

"It's they own fault," Bibb said. "They started this war."

He had felt no pity for the Japanese, only mild curiosity. The sound of firing grew louder as they neared the line. A soldier ran out into the road and flagged them down.

"You got any thirty caliber?" he shouted urgently.

The lieutenant looked at Bibb. Bibb shook his head. This was not a mixed load.

"Afraid not," the lieutenant said. "Just sixty millimeter."

"Crap," the soldier said. "Those sons of bitches back there."

"Hey, man," Bibb said. "Where is it they doin' all the yellin' for sixty-millimeter mortar?"

The soldier looked at him, surprised he and not the white driver should be asking directions.

"Straight up the road about eight hundred yards and off to the right," he said. "But you better not try to take that thing all the way in. You get past that hill up there, the Japs got observation on the road. You know if there's any thirty caliber coming up?"

"Must be," Bibb said. "They movin' all kinds of stuff up fast as they can load it on the trucks."

He was grateful to the soldier for warning him about the road but he wished people would quit calling his Duck a thing. The soldier grinned. He had noticed the insignia on the side of Bibb's amphib.

"Okay, Ace," he said. "Take it easy."

"Take it easy," Bibb said, feeling closer to the soldier in the brief exchange than he ever had with Lieutenant Lefko.

When they reached the hill the lieutenant pulled the DUKW off to the side of the road and cut the engine.

"What do we do now?" he asked.

That was one of the things Bibb liked about the lieutenant. He wasn't always acting like he knew everything.

"I'll go up and see where it is they want the stuff," Bibb said. "I expect they goin' to hand carry it up from here."

He wasn't going to take a chance on anything happening to his Duck, not after all he'd been through with it.

"I'll go with you," the lieutenant said.

"Ain't no sense in both of us gettin' out there, Lieutenant," said Bibb.

The lieutenant was always taking chances he didn't have to. Just like making this run when he was supposed to be back at the motor pool. He had even made a round trip from the landing ship with Bibb on X-Day, taking ammunition to the beach and bringing back wounded.

"For a change I'd like to see what they do with all the ammo you deliver," the lieutenant said. "All I get to see of the war is spare parts and grease guns."

Beyond the hill the road was quiet but heavily cratered. In places the earth was freshly disturbed, showing some of the shelling was recent. They kept off the road in the shelter of the encroaching high ground on the right until the terrain began flattening out.

"This must be where he said," said Bibb.

There was a stream up ahead and beyond it a ridge. Two Sherman tanks and a 105-mm. self-propelled gun were lobbing shells into the ridge. Beyond them a battery of field artillery was firing over the ridge toward Shimmachi. A stack of empty mortar ammunition crates told Bibb they had reached their destination. A sergeant eating a candy bar approached them and crammed the last bite into his mouth before speaking. He threw the wrapper on the ground. It was an Oh Henry. Where does a man get himself a Oh Henry out here, Bibb wondered.

"You looking for something, Lieutenant?" the sergeant asked.

"I'm just along for the ride," the lieutenant answered.

"I got a load of ammo," Bibb said.

The sergeant looked out at the road.

"Where?" he demanded.

"Back around the hill."

"Back around the hill? That don't help us none here."

"The road's under enemy observation," the lieutenant said.

The sergeant grunted.

"You think we ain't right here?" he said, adding as an afterthought. "Sir. Any thirty caliber?"

"Jess sixty millimeter," said Bibb.

"The Old Man ain't gonna like that," the sergeant said. "Come on to the CP."

He led them to the company command post. Less than a week ago it had been a Japanese bunker. A jeep was parked in a hole outside with only a pedestal-mounted machine gun showing above the ground. The bunker had electric lights run by a portable generator. There was not room for a tall man to stand erect but otherwise the bunker was spacious. It was furnished with two cots, two folding stools, a radio and a wooden table on which the previous occupants had carved crude Japanese ideographs. There were a captain, a first lieutenant and three enlisted men in the bunker, one of the latter tinkering with the radio and muttering obscenities.

"Captain," the sergeant said, "here's the man with the ammo. No thirty caliber."

"No thirty caliber!" the captain exclaimed, looking angrily at Lieutenant Lefko. "I told you bastards we needed thirty caliber. What the hell's going on back there?"

"I wouldn't know, Captain," the lieutenant said calmly. "I'm a maintenance officer myself. And Corporal Bibb here, he just brings what they load on his Duck."

"A maintenance officer? What are you doing up here?"

"He came along for the ride," the sergeant said helpfully.

"No wonder we can't get what we need," the captain said. "Everybody's out sightseeing. I suppose you came up here looking for a samurai sword for yourself."

"I'm Lieutenant Howard," said the other officer. "That's my battery out there. You bring anything for us?"

"No, sir," said Bibb. "Jess sixty millimeter."

"That figures," Lieutenant Howard said. "You get attached to an infantry company you always end up sucking hind tit."

"Elditch, you got men unloading that mortar ammo?" the captain asked the sergeant who had brought Bibb and Lefko to the command post.

"It ain't here, Captain," the sergeant replied.

The captain stared at him.

"Not here? Where the hell is it?"

"The lieutenant said the road's under enemy observation," the sergeant said sarcastically. "They left the truck back a piece."

"That's perfect," the captain said. "That's just perfect. Corporal, you get your ass out there and bring us that ammo. I mean right up to the front door."

"Yes, sir!" Bibb said smartly.

He was enjoying himself. He always did when things were going wrong for the officers.

"Come on, Corporal," Lieutenant Lefko said. "Let's go."

"Stick around and have a cup of coffee," the captain said. "Your boy can drive that thing, can't he?"

Lieutenant Lefko looked peeved, as Bibb knew he would. He hoped the lieutenant wouldn't make any big deal out of the captain calling him a boy. If it turned into an argument the loser was sure to be Aaron Bibb and nothing that lard-assed captain said could bother him in the first place. He'd been handling smarter and meaner men than that captain as far back as he could remember.

"Corporal Bibb made four trips to the beach and back in his DUKW X-Day and has been making regular runs under enemy fire ever since," the lieutenant said stiffly. "I'd say he can drive that thing."

God damn it, Bibb thought, if everybody didn't stop calling his Duck a thing he was going to say something about it. He felt kind of ashamed for the lieutenant. The way he was talking to the captain made him sound so prissy.

"Hey," the captain said, interested and unaware he had just been put in his place by the lieutenant, "is that what you're driving, a DUKW? One of you boys saved my ass X-Day."

He got up from the folding stool on which he was sitting and thrust out a hand.

"I want to shake your hand," he said.

Look at that old lieutenant, Bibb thought. Got a look on his face like he'd been bit by his own dog. He don't know what to make of this captain. He took the captain's hand and gave it a crunch. The captain winced.

"You got a real grip on you, Corporal," he said.

"Did I squeeze too hard, Captain?" Bibb said with feigned concern. "I'm so used to throwin' them shells around I forgets to squeeze easy with people."

"Speaking of shells," the captain said, "let's get that sixty millimeter up here pronto."

When they were on their way back to the DUKW the lieutenant turned to Bibb with a sorrowful expression on his face.

"You disappointed me back there, Aaron," he said.

"Sir?"

"I never thought you'd be an Uncle Tom."

That made Bibb mad. What did that simpleminded lieutenant really know, with all his college education and all his talk about everybody being the same? What did he know about Tomming and getting along with the least amount of trouble and not even knowing the difference between real Tomming and putting on just enough to make a fool out of the man? The lieutenant had talked up to the captain without the captain even paying any attention but he sure as hell paid attention when the old Ace of Spades took a hold of him. Bibb did not say anything. He let his face speak for him. Bibb had absolute control of his expression, something learned by every black man with natural wit who wanted to get along and get on in the world. He could smile when he smoldered inside or glower when he wanted to burst out laughing, or keep a poker face in either circumstance. Now he let his face go sorrowful, like the lieutenant's.

"I hurt your feelings, didn't I, Aaron?" the lieutenant said contritely. "I apologize for what I said. Okay?"

"That's okay, Lieutenant," Bibb said.

Oh, is that stud simpleminded, he thought. I don't see how he gets along in this world. If he was colored he'd be dead or in jail by now instead of being rich and a big officer. But for all that, he thought he liked the lieutenant. The lieutenant tried to do right. He didn't know how, but he tried. Bibb felt good. That captain back there had paid Duck drivers a compliment. And he hadn't made a big fuss about getting his hand almost broken.

He liked the captain some, too. Bibb felt more comfortable around a man like the captain than around one like Lieutenant Lefko. He started singing to himself as they hurried back along the cratered road.

I walked the road all night long,
With mah forty-four in mah hand.
I walked the road all night long,
With mah forty-four in mah hand.
I been lookin' for mah woman
An' I found her with another man.

"That's really good, Aaron," the lieutenant said. "Is it original?"

"Yessir," said Bibb.

Listen to him. Says he crazy about the blues and never even heard of Roosevelt Sykes. "44 Blues" was one of the most famous records the Honey Dripper ever made. Something whispered in the air. The explosion almost knocked off Bibb's helmet. The lieutenant yelled and fell down. When Bibb looked down at him he was sitting up holding his right elbow with his left hand. There was no arm below the elbow and blood was spurting out of the stump.

"Oh, Jesus, God, Lieutenant!" Bibb cried, kneeling beside him.

"Get a tourniquet on it quick, Aaron," the lieutenant said in a strained voice. "There's a handkerchief in my left pants pocket."

Bibb tied the olive drab handkerchief around the lieutenant's arm and twisted it tight with the bone-handled pocket knife he had carried all his adult life. There was blood all over the ground. Bibb had seen blood many times before, and not just since he'd been in the Army, but this looked brighter and uglier than he could remember blood ever looking. Even his own. He glanced around for the piece of the lieutenant's arm that had been blown off but did not see it. For some reason that bothered him.

"Can you hold on to the tourniquet your own self, Lieutenant?" he asked.

"I think so."

Bibb picked the lieutenant up in his arms and ran with him all the way to the DUKW. He propped him against the passenger side of the cab and scrambled into it, then reached down and pulled him up over the side. There were no doors on a DUKW. He leaned the lieutenant against the seat and slid past the clutches and gear levers to get under the wheel. He muscled the clumsy boatlike vehicle around as expertly as if it were a conventional truck and headed back for the Gunjibun road junction at top speed. The MPs there would know where to find the nearest aid station. The lieutenant was conscious but so weak from shock and loss of blood he kept sliding down in his seat. Bibb reached across to steady him but the cab was so wide it was difficult driving and holding the lieutenant at the same time. When they jolted over ruts the lieutenant would groan.

"Do it hurt real bad?" Bibb said.

"Yeah," the lieutenant gasped through clenched teeth.

"You jess hang on. I'm gonna carry you to a field hospital before you know it."

The DUKW, horn blowing, sped recklessly past other vehicles heading inland on the narrow road toward the line, forcing some of them to pull off to the side to avoid a collision. At the junction Bibb charged into the tangled traffic before jamming on the brakes. An MP ran toward the DUKW shouting, his eyes bulging with outrage.

"I got me a wounded officer here," Bibb shouted. "Which way's the field hospital?"

There was a signpost at the junction with a thicket of black-lettered white boards pointing in all directions. Bibb had no intention of taking time to search among them for the right one, if it was there at all.

"Thataway!" the MP shouted, pointing.

He ran to the Duck and scrambled up on the prowlike hood. He blew his whistle and waved aside other vehicles as they sped along the bumper-to-bumper traffic.

"Stop this thing!" he cried. "There's an ambulance."

Before the DUKW stopped rolling he jumped off and stopped the ambulance, and with it the whole line of traffic behind it. The ambulance driver and the MP came running with a litter. The MP started to climb into the DUKW to help Bibb.

"You stay down there and catch him real easy," Bibb said. "I don't need no help."

He took the lieutenant under the arms and handed him down gently.

"Don't you worry, Lieutenant," he said. "I'm goin' to follow you all the way to the hospital an' see they treat you right."

"They're waiting for that sixty millimeter," the lieutenant whispered. "I'll be okay."

"I want to be sure you all right," Bibb protested.

"You can come back later. Okay?"

"Yessir," Bibb said.

He did not turn the DUKW around until he saw the lieutenant loaded safely into the ambulance, despite the honks and curses from the vehicles stacked up behind him. At first he felt depressed, thinking about the lieutenant losing his arm, the right one, too, and how mad the Captain was going to be because he took so long getting back with the load. He hoped the lieutenant was going to be all right. The lieutenant had looked real bad when they slid the litter into the ambulance. Then his mood lightened and he began feeling an exhilarating sense of freedom. He had his Duck back with nobody wanting to rank him out of the driver's seat and until he got to where he was going there was nobody to boss him around. Getting shut of the lieutenant was a big relief although he was sorry it happened the way it did. It wore a man out just being around the lieutenant, trying to act like you knew he wanted you to, not saying and not doing so many things that came natural because the lieutenant said it gave mean whites something to make fun of, like the Ace of Spades on the Duck. Even when the lieutenant was preaching about how they were both the same it made him nervous and sometimes a little mad. His daddy didn't own no big laundry and he hadn't been to no college. He hadn't even finished high school. While the lieutenant was going to all those dances and football games he was out trying to scrape up enough gold to feed a wife and baby.

Yes, it was good to be driving down the road all by himself even if the road was on some island in Japan he'd never even heard of until they told him to land a load of ammo on it and even if they might start shooting at him and get him like they got the lieutenant. He began wondering if you got hit was it better to be killed than to lose your best arm like the lieutenant. He thought about the things you could do and couldn't do with just one arm. There really weren't any of the good things you couldn't do with just one arm, love your woman, drink, eat, throw dice. Drive a car, maybe. That would be hard with just one arm. He experimented with driving the Duck using only his left hand but decided it was not a fair test. The gear shift lever and special clutches were more complicated and harder to handle than in a car. He knew a man in Houston who didn't have but one arm and drove a car. The man did good, too, always having money in his pocket and nobody yelling at him for not taking a pick and shovel job because you couldn't expect a man to do that kind of work with just one arm. And they'd have to give him a pension, the Army would. He could take it easy the rest of his natural life. But it was better to have your two hands. Then you could take for yourself.

He started singing "44 Blues." That Lieutenant Lefko. Believing he'd made it up his own self. He was one dumb white man. The poor, one-armed son of a bitch. He wished more white men were like the lieutenant, though, as long as he didn't have to be around them himself. Before Bibb knew it he had reached the company area where the ammunition was supposed to go. The same sergeant came running up and looking as mad as that MP back at the road junction. And damn if he ain't eating himself another Oh Henry, Bibb thought. He must have found himself a Oh Henry mine somewhere.

"Where the goddam hell you been!" the sergeant demanded. "The Old Man's about to bust a gut."

Bibb climbed leisurely out of the DUKW and took a fond look at the Ace of Spades insignia before answering.

"You got another one of them Oh Henrys? I give you a dollar for it," he said.

The sergeant's expression went from rage to incredulity and back to rage again.

"What'd you say?" he bellowed. "I'm talking to you about our ammo, you black bastard!"

Bibb smiled, as if the sergeant had said something nice. That always made them go half crazy.

"I said you got another one of them Oh Henrys? I give you a dollar. Or you mad 'cause you think a dollar ain't enough, you white son of a bitch?"

He didn't have to take any crap off the sergeant. The sergeant was just an enlisted man like him, only with one more stripe, and he wasn't even a sergeant in the amphib company. The sergeant dropped his rifle and doubled up his fists. Bibb hoped he'd throw and hoped he wouldn't. He'd love to put that loudmouthed trash flat on his back but if he was to hit the sergeant he could get himself in real trouble. When a black soldier and a white soldier got into a rogue it was the black soldier they always threw in the stockade. He had a buddy doing five on the rock pile. Bibb stood waiting for the sergeant to throw, his face impassive. Maybe the sergeant would realize it wasn't a good idea. Bibb was five-feet ten of gristle, tempered by a life of hard labor, and his arms were as thick as some men's thighs. He was broad-nosed, thick-lippd and mean-looking when he did not bother to look pleasant.

While the sergeant was making up his mind the captain stuck his head out of the command post bunker and yelled, "What the hell's going on out there?"

He saw Bibb and the DUKW.

"Where the hell you been?" he cried, coming outside. "You could have dumped the sixty millimeter and been back with a load of thirty caliber by now."

"Sorry, Captain, sir," Bibb said. "The lieutenant got his arm blowed off walkin' back and I had to carry him to the hospital."

"Christ!" the captain said. "His arm? Will he make it okay?"

"They say so, Captain. Where you want this here load?"

Bibb could tell by the captain's smile he had just noticed the Ace of Spades insignia. The sergeant looked like somebody had run off with his last Oh Henry. Bibb hoped he would run into him in town some night, if there were any towns left by the time they got to them. He would like to see the sergeant try to finish what he had started.

Instead of answering Bibb, the captain turned toward the bunker and called, "Hey, Willie, come out here a minute."

A lieutenant Bibb had not seen before came out of the bunker.

"Look at this," the captain said, pointing a thumb at the DUKW.

The lieutenant laughed.

"That's rich," he said. "That's really rich."

For the first time Bibb had an inkling of what it was Lieutenant Lefko had objected to about the insignia. He felt the same as he had when, as a boy, he had taken his shine box to the newspaper office on Polk and Dowling and some of the reporters rubbed his nappy head for luck. But to hell with all of them. He liked being the Ace of Spades. He just wouldn't cut the fool with these officers and cater to them. Even if the sergeant started bad-mouthing him.

"You want this load, Captain?" he said. "They waitin' for me back at the depot."

He waited to see if that made the captain mad. He could see the sergeant was waiting, too.

"Don't stand there with your head up, Elditch," the captain said to the sergeant. "Round up a detail and help this man unload."

"I'd 'preciate that, Sarge," Bibb said, poker-faced.

Oh, he thought, if that ain't one mad white boy. Even though he knew now if the sergeant had started throwing, the captain probably would have been fair about it, he was glad it had worked out as it did. This was more fun than whipping the sergeant.

"It scare you to get shot at, Corporal?" the captain said.

"Yessir," Bibb said. "Some."

"If you'd said no you'd be a goddamned liar," the captain said. "What I'm getting at is I've got my weapons platoon strung out from here to Canarsie and not one company truck available. And Baker Company's screaming for sixty millimeter, too. Think you'd get yourself in trouble with your CO if you took time to deliver door to door?"

"I could do that, Captain," Bibb said.

He was getting to like this stud better all the time.

"That's damn white of you," the captain said.

When he realized what he had said, he laughed without a trace of Lieutenant Lefko's self-consciousness. Bibb thought it was kind of funny, too, but he did not smile. He wasn't going to do any catering.

They were taking off the crates the captain wanted left at the command post when they heard the plane. The engine was cutting in and out and making a popping noise. Bibb could see it in the distance, a silvery speck trailing black smoke. The captain came running out of the bunker to see what the yelling was about.

"Get a panel out so if he has to jump he'll know when he's over friendly territory," the captain ordered. "The rest of you men get down. They're not shooting blanks from that ridge."

Most of the fire from the Japanese-held ridge, however, now appeared directed against the crippled aircraft. The tanks and self-propelled gun which Bibb had seen earlier had gone off but the field artillery battery began firing continuously. The enemy guns were on the far side of the hill and the battery's howitzers pointed at a high angle to drop their shells on the invisible emplacements. It was impossible to see what effect they were having. One of the company's sixty-mm. mortars was set up not far from the command post. It began firing as well. The mortar, though much closer at hand, sounded like a popgun to Bibb compared with the 105s. Next to being a Duck driver he would have liked being an artilleryman. When he was in the engineers he had seen colored artillerymen and envied them.

Flames began washing over the plane, streaming from the engine back to the tail.

"He'll never make it to the 'zaki strip," the captain said.

Ignoring his own order to the men to take cover, he had remained standing.

"Jump, you son of a bitch!" he shouted.

Others began yelling for the pilot to jump. Bibb thought that was simpleminded of them. The pilot couldn't hear them. He might even already be dead. On X-Day he had seen a Hellcat ditch perfectly but the DUKW driver who had got to it as it was sinking told him later the top of the pilot's head was blown off and he had to have been dead before he ever hit the water.

The captain took the binoculars from a case hanging from his shoulder, removed all four lens caps, wiped the lenses with his handkerchief and put the binoculars to his eyes.

"He's bailing out," he said.

Even as the captain spoke Bibb saw a lump emerge from the smoke and flame engulfing the plane. A few seconds later a package rose above the lump and blossomed into a white umbrella. The lump, assuming the shape of a man, swung beneath it. The plane, burning fiercely, began sliding off toward the south. It did not explode until it hit the ground. The pilot drifted down slowly, still swinging beneath the parachute and moving perceptibly toward the fairly level ground between the ridge and the American position. The captain, watching through his binoculars, kept up a running commentary for the men around him.

"Looks like he might come down on the wrong side of the crik," the captain said. "God damn it."

Funny how an educated man like the captain said crik instead of creek, Bibb thought. He remembered how some of the amphib drivers who were from up East made fun of him the first time he called a river a bayou.

"He's pulling on the risers," the captain said excitedly. "He's trying to steer the chute this way. He must have seen our panel marker."

The pilot and the parachute grew larger as they came lower and drifted slowly toward them.

"It's going to be close," the captain said. "Elditch, get a detail ready to run pick him up if he lands on our side."

"He land on the other side, I can get him in my Duck, Captain," Bibb said.

"Good idea," the captain said. "Hold up, Elditch. Get the ammo out of that thing pronto."

He swept the ground on the other side of the stream with his binoculars.

"I see movement," he said. "There's some Jap bastards must be dug in on this side of the ridge. Crap."

Several men had already begun taking crates of 60-mm. shells out of the Duck.

"As you were," the captain said. "It's no use."

"Shit, Captain," Bibb said. "You ain't afraid of them little bitty sons a' bitches is you?"

The captain looked at him.

"It's your ass, Corporal, not mine," he said. "You know what those little bitty sons a' bitches can do?"

"I reckon," said Bibb. "It's about time they seen what the old Ace can do."

The captain gave him another look, this one admiring.

"Come on," the captain said.

He started running toward the DUKW. Bibb followed, passed him, and was over the side and under the wheel while the captain was still trying to clamber over the boatlike gunwale to the passenger seat, swearing. Bibb slid over and pulled him up, thinking he sure does like to cuss.

"Good thing Elditch didn't try tangling with you," the captain said. "You're strong as a bear."

So the captain knew all about his run-in with the sergeant. And hadn't let on. Yes, sir, he liked this stud fine.

"You going to sit there with your head up all day?" the captain snapped. "Get this thing moving, Ace."

Bibb started the engine and threw the Duck in gear. As they bounced toward the stream, the captain clutching the dashboard and swearing, the pilot, doll-size at that distance, hit the ground a couple of hundred feet on the other side and went rolling head over heels. The captain let go of the dashboard to put his binoculars to his eyes, bounding around in the seat.

"You should have safety belts in this thing," he said angrily.

"Captain, sir," Bibb said. "This here's a DUKW an' I'd sure thank you not to call it no thing."

It was something he had never said to Lieutenant Lefko. The captain did not answer.

"There's three, four Japs come out of their holes," he said. "Step on it. I hope that damn mortar's got sense enough to lay some fire on them."

The pilot had stopped rolling. The parachute came loose and went blowing along the ground. The pilot must have cut himself loose to get rid of it that fast. He hobbled toward the stream, favoring one leg. Bibb drove into the water and when he felt the rear wheels stop biting threw the Duck into propeller drive. Behind him, over the noise of the engine, he heard rifle fire, a machine gun and the pop of the mortar. The captain heard it, too.

"That'll give the bastards something to think about," he said.

Japanese mortars began kicking up the surface of the stream. The pilot hopped toward the stream, head down. The captain scrambled over the windshield and onto the bow.

"This way!" he yelled to the pilot.

The front wheels touched bottom and Bibb shifted to truck drive. He took the DUKW up the bank instead of waiting for the pilot to reach them. The captain reached down and pulled the pilot onto the bow of the DUKW, dragging him belly down until he was aboard full length. Bibb heard cheers back on the American side. It made him feel good. The pilot lay face down, exhausted, while Bibb swung the DUKW back toward the stream. The captain was almost thrown off the vehicle by the abrupt maneuver.

"Watch it, you dumb bastard!" the captain shouted.

It did not bother Bibb. He would have said the same thing if the captain was driving and he was hanging onto the front. It did not bother him much to be called bastard, anyway, unless they put black in front of it.

The pilot's arms were outstretched, his gloved fingers spread as if attempting to clutch the smooth surface of the jouncing DUKW's bow. When he lifted his head, his face was only a foot or so from Bibb's. The pilot's expression went from mixed fright and relief to astonishment. Bibb knew there was a surprised look on his own face. The pilot was a Negro. Bibb felt a burst of pride and an instant kinship with him. This fighter pilot, from his insignia a captain just like the infantry company commander, was one of his own people. Bibb grinned at him and gave the thumb's up sign. The pilot smiled back.

The DUKW got back across the stream and behind the command post bunker without being hit. The rescue had started up a brisk little fire fight and no one had run out to meet the DUKW, though several men had stood up in their holes to wave and shout.

"Get that ammo away from the CP," the captain ordered Bibb before sliding from the DUKW and helping the pilot down. "Then get back here."

Bibb thought the bunker offered the best protection around but when a captain said move, you moved. The only decent cover was the depression where the jeep was parked. The depression had been made into a revetment by digging away the sides and mounding the excavated earth around it with a single row of sandbags on top. It apparently had been fashioned originally to hold a tank firing hull down, for it was much larger than necessary for a jeep and Bibb saw tread marks on the dirt ramp leading down into it. Leaving the DUKW engine running he jumped into the revetment and backed the jeep out into the open. Then he ran back to the DUKW and drove it into the vacated place. It was a tight fit and the top protruded but Bibb thought it was still the safest place in the area for his vehicle.

When Bibb got inside the bunker the pilot was propped on his elbow on one of the cots. His left flying boot and sock were off and the leg of his flying suit, slit to the knee, was spread open. The pilot's ankle as swollen. He smiled and pushed himself into a sitting position, holding out his right hand, when Bibb entered.

"I want to thank you for what you did, Corporal," he said. "Captain Tallichet told me it was your idea to come after me. You saved my life."

Something about the way the colored captain talked bothered Bibb. It reminded him of somebody. He thought about who it was while he was shaking the pilot's hand. Damn if the man didn't sound just like Lieutenant Lefko. Like a college boy. When you thought about it, though, there was nothing so funny about that. They weren't about to let no colored stud fly one of their airplanes unless he had himself a college education. Except for his color the captain didn't look too colored. Back home a lot of folks as light as the captain looked down on folks as black as he was. "If you white you right, if you yellow you mellow, if you brown stick aroun', but if you black git back." He remembered a barbecue stand in Houston that catered to whites. When he went there for ribs or hot links he had to come in the back and go outside to eat while white customers sat inside at the counter. Colored folks owned that barbecue stand. Light-colored colored folks.

"Corporal," the white captain said, "give me your full name and serial number. I'm putting you in for the Silver Star."

"You certainly earned it, Corporal," the colored captain said.

Funny how much fancier the colored captain talked than the white captain. Like they'd got their color mixed up. He purely did sound like Lieutenant Lefko except that he talked more like an officer was supposed to than Lieutenant Lefko did.

"It really wasn't nothin'," Bibb said. "That old Duck of mine is what did it."

"It's a handy vehicle to have around, I'll say that," the white captain said. "Some dark night you ought to steal it and put in with my company," he added, half seriously. "I'd see you didn't get in any real trouble. Might even find a way to get you another stripe."

"Yessir," said Bibb. "Only they takes your stripes when they throw you in the stockade."

The white captain laughed. The colored captain, his face set against the pain in his ankle, smiled faintly, looking as if he did not really want to. Bibb gave the company commander his name, unit and serial number. The captain wrote it down.

"You want a copy, too, Captain George?" he asked. "So you'll know who it was kept the Japs from grabbing you?"

Bibb was shocked and disillusioned. This stud he thought was so fine was calling the colored captain by his first name the way white folks back home called all colored folks. But the colored captain didn't seem to mind. There was something funny about that.

"I was on the verge of asking just that," the colored captain said. "And I've been remiss about giving the corporal my own name. Corporal Bibb, I'm Captain Clarence George."

"Yessir," Bibb said, relieved to learn the captain had not been talking down to the pilot and feeling a little strange about sirring another colored man.

He was mad at himself for feeling that way. Captain George was an officer just like any other officer and more important than most because he knew how to fly an airplane. And look how easy he was around that white captain, just like he belonged more with that white captain than with a plain old nigger like Aaron Bibb.

"Soon as we get the rest of the ammo off the Duck, Bibb will take you to get your leg attended to," the white captain said.

He went outside. Bibb looked at Captain George, hoping to strike up a conversation. The captain wasn't paying him any mind. He was bending over his swollen ankle, prodding it gingerly.

"Bibb!" Captain Tallichet's voice yelled from outside. "Get your butt out here!"

He sounded mad. Bibb wondered why. He ran outside. The captain was standing with his hands on his hips, glaring at his jeep. His face was red. There was a big hole in the jeep's radiator and the ground beneath it was puddled with the water that had run out.

"Did you move my jeep, Bibb?" the captain roared, his voice strangled with rage.

Oh, oh, Bibb thought, that is one mad captain.

The fire fight had stopped and several men were standing around. They were all grinning but kept their faces turned away from the captain so he would not see it. Bibb knew he would have been grinning, too, if the monkey was on somebody else's back.

"Yessir," he said meekly. "You told me to get the ammo away from the CP and that was the onliest place I knowed of, without leavin' it out maybe to get blowed up."

"I suppose better my jeep than a load of sixty millimeter," the captain said grudgingly. "What are all you men hanging around for? Get back to whatever you're supposed to be doing. And if you're not doing anything I can damn sure find you something."

The men scattered quickly and Bibb followed the captain back into the bunker.

"You know what this fool corporal did?" the captain said to the bunker at large. "Moved my jeep out of its revetment and got it all shot up."

"It's jess the radiator, Captain," Bibb said. "I bet I could find you one and bring it back tonight if the dispatcher says I can."

"Japs infiltrate the area after dark," the captain said.

"Ain't no Jap can see me at night," Bibb said.

The captain and everyone else in the bunker except Captain George laughed. Captain George looked peeved. Thinks I'm catering, Bibb thought. He's so high-toned he doesn't know the difference between catering and funning. If Captain Tallichet was the kind of officer you had to suck up to he wouldn't have made that kind of a joke. Captain George couldn't see that, he must be as simpleminded as Lieutenant Lefko.

"You come back here, I might not let you go," Captain Tallichet said. "I could use you and that Duck."

"I wouldn't mind that none," Bibb replied. "Long's they didn't get me down for AWOL."

"I think I could figure something out," Captain Tallichet said.

He was serious.

Captain George cleared his throat.

"My ankle's starting to throb pretty severely," he said. "And I should be getting in touch with base to let them know what happened to me."

"I'm sorry, Captain," Captain Tallichet said. "I've been so busy scheming to steal myself a Duck. Corporal, you really think you can get back here with a radiator after you drop the captain off?"

"Yessir, if you can stop 'em from getting me down for AWOL like you said, Captain."

Bibb noticed the captain had not once called him Ace since they picked up Captain George. The captain must think that colored captain was as high-toned as he did.

"You can count on it," the captain said.

He gave Bibb Captain George's sock and flying boot and helped Captain George out to the DUKW. Captain George eased himself over the sandbags and into the vehicle. A disapproving look crossed his face as he stepped down. Bibb knew he had noticed the Ace of Spades insignia for the first time. That stud was acting more like Lieutenant Lefko every minute. Bibb backed the DUKW out of the hole.

"Good luck, Captain," Captain Tallichet said.

"Thanks for everything, Captain Tallichet," Captain George said.

Bibb headed the DUKW toward the road and looked back. The captain and several others were waving. He waved back and gunned the DUKW to give them a little show. Captain George bit off a groan. The jolting hurt his ankle. Bibb slowed down and picked his route more carefully.

They had been on the road several minutes and the captain had not said anything. Bibb found the silence awkward but did not break it. Colored or not, the captain was a captain and he was just a corporal. He started singing softly to himself, "Key to the World." The Little Son Joe record had been one of his favorites on the jukeboxes back in Houston, long with "44 Blues." He looked at the captain out of the corner of his eye. The captain was listening and looked as if he liked it.

"You likes the blues, Captain?" Bibb asked.

The captain stiffened, as if he had been caught doing something he wasn't supposed to.

"No," he said sharply.

After a while, as if trying to make up for the way he had acted, he said, "Where are you from, Corporal?"

"Houston," Bibb replied. "Where is you from, Captain? Chicago?"

"Chicago?" the captain said. "What made you think that?"

"You talks like an officer I know from Chicago."

The captain laughed.

"That's the first time I've ever been accused of having a Chicago accent," he said. "As a matter of fact I'm from St. Louis, Missouri."

Bibb started to explain it was not the accent he was talking about but decided against it. He might say something that peeved the captain. He felt as uncomfortable with Captain George as he had with Lieutenant Lefko when the lieutenant was explaining to him how he ought to act. Next thing you know, this captain was going to want to drive, just like the lieutenant, except he couldn't because of his ankle. No, he thought, this captain wasn't about to want to drive no Duck. That was nigger duty. He bet if you put a plate of snouts and rice in front of the captain he'd say no thank you if he was starving. Now Lieutenant Lefko, if you did that he'd eat it and say it was the best cuisine he ever ate even if he hated it.

"You married, Corporal?" the captain said.

"Yessir."

It was easy sirring the captain now. He wasn't much different from any other officer, just a little darker.

"Any children?"

"I got me a pretty little girl. Rebecca. She pretty as Ernestine. That's my woman."

Captain George got that Lieutenant Lefko look on his face.

"You mean your wife?" he said.

"Yessir," Bibb answered, puzzled. "That's what I said."

"You said your woman," Captain George said. "That has an entirely different connotation. And not a flattering one. That's just one of the little things that reflect on our people."

Well, Bibb thought, that's the first time you let on you was a nigger.

"In the Army, we have a first-rate opportunity to correct the false impressions some people have," the captain said.

If I was to close my eyes, I'd swear it was the lieutenant sitting over there in that seat, Bibb thought.

"And it behooves all of us, regardless of rank, to take full advantage of that opportunity," the captain was saying.

Behooves my black ass, Bibb thought.

"Yessir," he said.

"About that emblem on this vehicle," the captain said.

Oh, Jesus, he was fixing to start up on that just like the lieutenant. What I'm going to do, Bibb thought, is carry him straight to the field hospital where they carried the lieutenant instead of back to the aid station at the Miyazaki air strip where he'd want to go if he knew it was there. If the lieutenant ain't too messed up to talk, and if the lieutenant is too messed up to talk he's the same as dead, they're going to get along just fine. They can sit up all night talking about equality and the Japanese cuisine.

"What are you grinning for?" the captain demanded. "I don't find that emblem a bit amusing. And you shouldn't, either."

"Oh, it ain't account of my 'signia, Captain, sir," said Bibb. "I jess thought of somethin' funny."

"Well," the captain said, sounding as if his feelings were hurt, just like the lieutenant did sometimes, "if everything I've said has fallen on deaf ears . . ."

Bibb did not answer. The captain leaned back against his side of the DUKW and busied himself with his own thoughts. As did Bibb. I might really try to find a jeep radiator and go back and throw in with that Captain Tallichet, he thought. He knows how to treat a man. And maybe I'll get me a chance to have a little fun with that trashy sergeant.

10

[Lieutenant Colonel Shohei Tochizawa]

Lieutenant Colonel Shohei Tochizawa, battalion commander, had slept but three hours in the past thirty-six. Except for a ten-hour stretch the previous week, closer to unconsciousness than slumber, and a few grudging minutes snatched now and again, that had been his average for more than a week. He was napping now, oblivious to the uninterrupted sound of urgent conversation and movement of messengers in and out of the command post deep within the hill and to the muffled impact of incoming shells. He had been asleep only ten minutes when he was wakened by something more subtle than the familiar bustle of the command post, a silent presence beside his cot. Colonel Tochizawa came awake slowly, the sounds and movements about him seeming to grow louder and busier as they impinged themselves more firmly on his consciousness. This growing lag between sleep and full awareness was a matter of some concern to him and one of the reasons he slept as little as possible. One circumstance fed on the other. The longer it took to come awake the less sleep he permitted himself. The less he slept, the greater the lag. For eighteen years, since his first days at the Military Academy in Tokyo, he had possessed the faculty of coming fully awake in the fragment of time it took to open his eyes. Now exhaustion had robbed him of it in less than two weeks. Fortunately any change in his immediate surroundings could still drag him from slumber, however slowly.

His orderly was standing patiently beside the cot, a tray in his hands.

"I apologize for waking you, Honorable Battalion Commander," the orderly said.

He said it matter-of-factly. He had served Colonel Tochizawa for more than a year.

"Do not concern yourself, Imamura," said the colonel. "I have slept long enough."

He did not, however, know how long he had been sleeping. He looked at his watch and saw it had been only a few minutes. This pleased him. It still troubled him that a week ago, for a period of ten hours, the battalion had been obliged to function without his direction. He swung his legs heavily over the side of the cot. He felt as if his bones had been replaced with lead. When he was a younger man his legs had felt so after marching day and night, but regained their resiliency after a few hours. Now they always felt as if he had been marching without respite.

"I have brought some lunch, Honorable Battalion Commander," the orderly said.

Colonel Tochizawa took the tray on his lap, his ears tuned to the curt orders and scraps of conversation about him. There was tea on the tray, a mixture of rice and millet of the sort eaten by the poorest peasants and, miraculously, a bowl of hot bean-paste soup. The colonel drank deeply of it and felt strength flow from his stomach to his limbs.

"Tell me, Imamura, how did you manage this?" he asked.

"The quartermaster found a little miso in his stocks," said Imamura. "I fear the Honorable Battalion Commander has found it spoiled and unpleasant to taste."

His expression of delight at the colonel's approval belied his words. He had cooked the miso soup himself in the underground kitchen, where the kettle hung over a wood fire vented through a slanted tunnel loosely filled with dried grass to trap the telltale smoke.

"It is truly delicious," the colonel said. "It puts strength in me."

Colonel Tochizawa had an unpleasant feeling there had been an abrupt change in the situation while he slept. He always felt this way after awakening from a nap, no matter how short it might have been. But confidence in his troops and long experience told him this could not be so. If the Americans had made a penetration anywhere, Major Goto, his executive officer, would have awakened him immediately. And the level of activity in the underground command post was no higher than when he had laid himself down on the cot.

The Tochizawa Battalion's complex of fortified positions in the third, and main, line of defense lay inland north of Hishida, only a little more than two miles from the Ariake beaches and within easy range of American naval batteries. The battalion had been subjected to continuous bombardment from the sea and air since the first days of the invasion. For a week now it had been pounded also by enemy field artillery, tanks and self-propelled guns. The battalion's western flank was protected by the Hishida River, which the enemy had made only desultory attempts to force. The outposts and antitank parties to the south and east had been overrun and for four days American tanks and infantry had been nibbling away at the main defenses. Despite this, the Tochizawa Battalion continued to function as a cohesive fighting unit.

Three miles to the southeast Shibushi had fallen. At Tohriyama cliff, west of Shibushi and a mile and a half south of the battalion, the battalion's Masuda Company, manning the second line of defense positions blocking the approach to the abandoned Shibushi Naval Airfield, had been wiped out to a man. A soldier, who had escaped the slaughter and made his way back through the tunnel connecting the Masuda Company with the battalion's main positions, had been executed at Tochizawa's order for disobeying the strict command passed down from Imperial General Headquarters through every echelon that no one was to abandon his post under any circumstances. Thereafter the colonel had ordered his troops to fire on anyone, American or Japanese, approaching the Tochizawa Battalion's positions from its front or flanks, accepting only the survivors of the battalion's own nightly raiding parties. It had taken the colonel much thought to reach the decision to except his own skirmishers since, difficult as it was for him to accept, it was possible that even among his own men there might be one so lacking in Japanese spirit that he would return from a raid without having accomplished his mission.

Colonel Tochizawa thought of his battalion as a great rock in an angry sea against which the waves dashed themselves futilely and which sheltered all behind it. The Americans had overwhelmed the first line of defense on the beaches, ground through the second line, and on either side of his battalion driven deep into the main line of defense. But, though their engineers were improving Shibushi Naval Airfield within view of the naked eye, the Americans had bloodied themselves with repeated assaults and littered the broad fields south of his positions with the hulks of their Shermans without piercing his fortifications. And, a mile behind the bastion of the Tochizawa Battalion, the division command post remained inviolate.

Had the achievements of his battalion been a true measure of the tide of battle the colonel would have looked forward to his inevitable death with serenity. The rules which had always governed him were simple, and as much a preparation for death as a way of life. The code of Bushido declared that "a samurai lives in such a way that he will always be prepared to die," and the principle of Bushido was "the way to die at the right moment in the right place and for the right purpose." The Imperial Rescript to Soldiers and Sailors said, "Be resolved that duty is heavier than a mountain, while death is lighter than a feather." But, though he believed his death would be as pure as a cherry blossom floating to the ground, it angered him that it would be in a lost cause when, if everyone had displayed proper spirit, Japanese determination would have been more than a match for American technology. Those who had not succeeded in holding the enemy at bay had failed not because the Americans had too many guns, tanks and planes but because they did not have enough Japanese spirit. He felt a personal sense of betrayal in that failure and, worse, that it had caused him to give false encouragement to Kuniyoshi, his fourteen-year-old son.

Before all except radio communications with the north had broken down he had written his son often, always stressing two things. One, of course, Kuniyoshi already felt in the marrow of his bones, for he was a worthy son of a Tochizawa. Should he be given the opportunity to die for his Emperor he should do so joyfully. Yoshi had, in fact, months ago written that he was a member of his middle school Volunteer Combat Team and hoped the Americans would attempt to storm the Kanto plains as well as southern Kyushu so he would get his chance to fight them. The other thing which the colonel always stressed because Tokyo, where his son was, was filled with cowards and traitors, was that should the Americans carry out their anticipated foolhardy plan to come ashore at Ariake Bay, they would be dealt a bloody defeat such as the world had never seen. Yoshi had written him in fury that some of those to whom he had related his father's words had mocked him. "Honored father," he wrote, "if I were not saving all my strength to fight the Americans I could have killed them." Of all his son's letters the colonel treasured this one the most and always carried it on his person. When he reread the letter, as he often did, his bitterness at having been a poor prophet was somewhat allayed by the knowledge Yoshi must surely know that the Army's failure had not been his father's.

Tochizawa felt as much betrayed by the high command as by those who had permitted the Americans to take their positions. Had he not been assured that if he could prevent the Americans from breaking through for only eleven days after the landings, massive reinforcements moving down from the north would counterattack and drive them into the sea? The Tochizawa Battalion had held the Americans at bay for more than eleven days yet the great counterattack had never come. The 25th Division had marched thirty-five miles from Kobayashi and the 216th Division more than twice that distance from Kumamoto City. What was left of them and the thin-skinned Chi-He medium tanks of the 6th Independent Tank Brigade after running the gauntlet of American planes had streamed past the battalion and been thrown piecemeal into the battle. They had slowed the Americans to a snail's crawl but had not pushed them into the sea. Yet when the radio was functioning and the infuriatingly incompetent cipher clerk succeeded in performing his duty the colonel continued to receive messages that the Mutsu Plan was going as expected and in a few days the forces assembling in the Kirishimas would strike the decisive blow. The colonel had observed the Americans' growing strength and knew the opportunity for a decisive battle had been lost.

There were times when Colonel Tochizawa wished he were a simple soldier like his orderly Imamura, who believed the optimistic nonsense of his superiors and daily awaited the miracle which would drive the Americans from the sacred soil of Japan. Nevertheless, he was not completely without hope. There were those in high places who had foreseen the Americans could not be driven back into the sea but believed they might lose heart if final victory proved too costly. The Americans' limited successes thus far had indeed proved very costly. They might still lose spirit and accept the reasonable demands of War Minister Anami for an honorable peace. The colonel believed it an honorable peace only because it was said the war minister and Army Chief of Staff Umezu were willing to end the war without a clear-cut Japanese victory if the Americans agreed to certain conditions. For himself, he would prefer that he and all Japanese perish.

To Tochizawa, anything short of victory was defeat. There was nothing in between. And had not General Anami himself been reported in Tokyo to have said that a hundred million Japanese would gladly prefer death to the dishonor of surrender and would thus leave the Japanese people's mark on history? Not since the great victories in the Philippines early in the Pacific war had the colonel been so proud of being Japanese as when he learned what the war minister had said. The fact that such resistance meant Yoshi would not grow to manhood concerned him somewhat but his concern was outweighed by his pride as a father and a soldier. Yoshi, though only a boy in years, was no stranger to the code of Bushido and was already a man in his sense of duty. If he died for the Emperor he would do so gladly and gloriously and it would be a far better thing that he join the ancient heroes at Yasukuni Shrine at such a tender age than live out his years a slave to foreign conquerors.

The way Yoshi had turned out bolstered the colonel's conviction that the gods looked with favor on the strong and brave even though at times it might not seem so. It had been such a time six years ago when Yoshi's mother died. In his grief Colonel Tochizawa had thought heaven was not on his side, that the gods were against him. But in the months during which the war began going badly for Japan he had come to understand that his wife's death had precisely the opposite significance. Had she lived to influence Yoshi with her meekness and irresolution the boy might not have grown into so worthy a soldier's son. She had fainted when Yoshi was brought home with a broken arm at six years of age and later, while the arm was being set, she had wailed and raised her voice against him, her husband, for the first and only time when he stood beside Yoshi with his riding crop and promised him a beating if he cried out in pain. When she died less than three years later he should have understood it was a sign she was not a proper wife and mother to descendants of samurai despite her beauty and goodness. And yet there had been times, even in the past crowded weeks, that he missed her.

Shohei Tochizawa had married at twenty-two, young for a penniless Army officer. He had graduated from the Military Academy in 1931 with the 43rd Class only a year earlier. He was the second oldest son in a large family, son of the improvident owner of a tiny coal-mining property in Shikoku's Tokushima Prefecture, and hoped to restore luster to the family name, though not necessarily mend its fortunes, through a brilliant career in the Army. His grandfather was a samurai who as a young man had fought against the Tokugawa Shogunate. His warrior grandfather had been pensioned off after the Shogunate was overthrown and the Emperor Meiji made preeminent. The family had declined thereafter.

The disadvantages of an early marriage to a young man whose sole concern was to perfect himself in his profession were overbalanced by the advantages of this particular union. Tochizawa's record at the Military Academy had been only average and he had not attracted attention. The girl's father, though but a minor contractor of military supplies, was well-to-do and had fairly good connections in the Army's middle echelons. And he was just as anxious for Tochizawa to rise in the service as Tochizawa himself. Despite his father-in-law's supposed influence, Tochizawa's rise in the service had been hardly meteoric. He seemed never to be in the right place at the right time for recognition and advancement. In Manchuria and later in Burma he achieved a reputation of sorts for his bravery and an ability to instill his men with his own steely determination but he lacked the kind of brilliance and imagination which might have set him more clearly above his contemporaries. As company commander and then battalion executive officer in Burma, however, his qualities had been sufficient to earmark him for the command of a battalion. Before the prospect materialized he contracted typhus and was shipped back to Japan for convalescence.

His humiliation at having been so physically imperfect as to fall ill was no less than his disappointment at failing to get a battalion of his own. The fact that it meant being reunited with his son did not compensate for the misfortune. He would not even permit Yoshi to visit him in the military hospital because he thought it a disservice to the boy to allow him to see an officer of the Imperial Army and his own father in such a state. Even later in his convalescence, when he went to live in the home of his father-in-law, he did not allow Yoshi to enter his presence freely until he had regained his strength.

After his recovery he was to his disappointment assigned to a minor staff position in the War Ministry at Ichigaya Heights in Tokyo instead of a command in the field. He had neither the mind nor the inclination for staff work and his disposition grew bitter as his career languished. In March of 1944 he fell out with his father-in-law when the older man was frightened by the American fire raids and wanted to remove the household, including Yoshi, from Tokyo to a safer place in the country. It ended with Tochizawa calling his father-in-law a coward and defeatist and sending Yoshi to live elsewhere in Tokyo with the family of a fellow officer. The boy made his father very proud of him by indignantly refusing his grandfather's pleas and declaring he could not survive the disgrace of running away from danger if, indeed, there actually was any danger. The two grew even closer together once Yoshi was free of his grandfather's decadent influence. Tochizawa had not realized before that his father-in-law had the same weaknesses as his daughter, Yoshi's dead mother.

Tochizawa's faith in human nature had been shaken again in July when the great leader, General Hideki Tojo, was stripped of his power and replaced by men less resolute in marching toward the final victory. A few weeks later, when he was posted to Kyushu to take part in the formation of a new division, the 186th Infantry, instead of an active theater, he thought it but another dead end even though he received a long-delayed promotion to lieutenant colonel and was given a battalion. The quality of his troops and the shortage of weapons for them, even rifles, did nothing to change his opinion. The bulk of the men were raw conscripts, farm boys, clerks, students, small merchants and laborers. Many were under eighteen or over thirty. Few of those in between, who should have been in the prime years of their young manhood, were actually koshu gokaku, Class A physical specimens. Such men were greatly outnumbered by the heishu, the lowest acceptable category, and Tochizawa suspected many of the latter would have been rejected out of hand for military service in less desperate times. As for weapons, at first there was but one rifle for every six men and none of the rifle squads had the light machine gun in the Table of Equipment.

The machine gun company had less than a quarter of its guns and the artillery platoon had a promise of one 70-mm. cannon. The battalion had a single truck, which broke down regularly, and only half its 90 horses.

The horses provided Tochizawa with the one bright spot in an otherwise bleak situation. They were farm animals requisitioned from the local peasants but among them was a gray stallion which obviously had been the property of someone of means. Normally such a fine animal would have been taken for his own use by some high-ranking officer long before it could have been passed down to battalion level for use as a draft animal. The stallion, however, was gaunt, with lackluster, crusted eyes, obviously sick. Despite its appearance Tochizawa recognized it as an exceptional beast. In his days at the Military Academy he had developed a passion for riding. For a while in Manchuria, when he was a lieutenant, he had owned a fine horse bought with money brought to him by his marriage. Instead of berating the quartermaster for having fobbed off so obviously unfit an animal on his battalion the colonel went looking among his men for someone with a knowledge of horses. He found such a man, a thirty-seven-year-old first year soldier who until recently had been employed by a prosperous farmer with a number of horses. The conscript had worked with horses the year around and in the spring, summer and autumn had assisted the veterinarian when he came for chizashi, the regular treatment given the stock three times yearly. The conscript looked at the gray stallion's hooves and gums and saw it had not had chizashi in a long while. He built an open framework of construction timbers and secured the stallion within it with ropes. When this was done he heated a stone, wrapped it in a piece of blanket and rubbed the horse all over with it. Then, while Tochizawa watched with keen interest, he bled the drooping animal from a cut in its gums and another in its rump. There was no visible improvement. The colonel began angrily to describe the kind of punishment meted out in his battalion to liars and incompetents.

The terrified soldier fell to his knees in unmilitary fashion and explained this was only the first part of the proposed cure. He begged permission to search the surrounding fields and hills for healing plants and to seek out a kitoshi, a healing priest, to make the necessary prayers. Tochizawa had faith in a peasant's knowledge of healing plants but not in the healing power of prayer; had not prayer failed him utterly when typhus struck him down in Burma? Nevertheless he granted both requests and gave the soldier the handful of rice he said he must have for the kitoshi. The power of some prayers was strengthened by fasting, the soldier said quite seriously, but this particular kitoshi was known to pray better on a full stomach. Two or three officers who had been amusing themselves watching the soldier's bizarre attentions to the stallion burst out laughing at that. Tochizawa silenced them with a few stern words and sent them away to put their time to better use. He did not do so to protect the soldier from their ridicule but simply because he thought their laughter indicated an unbecoming frivolous nature. Colonel Tochizawa was not noted for his sense of humor.

Whether due to the leaves and grasses the soldier mixed with the stallion's doubled allowance of fodder or, as the soldier insisted, a combination of this and the kitoshi's prayer, the stallion's health improved remarkably. Within three weeks it was sleek and spirited, altogether a different animal. Tochizawa would have named the stallion Uranus after the famous jumper on which Baron Nishi won the gold medal at the 1932 Olympic Games in Los Angeles, California, had he not considered it unfitting to give his horse a foreign name at such a time in history. Instead he named it Gekko, "Moonbeam," because of its color. The horse's gray coat had taken on a silvery sheen.

The colonel relieved the soldier, whose name was Nishihara, of all his squad duties except military training and made him Gekko's groom. Nishihara slept in Gekko's stable behind the colonel's billet instead of with his squad. Every night he rubbed the stallion down with handfuls of rice straw. Tochizawa himself gave the stallion its fodder when he was not too occupied with battalion affairs. He did not wish Gekko to become too attached to Nishihara. Tochizawa rode Gekko everywhere except when senior officers from higher headquarters were in the battalion area. Because it was Army property he felt he would be obliged to surrender the horse if a superior were to compliment him on his mount. Had he purchased the stallion privately their possible envy would not have concerned him.

For the next few months Tochizawa devoted himself single-mindedly to making soldiers of his men and competing with the other battalion commanders of the regiment for scarce equipment, his only diversions Gekko and correspondence with his son. Within the limits of his authority he expanded and enhanced the division's stringent training program. If the companies of other battalions made a twenty-four-hour training march without sleep, the companies of the Tochizawa Battalion marched for thirty hours. Soldiers without weapons customarily performed rifle drill with wooden sticks. Tochizawa's men also performed rifle drill with wooden sticks but within the squads in addition they performed rifle drill with borrowed weapons after normal duty hours. It was traditional in the Army that the rifle was the soul of the infantryman. Tochizawa did not believe it possible to impress this on an ignorant conscript if he had never had a real rifle in his hand. On the arduous marches he rode among his men on Gekko, going without sleep as they did and often dismounting to walk with them. It became a joke in the division that "If you see a soldier who can only sleep comfortably with one eye open and while climbing a hill, he surely is a soldier of the Tochizawa Battalion."

It was Tochizawa's conviction that the only indispensable ingredient of victory was Japanese spirit. If there were no weapons they would somehow appear when needed. If a Japanese had breath in his body, no matter how inadequate that body, an infusion of the warrior spirit would make him stronger than ten enemies. He was determined that no man in his battalion would lack the indispensable ingredient. Not all the officers in the south shared the colonel's zeal. Like Tochizawa, many of them felt they had been shuffled off to a backwater of the war, that their careers were languishing while others no more worthy were winning glory and immortality in desperate battle with the enemy. Unlike Tochizawa, some of them performed their duties only perfunctorily because of it. The colonel observed this and was not hesitant about commenting on it. In consequence he had few friends. If he had noticed this, which he did not, it would have been a matter of no concern to him. His battalion occupied him fully.

Beginning with the American invasion of the Philippines in October, Tochizawa knew several months of great frustration. Japan had been given the opportunity to smash the enemy and he was forced to stand idly by thousands of miles away. When would the division receive its call to join the battle and help change the course of the war? His frustration reached its peak in November when Japan's premier declared to the nation that Leyte was the nation's second Tennozan, after a battle fought four hundred years before in which the samurai Hideyoshi won the victory leading to his control of all Japan. If this were so, he would be cheated of a share in the war's decisive battle. When Leyte fell, and after that all the Philippines, Tochizawa was perversely gratified. He might yet get his chance. It was not until April and the invasion of Okinawa that he understood the battle might be fought in the homeland, that his battalion would not be sent off to meet the Americans but would fight them on the soil of Kyushu. Like his wife's death, his assignment to a backwater of the war had been a blessing in disguise.

He learned of the plan called Ketsu-Go in May and his men entered into preparation for the decisive confrontation. A general with the same name as Gekko's groom, Nishihara, was given command of the 57th Army, of which the Tochizawa Battalion was a part. The colonel's staff joked about it until Tochizawa ordered them to desist. He thought the coincidence interesting but in no way amusing. And to make a joke of any kind about the name Nishihara was to insult the commanding general. Tochizawa's officers quickly learned not even to say "First Year Soldier

Nishihara" in the colonel's presence and if they slipped and did so most certainly not to smile.

The 16th Area Army's new chief of staff, Lieutenant General Masazumi Inada, came down from headquarters in Fukuoka in northern Kyushu to take charge of defense preparations. He was a man after Tochizawa's own heart, brimming with Japanese spirit. The colonel saw him more than once passing through on quick inspection trips, missing nothing, and was pleased that the sharp-tongued general found little to criticize in the performance of the Tochizawa Battalion. He had heard tales of Inada's scathing comments and ruthless actions where things were not to his liking.

Life was again exciting for Tochizawa and deeply satisfying. Civilians labored alongside his troops as the battalion's underground positions took form. In June, the Ketsu-Go Transportation operation brought stockpiles of ammunition, fuel and rations, and his battalion was at last fully equipped with weapons. Despite that month's heavy rains the digging and building continued without pause. In July a great personal loss marred Tochizawa's happiness. Nishihara was slow in getting Gekko to shelter during a bombing attack and the stallion was killed. Although the colonel had not struck a soldier since his days as a lieutenant in Manchuria, he beat Nishihara into insensibility. In great sorrow he wrote Kuniyoshi of Gekko's death. The boy had asked news of the stallion in every letter. Tochizawa overcame his grief with work, heartened by a letter from his son. The boy brought honor to his father by the fortitude with which he accepted Gekko's death.

"If it is permissible for an animal to enter Yasukuni," Yoshi wrote, "Gekko is waiting impatiently there for you and if I am fortunate enough to earn a glorious death I will see at last the two of you together. This is something of which I have thought many times since first you wrote me of Gekko but which I have not dared hope until now."

When the Soviet Union invaded Manchuria in August, Tochizawa was more indignant than shocked and no less confident that Japan would somehow confound her enemies. It was just what one would expect of the Russians, he thought—waiting until they believed Japan was on her knees before risking an encounter. They would learn, as would America and the rest of the world, that Japanese soldiers fought hardest when the outlook was bleakest.

By September the positions were completed. The Tochizawa Battalion's maze of interconnected fortifications covered a roughly kidney-shaped area a mile and a half broad and a mile deep. It was an "all-around" position, prepared to repel attacks from any direction. There was some level ground within the perimeter but most of the positions were dug into the hills, some commanding the approaches from the sea and others on slopes facing away from the coast. Key hills were honeycombed with caves and tunnels. Some of the caves were several stories high with openings at various levels. Every cave and every underground position had one or more concealed exits, not for escape but to enable the defenders to launch surprise attacks on the enemy's flanks and rear. All of Tochizawa's artillery pieces had two or more firing ports connected by corridors piercing the hills. The cannon could be wheeled from one port to another within the hills. Ammunition was stockpiled in chambers near each port and more could be brought in over concealed paths or through tunnels connecting with underground dumps. Some of the gunports were situated so that the shells fired on the beaches would just clear intervening hills and appear to have come from them rather than the Tochizawa fortifications. The troops lived underground in caves and tunnels accessible by systems of tunnels and ladders. Food, ammunition, medical stores, the dispensary and cooking facilities were also underground. The battalion electrical generator was concealed in a cavern twenty feet wide and thirty feet high. There was ample water from the Hishida River but Tochizawa had wells dug within the perimeter so that his battalion would not be dependent on it.

In mid-September, after a high-level survey of the Ariake defenses, regiment gave the battalion another infantry company, bringing battalion strength within the main perimeter to the standard three infantry companies in addition to the company deployed a mile and half to the south in the high ground immediately south of the unused Shibushi Naval Airfield. There was also a machine gun company and an artillery platoon within the main perimeter. Tochizawa had more than a thousand men in his main positions armed with rifles, machine guns, grenade launchers, mortars, four 47-mm. antitank guns, four 37-mm. antitank guns and four 70-mm. cannon. There were an additional three 75-mm. guns from division artillery. Each of the infantry companies had its own tightly integrated set of defenses and a detachment from the machine gun company. Within each company the three infantry platoons had their own integrated positions. The companies were linked to battalion headquarters by field telephone and the platoons to company headquarters by radio. Within the platoons, squads communicated by runners and bamboo voice tubes. Around the battalion's main defenses were ranged tank traps, antitank defenses and a series of outposts. When the attack began, these outposts would be manned by riflemen and antitank parties abundantly equipped with explosive charges. The outposts ranged from fairly elaborate positions in which a squad could survive for days without emerging, to holes in which a single demolition man could wait in ambush.

Tochizawa's headquarters and command post was in the heart of the battalion position, dug into a hill dominating the area. It was on three levels, the highest containing an observation post near the crest. Here Tochizawa had made lavish use of the limited amount of concrete allotted his battalion. None of the concrete work was visible from outside the observation post.

A number of dummy gun and troop positions were constructed at points of little tactical value and only partially concealed. These were attacked regularly by American bombers and fighters. Tochizawa was gratified by the accuracy of the attackers.

The command post, the companies, the platoons, the gun emplacements and the outpost positions were linked by tunnels and crawl holes deep enough to be impervious to the heaviest bombs and shells. Some of the tunnels, and all those leading to the artillery positions, were large enough to admit a horse-drawn wagon.

Tochizawa's men did not find themselves with time on their hands when the major work of digging the positions, the tank ditches and the thousands of yards of tunnels was completed. There could be but little activity above ground during the daylight hours because of constant enemy surveillance but Tochizawa kept his men busy enlarging and improving the fortifications. At night and in bad weather, when cloud cover hid the ground from enemy observation, Tochizawa drilled his men in close-combat tactics, ambushes, surprise attacks and the destruction of tanks with explosive charges carried in the hands or at the end of bamboo poles. Everyone, including Tochizawa himself, did strenuous calisthenics so that their muscles would not grow weak and their reflexes slow from the frequent long periods of confinement underground. Individual units were regularly required to man their positions around the clock for three or four days at a time to simulate siege conditions. At other times they were required to go without food, water and sleep for twenty-four hours and then were led through a defense exercise against an all-out frontal attack by the enemy. It was said throughout the division that all the men of the Tochizawa Battalion prayed that the assault on the Ariake front would come quickly because anything the enemy might hurl against them would be easier to endure than Colonel Tochizawa's training program.

It remained Tochizawa's conviction that spirit was even more important in achieving victory than guns and fortifications. Because of this, and because opportunities for battalion-strength military drills and maneuvers were limited, he stressed the spiritual training of his troops. His noncommissioned officers tested the men frequently on their knowledge of the Imperial Rescript to Soldiers and Sailors and his officers instructed them in the code of Bushido and filled them with tales of Japan's ancient heroes. Tochizawa himself spoke of these things to groups as small as a squad of riflemen to impress them with the importance of Gunjin Seishin, warrior spirit. The colonel liked his troops to sing martial and patriotic songs. He believed it a measure of their spirit that they could sing even while enduring the most arduous training without food or sleep. His favorite was a song that went: "The infantryman's color is the color of the cherry blossom. Look, the cherry blossoms fall on the hills of Yoshino." When he heard his men singing it he did not regret having been commissioned in the infantry instead of the cavalry so long ago.

The great typhoon of October flooded or washed out fully a quarter of the Tochizawa's Battalion's fortifications, ruined some of its food and medical stores, and disrupted communications with higher headquarters. As soon as the rain and winds began abating, Tochizawa had his men out repairing the damage. When word came over the radio from Tokyo that the typhoon had smashed the American invasion fleet at Okinawa he felt cheated. He wanted to see the enemy routed not by a Divine Wind but by Japanese spirit and he wanted to play a significant personal role in the victory. The fortunes of war had thus far denied him the opportunity to fight Japan's greatest foe, the Americans, and the lack had grown more galling with every unopposed attack on the homeland.

After the initial impact of the reports from Tokyo dissipated itself he realized the announcements were intended to encourage the masses. His common sense and military experience told him no typhoon could smash a modern and widely dispersed armada as the kamikaze had done to the fleet of Kublai Khan almost seven centuries ago. The kamikaze which would defeat the Americans must emanate from the soul of the Japanese people. He issued orders forbidding his men to speak of an American debacle and exhorting them to prepare for the coming decisive battle with even greater vigor than before. Under his relentless bullying, fortifications that had taken months to construct were rebuilt in weeks. When the Americans came ashore on November 12 the ravages of the typhoon had been completely erased.

His troops remained underground during the steady bombardment of the following days and suffered relatively few casualties. The division and battalion artillery joined in the attack on the landing areas. When one of Tochizawa's 70-mm. guns was knocked out, acting without specific orders he had the three remaining cannon drawn back deep within their caves to save them for the time when the Americans posed a more immediate threat to his position.

The colonel made regular personal inspections of his outposts to inspire the troops with his presence.

"Yours will be the honor of being the first in the main line of defense to engage the enemy," he told them. "If any man fails to take ten of the enemy with him in death he will have failed the Emperor. It is unnecessary to inform you that you should consider your position your grave, but let no man give his life foolishly or for mere glory."

One of the outposts was manned by a raiding party comprising members of the squad which included Private Nishihara, Gekko's derelict groom. Tochizawa punished Nishihara by sending him back to a less exposed position. Gekko's murderer would be denied the honor of drawing the first American blood.

Tochizawa made his way to the outposts above ground, disdaining the cramped safety of the tunnels connecting them with the main defenses. He longed for Gekko. Had the stallion lived he would have made his inspection tours on horseback. Tochizawa did not find this inconsistent with his admonition to his troops not to give their lives foolishly. He believed heaven was on his side and he would not die through some stupid mischance. He would not die until he had seen his battalion blunt the thrust of the American attack.

The first reinforcements from the mobile reserve began arriving before the Americans had broken through the second line of defense. They streamed past the battalion in the night by the weary hundreds on their way to counterattack. They were loaded with explosives and ammunition but had been forced to abandon much of their heavy equipment. Among the arrivals was the 37th Tank Regiment with only 27 of its 43 tanks and self-propelled guns. The others had been lost before they could fire a shot, some detected in the flares of the enemy's night air patrols and others damaged beyond use or hopelessly stuck negotiating the tortuously narrow and bomb-cratered roads. Tochizawa saw the surviving tanks knocked out one by one as they dodged toward the front. Two of the seventeen-ton Chi-He mediums were knocked out by a single murderous naval salvo as he followed their progress through his binoculars. One of them did not burn and he made a note of its position so that he could send out a party after dark to recover its 47-mm. gun. He saw another engage a Sherman and score direct hits that failed to penetrate the armor of the thirty-five-ton American monster. The Sherman destroyed the Model 1 almost disdainfully with the second round from its 75-mm. gun. In a rage, Tochizawa had one of his 70-mm. cannon moved into firing position and engage the Sherman with antitank shells of German design. The gun killed the Sherman with its fourth shell. Tochizawa was furious with the crew for its poor gunnery and resolved not to commit one of his precious guns against tanks again except at close range. His supply of antitank shells was small.

The heavy fighting south of the Shibushi Naval Airfield appeared so close that Tochizawa felt he could reach out and touch the combatants. The valor of his troops in the second line of defense filled him with pride. For one irrational moment he considered launching a counterattack through their positions. He was confident that his restless, well-trained men could drive a wedge through the American lines all the way to the sea. Wisdom and discipline quickly regained control. To penetrate the American front without a sizable force in reserve to exploit the victory would be meaningless, and the withdrawal of his troops from their assigned positions would leave a disastrous weakness in the main line of defense. His duty was to stand fast. Other units had been assigned the task of counterattack. That they had been unable to achieve a significant victory did not alter the situation. Despite the mounting pressure on the positions guarding the open ground of the airfield and his admiration of the defenders' prowess, he continued hoarding his artillery and supported the Masuda Company with only mortars and heavy machine guns.

When it was obvious that organized resistance had crumbled within the Masuda Company positions, Tochizawa's admiration turned to contempt. If Captain Masuda had led his men with enough spirit they could have held out at least another day or two. It was Tochizawa's belief that a truly dedicated soldier could always do a bit more than the possible. Were it not folly to risk leaving the battalion leaderless he would have crept through the long tunnel beneath the airfield to rally the company for a final stand.

After the reduction of the Masuda Company positions, the Americans had probed the Tochizawa Battalion's outer defenses with tanks and infantry. The enemy formations approached the battalion along the most obvious route, the wide, level airfield. There was no subtlety about the attack. The Shermans moved forward slowly on a broad front, well spaced. Infantrymen ran ahead of the tanks, bent low, and others skulked among the Shermans. Some of the tanks mounted flame throwers instead of the usual 75-mm. gun. Tochizawa, directing his defense from the observation post, gave them first priority. His positions were almost impervious to shelling except for direct hits in openings but flame throwers could force his troops deep inside their caves and could set fields and hillsides ablaze. His 47-mm. antitank guns had an effective range of only a quarter-mile against the heavily armored Shermans—how he envied the Americans their beautiful and deadly tanks—so he did not commit them. He could use his 70-mm. guns only sparingly lest the enemy pinpoint them and knock them out with air strikes and counterbattery fire. His tactic was to permit only a few well-aimed rounds from an emplacement before withdrawing the gun to safety within its tunnel or shifting it through the corridor to another position. His chief weapons against the Shermans at this stage were the individual soldiers concealed in the outpost positions with explosive charges to be carried to the target. The screen of infantry advancing with the tanks was to protect them from such suicide attacks. Tochizawa set about stripping the infantry from the tanks with machine gun and mortar fire. The infantrymen accompanying the Shermans began falling back or taking cover. When the Americans neared the outposts Tochizawa's riflemen opened fire on the infantrymen still with the tanks. The antitank parties remained concealed. The Shermans continued to creep forward firing all their weapons.

One of the 70-mm. guns scored a hit on a flame-throwing Sherman. The tank erupted in an enormous orange ball edged in black. The first Shermans reached the forward positions. They fired point-blank into the dugouts or washed them with liquid fire. Tochizawa knew that many of his men were crawling underground from the positions under attack to vantage points to the enemy's flanks or rear. Men popped out of holes and ran toward the Shermans. Many of them were cut down by rifle fire or the tanks' machine guns but some reached their targets. They climbed upon the Shermans and pulled the fuses of the satchel charges they carried. Some, using long poles, thrust charges beneath the tracks. After awhile the Shermans began pulling back, firing as they withdrew. Within half an hour formations of planes roared in to bomb and strafe. The air attack was followed by an intense hour-long artillery barrage. Shells continued to fall among the battalion's positions after the bombardment had passed its peak. However, the Shermans did not return that day.

Tochizawa sent men forward through the tunnels to learn if the Americans had occupied the dugouts they had overrun in the probe. They had not, although they had blocked caves and tunnel exits with demolitions. The battalion had lost a hundred men and one of its three remaining 70-mm. guns. Tochizawa did not consider the loss of the troops as significant as the loss of the gun. The stream of reinforcements from the north had slowed to a trickle but now that his battalion was actively engaging the enemy he expected some of them would be made available to him. The Americans, he was sure, had lost heavily in the attack and he counted seven wrecked Shermans scattered among his advance positions. That night, when he sent raiding parties behind the American lines to harass the enemy and gather information, he sent parties to occupy the Sherman hulks and use them as pillboxes in the next day's inevitable attack.

It began raining shortly before midnight. Rain continued to fall throughout the night and all the next day. Tochizawa received reports that some of the positions were flooding and with his executive officer Major Goto, went to inspect them. The flooded positions were chilly and ankle deep in mud and water. He reprimanded the noncoms in charge for not setting men to work digging drainage trenches from the low places on the surface which were pouring water into the underground chambers. In one position, where the men appeared unusually highspirited, he gave the squad leader a precious cigarette with instructions that the soldiers were to draw lots for it. In another, which had lost several men to an unlucky hit from a Sherman the day before, he inspired the troops with an account of an action in his Manchuria days when an entire squad had died gloriously in the successful defense of its post. Every man was profoundly affected by the fact that the battalion commander had personally visited their positions and in some instances spoken directly to ordinary soldiers. Although the men in the flooded positions were inspired and deeply honored by his visit, none breathed easily until he had gone.

The enemy resumed his attack in the afternoon, this time using his tanks differently. They remained in the rear while the infantry advanced cautiously with strong artillery support, probing for Tochizawa's remaining forward positions. When the foot soldiers encountered opposition they took cover and called in more artillery fire. Tanks would then move up in small numbers to attack the positions pinning down the infantry. The tactic generally was for a flame-throwing tank to move up under the guns of standard Shermans. It appeared to Tochizawa that the function of the latter was to locate and attack the battalion's guns when they engaged the flame-throwing Shermans. None of the tanks ventured beyond the probing infantrymen. Tochizawa's demolition men attempted in vain to break through the protective screen of infantry and attack the Shermans with satchel and pole charges. Tochizawa, while grudgingly acknowledging the soundness of the American commander's tactics, despised him for his timidity. Had their positions been reversed, had the Americans been fighting the defensive action and he been attacking them with overwhelming superiority in armor and artillery, he would have crushed them quickly with a determined attack employing all available forces. He was both pleased and disappointed that the Americans had no stomach for costly frontal attacks. Had they enough martial spirit to attack as he would were he in their position, his unyielding troops would be enabled to catch them in the open and smash them with hammer blows. Instead the Americans were nibbling away at his strength like mice at a bound tiger. It was said that when the Americans suffered great losses in men, even though it was in the course of achieving a great victory, the military leaders were reviled by their own government and the populace. It was really unspeakable that such a faint-hearted race had by mere abundance and technology been able to push its way across thousands of miles of the Pacific against a morally superior people.

Unable to halt the attrition of his forward positions, Tochizawa had arranged a trap. He ordered the forward positions in his center to permit the Americans to pass through them without resistance unless directly attacked. He augmented the antitank parties in the sector with demolition men moving up through tunnels from the main fortifications and sent two of his 47-mm. antitank guns to cover the most favorable tank approach. The tunnels were not large enough to admit the guns but natural terrain features and camouflaged trenches permitted their undetected movement. In the months of preparation the area between the Tochizawa Battalion and the sea had been divided into sectors and marked on grid maps, and the fire of the battalion's artillery preplotted for each sector. The battalion's two remaining 70-mm. guns were now ordered trained on the sector to which the Shermans would be admitted, with orders not to engage the enemy tanks until a quick hit was assured. He did not request division artillery to participate in the action. Tochizawa was not sure higher headquarters would approve of his trap.

The Americans soon found the apparent gap in the defenses and began moving through it. They advanced cautiously at first, taking cover from the mortar and machine gun fire which Tochizawa rained on them so they would not suspect they were being lured forward. When the American soldiers stumbled upon burrows concealing one or two demolition men they were permitted to attack and kill them without opposition from undiscovered supporting positions. More American infantry streamed into the gap. Soon tanks moved in behind the soldiers. Tochizawa received word from his forward observation posts that the enemy was converging on the gap from all along the front. Tochizawa knew it would soon be time to spring the trap. If he permitted too many Shermans to enter his defenses the enemy might turn his ruse to their own advantage and achieve a genuine penetration. The infantry, with a dozen Shermans among them, had advanced several hundred yards when Tochizawa gave the order to fire the signal flare. The dragon flare arched through the rain, its green fire brilliant against the gray skies.

The two antitank guns and the 70-mm. cannon opened fire with one voice. Demolition men sprang from their hiding places among the enemy and ran toward the Shermans. Four of the Shermans were knocked out in the first moments and two more before their commanders grasped the situation. The remaining six began withdrawing through a gauntlet of demolition men and shellfire. Two of them were destroyed before Tochizawa reluctantly decided it was no longer profitable to keep his artillery committed. Answering fire had already knocked out both antitank guns and one of the last two 70-mm. cannon. From now on he would be almost solely dependent on the jealously hoarded division artillery.

The American infantry withdrew deliberately, killing the surviving demolition men and wiping out the positions in their path. They did not retire all the way back to their jumping-off point. Instead they captured and occupied some of the forward positions they had bypassed and began digging additional shelters among them. Though Tochizawa's trap had been effective, the Americans had turned it partially to their advantage and succeeded in driving a wedge into his outer defenses.

Division headquarters ordered a night counterattack to eliminate the salient, a move Tochizawa anticipated and for which he had already begun planning. That night he sent men armed with grenades and explosives against the Americans' newly won positions north of the airfield. The tunnel system proved useless, for the Americans had searched out and blocked the exits. Tochizawa's men did not succeed in infiltrating the American lines in effective strength. The enemy was alert and quick to fire at anything moving among its positions. When they realized they were undergoing more than the usual harassing action they sent up flares and caught Tochizawa's men in the open. The colonel learned from a shaken young sublieutenant who had survived the attack that the enemy had brought up reinforcements and a number of light mortars and machine guns, a development which had not been detected by the forward observation posts. Though the information was useful, albeit several hours too late, Tochizawa did not commend the officer for his alertness. Instead he reprimanded him for returning alive without having accomplished his assigned mission. It seemed to Tochizawa that the Army had grown criminally lax in determining the qualifications of men it honored with a commission. A few hours later Major Goto informed the colonel that the young officer had killed himself. The lieutenant did have a spark of self-respect after all, Tochizawa thought, but was a fool to have needlessly taken a life which belonged not to him but to the Emperor. It would have been far more seemly if he had let himself be killed by the enemy while performing his duty as a soldier.

In the days that followed, the Americans had continued to grind into the core of Tochizawa's defenses. Shermans and infantry probed tirelessly for weak spots. Shells fell among the positions without pause and only rarely did a whole hour pass without a visit from American planes. It was impossible to move above ground in any numbers by day and dangerous to do so even at night except where the terrain offered shelter from American artillery blindly showering the hills and fields. Tochizawa was often denied even the cover of darkness. Flares from the ground and from the air, and star shells from warships in Ariake Bay, illuminated the night. The pressure on the battalion increased as the enemy drove into the division's main line of defense positions on either side of Tochizawa's command. Because the Tochizawa Battalion was holding its own for the moment, the bulk of division artillery support was diverted to points where the enemy threat was greater, and Tochizawa was not given the replacement troops he had expected and to which he believed himself entitled.

The days and nights took on a pattern. The ever-pressing enemy would be fought to a standstill among the intricate fortifications and would call in reinforcements, air strikes and artillery barrages to support new attacks. Sometimes they attacked behind dense screens of smoke, firing through them with profligate blindness. Tochizawa lacked the ammunition to do likewise. Occasionally the Americans would come without a preliminary artillery barrage, hoping to achieve surprise, but more often they would attempt to pin down Tochizawa's men with a massive bombardment. Such bombardment was largely ineffective. When shells began falling in great numbers Tochizawa's men would withdraw deep into their caves and tunnels, confident the Americans would not attack through their own barrage. They would return to their firing positions when the bombardment slackened to permit the attackers to advance. Tochizawa allowed himself to be tricked once by the Americans. There was an exceptionally violent and concentrated bombardment of the Ikebuchi Company's sector on the battalion's left front. Captain Ikebuchi, having been given no orders to the contrary, rushed his men to their posts when the barrage ended to engage the waves of Shermans and infantry which had always followed such a bombardment. The enemy appeared to be disposing himself for his standard attack but instead held fast and five minutes later the bombardment was resumed with full fury, catching many of Ikebuchi's men in their shelter entrances. The company beat back the attack that followed but when the action was over Captain Ikebuchi came to the battalion command post to offer his abject apologies. Tochizawa attempted to console him but was so vexed with himself for failing to anticipate the tactic his anger deprived his words of their intended effect.

"It's no use biting one's navel, Ikebuchi," he said harshly. "You carried out the orders of your commander. Had you done otherwise I would be compelled to relieve you of your command."

He was too weary and too preoccupied with more important matters to say more. And he thought if his company commander was so weak-spined that he needed further reassurance Ikebuchi was not worthy of his attention. But the captain was a soldier of the old breed.

"You have given me new spirit," Ikebuchi said. "I beg your permission to counterattack at once."

"You will defend your positions as planned," Tochizawa said, unimpressed. "I will decide when it is appropriate to go over to the attack."

Chastened but no longer abject, the captain returned to his company. Tochizawa knew that as long as Ikebuchi remained alive the battalion's left was in the best possible hands.

Though the men of the battalion fought desperately and died gallantly at their posts or in ferocious counterattacks, one strongpoint after another fell to the persistent enemy. Morale continued high under Tochizawa's aggressive leadership but the troops deteriorated physically. Hammered unremittingly by bombardment and ground attacks, the men got but little more sleep than their commander. Many suffered from diarrhea. The water from some wells proved bad and the underground latrines became foul centers of infection when scores of men were unable to wait until nightfall and use the outside latrine trenches. Grenades and mortar and heavy machine gun ammunition ran low, though with only one 70-mm. gun left there was still ample ammunition for it. The steady fighting had reduced the stockpiles more rapidly than expected. The quartermaster had stored the rice bags improperly and a quantity of the battalion's rations was spoiled by water seeping down into the storage cavern. The men were obliged to supplement their rations with sen giri, "thousand slice," dried shredded daikon radish which some of them used also to pad their sleeping places. The sen giri was filling but hard to digest and not very nourishing.

To compensate for the shortages and privations Tochizawa had his subordinates conduct physical and spiritual training with all the vigor circumstances permitted. Physical weakness, he believed, could be overcome by exercise and willpower. At night they were regularly led outdoors in small groups for calisthenics and deep-breathing exercises in the shelter of ravines and hillsides. Recitation of the Imperial Rescript to Soldiers and Sailors, discussion of the Bushido Code, and the retelling of heroic legends were resumed. Tochizawa regularly made the rounds of his positions to encourage the men by personal example. Slogans were lettered on banners and wooden slabs and placed on display throughout the battalion. "Be resolved that duty is heavier than a mountain, while death is lighter than a feather." "If we are born proud sons of the Yamato race, let us die on the fields of battle." "We believe in the Merciful God of War." "Long live the Emperor."

Now, as Tochizawa sat on his cot in the command post drinking the miso soup brought him by his orderly, he had ample reason for a nagging feeling there might have been a change in the situation while he slept. The enemy had forced his way past the battalion on both flanks and was threatening the division command post northeast of it. The Americans were drawn up in strength in an arc extending from the left flank to the far bank of the Hishida River on the right and applying continuous pressure. Their artillery ringed him in a two hundred and seventy degree noose which for the past seven hours tanks and infantry had been battling to close. More tanks and troops blocked all routes by which reinforcements might reach him except those to the immediate rear. For some reason—he suspected it was because division was hoarding troops to defend its own command post and headquarters—few reinforcements had been sent through the gap. Yet division continued to bombard him with exhortations to hold fast so that the great force assembling in the Kirishima Mountains could strike through his positions and split the enemy in half. Messages poured into the command post from all three companies, reporting heavy fighting and increasingly bold forays by enemy tanks. The Americans had swept over a platoon of the Ikebuchi Company and were now exterminating the survivors in their caves with demolitions, flame throwers and white phosphorous grenades. The main positions of the Doi Company, in the center, were still intact but Captain Doi reported spirited fighting everywhere along its front. On the right, the Yamaguchi Company, protected by the Hishida River, was being pounded unmercifully by a great variety of weapons.

While he ate, Tochizawa studied sheaves of messages his executive officer thought required his attention, and exchanged brief remarks with other staff officers who hurried to him. He finished his rice, not noticing or caring how much of it was millet because even in the best of times what he ate had been of little importance to him and, with Major Goto at his heels, climbed the ladder to his shattered observation post. Although it still afforded protection from shelling and enemy eyes, it was a shambles. Artillery and bombs had stripped away the earth concealing the inner core of concrete and thereafter American guns had pounded the thick walls to rubble. The front of the observation post was a gaping hole and its floor was heaped with broken concrete. The roof was firm enough, being twenty-five feet of hilltop. The position was still usable as an observation point as long as Tochizawa kept low amid the rubble. The telescope and its tripod had been smashed but he had powerful binoculars. They were Zeiss, a gift from his father-in-law eight years ago. Tochizawa had thought them no better than Japanese binoculars but prized them because in those days he respected all things German. When Germany fell he no longer prized them so highly. He tried to exchange them for a Japanese instrument but by then comparable Japanese binoculars were difficult to come by. His dismay at the fall of his nation's only ally was tempered by this revelation to the world that Japan was history's most unyielding warrior race. Japan would never surrender so abjectly while millions of its subjects were still capable of resistance. Before the surrender he had considered the Germans worthy partners, equating their defense of Brest with the defense of Tarawa and, in fact, had even admitted to himself the superiority of German arms. Afterward he had come to understand that even Tiger tanks and 88-mm. guns meant no more than Shermans and swarms of planes if proper spirit was lacking. There was, after all, no substitute for the spirit of the Yamato race.

A telephone line led from the observation post to the command post below it. On it Tochizawa could receive information and issue orders. From his vantage point he could view the entire battlefield except some areas blocked by ridges. The woods on slopes and the patches of rough, uncultivated ground no longer afforded concealment for friend or foe. The trees lay shattered or thrusting upward in blackened nakedness. The desolate earth was torn and smoking. It put Tochizawa in mind of a picture of the Christian Hell he had seen in an American book when he was studying English in the upper school. It was fitting, he thought, that the same Americans who had created such desolation on Japanese soil were being given a taste of the Hell which they were said to fear so greatly. It was little wonder they placed such value on their meaningless lives if they truly believed such a place existed. Perhaps it did. Only the Divine Race merited Yasukuni.

The area still firmly held by the Tochizawa Battalion had shrunk to half its original size. In places the enemy had pushed narrow, shallow salients into the shrunken perimeter, holding some of them against the inevitable counterattacks, and being pinched off and wiped out or driven back in others. Shermans were as thick as fleas from a few hundred yards beyond the perimeter to as far away as the eye could see. Tochizawa observed with satisfaction that numbers of them were useless hulks. Far in the distance enemy convoys moved on roads still being repaired and improved by tireless dump trucks and bulldozers, and an occasional plane took off or landed at the Shibushi Naval Airfield. Two days before, Tochizawa had sent a strong raiding party to disrupt activities on the airfield but there had been no indication of success. The enemy had concentrated troop positions and gun emplacements around the field, laid down pierced steel mats for runways, and pushed up mounds of earth to shelter his planes.

It was often difficult to engage the American soldiers attacking with the Shermans. They made such good use of cover they must be veteran troops, Tochizawa thought. The infantry worked efficiently with the tanks and were very difficult to dislodge from the strongpoints they captured. Some of them now occupied what had been his own forward positions. The number of these positions was small because almost always the enemy had to destroy the fortifications to kill the defenders. His men fought bravely until the last and the Americans did not dare to come into the caves and tunnels after them. The Americans resorted to barbarous and craven tactics rather than face his troops in close combat. When they detected a cave entrance their Shermans fired phosphorous shells into it until smoke drifting out revealed the other apertures with which the cave connected. Then they would seal the cave entrance and the apertures, suffocating the men inside. Once they had managed to thrust the end of a long hose into an Ikebuchi tunnel system and pump gasoline into it from a tank truck. The earth shook with the explosion when a phosphorous shell from a Sherman ignited the gasoline. Not the least maddening aspect of this incident was the demonstration of the enemy's enormous supply of fuel. Japan had not possessed enough gasoline to give even its special attack pilots proper training and had been forced to convert its trucks, when it still had trucks, to charcoal fuel. Yet the Americans could squander hundreds of gallons to reduce one strongpoint.

The colonel swept the ravaged countryside with his binoculars. From the enemy's dispositions and movements he estimated the force besieging his positions was no less than 2000 and that it was but a fraction of American strength on the Ariake front. His radio spoke of tens of thousands of fresh Japanese troops massed in the mountains for an imminent counterattack but thus far he had seen no evidence of their existence. The Americans had tanks and self-propelled guns in abundance—it seemed for every one destroyed ten more appeared—and unlimited artillery and air support. They expended shells and bombs as if their entire campaign centered on his positions, yet he knew they were doing the same all along the main line of defense and in several points beyond it. He had seen their wounded evacuated on litters to be treated at leisure, and parties of able-bodied troops moving toward the rear out of forward positions, obviously to be given a rest from the battle. His forward observation posts reported relays of American troops being relieved in the midst of the fighting merely to be given hot food in such quantities that some of the soldiers were observed emptying their mess cans on the ground.

Opposing them, Tochizawa had by the latest count some 400 men, including the wounded and the handful of replacements allocated him from the remnants of units moving down from the north. They had been fighting without respite for ten days, sleeping but three or four hours in twenty-four. Those too severely wounded to fight lay crowded in the underground dispensary and with but a single doctor left to attend them. There had been no hot food in days and food of any kind was dwindling. He had no more battalion artillery. What fire support he had against prowling Shermans came from one division 75-mm. within his perimeter and regimental and divisional batteries well to his rear. And the latter were being systematically destroyed by enemy aircraft and artillery directed by observations planes hovering always overhead. He had lost most of his machine guns and trench mortars and could employ those remaining only sparingly because ammunition was running low. Nevertheless Tochizawa believed he could hold his positions another five or six days regardless of what forces the enemy hurled against him and even if the promised counterattacks proved mythical. The enemy had numbers and material. His men had spirit.

As he scanned his positions Tochizawa saw a soldier emerge cautiously from an opening behind the Yamaguchi Company positions on his right front. Tochizawa watched him curiously, wondering what errand could be important enough to send him from his post. Perhaps, as had happened with the less strong-willed men, the days of living underneath the ground had weakened his spirit and an overindulgent commander had sent him out to restore himself with a view of the open sky. It was unwise for even a lone man to show himself. The Americans were so profligate with their artillery that Tochizawa had known them to fire on a single man with large-caliber shells. Though this man was too far back in the fortifications to be observed he might well fall victim to the steady bombardment lashing the entire battalion area. Whether or not the soldier survived his excursion on the surface was of little concern to Tochizawa. Though he needed every man, he could most easily spare one unable to perform his duty properly. The soldier moved erect and without haste, as if indifferent to the shelling. Tochizawa thought him either very brave or so lacking in moral fiber he had lost his wits. The soldier relieved himself against a mound of earth and continued his leisurely walk. He entered a level-floored gully in the fold of a hill where vegetation grew in orderly rows. It was a battalion vegetable garden which because of its location had gone unscathed. The Tochizawa Battalion, like other Kyushu units, had been encouraged to grow as much of its own food as possible. Every company had its own gardens inside the perimeter and until shortly before the American landings had cultivated larger tracts in the countryside where fields had been left unworked because of the civilian labor shortage.

Feeling among his clothing the soldier produced a white object. It appeared to be paper, a letter, perhaps. From the manner in which the soldier unfolded it the colonel assumed it was a letter. Had the sentimental weakling left his post simply to reread a letter in privacy? The soldier tore a piece from the paper and returned the remainder to his pocket. He reached into another pocket, dribbled something into the paper and rolled it into a tube. He put the tube in his mouth and dipped into his pocket again. From the movement of his hands it then appeared he was striking a spark. Many of the men carried wicks which they were adept at lighting with bits of flint and steel. It was the ordinary soldier's lighter when there were no matches. The soldier blew out a puff of smoke. This man was no weakling, Tochizawa realized, except perhaps in his addiction to smoking. There was no addiction strong enough to make a coward risk his life for a cigarette. The spectacle made Tochizawa realize how much he himself craved tobacco and he felt a sudden animosity toward the soldier. Tochizawa had no bodily craving he could not control fully but the unexpectedness of the soldier's action had caught him off guard. He deeply resented being trapped into momentary weakness. And it was probably not even tobacco the soldier was smoking.

The men took a grass called itadori, shredded and dried it, and used it as a substitute for tobacco. It must be that the soldier was smoking.

Tochizawa's anger deepened when the soldier picked up a mattock and began to dig among the plants. The imbecile had left his post to work in the garden. Tochizawa was on the verge of telling Major Goto to have the man dragged back to his position and punished when a second soldier came out of the ground and crawled to the gully. Without standing erect he reached up and tugged at the gardener's sleeve. He appeared to be remonstrating with him. After a minute or so the man laid down his mattock and permitted himself to be led like a child back to safety. He was obviously demented. Tochizawa told Major Goto to have the man identified and sent to a forward position from which he would be unable to return to the garden. The soldier's abberation should not impair his fighting ability. Major Goto made a note of it in the little book he always carried.

Imamura, Tochizawa's orderly, poked his head into the observation post and reported the battalion commander was urgently required in the command post. Imamura spoke as calmly as if he were announcing dinner. His orderly was brave, devoted and unburdened by imagination, Tochizawa thought. A perfect soldier. In the command post, a private bleeding from several minor wounds stood at ease. He came to attention at Tochizawa's approach.

"Much trouble at the Ikebuchi Company," a staff officer said. "I thought you'd want to question the runner yourself."

The soldier answered Tochizawa's curt questions nervously, more shaken by the battalion commander's presence than by his wounds. The Americans were attacking heavily out of the Third Platoon positions they had seized earlier in the day, and Captain Ikebuchi did not think he could hold indefinitely without a counterattack by the reserve platoons and some support from division artillery. He had sent a runner back through the tunnel system because the telephone line had been severed and none of his remaining radio transmitters were functioning. The runner said the Americans were employing more than a thousand men and at least a company of Shermans in the attack. Tochizawa demanded to know if that was Captain Ikebuchi's estimate or the runner's own. Stammering, the soldier assured him he was repeating the exact words of the honorable company commander. Even then Tochizawa doubted the accuracy of the estimate. Despite the enemy's overwhelming strength he did not believe the Americans could concentrate so many troops so quickly, even though he did think them foolish enough to crowd them into an area so cramped it denied them adequate cover and fighting room.

Tochizawa was annoyed with Captain Ikebuchi and with himself for having overestimated the company commander's spirit. What had the world come to, he wondered, with Japanese soldiers leaving their posts to scratch among pumpkin vines and seasoned officers showing panic under a little pressure. A true warrior's determination should grow firmer as the pressure increased, just as when food grew shorter one's appetite should shrink, and when there was no time for sleeping one's need for sleep should grow less. He sent a staff officer with the runner to bring back a firsthand and more reliable estimate of the situation and to order Ikebuchi to launch a series of small attacks without delay. Should the enemy succeed in breaking his front he was to counterattack immediately with all available forces. The Americans must be prevented from consolidating any gains. When they seized a strongpoint they were adept at exploiting it as an assembly point from which to attack surrounding positions.

"You will inform Ikebuchi the only further report I will accept from him is that the enemy has been thrown back," Tochizawa told the staff officer.

As they were leaving, Major Goto gave the runner an encouraging pat on the back and said, "Hard work."

If his executive offlcer had a weakness, Tochizawa thought, it was his tendency to be overindulgent with the troops.

Tochizawa returned to the observation post, which was exerting a growing fascination for him. Although Tochizawa could draw a clear picture of the complex situation from reports entering the command post, there were delays and breakdowns in communications from the companies and on occasion, as with the latest report from Ikebuchi, the information was questionable. From the observation post he could see much of what was happening as it happened and often reach decisions even before reports arrived from the scene. And, alone in the observation post, he was not obliged to conceal his weariness from his staff. It strengthened their spirit to see him ever tireless.

He was thirsty and thought tea would be most welcome. Imamura somehow always managed to have tea for him when he wanted it. Major Goto had chosen well when he assigned Imamura to orderly duty. But to set Imamura to making tea now would be to give in to an unworthy bodily craving. Instead he sipped flat-tasting water from the canteen he always carried.

From the observation post he could see enough of the Ikebuchi Company's sector to determine the Americans were attacking recklessly as if sensing its imminent collapse. Tochizawa was not dismayed by what he saw. On the contrary, he was pleased because it confirmed the wisdom of his instructions to Captain Ikebuchi. He recalled as clearly as if the pages were before his eyes General Tanaka's words in his memorable article, "The Way to Sure Victory."

"American troops, when the military situation develops somewhat favorably for them, tend to launch bold and reckless headlong rushes. That very time is best to deal them a heavy blow by conducting surprise attacks."

The truth of General Tanaka's analysis was not altered by the fact he had been proven wrong on another point. "If we risk our lives and kill several enemy soldiers with one," the general had written, "I think we will be able to break the enemy's will to fight." The Americans, though at times inclined to be overly cautious when resisted with sufficient spirit, showed no signs of breaking.

Tochizawa could also see enough of the Doi Company's sector to tell the enemy was preparing a thrust into its center. He abandoned a half-formed plan to send part of the Doi Company's First Platoon to relieve pressure on Ikebuchi Company's right flank with a counterattack if the Ikebuchi situation grew more critical. Adding to his problems, Major Goto informed him by telephone from the command post that something was developing on the relatively quiet Yamaguchi Company's Hishida River front. The enemy had intensified his bombardment of the hillsides facing the river and was bringing up quantities of bridging materials, obviously preparing for a large-scale attempt to force a crossing. Of the three threats to the battalion, Tochizawa considered this potentially the gravest. Yamaguchi Company's fortifications were the most thinly spread, and of the three company commanders he considered Captain Yamaguchi the least able, though his spirit was unquestionable. It had perhaps been an error in judgment to place such reliance on the river barrier in planning the battalion's defenses. But when the Hishida positions were constructed it was expected the battalion would have sufficient artillery support to break up enemy concentrations large enough to endanger its right flank. Such support was no longer available. He considered radioing a demand to division that it assign all its remaining artillery to provide call fire for the Yamaguchi Company if the enemy activity did not prove to be a feint. He decided to withhold his decision until he had studied the American preparations with his own eyes.

He descended to the command post and, accompanied by Major Goto, climbed down the ladder to the battalion headquarters on the first level and through the tunnel to the Yamaguchi fortifications. The first part of the tunnel was large enough to walk through at a crouch. It opened into a troop shelter. There were a handful of troops in it, too severely wounded or ill to handle weapons. Those who were conscious attempted to get to their feet when the battalion commander entered. He stopped them with an impatient gesture. Tochizawa paused long enough to assure himself none of them were capable of fighting if instructed forcefully in their duties as soldiers of the Emperor. Major Goto went from man to man offering comforting words. Motioning the executive officer to follow him, Tochizawa gave the wounded men a perfunctory "Hard work" and continued forward. The tunnel narrowed and he was compelled to go hands and knees. He was almost overcome by a weariness to which he refused to surrender. There was considerable traffic through the tunnels connecting the Yamaguchi positions, and the soldiers crawling through them bawled out their errands for priority in the one-way passages. Emergency duty had first priority. Tochizawa permitted those on such duty to take precedence. All others were obliged to wait until he had passed, Major Goto calling out at regular intervals to advise all within hearing that the battalion commander was coming through.

Captain Yamaguchi sprang to attention in the company command post. He appeared confused but undaunted by the new development on his front. He led Tochizawa and Major Goto through yards of tunnels to the most advantageous position for viewing the enemy's preparations. They were obliged to crawl.

The position was a small one, manned by a light machine gun squad. The gunners had to be sent out into the access tunnel to make room for the three officers. The position was two-thirds of the way up the side of a hill sloping down at a steep angle to the bank of the river. Hills verged on the river all along the Yamaguchi Company front, rendering tanks unemployable in any crossing. Only infantry could make a direct assault on the river fortifications. Tochizawa could see a considerable stretch of the greenish-brown river on either side of the machine gun position. He had had the banks cut vertically when the fortifications were constructed. That should give the Americans something to think about. There was a marked difference between the area occupied by the Yamaguchi Company on one side of the river and that now held by the enemy on the other. Both were heavily scarred but there was still greenery in the level fields on the American side of the river and only an occasional shower of earth from exploding shells. Every yard of Yamaguchi Company's sector was scorched and pocked, and a steady rain of projectiles sent dirt, rocks and charred vegetation flying into the air. The situation was exactly as it had been described to Tochizawa. Armored amphibian personnel carriers and ungainly truck-boats were deployed across the fields just beyond the range of his machine guns and behind them tanks and artillery for supporting fire. Some of the vehicles were piled high with sandbags, heavy timbers and what appeared to be prefabricated bridge sections. Pontoons hung from the sides of many vehicles.

Captain Yamaguchi looked eagerly to Tochizawa for some indication of his intentions. The colonel surveyed the American lines without expression, committing every detail of the terrain and the enemy's dispositions to memory and dictating notes to Major Goto. The executive officer wrote them down in his little book and, at Tochizawa's direction, made a rough diagram of the American dispositions. Tochizawa did not speak to Yamaguchi until they returned to the company command post.

"Is the radio functioning?" he asked.

"Yes, Honorable Battalion Commander," the captain said with a trace of pride.

"Get me division," Tochizawa said.

Yamaguchi's face fell.

"It has insufficient strength," he said apologetically.

"It doesn't matter," Tochizawa said. "It's better I have my overlays before me when I confer with division."

"Is the situation grave, Honorable Battalion Commander?" Yamaguchi asked hesitantly.

"Only for the Americans, if your men display proper spirit."

"They will!" Yamaguchi shouted, startling Major Goto with his vehemence. "There is not a man in Yamaguchi Company who is not anxious to give his life for the Honorable Battalion Commander."

"The lives of all of us belong to the Emperor," Tochizawa said severely. "I dislike such talk."

"I apologize, Honorable Battalion Commander," said Yamaguchi, shaken.

"The Americans must not cross the river," Tochizawa said. "I am depending on you. You will have artillery support from division."

"I am deeply honored that the Honorable Battalion Commander is pleased to place such trust in me," Yamaguchi said.

As he passed through the troop shelter on the way back to the battalion command post Tochizawa saw that one of the wounded soldiers had died. He had Major Goto take the body outside. It was not good for the morale of the wounded men to have a dead comrade among them and, more important, in a day or so the corpse would create a health problem in the shelter. It was a pity time could not be taken to cremate the bodies of fallen soldiers and that their families would have no ashes to memorialize their valor.

When he reached the command post the staff officer he had sent to Ikebuchi Company was waiting with his report. Though Ikebuchi's estimates of enemy strength had indeed been on the high side the company commander had displayed no sign of faltering spirits and, if anything, appeared to have become even more resolute on learning he must defend his positions without assistance from battalion. Tochizawa had the map overlays brought to him while the radio operator was contacting division. Using the map overlay, his memory, his notes and Major Goto's diagram of the Hishida dispositions, he worked out the coordinates for the artillery concentrations he thought necessary. Tochizawa asked for the division commander when contact was established. The division commander was not available at the moment. When Tochizawa insisted it was a matter of the greatest urgency, he was informed brusquely that the general was occupied with other matters of the greatest urgency. Tochizawa at last succeeded in getting a staff officer of the artillery regiment. The staff officer took the coordinates and promised to provide concentrations from a 150-mm. battery when Yamaguchi Company requested them. Tochizawa had a feeling he could expect no assistance from regiment. The staff officers at regiment and at division as well, always thought they had a better grasp of the situation than the local commanders. If only they would permit him to speak with the division commander.

He was still fuming when he climbed to the observation post. Major Goto accompanied him. Tochizawa felt his proper place as battalion commander was in the command post, where he could receive incoming reports as they arrived instead of being dependent on a single telephone and Imamura's legs, but he functioned better when he could follow the battle with his own eyes. This was one of the limitations that had slowed his advancement in the Army.

The gravest threat erupted unexpectedly in the center. On the left, surprise attack by the Ikebuchi Company had thrown the enemy off balance and the Americans appeared to be regrouping. On the right the Americans were contenting themselves for the moment with a thunderous bombardment of the river defenses. Tochizawa saw the situation developing in the Doi Company sector before the first report reached the command post. A platoon-size force of American infantry suddenly appeared on the crest of Hill 91, a ninety-one-meter hump more than a hundred yards inside the Doi positions. They had somehow managed to creep up a shallow draw without being detected and surprise the defenders of the forward slope with a shower of grenades that drove them from their firing apertures. The Americans closed the cave entrance with satchel charges and scrambled to the top of the hill, where Tochizawa saw them. Meeting no resistance at the top they charged recklessly down the reverse slope. Tochizawa was already on the phone demanding to know what had happened to the machine guns and mortars commanding the reverse slope when Doi Company troops piled out of their holes and drove the Americans back up the hill. Tochizawa sent Major Goto down to the command post to monitor incoming reports and inform him immediately of any change in other sectors so that he could be free to concentrate on the Doi Company action.

The Americans began digging in to make a stand on the crest under heavy cross fire from surrounding strongpoints. The first counterattack failed to dislodge them but a second, after fierce hand-to-hand fighting drove them down the forward slope. Some of the soldiers attempting to pursue the Americans were cut down by a storm of shrapnel from American artillery and the rest were forced to retire to their positions on the reverse slope. The Americans brought up reinforcements through the draw to consolidate their hold on the forward slope. Captain Doi mounted another counterattack that was broken up by an even greater concentration of fire than that which had swept his men from the crest in the previous attack. It was obvious to Tochizawa the Americans were building up to a new and heavier assault.

It was imperative that the enemy be denied the crest of Hill 91 from which to mount one of his deadly straddle attacks on the reverse slope positions. It was a tactic much used by the Americans. They had shown a preference for attacking cave complexes from above so that the defenders could not resist without showing themselves. If they succeeded in taking the top they would almost certainly be able to reduce the reverse slope strongpoints and control all Hill 91. With the hill in their hands they would have driven a wedge into the Doi Company fortifications and could move up heavy weapons with which to support new assaults.

Tochizawa had one of his rare moments of indecision. He should return to the command post where there was a steady flow of reports and where his staff could supply him with any supporting information he might need. It was not enough that Major Goto was screening the information for him as it came in even though the executive officer was so familiar with his battalion commander's methods he sometimes seemed able to think with Tochizawa's mind. But Tochizawa did not like being unable to view the scene of battle at such a critical time. And he did not look forward to the climb down to the command post. His legs felt lifeless and it had become increasingly difficult to negotiate the narrow ladder. He must have Imamura knead his legs for him. Imamura's hands were strong and cunning as a bath attendant's. Tochizawa phoned down to the command post and directed Major Goto to send the reserve platoon that had been denied Ikebuchi to reinforce the Hill 91 defenses. Goto informed him there had been no word from Ikebuchi for twenty minutes. Tochizawa ordered him to send a staff officer to investigate and instruct Ikebuchi to send back a report immediately if there was any change in the situation in his sector. Yamaguchi Company, Goto said, had reported only continued intense bombardment. When Goto completed his report Tochizawa told him to send Imamura up to the observation post.

Tochizawa lay on his stomach, propped on his elbows, his binoculars fixed on Hill 91, which was quiet for the moment. Only occasionally did he turn them on other sectors to assure himself that Ikebuchi Company still held firm and the Americans were not attempting to move across the Hishida. At first he scarcely felt Imamura's fingers pressing into his calves. Then, as the muscles began to loosen, it felt as if the orderly were untying knots in his legs. It was not painful. Imamura did not prod or twist. His fingers coaxed. If Imamura could only do the same for his eyes, thought Tochizawa. They sometimes felt as if they were held in his head by elastic bands stretched so tightly they would be pulled back inside his skull. He put down the binoculars, took off his glasses and rubbed his eyes.

"Enough," he said.

"Thank you, Honorable Battalion Commander," Imamura replied.

Imamura had removed his tunic to work more freely on Tochizawa's legs. He wore a senninbari, a "sash of a thousand stitches," around his waist as a good luck charm against enemy bullets. Major Goto had told Tochizawa Imamura's wife had spent days outside a department store in Okayama getting passing women each to sew a single stitch in the waistband. Though Imamura had never been wounded Tochizawa doubted if the senninbari had a great deal to do with it. But it undoubtedly must be a great comfort to a man to have a wife so devoted she would stop a thousand women on the street. Yet a soldier should need no such comfort. The assurance that one had done one's duty was sufficient. He thought of his dead wife. She would never have accosted a thousand women in such an endeavor. It was not that she would not have wished to do so. It was because she was too shy. She had not lived to see Japan ravaged by barbarians. Perhaps fate had taken her for that reason as well as to preserve Yoshi's manhood. It was strange that he should think of her at such a time. This was hardly the moment for sentimentality.

The sun was setting. Tochizawa was relieved. He did not think the Americans would attack over Hill 91 before dawn. They had little stomach for fighting in the dark. They thought night was for sleeping. He must sleep a little himself. It was not an indulgence. He could remain awake indefinitely if necessary but an hour or two of sleep would help him think more clearly. Fatigue was a drug which deadened the senses as well as the muscles.

"Shall I bring blankets, Honorable Battalion Commander?" Imamura asked, as if sensing the colonel's decision. "It has grown cold."

Tochizawa had not noticed. He was insensitive to heat and cold except when they were extreme. He put his hand to his cheek. His face was cold to the touch.

"I'm going down," he said.

Before lying down on his cot he ate a tin of fish and a little cold rice. While he was eating he conferred with Major Goto and spoke at length on the telephone with Doi and Yamaguchi. There was still no telephone contact with Ikebuchi. Tochizawa told Major Goto to send a man out to find the break and repair it. Major Goto said he had ordered the communications officer to do so shortly after the break was reported. The communications officer was sent for. Yes, he had sent a man as ordered but he had been killed. Why had this not been reported? The communications officer said he had not done so because he still expected to find and repair the break. Tochizawa berated him in a loud voice. That should remind the other staff officers they should not attempt to conceal failures from him or be lax in their duties. The colonel sent one of his own signals men to put Ikebuchi's radio back in order, hoping it was not out for want of a part. He had no spare parts left. He sent a written order with the signals man. If neither telephone or radio contact could be reestablished Ikebuchi was to send back an oral report every half hour whether or not there was increased activity in his sector. The enemy was too quiet, Tochizawa thought. Perhaps he should not sleep until he had a better idea of what the Americans were up to.

Captain Doi requested permission to counterattack and drive the Americans from the forward slope of Hill 91. Tochizawa considered the request for a moment before rejecting it. The enemy might anticipate such an attack and prepare a trap. He ordered Doi to send out a patrol instead. He ordered Yamaguchi to slip men across the river to observe the enemy's movements and send up signal flares if attack appeared imminent. Only then did he lie down and close his eyes.

When he was awakened by Major Goto five hours later he could not believe he had slept at all until he looked at his watch. It was eleven minutes after midnight. The Americans were moving across the Hishida. Yamaguchi's patrol apparently had been ambushed for it had given no warning of the enemy preparations. The first wave had crossed silently in rubber boats and attacked the hill positions while engineers bridged the river in two places. Yamaguchi wanted to know if he should risk a counterattack or concentrate his efforts on maintaining the integrity of his interconnected fortifications.

"Attack at once!" Tochizawa shouted into the phone. "Drive them back into the river at all costs!"

He slammed the receiver back into its cradle. He would have liked to say more but Yamaguchi already had wasted too much precious time. What an incompetent wretch he was not to have sallied out the moment the Americans revealed their presence on the east bank. The enemy's massed artillery would have been helpless to support the assault party in mixed hand-to-hand combat. Once they secured a bridgehead in strength it would be impossible to dislodge them even if they were denied artillery support.

While he radioed division for the promised artillery concentrations he studied the reports that had come in from the other two companies while he slept. Telephone communications with Ikebuchi Company had been restored. Both companies reported only enemy patrol activity. Tochizawa scrambled to the observation post to observe the response to his message to division. The American side of the river was pricked with countless muzzle flashes and the Yamaguchi sector was raddled with exploding shells. Tochizawa hoped Yamaguchi had been wise enough to mount his counterattack underground through the hill positions. He regretted losing his temper and not giving Yamaguchi more explicit instructions. On the American side of the Hishida there was only an occasional transient glow as regimental artillery delivered its promised concentrations. It was an accurate measure of the disparity in firepower. It was clear to Tochizawa he could not expect the regiment's guns to alter the course of battle. Everything depended on the spirit of Yamaguchi Company. Now that Yamaguchi had been told what to do it was possible he might bring it off with raw determination. Tochizawa had a fierce desire to take over the counterattack personally but he knew it would be disastrous if American attacks in other sectors caught him away from the command post. He must continue to put his trust in the fighting spirit of his commanders and his troops.

The counterattack failed with significant losses to Yamaguchi Company. When morning came the Americans were firmly established on the east bank of the Hishida, having taken the forward slopes of the hills on the river. Two pontoon bridges spanned the Hishida. Shermans were ranged along the west bank to forestall any counterattack over the hillcrests. Tochizawa requested artillery concentration on the tanks and bridges but was informed the regiment's guns had come under heavy counterbattery fire during the night engagement and were being shifted to new emplacements. He attacked the bridges and the bridgehead with every mortar that could be moved within range and drew down a prolonged fire bombing which killed several mortar squads and forced the others to pull back into their tunnels.

A more immediate threat developed in the same place as the day before, around Hill 91. Fighter bombers came over in endless flights of three to hit the reverse slopes and surrounding hilltops with high explosives and napalm. Then howitzers and heavy mortars laid down densely patterned fire over the entire area. After this the planes returned with smoke and when it cleared there were Shermans at the base of Hill 91 and troops on the crest in considerable strength. The troops made little effort to dig in. The source of their daring was soon evident. When the Doi positions ringing Hill 91 engaged them, the waiting Shermans crept forward, pumping 75-mm. fire into the positions. Tochizawa watched helplessly while the

American infantry completed its straddle attack on the reverse slope fortifications. Grenade and automatic weapons squads kept the defenders pinned inside the caves while demolition squads swung satchel charges into the entrances at the end of ropes. They moved carefully down the slope, shooting flame and throwing phosphorous grenades into the smoking caves. Smoke drifted out of an heretofore undetected aperture near the top of the hill. A number of American soldiers gathered around it. One of them scrambled down the hill to a flame-throwing Sherman and climbed back dragging a long hose. He thrust it into the opening. Black smoke spewed out of half a dozen crevices in Hill 91.

A burning figure, at that distance from Tochizawa no larger than a child's thumb, emerged from the earth and ran across open ground. He covered only a few yards before falling. Tochizawa did not know if he had collapsed from his burns or had been cut down by enemy fire. A second figure dashed from concealment and threw itself beneath a Sherman. There was a bright flash and one of the Sherman's tracks lay spread over the ground. Hatches opened and the crew ran away. In a few minutes another Sherman dragged the tank back behind the hill at the end of a cable.

The Americans advanced over the level ground beyond Hill 91. They were halted by determined fire and fell back toward the hill, taking their wounded with them. Then Tochizawa saw a sight that horrified and infuriated him. A splash of white rose out of the earth between the retreating Americans and the hill, and after it a man. Tochizawa was so stunned it was several seconds before he comprehended the enormity of what was happening. A Tochizawa Battalion man was surrendering. Retching and almost inarticulate with fury Tochizawa screamed into the telephone for every weapon to fire on the traitor. In the several minutes required to relay the orders the captive reached shelter. Tochizawa ordered an immediate attack with every available man to retake the hill and kill the coward who had dishonored the battalion. He rescinded the order with his next breath. He must expend his men frugally. And the traitor was already worse than dead. If the Americans did not kill him he would be haunted by the knowledge he had dishonored his Emperor, his country and his family, and betrayed his fallen comrades.

It took the Americans two and a half days of bloody and continuous fighting to reach Tochizawa's command post. The enemy was like a scaly pangolin in an ant colony, probing methodically among the battalion's fortifications and exterminating the defenders of each strongpoint before moving on to the next. They fanned out from Hill 91 to isolate the center company's main fortifications, overran the riddled Ikebuchi positions in waves of infantry and armor, and burst out of the Hishida hill line by sheer weight of numbers. Though resistance might have been prolonged if the defenders had fallen back through the tunnel network for a final stand in the heart of the battalion's positions, they did not do so. They had been ordered to defend each strongpoint to the death and with but few exceptions did so.

When it was clear to Tochizawa but little time remained, he sent Imamura and other headquarters soldiers to the troop shelters, where many helplessly wounded men lay, with hand grenades so the casualties would not be dishonored by capture. Those strong enough to move were sent forward to positions where resistance still flared. With Major Goto, he went himself to the dispensary to render the men there the final service a commander could provide troops who had fought so gallantly. The dirt floor of the dispensary was piled with dead and wounded. The stench of blood and putrefaction rose above them like a mist. The battalion's last surviving doctor reeled among them, his face a mask of fatigue and horror as he fumbled mechanically to minister to their wounds. Tochizawa looked at him contemptuously. There was nothing a doctor could do here now. If he were a worthy son of Japan he would be fighting side by side with his comrades in arms. One of those in the tangle of recumbent forms rose, reeling, and saluted when Tochizawa entered the reeking chamber. Tochizawa was at first moved profoundly that a mortally wounded soldier possessed such unquenchable spirit. On closer examination he saw the soldier, though bloody, displayed no wounds.

"What are you doing here?" Tochizawa demanded.

The soldier gestured fearfully toward a corpse at his feet.

"Honorable Battalion Commander, I brought the honorable squad leader for attention. It proved useless."

"Who ordered you to leave your post? Why are you still here?"

The doctor was crouching beside a soldier with half a face. He looked toward them.

"He was utterly exhausted when he brought the sergeant in," he said placatingly. "I ordered him to rest a moment before returning to his post."

"You exceeded your authority," Tochizawa said. "You will return to your post immediately," he told the soldier.

The man did not move. He stood among the bodies, weaving.

"I . . . ," he said, "I . . . ,"

Major Goto," Tochizawa said without looking at the executive officer. "Kill him."

Major Goto drew his pistol and shot the soldier.

The doctor jerked to his feet, as if to protest, but said nothing. No one else in the cavern reacted in any way. Major Goto, his face impassive, put his pistol back in its holster.

"The Americans will arrive in a matter of hours," Tochizawa said. Have you anything . . . ?"

He nodded toward the supine troops around them.

"Nothing," the doctor said hopelessly. "Nothing to save them and nothing to kill them."

"Those with sufficient strength will manage for themselves," Tochizawa said. "The others . . ."

He nodded at Major Goto, who held out a pair of hand grenades. The doctor drew back, shaking his head.

"I command you," Tochizawa shouted. "Do you call yourself a soldier of the Emperor?"

The doctor kept shaking his head as if powerless to control his own body. Tochizawa unholstered his pistol and shot him.

"The Americans will be here shortly," he announced in a loud voice. "You have done well. You have held long enough for the great counterattack to form in the Kirishimas. You have two minutes to do what must be done."

He looked at his watch. Several of the soldiers struggled to their knees and thrust bayonets into throat or abdomen. When two minutes had passed he picked his way to the cavern exit, took the two hand grenades from Major Goto, rapped them against his sword scabbard to activate them, and threw them among the dead and wounded men. He was well back in the tunnel when they exploded close together. He felt a rush of air.

Major Goto spoke for the first time since leaving the command post.

"Do you think two grenades are sufficient?" he asked. "Should I . . . ?"

"No," said Tochizawa. "We will return to the command post."

Tochizawa regretted there was insufficient time to see to each man individually. But they were soldiers and would understand. He felt grim satisfaction in having executed Captain Orita and the wretch who deserted his post. It was a stroke of fortune he had discovered their weakness in the nick of time. It baffled him that anyone would cling to life when living no longer served a useful purpose. To die in battle was but to fall like a cherry blossom, to live without honor disgusting.

When Tochizawa and his executive officer returned to the command post, the Americans had penetrated at some points to within less than a quarter-mile of it. The headquarters staff had been awaiting his arrival so that he might lead them in the final attack when the enemy drew within striking distance. The idea of dying in a gallant charge appealed to the colonel but it would not do. There were no doubt isolated strong points still resisting and he did not wish his death to precede their fall. And the thought of perhaps being killed at a distance by some overfed American lout was distasteful to him. He would pick his own time and place to die and at the hands of a true warrior. Himself. No American would win unmerited honor by ending the life of Shohei Tochizawa.

Major Goto produced a bottle of Old Par whiskey and Tochizawa drank one farewell toast with his staff. The lights went off while he was doing so. The Americans had either taken the generator cave or discovered the power cable and cut it. They might be digging at the buried cable this very moment to see where it led. The command post was in complete darkness until someone lit a candle. Tochizawa sent a last radio message to division before turning over command of the battalion to his adjutant.

"The Americans are less than two hundred meters from the command post. My troops have fought like the warriors of old and each has taken ten of the enemy with him in death. Though a hundred million Japanese perish, the world will not forget Tochizawa Battalion. Long live the Emperor. Tochizawa."

The staff was drinking toasts in boisterous high spirits when Tochizawa climbed to the observation post. He took Major Goto with him for kaishaku, assistance in committing hara-kiri. He did not expect to require active assistance but tradition dictated the presence of a trusted aide to witness the act, give a finishing thrust if necessary, and follow him in death. With Goto's assistance he pulled up the ladder and blocked the crawl hole with jagged slabs of concrete.

Tochizawa made a last sweeping survey of the hills and fields which the thousand men of his battalion had held for so long against the planes, armor and swarming troops of the enemy. The landscape was alive with their Shermans and infantry. He was struck once more by its resemblance to the picture he had once seen of the Western notion of Hell. Wrecked Shermans lay in ones and twos and even threes. The Americans had paid a great price in blood and time for their victory. He was almost content. Yet he wondered if he had been a bit more cunning, if his troops had displayed a bit more spirit than could be expected of ordinary men, the battalion might not have resisted a few more days. When he had drunk it all in he shattered his binoculars against the concrete. No American soldier would ever wear them dangling from his neck. Tochizawa no longer needed them to see the enemy troops closing in on the hill concealing the command post.

When the Americans were little more than a hundred yards distant the battalion staff sallied out of the command post, shouting, the officers flourishing their swords, the men carrying rifles, grenades and sharpened stakes. All were cut down by the advancing Americans before they could draw blood. The time had come at last. Except for himself and Major Goto the Tochizawa Battalion no longer existed. Perhaps somewhere among the shattered positions a few men still lived and fought. He preferred to believe not. Tochizawa stripped to the waist. He was mildly surprised at how plainly each rib showed. He had not seen his own naked body for many days. He thought of his son, Yoshi. It would be good if he could leave a final message for his son so Yoshi would know how his father had fought and died. But Yoshi would require no such message. He knew his father well enough to know how he would die. When the Americans came to the Kanto, Yoshi would die well, also. Perhaps, as Yoshi hoped, they would meet at Yasukuni.

Grenades were exploding in battalion headquarters on the first level. Tochizawa tore the letter from Yoshi he had been carrying on his person into tiny pieces. It would not become a souvenir for some American soldier. He took the tachi, the long sword of his samurai grandfather, from its scabbard and broke it between two blocks of concrete. That also, would never become a souvenir. And there would be no Tochizawa left alive worthy of bearing it, excepting Yoshi. He spread out the rectangle of white cloth he had brought for the purpose and knelt upon it. On one side he laid the two pieces of the tachi. On the other, his grandfather's short sword, the shoto. That he could not break, even to preserve it from the Americans. It was required for his death. He turned and looked at his executive officer. Major Goto's face was sad. Tochizawa was surprised. Surely Goto must understand the beauty of this moment.

"Major Goto," he said. "When I am dead you will break the sword. It must not be left for the Americans."

"I understand," Major Goto said.

Jagged bits of concrete dug into Tochizawa's knees but he felt no pain. From far below in the bowels of the hill came muffled voices. The Americans, encountering no opposition after tossing in grenades, had broken into battalion headquarters. Tochizawa wondered if his staff had destroyed all secret documents before sallying out. He had neglected ordering it done. The oversight annoyed him. There were explosions in the command post now. The Americans were throwing grenades into it from the headquarters on the first level. Now the Americans were in the command post. He could hear their voices. It is time, he thought.

"Good-bye, Goto," he said. "You have served me well."

He thought he saw tears in the eyes of his executive. Incredible. Was it possible he had chosen unwisely for kaishaku? No, Goto would not flinch. Often the twin belly cuts of seppuku did not bring quick release but a lingering, agonizing death. In the old days a beheading sword stroke by the chosen aide followed disembowelment. Less than seventy years ago the great Saigo Takamori had died thus at Kagoshima City after the failure of his rebellion against the new Meiji regime. Goto would be obliged to deliver no such stroke. A simple neck thrust would suffice. But even that would not be necessary, Tochizawa thought. His death would be simple and pure.

Something rammed against the concrete blocking the crawl hole. Tochizawa knelt on the rectangle of white cloth, facing north, toward the palace of the Emperor. He took the hilt of his grandfather's short sword in both hands. He thrust it into his belly and drew it from left to right. The pain was the first sharp physical sensation he had felt in many days. Somehow he had expected to feel nothing. Although it took him by surprise he uttered no sound. His death must be simple and pure. He turned the blade and pulled it upward. The concrete blocks over the observation post were shifting. The pain was intense and he felt himself weakening. The shouts of the Americans faded. When his body began to topple he forced it with his last strength of will and muscles to fall forward, as if bowing. He lay with his face pressed in the dirt and gritty shards of concrete, barely conscious.

Simple and pure, he thought, a perfect death.

11

[Private Eishun Murakami/Sergeant Oscar Knolle]

Sixty-three soldiers of the Tochizawa Battalion's thousand were taken prisoner. Four of these surrendered. The other fifty-nine were unconscious or too severely wounded to kill themselves. The last man to die in the battle was one who had not sought the honor and did not comprehend it when it came. He was an ordinary private, Eishun Murakami, a second year soldier. Private Murakami was the soldier Colonel Tochizawa had seen working in the garden in the midst of battle.

He was thirty-two years old and a farmer in Kyushu's Kumamoto Prefecture when he was called into the Army in May 1944. He had been rejected in an earlier call-up because he had no trigger finger on his right hand. He had been accused of deliberately maiming himself until it was ascertained he had lost the finger during rice harvest in 1937. Despite the condition of the stump, the authorities had refused to believe his explanation until official confirmation arrived from his village. Even while he was being reviled and pummeled by the hanchos at the receiving barracks he had not thought to point out the absence of the finger impaired his efficiency but little. He was ambidextrous. Born lefthanded, he had been forced as a schoolchild to use his right hand and only after his accident had reverted to his left. He did not deliberately conceal the information to avoid conscription. Though he had no great desire to become a soldier he would not have dreamed of evading his duty. It was simply that no one asked.

The life of a soldier was as unpleasant as he expected. It was particularly bad the first year when his family and his fields were fresh in his memory and he and the other first year soldiers were the butt of everyone above them. He was scolded, slapped, lectured, given all the extra details, and drilled interminably. Although the Army fed him, housed him, and clothed him, the six yen a month he received in pay was as much cash pocket money as he had been accustomed to in civilian life, and the work only occasionally more arduous than that on the farm, everything seemed strange and oppressive. On the farm, every season was different and had its own special tasks and celebrations. There were some things to be done in spring and autumn and others to be done in summer and winter. On rainy days one did this and on fine days one did that. In the Army one day was like another except that in summer one sweated and in winter one shivered. And on the farm he could see the results of his labor in the earth about him and in his storehouse, in the clothing his wife and children wore and in the food they ate. In the Army, no matter how long one marched or drilled, at the end of the day there was nothing to show for it but weary muscles. Sometimes when he had been drilled until his feet burned in the unaccustomed prison of Army boots or he had been cuffed because there was a loose button on his tunic or a private first class had been reprimanded by the squad leader, he thought wryly of the song he had been taught in the first year of primary school and whose words he had never forgotten.

With his gun over his shoulder the soldier marches,
To the sound of the bugle he marches;
The beautiful soldier, I love the soldier.

Soldiers were not beautiful and when they marched their feet hurt and the rifle grew heavy on their shoulders. It was inspiring that the Emperor was pleased to have his own chrysanthemum symbol on every rifle but it made them no lighter. The song said nothing of these things. Once, after a long march, he had sung the song without thinking and his comrades ridiculed him and called him an infant. They had been taught the same song in primary school but did not relate it to their own condition. Some of the men, he knew, thought him rather stupid because he had difficulty adjusting to Army life and seldom spoke of anything but farming. After he became aware of their opinions he hardly spoke at all because little else interested him.

Murakami knew his first contentment in the Army when his platoon was assigned a plot of land to cultivate as an extra duty. To plant and cultivate was almost like returning home again for a few hours. What he felt for the land was not love. It was respect. And gratitude. One put seed and his sweat into the ground and the ground repaid him with a livelihood. It put food in his belly and clothes on his back with enough left over for a pipe of tobacco and on special occasions a cup of sake. He preferred the ruder shochu but it took sake to make a celebration elegant. The vegetable garden, moreover, won Murakami a certain condescending popularity. No man in the platoon knew as well as he how to coax cabbages and pumpkins from the ground, and he was always ready to take a comrade's duty in the garden without the customary inducement of a cigarette or a sweet from home.

In the spring of 1945, when General Inada came down to speed the construction of the southern Kyushu defenses, the Tochizawa Battalion was shifted to build the network of fortifications it would occupy. It was necessary to abandon the platoon garden with its spring vegetables too young for picking and the taro, cabbages, daikon and pumpkin still to be planted. Murakami felt the loss as keenly as Colonel Tochizawa might have felt the loss of a key position to the enemy. While he labored in the earth with pick and mattock he thought how much more useful it would be to be working the soil instead. He thought constantly of the crop he had left behind, following in his farmer's mind the days of seeding, of cultivating, of watering and fertilizing and the ripening and gathering. When he calculated the produce was at its peak, he asked his squad leader for one day's leave to return to the garden and bring back what might have survived neglect. He was slapped and ridiculed.

"Do you think the Tochizawa Battalion left only ghosts behind?" the honorable squad leader demanded. "There are plenty of hands back there to tend your precious garden, and more than enough mouths to eat your cucumbers."

When Murakami heard that he felt cheated, but also relieved. Others would profit from his labor, but at least it would not have been wasted. He was accustomed to having others profit from his labor. He had been indebted to the rice broker for as long as he could remember while the broker grew richer and richer as the war went on. He hoped no rich man shared the produce of his garden, only poor farmers like himself.

In July, though work on the fortifications continued night and day without relief, the platoon was again assigned land to cultivate. This time it lay within the positions and Murakami knew he would never have to leave it as he had the other. The platoon worked two plots, the larger on open, level ground where it got the full sun and also helped disguise the presence of a military installation. The other was tucked in the fold of a hill where it could be worked and provide food in the event of a prolonged siege. Although it was late in the season the platoon planted taro, cabbages and pumpkins. At first, though he would have liked to spend more time in the garden, Murakami was too weary for more than his own duty period. He resented the interminable burrowing that exhausted him and kept him from useful work. The principal work on the Tochizawa positions was finished in August and despite the fact that military training grew more stringent Murakami was again able to spend extra hours in his gardens. Although he shared them with the sixty-odd men of his platoon, in his mind they were his. The others, even the farmers among them, begrudged the weary hours they were obliged to spend among the plants when their regular duties were done.

The October typhoon severely damaged the gardens but the platoon was given no time to restore them until the washed-out fortifications were rebuilt. Although Murakami took the setback philosophically—he was accustomed to natural disasters—he fretted during the entire period the construction work kept him from his gardens. During the period of waiting for the enemy attack after the positions were repaired, platoon duties became comparatively lighter. Murakami spent all his free time in the gardens, determined that the plants that survived the typhoon should flourish. He weeded and cultivated and brought buckets of night soil from the latrines to fertilize them. The other soldiers avoided him as much as possible because of his smell and began calling him Koetago-San, "Mr. Honey-Bucket." When he worked in the gardens by day he wore, like the other soldiers so employed, an umbrellalike hat of woven straw to add to the illusion he was an ordinary farm worker should American fighter and reconnaissance planes appear unexpectedly.

There were cabbages in the garden by the end of the month and prospects of fine pumpkins in a few weeks, taro root in another month. Before they could be harvested, the garden on open ground, the larger of the two, was completely destroyed by enemy shells and bombs a few days after the Americans landed on the beaches of Ariake Bay. This inflamed Murakami against the enemy as had nothing before. For the first time their wanton barbarity was made tangible for him. But his anger gradually faded with his growing concern for the little garden in the fold of the hill. He brooded over it as if it were a last surviving child. Although there was no fighting in the area no one was permitted outside the positions by day without specific orders. The enforced idleness underground while his garden went untended deeply disturbed Murakami. He became irritable and at times abstracted. There were occasions when he imagined the pumpkin vines and taro were calling him. He stole time from his evening rest periods between the calisthenics and deep-breathing exercises to tend the garden as best he could. A week after the invasion he managed to work almost the entire night through. The moon began rising just at sunset and only a few scattered clouds shadowed the clarity of the night. A few hours before dawn the temperature fell to less than forty degrees but he did not notice the cold. During the next day's rest period his sleep was untroubled for the first time since the destruction of the larger garden.

When the Americans reached the forward positions of the Tochizawa Battalion and all troops were required to remain at their posts or relief stations around the clock, Murakami's concern for his garden became an obsession. If he listened carefully he could hear the voices of the pumpkin vines and taro plants above the sounds of battle. When he could resist their call no longer he began stealing back through the tunnels to tend them in the intervals between duty periods on watch at the firing aperture. Such excursions were almost always at night, though occasionally when the demands of his garden were irresistible he went out by day. It was on such an occasion that he was seen by Colonel Tochizawa.

He was unable to absent himself even a few minutes either by day or night after the Americans broke into the Yamaguchi Company positions. He imagined all sorts of dreadful things happening to his plants. Shermans grinding them beneath their treads, American troops kicking them down with their heavy boots, or the plants themselves shriveling spitefully because he no longer answered their summons. He tried to leave his post more than once, only to be dragged back by a comrade. Murakami's position was one of the last to fall. When the Americans began attacking it and engaged the attention of all the defenders he managed to creep away undetected. When he emerged into the sunlight he began running despite his weariness and the stiffness of long confinement underground. His spirits lifted when he saw the pumpkins plump and undisturbed among their vines and the taro plants still green and full-leaved. It seemed to him they called a greeting when he appeared among them. He fell to his knees and crawled between the taro plants, searching the night-soil enriched earth for weeds.

He had finished his weeding and was turning the ground with his mattock when an American soldier, moving cautiously at the foot of a nearby slope, spied him. The soldier had seen the garden before detecting Murakami's presence and, since the last Japanese strongpoints were being mopped up and no one had fired at him in the past several minutes, had come over to investigate. He was himself a farmer.

Sergeant Oscar Knolle's family grew sugar beets in Nebraska. They also kept a large table garden. When he was a boy he had worked in the garden with his brothers and sisters. Wherever he was stationed in the Army he had made a point of learning what was being grown in the area and how.

That summer, when the division was training on Luzon, he had spent most of a three-day pass visiting the quartermaster farm at San Miguel. He hoped he would never have to apply what he learned there. The soil was exhausted from overcultivation, there was not enough water and there were all sorts of other difficulties with labor, seed and equipment. Japan had surprised him. He had expected to find the land exhausted on Kyushu, too, and every inch under cultivation. Kyushu, to his farmer's eye, was extraordinarily beautiful, at least he knew it would have been had it not been fought over. The fallow rice paddies looked rich and as neat as if laid out on paper with a pencil and ruler. He liked the orderly, clean way the terraces climbed the hillside and the little diked fields patterned the valleys. There were trampled vegetable gardens wherever he looked. The waste bothered him although he knew a soldier fighting for his life could not be expected to watch where he put his feet. He knew many of the plants growing in the gardens. Some of them, like cabbages, pumpkins, onions and carrots, grew in the table garden on the family farm. He was surprised to discover that southern Kyushu was not all farmland. There were groves of bamboos and forests of pines and cedar, rough land and untouched hillsides. He was a little sorry it had been necessary to ruin so much of it blasting the Japs out of their holes. The one thing he did not like about the land was the pervading odor, where battle smells did not mask it, of the human excrement used to fertilize some of the fields.

When he stepped around the last hill in the Yamaguchi Company fortifications and saw a garden in the heart of the enemy's positions he could scarcely believe his eyes. His astonishment was even greater when he approached the garden and saw a man back in the fold of the hill swinging a broad-headed hoe as if unaware of the bloody struggle that had just ended. Sergeant Knolle's first instinct was to shoot the Japanese, but the man's back was to him and he was unarmed. And Knolle's curiosity was aroused. He moved a few steps closer and aimed his rifle at the Japanese soldier.

"Hey, you!" he shouted. Murakami looked around, the mattock lifted for a downstroke, glanced at Knolle without acknowledging his presence, turned away and continued working.

"Drop it, you dumb son of a bitch!" Knolle cried angrily.

Maybe it was a trick. The Jap wanted him to get close enough to clobber him with that hoe. His finger tightened on the trigger. If it was a trick the little bastard was the coolest customer he had ever seen. He wasn't missing a single lick with that hoe. And he really knew how to handle it. That was about the best-kept little garden he'd ever seen. The pumpkins were about half the size of those they grew back home. Those green plants looked a lot like the taro he'd seen in the Philippines. Knolle moved close enough to nudge Murakami's shoulder with the rifle muzzle, ready to fire if the Japanese tried to get him with the hoe. Murakami looked around, annoyed. Hadn't the Americans already interfered with his work enough? He had to finish the row and get back to post before anyone noticed his absence.

Off his rocker, Knolle thought. He wouldn't have believed it if he hadn't seen it. He had thought the Japs never got combat fatigue. Too damn fanatical. Well, it proved this one was human, anyway. The captain was always screaming to bring in some prisoners. Knolle wondered what the captain was going to say when he brought one in that was crazy. They'd have themselves one hell of a time getting any sense out of this one.

"Come on," he said, gesturing with his rifle. "Let's go."

Murakami stared at him, still annoyed.

Maybe I ought to bust him one and carry him back, Knolle thought. He could not do it. The Jap was so little and skinny and looked like he didn't even know what was going on. Maybe there was some other way. Knolle pointed at a pumpkin and touched it with his foot.

"Pumpkin," he said.

When he saw that Murakami showed interest he said it again. Murakami nodded his head.

"Kabocha," he said.

"Kabocha," Knolle repeated after him. "That's Jap for pumpkin?"

He pointed at the pumpkin as he spoke. Murakami nodded his head more vigorously. Now I'm getting somewhere, Knolle thought. He took out his cigarettes and handed one to Murakami. Murakami hesitated then took it. Knolle lit Murakami's cigarette and then his own. Murakami smiled and thanked him. He would have liked a closer look at the American's lighter but was too shy.

"Let's go," said Knolle. "Okay?"

He motioned for Murakami to walk ahead of him. The American wanted him to leave his garden, Murakami thought. It would be safe enough, the American respected his pumpkins. And he should be getting back to his post. He must certainly have been missed by now. Murakami started walking back toward the hidden tunnel entrance. An American soldier came around the hill with a Browning automatic rifle slung across his shoulders, his arms hooked over it carelessly. He saw Murakami before he noticed Knolle. He jerked the BAR from his shoulders and fired with one smooth action. Murakami fell dead.

"Watch it!" Knolle yelled at the same instant. "You tryin' to kill me, for Christ's sake!"

"Didn't see you," the BAR man said calmly.

"Goddam it, you killed my prisoner!"

"How the shit did I know he was a prisoner?"

"Didn't you see he didn't have no rifle?"

"I wasn't about to take the time to look. Why you so pissed off anyway? He's just a Jap."

Knolle looked down at Murakami. His eyes were open and the cigarette was still clenched between his teeth, smoke curling from it. The poor starved crazy little son of a bitch, Knolle thought. That's what they'd been fighting and had given them so much hell. Seeing him working in the garden and now lying dead on the ground with his belly all shot full of holes he just couldn't hate Japs as much as he had before.

"I heard we took their battalion headquarters," the BAR man said. "Come on, let's get there before all the good stuff's gone."

"Okay," said Knolle.

The two of them started walking toward a dominating hill a hundred yards away. Knolle turned around once to look at the small body on the ground among the taro.

12

[Corporal Lester Waddell]

Corporal Lester Waddell of the 5th Marine Division did not know how many Japanese he thought he had killed when he first discovered the trick they were playing on him. Five, at least, that he could be sure of. These were Japs he'd aimed at and seen drop and did not include any he might have lucked out on popping at hot spots in hills and trees or at suspicious sounds in the night. Or any who had been hiding in the caves and holes he had helped blast or the eleven certains he had racked up in the fourteen months before he came ashore X+2 on Beach Stutz Yellow Two. That eleven averaged less than one a month for the fourteen months he had been overseas but it was still pretty darn good when you figured less than a third of that had been actual combat and he hadn't included any he hadn't got all by his lonesome with an M-1. Whenever anybody wanted to argue about who got who, he just said to heck with it and let them have it, like when you were bird hunting with somebody and shot at the same quail. And when you just threw a grenade where they were he didn't count that either, any more than you'd brag about how many fish you got dynamiting a pond. To do that you didn't have to be able to hit the side of a barn with you inside and the door closed.

But the five, or anyway what he thought was five before he found out about the trick, was almost two a week since he hit the beach and would have been a lot better than that if the pesky little codgers didn't use their holes as clever as woodchucks. You hardly ever caught one out of his hole and when you did the way he ducked into it at the crack of the rifle you never knew whether you had really got him or not. Of course when you had an eye like he did you could be pretty sure but he didn't count pretty sures. If he'd just had his scope-mounted Savage Hornet from back home there wouldn't be any two ways about it. He'd begged and begged the platoon sergeant to get him a scope but the bowlegged cowboy son-of-a-buck just said scopes were for snipers and the last time he'd looked at the T O and E Waddell's squad wasn't authorized any sniper. Which was Sergeant Youngblood's cute way of saying "Semper Fi."

The first three he hadn't gotten much of a look at after he bagged them. The very first one had been a real piece of luck, it had come so quick and easy and unexpected. Just a case of being in the right place at the right time, not getting flustered and, naturally, being one heck of a snap shooter. He hadn't been off the LCVP five hours and wasn't even up in the line yet when it happened. The platoon leader had detailed half the squad to making up machine-gun belts while they were waiting to go up and relieve an outfit that had been pretty well chewed up the first two days of the invasion. They were sitting there loading .30 caliber into the belts when off to one side the Jap popped out from between the roots of a big pine that had a Spruance haircut down to about fifteen feet from the ground. He was waving one of those swords like they did and before anybody knew what was going on he took off a Marine's head neat as a chicken's and was bearing down on another one, yelling the whole time. He was at least twenty yards away but the loading detail jumped up and lit out for cover, scattering ammo all over the ground. Except Waddell. He reached over to where his M-1 was propped against his pack and got off two shots without getting up and without hardly aiming. Both of them got the Jap square in the back. It was close enough he heard them hit. "Thunk." "Splat." One must have hit bone. It wasn't much for distance but it was darn fair snap shooting.

There was a bunch of Marines over where the Jap had come charging out. They ran over to where he was laying on his face and started scrambling for his sword a heck of a lot faster than they'd scrambled to get their pieces into firing position. Waddell couldn't understand why they were so hot for that sword. It had the blood of a good old American boy all over it. With the sword and all, it had to be an officer and it was the first Jap officer Waddell had ever got that he knew of so he started over to take a closer look. He didn't get halfway there. One guy started through the Jap's pockets and two others got into an argument over his wristwatch. It made Waddell want to vomit. It seemed there were always a buzzard or two like that around. You wondered how guys like that ever got in the Corps. Waddell just went back and started shoving .30 caliber in the links again and didn't get up until the company commander came over to shake his hand personally and tell him he was going to put him in for the Bronze Star. If he got it, it would be the second one. He got the first one on Iwo and a Silver Star, too. He was the most decorated enlisted man in the platoon and some of the guys thought he should be at least a sergeant by now but Corporal Waddell didn't care that much about stripes. A rifleman had his job to do and what counted was how good he was at it, not how many stripes he had on his arm. He didn't think he was cut out for sergeant, anyhow. It wasn't his place to tell other guys how to do their jobs.

Getting the Jap officer so easy made him think he was off and running but it was two whole days before he got his next certain, when they were busting through the hills just east of the coast. It had been an easy two-hundred-yard-shot. The fool Jap had stuck his head and shoulders out of a hole to take a look around. Just like a chuck. He hadn't got a close look at the Jap because the squad was moving off in the other direction but he knew the little fellow was dead from the way he lay there half outside the hole. It was another four days before he got number three. It wasn't from any lack of Japs—there were so many of them it took that long to push two miles to the railroad near a little place called Yunomoto—you just didn't catch one out in the open. It was nothing but grenades and satchel charges day in and day out. There had been a ridge at Yunomoto with a neat row of caves running all along the bottom. They were almost big enough to walk into standing up and weren't camouflaged or anything and there wasn't anybody in them but a few scared civilians and the bodies of more civilians who had been so scared they had killed themselves. The Jap soldiers were on top of the ridge and the reverse slope. Waddell got number three when they were moving on the ridge and the Jap raised up to lob a grenade. He never got a close look at that one, either, because the other Japs dragged the body back out of sight by the feet. Waddell had happy memories of Yunomoto for another reason, too. They had been held up there for half a day waiting for reinforcements to come up and everybody had had a nice bath in the natural hot spring water that came up out of the ground. Once he got used to the smell it was as good a bath as he'd ever had.

It took another ten days to get number four. That was after the battalion had joined up with the 2nd Marine Division to take Ijuin. The Japs put up a heck of a fight at Ijuin; the lieutenant said the Jap 40th Army Headquarters was there, but it was just his luck he never got a clean shot at one of them even halfway out in the open where he could be sure if he really finished one. But when he did get number four, about eight hard-fought miles inland from Ijuin, he got a good look at him. It was on a reconnaissance patrol. They had come quite a piece without drawing fire by staying low and keeping off the paths. It was hard climbing at times and some of them were blowing pretty good. The squad leader pulled them off into a gully to take a break in among some bamboo. He wouldn't let anybody talk or smoke, which didn't make any difference to Waddell because he didn't smoke anyhow. Smoking was unhealthy and some even said it was sinful.

There was a rustling at the far end of the gully and a Jap soldier came walking into it bent over and putting one foot ahead of the other like an Indian. He stopped and looked around like he was checking out the gully. The Jap had hardly set foot in the gully when Waddell had his M-1 to his shoulder but the squad leader grabbed hold of his arm and shook his head, no. Waddell was disappointed but he had to admit Sergeant DiVita was right. The Jap was acting like he was point man for a patrol and if he didn't spot them they could maybe catch the whole patrol. If he did see them back in the bamboo they could still drop him before he could duck back out of sight. He must not have seen them because he turned around and gave a hand signal not much different from the kind Americans did. Waddell's patrol had an M-3 submachine gun and DiVita motioned the M-3 man to hold his fire until he gave the signal.

The first Jap came deeper into the gully and right behind him were four civilians. Two of them had hold of the handles of a wooden wheelbarrow with what looked like a keg mounted on it. A third civilian was holding on to the side of the wheelbarrow to steady it. The other one had a pillow charge in one hand and a spear in the other. They weren't plain civilians. They were GUs, volunteer combatants. Waddell had heard a lot about them but these were the first ones he'd seen that he could be sure weren't plain civilians. He'd never shot at any of the plain civilians the way the trigger-happy guys did. He felt kind of sorry for civilians, even if the Japs did deserve everything they got for Pearl Harbor and all. But these were GUs so it was okay. Another Jap soldier brought up the rear. The M-3 man got itchy and started firing before Sergeant DiVita gave the signal so everybody else started shooting too. The lead soldier and the GUs went down before they knew what hit them but the other soldier had lagged behind and would have gotten clean away around the hill if Waddell hadn't put a bullet between his shoulder blades. Waddell got him twice more while he was going down which was a waste, but it had been such a long time since he had a clean shot he just kept squeezing them off.

Waddell rolled him over and took a look at him when they were going over the bodies for intelligence stuff––insignia, documents, letters, snapshots and that kind of thing. He was a tough, feisty-looking little codger, skinny as a lost cat. He had a scraggly beard and mustache not like he'd grown them on purpose but because he hadn't had a chance to shave in a while. There was a two-sided scar about half-healed over his right eye. His upper lip was pulled back in a kind of crazy grin and you could see a tooth missing right in front.

The whole patrol gathered around the wheelbarrow to look it over except for one man DiVita put at the end of the gully in case more Japs came to see what the shooting was about. There was a rifle stuck in the back of the keg and if you looked in the round hole in the front you could see what looked like the nose of an artillery shell. DiVita said it looked to him like some kind of close-range antitank deal and he was breaking off the reconnaissance to get it back so somebody who knew ordnance could check it out. They all laughed and said they'd hate to be around when anybody pulled the trigger of that rifle stuck in the keg. They got it back okay but they never did get the official word on exactly what it was supposed to be. They did hear that the Jap soldiers were from the 216th Division, which wasn't the one they'd been slugging it out with for the past two weeks. DiVita got a commendation for that.

Four days later he got number five when they crossed the Kotsuki River a mile and a half north of Kagoshima City, and took a road junction on the drive toward Kawakamicho. It wasn't much of a junction, just a couple of narrow dirt roads. Number five came sprinting out of a burning thatch-roofed house and set sail for a paddy field hedge. Waddell caught him in full stride and he jumped headfirst about seven feet with his arms stretched straight out. It was so much like somebody trying to make a flying tackle Waddell couldn't help but laugh out loud. They were working with tanks then, including a tankdozer that would creep ahead and take down paddy hedges and dikes and shove dirt into the holes on the other side, so he was able to check out the Jap without getting his own tail shot off. The Jap had rolled over after he hit and was on his back with his arms and legs stretched out. When Waddell got a look at his face was when he realized something fishy was going on. The Jap had a scraggly beard and mustache and a half-healed twosided scar over his right eye. He looked like the son-of-a-buck Waddell had got back in the gully. Waddell pushed back the Jap's upper lip with the end of his rifle and sure enough there was a tooth missing. It gave him a creepy feeling, like a thousand-legs was crawling down his collar. Kulik, who had been in the gully with him, wasn't far away. Waddell called him over.

"Look at this," he said, breathing hard, touching the body with his rifle.

Kulik looked at the body and then, uncomprehendingly, at Waddell.

"Yeah?" he said.

"Remember the little codger I got last week?" said Waddell. "Back in that gully?"

"Yeah," Kulik said. "What about it?"

"He looked like this one."

"Hell, what's so great about that? They all look alike."

"No," Waddell said impatiently. "No. I mean just like him. Scar and all."

Kulik took a closer look.

"Naw," he said. "That one you got didn't have any whiskers. And I didn't see no scar on him, either."

"Gol darn it!" Waddell cried. "I ain't talking about the front one. I'm talking about the one I got. The one in back."

"Don't get your shit hot," Kulik said. "I don't remember if either one of 'em had a beard. What the hell difference does it make, anyway?"

Waddell wished Sergeant DiVita was there because he would have remembered but DiVita had got himself killed the day before crossing the Kotsuki. Waddell puzzled a day and a night over the two Japs that looked exactly alike. Japs mostly looked pretty much alike, but not exactly. And to have the same scar and the same missing tooth. It was enough to make you think it was the same Jap. That didn't make any kind of sense at all, but there it was. There was something fishy about it no matter which way you looked at it and he was going to find out what.

The drive pushed on a mile or so and turned north for Kawakamicho. Waddell got the chance he was waiting for when the Japanese made a stand near Sanekata, where a hill dominated the only road, and stalled the drive. Hill 186 it was called because it was one hundred eighty-six meters high. The Marines called it Big Nose because somebody said it looked just like the CO's nose, and was just as hard. He was on patrol duty again, looking for the best way around it, when they all saw the Jap soldier duck into a cave. They didn't know if it was just the one soldier in there or a whole raft of them the way it was sometimes. Or whether it was just a plain natural cave that didn't go anywhere or was the entrance to a tunnel and by now the Jap was either off somewhere reporting them or sighting down on them from another entrance. They didn't have any demolition charges with them, only grenades, and the staff sergeant running things couldn't make up his mind what to do about the cave. Waddell volunteered to take a look. The sergeant let him, glad to be off the hook. The rest of the patrol got down and covered the entrance while Waddell crawled up to it from the side. He reached around the mouth of the cave and threw a rock in. He thought he heard something moving around in there. He threw in another rock.

"Grenade you dumb bastard!" the sergeant yelled. "Use your grenades."

Waddell didn't pay him any mind.

"Hey, Jap," he called. "I'm gonna come in and get you."

He could hear heavy breathing inside. Just one man. It must be one of those little natural caves that didn't go very far back. He got up and made a lot of noise with his feet, like he was coming in. A rifle popped back in the cave and a shot came zinging out. While the sergeant was screaming for him to throw in a grenade Waddell stuck his rifle into the cave entrance and got off all eight rounds as fast as he could, moving the barrel just enough to give the inside a good spraying. He didn't want to mess the Jap up with any grenades. The Jap yelled, then Waddell heard him thrash around a little and lie still. He crawled inside and dragged him out into the sunlight where he could get a good look at him. The rest of the patrol came running up, the sergeant cussing him for taking such a damn fool chance, but Waddell was too busy looking at the Jap he had killed to take any notice. He felt cold all over when he saw the face. It was the same Jap he had killed back in the gully and again at the road junction. He wished Kulik was there so he could ask him what he thought about it now but Kulik hadn't come on the patrol. Maybe if he could get the body back Kulik wouldn't talk so blamed smart. But he knew he couldn't do that. He wished he had a camera to take a picture.

All during the rest of the patrol he thought about how it could be he had killed the same Jap three times, maybe even six for all he knew because he hadn't seen the faces of the first three. Except the first one had been an officer and the Jap couldn't have been an officer and an enlisted man both. Then he hit on a thought that kind of made sense out of it. They'd been killing Japs by the bushel for more than three weeks now but it looked like every time they cleaned up one bunch there were twice as many waiting at the next place. You'd think the Japs would be running out of troops. Unless everybody was killing the same one over and over again, like he was. The only thing was, if they were, why hadn't anybody said anything about it? Maybe they just hadn't looked.

When he got back off patrol he started asking around. At first they would all laugh but when they saw he meant it they gave him funny looks. Either they wouldn't admit the same thing was happening to them or they just didn't believe him. If it was because they didn't believe him then it was a sign he was the only one it was happening to. And if he was the only one the Japs were doing it to, what was the big idea? That was when he started getting angry. Why were the Japs picking on him? What were they trying to pull, and why? He'd show them he was on to their trick. Then maybe they'd start leaving him alone.

It was several days before anyone noticed Waddell had stopped firing his rifle and was taking all kinds of foolish chances. By that time they were past Big Nose Hill and almost to Kawakamicho. The squad leader called him on it first and then the platoon sergeant. Waddell knew what he was doing but he did not try to explain it to them. He'd had just about enough of Marines looking at him like he had rocks in his head. He wasn't going to shoot another Jap until he got close enough to get a good look at his face and make sure he wasn't just killing the same one over again. That was how he would show the Japs he was on to their trick. But just to get the sergeant off his back he started popping away at every hot spot just like the others. Only he wasn't really trying to hit anything. What was the use if he was only going to kill the same Jap over and over again? What he needed was binoculars so he wouldn't have to get so close to make sure it was a new Jap he was after. There was a Pfc over in First Platoon had a good pair of binoculars he had taken off a Jap officer somewhere back down the line. The next time Waddell was sent back for hot chow he went looking for him. He was in luck. The private first class had been sent back for a hot supper, too, and had the binoculars with him. Waddell got them off him for almost a month's pay, three twenty-dollar bills in real American money he had been carrying in his billfold ever since he shipped out. Waddell was really glad he had held on to them even back in the Philippines, where he could have got five times what they were worth back in the States.

The binoculars turned out to be the worst buy he ever made. The very next day after he bought them he got himself a Jap. He first spotted the Jap away off, crawling through the trees and dead grass on the side of a hill with only his helmet showing and some zookie grass stalks sticking out of it for camouflage. Waddell was the only one with binoculars so he was the only one who saw him. He started working his way toward the Jap, hoping to get a look at his face. After a while the Jap raised up a little and took a look around. Waddell froze. Before he could sneak the binoculars up to his eyes the Jap put his head back down and started crawling again. Waddell took a chance and ran a few yards paralleling the Jap's course and then flopped down. He looked through the binoculars and waited. Sure enough, before long the Jap raised his head for another look around. Waddell could see his face as plain as if he was in the next pew in church. He didn't look anything like the Jap Waddell had been killing except in the usual ways Japs looked alike. Unshaven but nothing you could call a mustache or whiskers, more nose and less chin than the face he knew as well as his own. Waddell couldn't tell if he had a scar over his eye or not because the helmet had slipped down low over the right eye.

Waddell figured out where the Jap would be when he rose up for another look if he didn't change his pattern and slipped over to where there was the best chance of a clean shot at him. He steadied his M-1 in the prone firing position and waited. The Jap raised up for a look around almost where Waddell figured he would. That was one dumb Jap. Waddell wondered how he had managed to stay alive this long. He held his breath and squeezed off a round. The Jap's head went down with the crack of the rifle. The grass where he had been hiding didn't stir. Waddell knew for sure he'd got him. He jumped up and ran toward the spot. Before he got halfway there somebody started shooting at him from up the hill and he had to crawl the rest of the way on his belly. The platoon let loose at whoever it was shooting at him and the firing from up the hill stopped.

The Jap must have been on his hands and knees when he got hit. He had fallen forward with his face in the dirt and his tail sticking up, like he was praying the way they did. Waddell gave his tail a little shove and he toppled over sideways. His eyes were open and looking straight into Waddell's, but he was dead. And he had a mustache and whiskers. Waddell pushed back the upper lip. There was a tooth missing. He didn't have to push up the helmet for a look above the right eye but he did it anyway. The two-sided scar was there. He should have known the little devils were too smart for him. If they knew how to make him keep killing the same Jap over and over again they sure as fire were smart enough to trick him into thinking he was getting a fresh one. If that was the way it was going to be he might just as well give up and go home. He wasn't doing any good here.

Waddell got to his feet and started walking down the hill to where the platoon was. The Japs on the hill started shooting at him again and the guys in the platoon yelled at him to get down. Waddell just kept going. It didn't matter much one way or the other if he got hit or not. What was the use if he was just going to keep killing the same Jap over and over and over again? But he did not get hit. Not just the platoon but tanks and artillery and everything opened up on the hill where the Jap had given their ambush positions away. When he got to where his squad was holed up he kept right on going. The squad leader ran after him and grabbed him by the arm.

"You hit?" the squad leader said. "Can you get back to the aid station by yourself?"

Waddell pulled his arm loose and kept walking.

"Where the hell you think you're going?" the squad leader yelled, mad now.

"I quit," Waddell said.

The squad leader grabbed his arm again and spun him around.

"What'd you say, you son of a bitch?" he bawled.

"I ain't doing any good here," Waddell said patiently. "I quit."

"You quit? You dumb son of a bitch you know goddam well—"

The squad leader shut up in the middle of the sentence and just looked at him, letting go of his arm. Waddell turned around and started walking toward the rear again. The squad leader ran around in front of him and walked backward, facing him.

"You'll be okay," the squad leader said. "I'll send somebody back with you."

"What for?" Waddell asked. "I don't need anybody to show me the way."

The squad leader called that bald-headed Jones over from the squad and Waddell heard them whispering behind him. He heard the squad leader say "battle happy" and that made him sore. Like he had that combat fatigue like some of the yellowbellies that quit when the going got rough. It wasn't anything like that. He wasn't scared. He just wasn't doing any good any more so why hold back the squad on account of it. He explained that to Jones as they walked back toward the rear and Jones nodded and said sure, he knew just how it was and would show him where to find somebody to quit to. But instead of going to company headquarters with him Jones took him to the aid station.

"I'm not hit," Waddell protested.

"I know," Jones said, like he was talking to some little kid, "but this is where they take applications to quit."

Waddell knew better than that. The Marines didn't take applications to quit. He didn't want to quit the Marines anyway. He just wanted to quit trying to kill Japs because it wasn't any use. Maybe they could find him something to do where the Japs wouldn't be able to make a fool of him. But he went along with Jones just to be shut of him. He'd find somebody with more sense to explain it to. Jones said, "Take it easy, Waddell," and went off and left him with a clerk inside the aid station.

The aid station was a big sidewall tent. It was divided off in front by a canvas flap to make a place for the clerk and a folding table and an old-looking corporal. Marines were sitting around on the dirt floor with first aid bandages on them and one was out, flat on his back, and getting blood in his arm from a corpsman. Another one had his head down between his knees, crying. He wasn't hit that Waddell could tell. Some of the Marines were talking and some were just sitting there. There had been more Marines sitting around outside the aid station waiting their turn. From behind the flap Waddell could hear moaning and cussing and doctor talk. He didn't feel right about being here with all the guys who had been hit when he was all right. The clerk took down his particulars and told him to sit down with the others and wait. The clerk pulled back the flap and went into the back of the tent. Waddell could see men lying all over the floor and some on tables being worked on. The old-looking corporal took his M-l and gave him a receipt for it with the serial number and all and told him if he wasn't evacuated to the rear he'd get it back. Waddell didn't care if he never got it back. He'd really liked that M-1 even if it wasn't a patch on the Savage .220 Hornet he had back home, but what was the use of having it if all it did was kill the same Jap time after time? The clerk came back and sat down at the table and told him it wouldn't be but a little while.

A doctor wearing a white apron with blood all over it and a doctor mask hanging down from his neck, pulled back the flap and said something to the clerk. The clerk nodded his head toward Waddell and said, "Him." The doctor walked about halfway over to Waddell and looked him over a minute. Waddell could tell he was anxious to get back to whatever he had been doing behind the flap. Waddell got to his feet, not knowing if he was supposed to stand at attention or what.

"Nerves all shot?" the doctor said.

He looked like he hadn't shaved lately and could use some sleep.

"No, sir," Waddell said.

"That seems obvious enough," the doctor said. "Headaches? Nightmares?"

"Sir?"

"Does your head hurt all the time? Ever have bad dreams or wake up in a sweat? Any trouble sleeping?"

"No sir. I feel okay. It wasn't my idea to come here."

"I know," the doctor said. "What's this about not doing any good?"

Waddell told him. The doctor looked more and more interested and less and less anxious to get back to work. When Waddell finished telling him the doctor rubbed his stubbly chin and said, "I see." Waddell thought maybe he really did because he didn't act like there was anything funny about it. The doctor went over and said something to the old-looking corporal and the corporal took Waddell outside to a jeep with a red cross on it and said something to the driver. He didn't offer to give Waddell his M-l back. There was a litter with a man on it fastened on both sides of the jeep and three Marines all bandaged up squeezed in the back seat. The driver told Waddell to get in the seat by him and they took off down the road.

"Where we going?" Waddell asked.

"Kagoshima City," the driver said, acting like it was more trouble to talk than it was worth. "Hospital."

"Me, too?" Waddell demanded. "I ain't hit."

"Yeah. Pops told me."

Waddell didn't like the way the driver laughed when he said that. It was like he was making fun of him. It was then Waddell realized what a mistake he'd made telling them he wanted to quit, and why. Everybody thought he had combat fatigue. That was the dumbest thing he ever heard. It came to him clear as spring water what he should have done and what he was going to do now that he finally had it all straight. Where he had gone wrong was thinking the only way he could do any good was to kill Japs. And that was just what the clever little codgers had figured on him thinking. But what if he didn't try to kill any? What if he just caught them? They sure as fire couldn't make him catch the same one over and over again because if a Jap was off somewhere in a stockade he couldn't be somewhere else at the same time. And what was so keen about the whole proposition was that from all he'd heard the Japs hated being caught worse than they hated being killed. That would really get even with them for playing such a smart-aleck trick on him. He could have kicked himself for not thinking about it sooner. Thinking about the surprise the Japs were going to get made him want to laugh out loud. And he did.

The driver looked over at him about half scared.

"Stop this thing," Waddell said.

"What do you mean, stop?" the driver said.

"I ain't going to no hospital."

The driver looked around in back where the three wounded Marines were jammed together.

"Any of you guys in any shape to give me a little help if I need it?" He said anxiously.

One of them, a big one with his left arm in a sling, said "I reckon" in a deep voice, and the driver turned back around to Waddell and said, "Oh, yes, you are."

That made Waddell mad, that yellowbellied driver thinking he was a troublemaker and then trying to get some poor old wounded Marine to do his dirty work for him to boot. Waddell pointed at his corporal's chevrons.

"See these?" he demanded. "No dad-blamed private's gonna tell me what I'm gonna do and what I'm not gonna do."

"That ain't the way it works, Mac," the driver said. "I got orders from the captain to take you to the hospital."

"Oh," Waddell said, sitting straight back in his seat.

The smart-aleck driver had him there. A corporal didn't amount to a hill of beans up against a captain. He was going at it the wrong way, just like he had gone at the Japs the wrong way.

"Look here," he said. "I'm all right now. I mean I don't want to quit any more. I just want to get back to my outfit."

"Too late now, Mac. Tell it to the psycho doc."

"See these binoculars?" Waddell said. "They came off a Jap officer. Cost me sixty bucks. If you let me go back to my outfit I'll give 'em to you."

The driver gave the binoculars a greedy look.

"I don't know," he said doubtfully. "I could get my ass in a sling."

"Who'd know the difference? You think all that captain's got to do is check up and see if some Marine got to the hospital or not?"

"I guess not," the driver said. "But if he does I'm gonna say you jumped out and took off before I could stop you and if they come looking for you, you got to promise to say that's how it was."

"It's a deal," Waddell said.

The driver stopped the jeep and Waddell handed over binoculars and crawled under the litter fastened across the side.

"Remember now, if you get picked up you took off before I could do anything about it," the driver said anxiously.

Waddell didn't answer doodledy-boo. He started back up the dirt road feeling good for the first time since he caught on to the trick the Japs were playing on him.

13

[Hajime Tsuyuki]

In thirty days of bitter fighting the Sixth Army ground its way through southern Kyushu's main line of fixed defenses and pushed inland at some points as deep as fifteen miles. On the west coast the Marines of V Amphibious Corps had taken Kushikino and Sendai, seven miles to the northeast, and driven through the narrow valleys of the Satsuma Peninsula to the eastern shore of Kagoshima Bay to take Kagoshima City, the chief port of southern Kyushu. Driving fourteen miles across the Osumi Peninsula from Beach Ford on Ariake Bay, XI Corps reached the eastern shore of Kagoshima Bay, taking the key airfield complex of Kanoya along the way. The defenses of Kano proved so formidable it was necessary to commit the Sixth Army's reserve division, the 11th Airborne, on December 2, X+22. On its right flank XI Corps took Shibushi and pushed north eleven miles to Aoki, only seven miles from the key depot and communications center of Miyakonojo. On the east coast I Corps took Miyazaki City and drove nine miles along the coast from Beach Chrysler to Fukushima on the Hitosuse River. South of Miyazaki City, I Corps pushed thirteen miles inland from Beach Cord to the mountain village of Aoidake, eleven miles northeast of Miyakonojo. The 98th Infantry Division, which on X+4 had landed on Beach Plymouth at the foot of the Satsuma Peninsula, advanced past the one-time kamikaze base at Chiran to Sesekushi on the western shore of

Kagoshima Bay, ten miles south of Kagoshima City. In these drives the Sixth Army opened Kagoshima Bay to U.S. shipping, obtained other harbors at Shibushi and Miyazaki City, seized airfields, split the defenses of the Satsuma and Osumi peninsulas, and isolated large Japanese forces manning coastal fortifications.

On the Kushikino front, the Japanese 303rd Infantry Division was smashed and the 206th Infantry Division south of it split. Farther down the Satsuma Peninsula the U.S. 98th Infantry Division had driven a wedge between the 125th Independent Mixed Brigade defending the southeast tip of the peninsula and the 146th Infantry Division defending the balance of the southern end of the peninsula. Both the 206th and 146th divisions, which had rushed to reinforce the 303rd Division, were decimated. The bulk of the 125th Independent Mixed Brigade, including its headquarters, was penned in its fortifications at the entrance to Kagoshima Bay. Sea and air bombardment had eliminated its artillery and the brigade was unable to interfere with U.S. shipping steaming into the crowded bay. On the Ariake front, troops of the widely deployed 86th Infantry Division had either been exterminated or isolated at the bottom of the Osumi Peninsula and the southeast tip of Kyushu. The 98th Independent Mixed Brigade, guarding the eastern shore of Kagoshima Bay to the west of the 86th Division, was split by XI Corps' drive across the narrow waist of the Osumi Peninsula. The 77th and 25th Infantry divisions and the 6th Tank Brigade, which had reinforced the 86th Division, were fragmented. On the Miyazaki front, the 156th Division and 5th Tank Brigade, which had borne the brunt of I Corps' assault, were reduced to tattered remnants. The 154th Division, pushing south to assist the 156th Division, was chewed up piecemeal.

More than half a million Americans came ashore in the first thirty days, exclusive of Navy shore establishments. The number included service troops and large elements of the Far East Air Forces. On December 2 the first of 130,000 Army Service Command "O" troops in the follow up echelon had reached Kyushu. The three deep U.S. enclaves were becoming stabilized rear areas, with hospitals, post offices, laundries and replacement depots. Fumigation and bath units, graves registration teams and military government units were operating. A dozen air groups, including one of Marine Corsairs, flew fighters, fighter bombers and light bombers from American-made strips or restored Japanese bases at Chiran on the Satsuma Peninsula, Kanoya on the Osumi Peninsula and in the Shibushi and Miyazaki City areas. Engineers and Seabees, often with the aid of hired Japanese civilian labor, were improving or constructing harbor facilities, roads, airfields, permanent living quarters and supply depots. Ninety-two thousand tons of construction materials alone were unloaded at Kagoshima City, Shibushi and Miyazaki City.

The United States had paid dearly for its foothold in Japan. Battle casualties, including the heavy Navy losses of the first four days, were 53,000, of which 14,000 were dead or missing. Navy losses included personnel in British Pacific Fleet elements participating in Operation Olympic. Nonbattle casualties were significant, the bulk of them combat fatigue. There were more than 13,000 cases, roughly comparable to Okinawa where, in the first two months of fighting, less than half as many combat troops had suffered 14,000 cases of combat fatigue. Japanese casualties were far greater. Though the Japanese fought from superbly planned fortifications they never withdrew when their positions became untenable but remained at their posts until hunted down and exterminated by the Americans' "blowtorch and screwdriver"— flame throwers and explosive charges. A hundred and five thousand Japanese soldiers died in caves, tunnels, pillboxes and bunkers, in assembly areas and on the trails and back roads from the north. The only surviving wounded, except for a few in American hands, were in rear areas. On the battlefront, the less severely wounded continued to fight. Those unable to do so either died from their wounds from lack of medical attention, were killed in the American mop-up, killed themselves, or had that last service done for them. Of 617 military prisoners less than 100 had not been too incapacitated to kill themselves or resist capture. Several hundred more whose efforts to surrender may or may not have been genuine rather than to lure their attackers within range were killed by wary American soldiers.

Eighteen thousand Volunteer Combat troops also died in action after the main lines of defense were pierced. The volunteers inflicted few casualties on American troops with their bamboo spears, reaping hooks and locally manufactured explosives. They did have considerable nuisance value, infiltrating bivouac areas at night, disrupting communications, ambushing small patrols, and setting up tank traps. Those who allowed themselves to be captured, as they did in some thousands, were a greater nuisance than those who fought. Unlike the civilian populations of occupied towns, who were permitted a certain freedom of movement, the quasi-military volunteers had to be confined under guard in barbed-wire stockades, fed, and given medical care. Attempts were made to screen them and release as many as possible to fend for themselves. The American soldiers called them "GUs," after "giyu," the Japanese word for volunteer.

Country folk, in the main, shared the popular beliefs about the barbarity of the invaders and either fled before the American advance or attempted to resist. In the larger and more sophisticated localities there was a wide divergence of attitudes. The arrival of American troops in force elicited fanatical resistance, occasional eager collaboration and every shade of reaction in between. The norm, in the larger towns, was numb, philosophical acceptance. Many civilians died fighting in Kanoya, where the mayor inspired the citizens to emulate the spirit of the peasant revolts of feudal days and "kill one samurai with ten civilians." In Kagoshima City, on the other hand, many bombed-out and hungry inhabitants joined labor crews rehabilitating the harbor when they saw the Americans were not bent on rape and slaughter but on the contrary paid them for their work. Even in Kanoya, as in Kagoshima City and the larger towns, when the situation stabilized and the Americans were firmly in control, some merchants resumed business in the broken buildings with such meager stocks as were left; the manufacture of bean curd, bean paste, soy sauce and shochu was begun on a limited scale, and some independent thinkers regarded the conquerors as liberators.

The opening of Kagoshima Bay and the seizure of other harbor, airfield and base areas, brought Phase II of Operation Olympic to a successful conclusion after weeks of battle as bloody as at Iwo Jima and Okinawa. Phase III, the occupation of Kyushu south of the general line from Sendi on the west coast to Tsuno, twenty-five miles north of Miyazaki City on the east coast, and the destruction of the remaining Japanese forces below that line still posed a formidable task. The hills and tortuous valleys of southern Kyushu swarmed with soldiers who had moved down from the north and with hundreds of thousands of partially trained Volunteer Combat troops. Though the Japanese had no fortifications to compare with those that had been smashed in the coastal zones they were indefatigable in preparing new positions and adept in turning the natural features of the mountainous and wooded terrain to their advantage. The soldiers and many of the GUs fought as tenaciously for every yard of Japanese soil as the troops who had fought to the death in the fixed positions nearer the sea. Infiltrators, bypassed units and a generally hostile rural population still harassed the American rear. The three U.S. Corps that stormed ashore on X-Day had yet to link up. Aoidake, which marked I Corp's deepest penetration, was twenty-five miles from Aoki and the nearest XI Corps troops. V Amphibious Corps, battling toward the northern end of Kagoshima Bay for a junction with XI Corps, had advanced only as far as Kawakamicho, nine miles southwest of the head of the bay. XI Corps, with a greater distance to cover, was just pushing out of Iwagawa, a small town on the Shibushi-Miyakonojo axis twenty miles southeast of Kagoshima Bay's northern shore.

As the campaign developed it had become increasingly obvious to the American staff, as it already had been for some time to the Japanese, that the key to control of southern Kyushu was Miyakonojo. Miyakonojo, after Kagoshima City and Miyazaki City the largest city in Operation Olympic's objective area, was the hub of communications between the coastal plains of Miyazaki and Ariake and the head of Kagoshima Bay. It was southern

Kyushu's principal road and rail junction. Japanese 57th Army Headquarters was on a hilltop at Takarabe, only five miles to the west. Such was the nature of the terrain and the inadequate road and rail net that the fall of Miyakonojo would cut the only serviceable link between the Japanese strategic reserve in central Kyushu and the forces confronting the Americans in the south and east. Depots and dumps for a great variety of military supplies were located in Miyakonojo. The city was strategically located in a sizable basin of comparatively even terrain in which large forces could assemble and armor could maneuver, and through which powerful American thrusts could be launched toward the north and west. And it was the logical anchor for drives to give the three American corps a continuous front.

I Corps at Aoidake was two-thirds of the way into the twisting twelve-mile corridor through the steep hills and forests separating the Miyazaki plain and the Miyakonojo basin. XI Corps at Aoki had but two miles of rugged terrain to negotiate before reaching the southern end of the basin. Once linked at Miyakonojo the two corps would have cut off all Japanese forces remaining in southeastern Kyushu and the way would lay open to Kokubu, at the head of Kagoshima Bay, from which to push toward V Amphibious Corps, pressing from the southwest. The twelve-mile-long corridor between the Miyakonojo basin and the head of the bay was favorable for armored operations except for the central four miles, where narrow valleys angled among steep hills up to a thousand feet high.

XI and I Corps concentrated forces for a two-pronged drive on Miyakonojo. Japanese soldiers and Volunteer Combat troops dug in around the city and reinforcements streamed toward it from mountain sanctuaries.

If his situation had not been so perilous Mr. Tsuyuki would have considered it preposterous. Preposterous that a respectable fifty-two-year-old merchant should be out of doors in such weather without a raincoat, digging a trench in the sodden earth instead of tending his shop as he had done for more than two decades. Despite the great changes wrought in his life by the times, Mr. Tsuyuki refused to acknowledge the fact that it had been some months since his shop existed and more months than that since he had honest cloth to sell.

It was preposterous that all about him equally solid businessmen and heads of families should be doing the same as he, side by side with excited schoolboys and weary women who in less insane times would be about their household duties. Preposterous and humiliating that he must endure in humble silence the abuse of the ignorant soldier no older than his second son and whom before the war he would not have hired to sweep the floor of the shop. Most preposterous of all that he should be doing this to prepare a place for brave Japanese soldiers to die without reason, and quite possibly himself, neither brave nor a soldier. The foolish scrap of cloth he wore on his breast did not make him a soldier any more than the bombastic slogans made him brave no matter how often they were repeated on the radio, spoken by local officials, or written on walls. "One hundred million people die in honor." "Better to die than seek ignominious safety." Such sentiments were for the politicians who in the end would try to save their own necks, as politicians always did, and for the militarists who valued neither their own lives nor those of their countrymen. It was one thing to choose war as your profession and quite another to have it forced upon you. If there was any sense to it he would be as willing as the next to give his life for his country, but surely it must be as obvious to the Honshu politicians and militarists as it was to a Kyushu merchant that it no longer made any sense to die.

The Army and Navy had been unable to prevent the Americans from seizing footholds at Kushikino, Miyazaki and Ariake Bay. Regular troops and volunteers in their tens of thousands had not stopped them in the narrow mountain valleys to the northeast and south of Miyakonojo. How could they expect to do so on open ground with the Americans advancing on the city, so it was rumored, from two directions? It was much more than a rumor, for he could hear with his own ears the American artillery booming out to the south and northeast, where the enemy had burst out of the mountains. It was foolishly optimistic to believe, as some professed, that the guns they heard were Japanese. He was no general with polished boots and a sword at his side but even he had enough common sense to realize that if the Americans could not be defeated in the fixed positions on the coast or in the mountains they most certainly could not be defeated here.

Mr. Tsuyuki sighed and put down his mattock to wipe the rain from his face. He pretended not to hear the disrespectful remarks of the young soldier, who resented even the briefest work stoppage. One could at least be grateful, Mr. Tsuyuki thought ruefully, that the rain had kept the American planes away and that it was not quite as cold as the preceding two days, when the temperature had fallen below the freezing point.

Hajime Tsuyuki was a lifelong resident of Miyakonojo, though in his youth he had gone away to the upper school at Kumamoto City. That, he still remembered, had been considered by his father's friends a waste of time and money, if not actually ostentatious, when he could have more sensibly made himself useful in the family business. He had taken over the guidance of both business and family in 1928 when his father had elected at the rather early age of sixty to go inkyo—enter formal retirement—and devote himself exclusively to contemplation, study and his archery club. It had always been a source of disappointment to the elder Tsuyuki that Hajime did not share his interest in the classic martial art. One of Mr. Tsuyuki's strongest childhood memories was of sitting quietly under the trees for hours while his father and his father's cronies in the archery club shot their arrows from the long, curving bows, talked, and drank shochu. His father did not drink shochu at home and had not kept it in the house after Hajime's grandfather died. At home his father drank sake, and much more sparingly than he drank shochu at archery club meetings. On Boy Day, after he had supervised the hanging of the carp banner outside the house, his father invariably had one drink from the bottle of English whiskey he had brought back to Miyakonojo from a visit to Tokyo.

The old man died in 1940. In the first year of the war Mr. Tsuyuki sometimes grieved that his father had not lived to see Japan's glorious victories. That grief had been engulfed by a greater one when the ashes of Kameo, Mr. Tsuyuki's elder son, came back from New Guinea in February, 1943. His sorrow was mixed with pride, for his son had given his life in his country's struggle to take its rightful place in the world. The white box containing the ashes was given a place of honor with the image of Amida and the memorial name tablets in the butsudan, above which hung the oil portrait of Mr. Tsuyuki's deceased father. Until Kameo's death Mr. Tsuyuki had considered himself smiled upon by fortune. His family enjoyed good health and harmony, he was highly regarded in the community, the shop did well. In the fifteen years since assuming control of the shop he had tripled the business that took his father more than thirty years to build. He had put both sons through upper school and had the war not intervened would have sent the elder to the university. Kazuko, his daughter, had finished middle school and proved remarkably capable in the shop, though she occasionally spent too much time whispering with young Asayama. He was the tea wholesaler's son, who had escaped both conscription and service in heavy industry because of a purported weakness of the lungs. He certainly looked robust enough to Mr. Tsuyuki and behaved far more frivolously than was fitting for a young man who remained home while others his age were winning victories for their country. Old Asayama had a substantial business and Mr. Tsuyuki acknowledged to himself he might have regarded young Asayama differently had the times been different.

Mr. Tsuyuki had been well content that his two sons were serving their country despite the inconvenience of having to hire outside help in the shop. There was too much business for himself and Kazuko to handle and Mrs. Tsuyuki had her hands so full with household and civic duties and had such a poor head for figures she was of little assistance. She was a leader in the Patriotic Women's Association and the Buddhist Women's Society. He was particularly pleased that his second son, Kazuo, had been accepted for pilot training by the Army. He was careful not to reveal in any way that he took special pride in this accomplishment. To do so might indicate, and falsely so, that he favored the younger son over the older and also might not sit well with those of his associates whose sons had not distinguished themselves.

After Kameo's death things seemed to change. Taxes rose and cloth became more difficult to find, rising in price and going down in quality. People watched their yen and business fell off to such a point Mr. Tsuyuki let the clerk go and ran the shop with Kazuko's help alone. The Army reached deeper and deeper into the city's male population until the sight of a young man not in uniform became a rare one. Young Asayama still had not been conscripted but Mr. Tsuyuki noted with some satisfaction he no longer behaved so frivolously and Kazuko cooled toward him, her eyes at last open to his lack of patriotism. There was no shortage of rice in Miyakonojo but it was said on good authority that Tokyo and the other big cities were feeling a pinch. Mr. Tsuyuki knew if that were so things would certainly get worse in Miyakonojo. The politicians were bound to try to ease conditions in the capital at the expense of the rest of the nation. The city lost an increasing number of its sons in battle and more often than not the report of a death in action was not accompanied by the hero's ashes. Despite continued victories by the Army and Navy, the enemy advanced steadily across the Pacific. This puzzled Mr. Tsuyuki until he decided that all the government reported was not necessarily true. In guarded, oblique conversations with Mr. Asayama and others he learned that while a few of his acquaintances entertained the same notion, most of them believed Japan was merely concentrating her forces and drawing the enemy into a trap to be dealt a mortal blow. Mr. Asayama, who was belligerently patriotic, was among the latter. His son's physical incapacity, he said in all sincerity, was the greatest sorrow of his life.

Near the end of January, 1945, when Mr. Tsuyuki was notified that Kazuo had died heroically earlier in the month in a kamikaze attack on the American invasion fleet at Luzon, Mr. Asayama professed to be envious. In public Mr. Tsuyuki displayed only quiet pride in the honor his son had brought him, but deep inside this conventional response was muted by grief. Mrs. Tsuyuki, unable to hide her feelings, took to her bed for several days. Hysterical, the neighbors said. What could one expect of a woman after all? The effect on Kazuko was quite the opposite. She raged against the enemy and wept because she was not a man and could not take her two brothers' place against them. Kazuko believed with all her heart that Japanese spirit would soon turn the tide, as the radio and all the local officials said, and that the staggering losses inflicted on the Americans by heroes like Kazuko would make them lose their stomach for conquest. Mr. Tsuyuki did not attempt to disabuse her of this. Only a few weeks before, a friend of his who spoke incautiously of the possibility of Japan's defeat had been arrested by the military police and was now in prison, leaving his family without a provider.

In February, Tokyo itself was attacked by American carrier planes for the first time. Iwo Jima fell the following month and in April the enemy invaded Okinawa. Planes from the naval air base at Miyazaki City flew over Miyakonojo on the way to attack the American ships and did not return. Even in Miyakonojo it was often difficult to purchase the three hundred and thirty-gram rice ration from legitimate dealers at the official price. Mrs. Tsuyuki was often obliged to turn to the black market for rice and other necessities at ten times the fixed price. They were often without salt and it was next to impossible to find soap. When Mrs. Tsuyuki did find soap, a bar that had cost ten sen before the war now cost more than ten yen. No sugar was to be had at any price. And now that the shelves of the shop were empty, Mr. Tsuyuki's old customers perversely began coming to him in increasing numbers, offering any price for cottons and woolens. They were sometimes unbearably rude when he told them he had nothing to sell them, even hinting they knew he had goods hidden away for his friends and those who had enough yen. Rudeness was the order of the day, Mr. Tsuyuki thought sadly. Not just in his shop but in every shop, and on the streets and in the queues for rationed goods, which meant virtually everything. There was mounting talk the enemy meant to invade Japan itself. Mr. Tsuyuki sometimes thought that the Japanese people might destroy themselves with their rudeness and selfishness before that happened.

Despite the shortages of everything, the military subdepots at Miyakonojo began filling up with munitions, clothing, provisions and medical supplies. The city bustled with rail and road traffic as men and supplies passed through it on the way to the coastal areas being readied for the anticipated invasion. The 57th Army established its headquarters at nearby Takarabe and swarms of soldiers added their rudeness to that of the residents of Miyakonojo.

July was a particularly discouraging month for Mr. Tsuyuki. First, both he and Kazuko were obliged to register for the Volunteer Combat Corps. What made it all the more distasteful was the fact that Mr. Asayama had been appointed to the staff of the local Volunteer Combat Telam and it was he who supervised the preparation of the enrollment list. Kazuko, now twenty years old, was delighted at the prospect of avenging her brothers. Then the daily rice ration was reduced to two hundred ninety-four grams. It was not so much the reduction that disturbed Mr. Tsuyuki as it was the implications. The government had acknowledged the increasing difficulty of feeding the nation. And finally, on the twenty-fourth of the month, American carrier planes struck a heavy blow against Miyazaki City, only thirty miles away. The next day refugees began arriving in Miyakonojo with tales of horror and destruction.

And things grew worse. In August the Soviet Union showed its true colors with a perfidious attack on Manchuria while Japan was preoccupied with the threat from the south. Early in September land-based American bombers attacked the railway station and the military barracks west of the city. Many bombs fell within the town and Mr. Tsuyuki's shop was among the buildings burned to the ground. He was more fortunate than the owners of smaller shops, whose places of business were also their homes. Mr. Tsuyuki's home in the outskirts was untouched. After the destruction of the military barracks, which had housed the 23rd Regiment of the 6th Infantry Division before the war, a young infantry lieutenant was billeted in Mr. Tsuyuki's home, giving him something else to worry about. He was handsome and filled with martial spirit and Kazuko was fascinated by him. Even after Mr. Tsuyuki investigated and found he was of good family, his presence disturbed Mr. Tsuyuki more than he cared to acknowledge. He was very polite and respectful and sometimes brought Mrs. Tsuyuki gifts of tinned fish, salt or soap, but Mr. Tsuyuki did not like the way Kazuko looked at him when she thought she was not observed.

Later that month soldiers and members of the volunteer corps were set to work erecting poles and digging glider traps in many level areas around the city. A rumor swept Miyakonojo that the city was considered a major objective of the enemy and American airborne troops might appear at any moment. Mr. Tsuyuki was not obliged to assist in the construction of the glider obstacles. Because of his experience with textiles and through a contact of the young lieutenant's, he was allowed to work at the clothing depot.

American planes began visiting the refugee-swollen city regularly. Half the town was burned, the public water system was wrecked, and night soil went uncollected. Everyone not obliged to remain began leaving for the safety of the countryside. A number of these who did not have family or friends in the country returned when they found the farmers inhospitable and food and shelter as scarce for outsiders as in town. Mr. Tsuyuki's family was among those remaining. Mr. Tsuyuki and Kazuko assisted the volunteer fire brigade of the Tonari-gumi, neighbor squad. Kazuko declared she would not leave the city until ordered to do so with her platoon and then, if it was to fight the Americans, she would do so gladly. The young lieutenant complimented her on her spirit. If the manner in which she simpered had not been so appalling, Mr. Tsuyuki would have found it amusing.

There was a brief period of optimism after the October typhoon even though its ravages added to the misery of the shattered city. The American invasion fleet had been scattered off Okinawa and the enemy was in disarray. The Divine Wind had once again come miraculously to Japan's aid. The Americans would now want to negotiate a settlement of the war which had been so calamitous for both sides. Mr. Tsuyuki prayed that the militarists in Tokyo would not be too demanding and would ask only that Japan be left in peace to bind her wounds. It quickly became obvious that the official reports had been, as always, greatly exaggerated. Hardly had the weather cleared when the American planes returned in greater numbers than ever before.

On November 11, Japanese planes flew over Miyakonojo for the first time in months. Mr. Tsuyuki grasped the significance of this immediately. The invasion of Kyushu was imminent. The planes were on their way to attack the American fleet. Before noon the next day everyone knew the Americans had attempted to land at Miyazaki City, Ariake Bay and below Kushikino. The first reports said they had been repulsed with staggering losses. Later reports, the gist of which filtered down to the civilians remaining in Miyakonojo, were ambiguous. Within forty-eight hours Mr. Tsuyuki, like everyone else, knew the Americans had succeeded in landing troops in all three coastal areas. Mr. Asayama, who because of his position on the Volunteer Combat Team staff had access to the latest information, said confidently that counterattacks now developing were certain to drive the enemy back into the sea. Troops, guns and vehicles, including the light tanks of the 1st Special Tank Unit which were to have defended the city against airborne invaders, streamed through Miyakonojo on the way to the fighting. It seemed that for once Mr. Asayama's information was sound. Mr. Tsuyuki had further cause for joy. The young infantry lieutenant billeted in his home, for whom Kazuko had displayed a growing infatuation, left for the front with his unit.

Mr. Tsuyuki's hopes were dashed within the week. American planes of all kinds ranged freely over the city, sometimes bombing or strafing but more often continuing on to other targets. Mr. Tsuyuki often heard their bombs and guns in the distance and saw columns of smoke on the horizon. Groups of soldiers entered the city from the east and north and passed through it on the way to the fighting. They were often in disarray and had to be reformed and reequipped before moving out. Members of Volunteer Combat Corps units miles distant from Miyakonojo brought in gravely wounded soldiers and civilians by the hundreds. All of them, it was said, had received their wounds behind the battle lines. The military and civilian hospital filled to overflowing and many patients were obliged to live in tents and shanties outside the main buildings. Mrs. Tsuyuki, who went to do volunteer work in the civilian hospital, said few civilians were admitted and that the overworked staff gave priority to military patients. She had yet to encounter a soldier who had been wounded in the coastal areas. They were all victims of American air attacks. It was said, she reported, that the brave Japanese soldiers to a man refused to leave the front even when gravely wounded. After the military hospital was bombed and the surviving patients moved to the civilian hospital, Mrs. Tsuyuki was kept so busy Mr. Tsuyuki hardly ever saw her for more than a few minutes.

Her sister, Mrs. Aoyagi, whose sons were in the Army and whose husband had been killed by the American planes, moved in with the Tsuyukis to take care of the house and prepare the meals, such as they were. She was a bad cook and often served appalling messes of rice and soybeans. She persisted in cooking them together even after Mrs. Tsuyuki patiently explained that rice took less than twenty minutes to cook properly and soybeans took hours. There was no serious lack of wood fuel, as there was said to be in Tokyo, so it was simply that Mrs. Aoyagi lacked patience. Although it was an affront to his dignity, Mr. Tsuyuki began seeing to the cooking of the soybeans himself. Even when properly cooked he found them unpalatable and lived on a little rice and an occasional potato. Potatoes, particularly the yellow ones, were still available although they were growing scarcer as the soldiers passing through the area foraged on the countryside.

Kazuko's platoon, which comprised younger women, young men with physical disabilities which kept them from regular service, and the more vigorous middle-aged men, was called up and sent off toward the mountains. A few had Model 38 rifles of 1905 vintage and explosive charges. The remainder had spears, kitchen knives or reaping hooks but were promised better weapons when they reached their unspecified destination. Kazuko went eagerly. Mr. Tsuyuki tried not to display emotion but it was difficult. He had no doubt he was seeing the last of his children march off to certain death. Mrs. Tsuyuki displayed remarkable strength of character and did not shed a tear until Kazuko disappeared from view. Even then she recovered quickly and went off to tend her wounded. Mr. Tsuyuki was as proud of her as he had been of his son Kazuo. Young Asayama was in the same platoon as Kazuko. Mr. Tsuyuki had observed his ashen face with satisfaction. Mr. Asayama, who had also come out to see the platoon depart, could not look Mr. Tsuyuki in the eye. Mr. Tsuyuki felt a rush of compassion for the elder Asayama. For all his bluster he was truly brave and patriotic and did not merit such dishonor. The situation afforded Mr. Tsuyuki some consolation for the loss of his own sons. It was better that they had died bravely than remain alive like young Asayama and shame their Emperor and their father.

This war that was destroying what remained of his country had cost him his family, he thought in sorrow and anger. Mr. Tsuyuki found himself dwelling more and more on the past because the present was unspeakable and the future unbearable if the wanton sacrifice continued. He thought about the little boy sitting under the trees in the tranquil countryside, watching his father shoot arrows from the long curved bow and drink and talk with his cronies, all dead now along with so many of their children and grandchildren; of his own family outings when the children were small, to see the Sekino-o Waterfall outside the city, and the kikko-iwa, the tortoiseshell-patterned rock along the Shonai River, the visits every spring to the Mochio Shrine south of town to view the cherry blossoms along the way and watch the Kumaso Dance at the festival. He remembered Kameo, as a boy, telling how he would go to America when he was a man and buy cotton to weave into cloth in the textile mill he would build with his father, and Kazuo boasting how he would become an admiral and come back to visit his mother all in gold braid with a sword at his side; Kazuko saying she would not marry when she became a woman but remain home to serve her parents when they grew old. She had forgotten that promise quickly enough, but all the same she would never marry now.

When word came that Miyazaki City had fallen to the Americans he felt a pang not completely related to a sense of national loss, for he remembered the promise that life had held for him when he took his bride there for a honeymoon in November of 1919. He had thought to take her to Tokyo and Kyoto, where he had been more than once on his father's business, for she had never traveled beyond Kumamoto City, but sentiment prevailed and he took her to the city where his father had taken a bride before him. They had marveled at the ancient mounds at Saitobaru, north of Miyazaki City, and to the south strolled with scores of other honeymooning couples among the betel palms and tropical plants of Aoshima islet and taken photographs of the rock formations at ebb tide. He supposed nothing remained now of the hotel where they had spent those first days of their marriage, or of Miyazaki City itself, and hoped the American naval bombardment had not reduced Aoshima to naked stone. It was as if his past as well as family were being wiped out.

Until Kameo died, though Mr. Tsuyuki was approaching fifty, he could not believe he was aging. He was as vigorous as ever, his digestion was the envy of his friends, and he enjoyed life. Now, soaked with rain, digging what might prove to be his own grave, he felt old indeed. Any man who survived his own children was old, and one who lived to witness the demise of his homeland was ancient. He was so old he could not remember the last time he had laughed aloud, or had slept a whole night through, had not known constant anxiety and aching sadness. And on top of it all, this bullying young soldier heaping abuse on an old man whose two sons had died in battle and whose daughter, for all he knew, might already have joined them. Asayama there, digging like the rest with his long face down, why didn't he speak up about it? He wore the armband of staff and even if it was only a Volunteer Combat Corps position it certainly gave him more authority than a common soldier. But no, he was as humble as the others. Mr. Tsuyuki knew that Asayama's mind was filled with but a single thought, that his craven son might find his manhood and die bravely. Did it truly matter how young Asayama died, except to his father? Bravely or like a dog, it would not affect the outcome any more than the new ditches they were scratching in the ground.

A sergeant came with a fresh work detail and Mr. Tsuyuki put down his mattock for the long walk home across the sodden fields and through the rubble-strewn muddy streets swarming with soldiers and horse-drawn wagons. In the kitchen Mrs. Aoyagi was just sitting down to a bowl of rice and beans with a pickled onion on top to ward off enemy bombs. Foolish woman, he thought, to actually believe it was this that had preserved the Tsuyuki house from the fate of so many others. She showed him a stricken face and led him to the bedroom he had shared with his wife for the seventeen years since his father's retirement. Mrs. Tsuyuki was in bed, her eyes bright with fever. Typhoid, Mrs. Tsuyuki whispered. The town was swept with it, as with typhus, diphtheria and dysentery. She had fallen ill at the hospital. There being no ward for infectious diseases or sufficient beds for even the badly wounded, she had been sent home.

Mr. Tsuyuki railed at Mrs. Aoyagi. What could she have been thinking of, filling her stomach in the kitchen while her own sister lay so gravely ill in the same house.

"Please," Mrs. Tsuyuki said weakly. "Ritsuko begged to sit by my side but I did not wish to infect her. And I insisted she eat before your return so she would be free to look after you. I am afraid I am of little use now."

Mr. Tsuyuki apologized to Mrs. Aoyagi but she left the room weeping. He studied his wife's face. The skin was dry and stretched tightly and had a shiny look. She could have been a woman of sixty. She was forty-six. He realized with a shock that she might be dying. In other times one did not die so quickly of typhoid and most victims of the disease recovered, but there was no medicine now and she had been weakened by poor food, overwork and constant diarrhea. He had thought heaven held no further blows for him but he had been wrong. Mr. Tsuyuki put on his wet straw sandals and hurried to the hospital. The rutted, rain-swept streets were full of people. There were few civilians among them and nearly all of those wore Volunteer Combat Corps patches.

The hospital was surrounded by tents and small temporary structures. A number of soldiers lay outside the hospital entrance with only their tent sheets for shelter. They did not move or talk and Mr. Tsuyuki wondered if they were dead. The halls were also filled with wounded soldiers. The air was warm inside the hospital and reeked of blood, filth and death. No one on the staff would stop to listen to Mr. Tsuyuki. They were all exhausted and irritable. A friend of Mrs. Tsuyuki, also doing volunteer nurse duty, recognized him and took a moment off to ask him what he wanted. She shook her head when he said his wife had typhoid and needed medicine but when he insisted told him where to find a doctor. The doctor's eyes were blurry, his cheek twitched, and his hands trembled. He was so weary he had difficulty speaking. When Mr. Tsuyuki explained his purpose the doctor's only answer was a shake of his head and a short bitter laugh. Mr. Tsuyuki realized he should have known the Army had no medicine to spare for civilians. But the Army had medical supplies. The subdepot at Miyakonojo had escaped the bombings. Perhaps Mr. Asayama could help him. He had influence with the military.

Mr. Tsuyuki went back out into the rain. It was dark now and colder than usual for that time of year. Mr. Asayama's home had burned some time ago. He and Mrs. Asayama and Mrs. Asayama's ancient mother lived in a hut knocked together from bits and pieces over their air raid shelter. Mr. Tsuyuki had never heard him complain about this though Mr. Asayama had once been a rich man. He might still be, for it was rumored that Mr. Asayama's tea had found its way to the black market. Mr. Tsuyuki, for one, did not believe it. He had never questioned Mr. Asayama's honesty except in matters pertaining to his son.

Mr. Asayama was already in bed. He was surprised to see Mr. Tsuyuki out on such a night and was very sorry to learn of Mrs. Tsuyuki's illness. There was little hope of prying anything out of the medical supply depot, he said, but he would certainly try even if it meant getting his ears boxed. While he was getting dressed Mrs. Asayama crawled out of the sleeping quilts and apologized for having no tea to offer Mr. Tsuyuki. She was terribly embarrassed. Mr. Tsuyuki was equally embarrassed for having put her in this humiliating position with his uninvited and unexpected appearance. But it could not be helped. Mr. Tsuyuki said tactfully that even if there were tea she would be unable to start a fire to brew it. The hut was too clumsily built not to let light escape and the blackout regulation was very strict. They both knew it was unlikely the American planes would be out in such weather but it appeared to relieve Mrs. Asayama somewhat. Mr. Asayama said it was better if he went to the depot alone and told Mr. Tsuyuki to return home. If he succeeded in getting any drugs he would bring them immediately.

Mrs. Tsuyuki was sleeping when he got home, with Mrs. Aoyagi sitting up, nodding, just outside the door. Mr. Tsuyuki apologized again for his earlier rudeness and ordered her off to bed. He sat down beside his wife and waited for Mr. Asayama to come with the medicine. He waited all night, napping from time to time. Mrs. Tsuyuki awakened frequently to ask apologetically for water. Mr. Tsuyuki feared she was growing weaker. During the night shells began falling in the city. None struck close by but the explosions could be plainly felt. Mrs. Tsuyuki urged Mr. Tsuyuki to go to the air raid shelter dug in the yard or to the big communal shelter dug into a hill not far away. It was out of the question for her to be taken out into the cold and damp and he refused to leave her. Mrs. Aoyagi also insisted on staying with her sister. Morning came and still Mr. Asayama had not arrived with the medicine. The shelling grew heavier. The walls of the house trembled. Mrs. Tsuyuki was very weak. Her lips were cracked and she seldom opened her eyes. She was dying, Mr. Tsuyuki thought helplessly. If he was ordered out on work detail he would refuse to go even if they executed him for it. He would not leave her.

It was late in the morning when Mr. Asayama arrived. Instead of medicine he had a rifle. He was excited and in high spirits. The deep creases were gone from his face and he seemed years younger.

"I didn't come earlier because they wouldn't let me have the drugs," he said. "I'm sorry, Tsuyuki. But I have some exciting news."

The platoon had been called up and Mr. Asayama was to lead it to its position. The Americans advancing from the northeast on the road from Miyazaki City had reached the Takagi River below its junction with the Hananoki, only five miles from the city. The regular troops were falling back into holding positions on the Okimizu, where they intended to halt the enemy long enough for the defenders of Miyakonojo to mass on the Toshimi, which ran through the northern part of the town. Only a handful of regular troops had been left in a two-mile zone between the Takagi and the Okimizu, and Volunteer Combat Platoons were being sent forward to augment them. The volunteers would form skirmishing and tank ambush parties.

"I expect they've called us up at last just to get us old relics out of the way," Mr. Asayama said, his eyes twinkling as if he were sharing a fine joke with Mr. Tsuyuki. "But isn't it splendid to get a chance to pitch in?"

Mr. Tsuyuki hesitated. He had vowed he would not go if called out on a work party but this was a development he had not foreseen. To refuse to dig a ditch was one thing, to refuse to fight quite another.

"What are you waiting for?" Mr. Asayama demanded. "I've come to you first particularly to help me round up the others."

His voice had an edge to it.

"I'll just tell my wife I'm leaving," said Mr. Tsuyuki.

"Yes," Mr. Asayama said more sympathetically. "I'm afraid it can't be helped, Tsuyuki."

Mr. Tsuyuki went in to give his wife the news but she had already overheard it. As had Mrs. Aoyagi, who was sniveling in her usual place outside the bedroom door. He reached out to touch his wife's hand. It was more like the claw of a bird than a woman's hand. She drew it back.

"The contagion," she explained.

"I don't suppose it's typhoid that's going to carry me off," Mr. Tsuyuki said, touching it anyhow.

"I suppose not," Mrs. Tsuyuki said.

Neither of them spoke for a moment.

"Well, old woman," Mr. Tsuyuki said at last. "I suppose it's good-bye, then."

"Good-bye, husband," said Mrs. Tsuyuki.

Mr. Tsuyuki said good-bye to Mrs. Aoyagi, who appeared on the verge of falling to pieces, and went outside, where Mr. Asayama made an attempt to conceal his impatience. He thought about his wife as they went about what was left of the neighborhood assembling the platoon. There was no doubt she was dying, but if die she must she had not picked such a bad time for it. She had no one left but that foolish older sister. And who knew what would happen when the Americans came? He did not believe even the Americans would harm a middle-aged woman, but with no one to look after her she might starve, even if the fever did not carry her off. If only he might have stayed with her until the end. It wouldn't matter then whether the Americans killed him or not. It was really unbearable going off this way and leaving her dying.

Most of the platoon was in the communal shelter and had been since the shelling began. The people in the shelter were frightened and besieged Mr. Asayama with questions. He told them brusquely to display a little Japanese spirit in the face of danger. And besides, the Americans were going to be thrown back at the Toshimi, if not the Okimizu, and there was nothing to worry about. Only one man was missing from the platoon. Shimamoto, the rice broker, had fallen in a well and drowned while running to his shelter in the dark. Someone commented that the farmers would not be too unhappy about that and another said, "If the Yankees do succeed in taking the town I hope they drink from that well. They'll most certainly be poisoned."

Mr. Asayama led them to a bunker, where every fourth man was given a rifle and fifteen rounds and the others given black powder demolition charges in rayon bags. This was where the cloth had gone, Mr. Tsuyuki thought. The rayon was of poor quality but even that would have been better than empty shelves.

The Toshimi bridge was out and Mr. Asayama sent members of the platoon scouting along the bank for boats to take them across. Mr. Tsuyuki could see Asayama changing before his eyes. Mr. Asayama was very abrupt and his voice rang with authority. That was the way it should be, Mr. Tsuyuki thought, for Asayama was now an officer. And, it appeared, a good one. It was reassuring to be led by a man who knew what he was about. The rain had stopped by the time they entered the paddy fields on the other side of the river and the skies began clearing. Mr. Asayama cautioned everyone to be on the alert for American planes. The mud was deep in the paddy fields. It made walking difficult. Except for a few youths of fifteen and sixteen the members of the platoon were Mr. Tsuyuki's age or older, most of them settled businessmen. They tired quickly and soon some of them were demanding a rest period. Mr. Asayama ordered them to save their breath for marching. One of the men, who had once held a civic office and seemed to believe he still retained prerogatives, persisted in complaining.

"It's unreasonable to expect us to march without rest and on empty stomachs," he said fretfully.

Mr. Asayama reached down and plucked a wisp of rice straw from the mud. He thrust it at the offender.

"Here," he said contemptuously. "Baby birds cry for their food but a samurai holds a toothpick between his teeth."

These were samurai, Mr. Tsuyuki wondered, looking about him at the panting businessmen and the twittering schoolboys. All the same, it was well said and certainly put old Obata in his place.

They floundered on through the mud. Other platoons were moving over the paddies just as raggedly, and in the distance Mr. Tsuyuki saw a line of troops streaming along the road toward the city. It was interesting, he thought, that regulars retreated while volunteers went forward to meet the enemy. Could it be that the military authorities did not wish to waste their troops uselessly but had no compunctions about volunteers? If Asayama had not suddenly become such a martinet he would ask the honorable platoon leader about that. Mr. Tsuyuki permitted himself a wry smile. Honorable platoon leader, indeed. When one came right down to it he was still only Asayama the tea merchant with a bit of cloth slipped over his arm. He wondered about Kazuko. Could she still be alive by some miracle? Perhaps she was with the soldiers falling back toward the city. It would be a gift from heaven if she were and could be at her mother's side when the end came. But that could not be. He only gave rein to such thoughts because fatigue and anxiety had made him light-headed.

The sound of planes was heard in the distance. The platoon scattered to seek shelter behind the earthen dikes and low hedges bordering the paddies. Mr. Tsuyuki lay face down in the mud. He had practiced the maneuver a number of times at platoon drill and had always felt foolish doing so. He did not feel foolish now, only frightened. The planes attacked the road with their machine guns and flew off again. It was stupid of the soldiers to walk on the road instead of across the fields, Mr. Tsuyuki thought when he got to his feet and began scraping the mud from his clothing, but he was grateful to them for having drawn the fire of the American fighters. They took cover from planes several times before they reached their position just south of Takaki Village. There was nothing left of the village but expiring embers. There were sounds of heavy fighting in the distance from the direction of the Miyazaki City-Miyakonojo road.

"The Yankees will never come this way," Mr. Asayama grumbled. "They've assigned us a position away from the fighting. They don't have any confidence in us after all."

There were holes along the path leading from the village to the road, dug either by the villagers or by soldiers, but empty now. Mr. Asayama disposed his platoon in them, ordering everyone to remain concealed until he gave the order to emerge. He spent the afternoon creeping forward to the Takaki River to see if any Americans might be coming their way. Between times he went from hole to hole making sure the men knew how to employ their pillow charges.

"If only soldiers come, remain hidden and wait for the Shermans that are sure to follow," he told Mr. Tsuyuki. "These black powder charges are not very strong and no good against armor. If the Shermans are carrying petrol tins place your charges among them. If not, try to place them on the treads near the driving mechanism."

The pillow charge fuses, activated by pulling a cord, had a ten-second delay. Theoretically that would allow the user time to get clear of the explosion. Mr. Asayama said the ten seconds should be used in placing the charge properly after the cord was pulled. Well, Mr. Tsuyuki thought, he had not expected to come out alive anyhow. If the American planes did not kill him he no doubt would be cut down by American soldiers before he came near a Sherman. Mr. Asayama had spoken as calmly as if this were merely another platoon drill, but there was a vast difference between creeping up on an unprotected farm wagon and trying the same thing with a Sherman. Mr. Tsuyuki did not mind admitting to himself that he was frightened. He wished he was as brave as Asayama. But, he could say in all honesty, it was not fear alone that made him so reluctant to meet his enemy. There was the matter of being obliged to leave his dying wife and the knowledge that his death would serve no purpose.

Except for the few inches of cold water at the bottom, the hole was quite comfortable. The sun shone and out of the wind the temperature was moderate. Mr. Tsuyuki dozed. He was awakened by someone humming in the next hole. It was one of the schoolboys pretending to be nonchalant. The song was "The Glow of the Fireflies," which children sang on graduation from primary school. Mr. Tsuyuki was filled with compassion for him, then with anger for those who had sent a boy out to die. Who but a child would remember such a song at such a time? It was so incongruous. Mr. Tsuyuki remembered the controversy in Miyakonojo after the war started when it was pointed out "The Glow of the Fireflies" had the same melody as a song known as "Auld Lang Syne" in the Western world. Many had insisted that it be dropped from the traditional graduation exercises because of this taint. Mr. Tsuyuki now recalled with regret that he had been one of them, even though he had himself sung "The Glow of the Fireflies" at his own graduation from primary school in 1906. Word had finally come down from Tokyo that the song was too firmly identified with Japan to be abandoned merely because Americans and Englishmen sang different words to it. Mr. Tsuyuki had grumbled about that and called it an indication of decadence. He was quite the fire-eater in those days. He was wiser now that it was too late to matter, he thought ruefully. It was then that Mr. Tsuyuki made up his mind he was not going to face the Americans if he could avoid it. Not just yet, at any rate. If they did not come before dark he would steal away and return to his wife's bedside. He would remain with her until she died. After that there would still be time to do what was demanded of him.

Late in the afternoon the Americans forced the Takagi River south of the platoon and advanced along the road toward Miyakonojo. The Asayama platoon was bypassed. Mr. Tsuyuki could hear the enemy tanks rumbling a mile or more away. In another hour or so it would be dark and he would try to make his way across the fields to the city.

Mr. Asayama was annoyed by the direction the battle had taken. He crowded into the hole with Mr. Tsuyuki and said so most emphatically. Then he launched into a discussion of what should be done about it. Mr. Tsuyuki understood that Asayama was not asking his advice, or even his opinion, but was speaking aloud to organize his own thoughts. If Americans did not appear in his sector by nightfall, Mr. Asayama said, he would move the platoon out and fall upon them from the flank. That should have been the instruction given him in the first place, he said. The platoon had a much greater chance of success if it attacked under cover of darkness. Asayama actually believed his pitiful platoon could accomplish something, Mr. Tsuyuki thought. How much easier it would be to die if only he could believe the same.

Mr. Asayama crawled off again after telling Mr. Tsuyuki he was going to have another look across the river and then reconnoiter the Yankee column moving west along the road. After only a few minutes he returned in a state of exhilaration. A small force of Shermans and infantry was approaching the ruins of Takaki from the east. There was a chance it would cross the river directly into their position. He repeated his instructions that the platoon was to remain concealed until his signal. That signal would be the sound of his pillow charge exploding on a Sherman.

"Until we meet at Yasukuni," he said before leaving Mr. Tsuyuki, rather pretentiously, Mr. Tsuyuki thought.

Asayama would have to wait a bit for that. Whatever the rest of the platoon did, he intended remaining out of sight until the Americans went by. There would be time enough to join Asayama at Yasukuni, and Kameo, Kazuo and Kazuko as well, after he had seen his wife through her final hours.

The Shermans were soon close enough to be heard, and then the shouts of the infantry accompanying them. From the sound of it they were fashioning some sort of bridge over the river. The tracks and engines of the Shermans made a terrifying sound as the tanks passed through the positions. Mr. Tsuyuki heard the soldiers calling to one another. Could Asayama have grown cautious at the last moment? It was dusk now. In another half hour it would be dark enough to leave for home. Mr. Tsuyuki raised his head cautiously and looked about him. There were but three Shermans in the force. Two of them had already passed beyond the position, following the soldiers, and the third, on which several soldiers were riding in full view, was in the midst of it. Mr. Asayama burst from a hole and ran toward the last Sherman. The soldiers riding on the tank shouted and began shooting at him. Mr. Asayama fell down, then rose again, staggering, and hurled himself at the tank. He fell down again before he reached it and then exploded. One of the soldiers was knocked from his perch either by the explosion or a piece of Mr. Asayama flying through the air. Poor Asayama. They had been friends since they were small children.

Mr. Tsuyuki knew then he was not going home. He could not betray his old friend. He sprang from his hole and ran after the slow moving tank. The soldiers were shooting at him. He could hear the bullets whisper past.

Mr. Tsuyuki pulled the fuse cord of his pillow charge and continued running toward the Sherman.

14

[Sergeant Maurice Stokes/Dr. Wakao Kuninori]

Sergeant Maurice Stokes steered the chaplain's jeep cautiously along the bustling and battered Kagoshima City quay. He wore an overcoat, gloves and two pairs of socks, one cotton and the other woolen. An olive drab GI muffler was wound around his neck. That would have annoyed his mother had she known. She was an obsessive knitter and needlepointer. But who could have anticipated the need for a muffler in the Pacific Theater? Sergeant Stokes had once accused her jokingly in a letter home of resenting the fact he had not been sent to Europe in midwinter to provide an outlet for a stream of mittens, mufflers and socks. She had not thought it funny. He had written back immediately to tell her the nights were sometimes chilly where he was and please make him an OD sweater vest. He had never worn it and had no idea what had happened to it. He wished he had it now.

The woolen cap Sergeant Stokes wore under his helmet was pulled down around his ears. Despite the cap, overcoat, socks and muffler he was chilled to his toes. And he resented it. It was supposed to be like Florida here. It wasn't much farther north than Jacksonville. And this was Satsuma, where the oranges came from. He'd seen the trees with his own eyes, bare now, and palm trees. But two days ago he had awakened to find the puddles frozen over. It was a good thing he had followed the directive and put antifreeze in the jeep even though at the time he had thought it a typically ludicrous Army precaution against every conceivable act of man or nature. Except those that happened. This morning it had been thirty-three degrees when he looked at the thermometer and a freezing rain was falling. Later it had turned to real rain, which was no improvement, and now for God's sake it was snowing. Sergeant Stokes grinned. The chaplain's assistant blaspheming the chaplain's own jeep. Captain Gautney had this notion of a God who was always eavesdropping to catch some poor soul taking His Name in vain. But if God was keeping an eye on the really important things, and sometimes Sergeant Stokes doubted it, He had no time for such trivia.

There was a snap missing on the driver's side and an icy breeze was blowing in through the gap in the side curtain. He'd have to talk Captain Gautney into requisitioning some plywood so he could close the jeep in permanently. It had already been done to most of the jeeps he had seen around and some had been rigged up with heaters working off the manifold. He wished he was handy enough to do that but he was not even sure he could manage plywood sides. Or that he could persuade the chaplain to requisition the plywood. Captain Gautney never seemed to notice whether it was hot or cold. Of course he could always steal some plywood the way everyone else did—there was a lot of it laying around in the rain with piles of everything else except chaplain's equipment—but he'd need a pretty good story about how he got it. The chaplain was awfully strict in his interpretation of the Seventh Commandment. Also the other nine. Stokes grinned again. That was just one of the occupational drawbacks of being a chaplain's assistant. Sergeant Stokes was from southern Michigan, where it got considerably colder than southern Japan, but it did not make the weather at Kagoshima City any more endurable. He had already seen enough cold and snow in his twenty-three years to last him the rest of his life. When the war was over and he went back to college he was going to transfer to Southern Cal or the University of Miami.

Captain Gautney was lucky to be there in the port commander's warm office. At the last minute he had been summoned to a meeting on morale. The chaplain was always being called to some meeting or other. Captain Gautney didn't like conferences, he liked working with people, which was one of the things Stokes liked about him. Even Jewish and Catholic soldiers came to him with their gripes. Captain Gautney had given him the jeep's distributor, which they always removed when they were not in the vehicle, to keep the jeep from being stolen, and sent him out alone to try and locate the missing equipment.

"You'd think they'd know exactly where to put their hands on anything that important," Captain Gautney had said. "Only a week until Christmas and all the extra services."

Stokes had the chaplain's list of missing equipment in his pocket.

"Ecclesiastical appointments, wood: One each, cross and crucifix, two each, candlesticks and vases. One each, altar cover, pulpit and lectern scarfs. (Shouldn't it be "scarves," Stokes had thought.) One each, National Colors and flagstaff. One each, chapel flag and chaplain's flag. (Stokes had wanted to put a miniature chaplain's flag on the fender of the jeep, the way a general had his star, but Captain Gautney had refused, saying, rather unaptly Stokes thought, "Render therefore unto Caesar the things which are Caesar's and to God the things that are God's.") One each, organ, portable, folding. One hundred fifty each, Song and Service Books. One each, chest; container for Song and Service Books."

The chaplain's equipment was supposed to have been aboard the same LST that brought them from the Philippines in seven and a half lumbering, wallowing days. Either the chaplain or Stokes, and often both, had remained at the ship during the entire unloading process without seeing the crate that Captain Gautney had personally stenciled. The movable altar, pulpit, lectern and chancel rail had arrived ahead of them on another ship but they had been unable to track down the missing field and chapel equipment. Increasingly distraught memos, phone calls on the frustratingly overloaded trunk line, and frequent tours of the crowded littoral from the harbor south to within rifle shot of Japanese holdouts, proved fruitless. The first trip along the shore of Kagoshima Bay had convinced Stokes the search was hopeless. Landing ships, tank and landing ships, medium were nosed against the shore for almost a mile, discharging cargo, and lighters plied between the land and transports, Navy cargo and Liberty ships anchored out in the bay among a hodgepodge of salvage and repair vessels, dredges and barracks ships. The harbor itself was small. There were always four ships being unloaded inside the breakwater and four more anchored outside waiting to get in. Continuous relays of trucks fought a losing battle with the growing mountains of supplies. But Captain Gautney still expected to find one little crate in all that mess. Talk about faith.

"You'll find it today, Maurie," he said when he handed over the distributor. "I have a strong feeling you'll find it."

Captain Gautney had even told him to hitch up the trailer to the jeep so he would have something to bring it back in.

"Once you've located it don't let them load it on a truck with a lot of other things so they can lose it again," he had cautioned. "And Maurie, while you're looking around, keep your eyes peeled for Christians."

The chaplain had been looking for Christian Japanese ever since they hit Kagoshima City. That was where Christianity had first come to Japan, he said. Saint Francisco de Xavier in 1549. Captain Gautney was a bug on religious history. Stokes considered the captain something less than an intellectual giant in many areas but he did know his history. History had been Stokes's minor in his three years at Michigan State and he had been a top student, but in Captain Gautney's own field the chaplain was way ahead of him.

Cold or not, looking for a needle in a haystack or not, it beat shuffling papers at battalion headquarters, which was what Stokes had been doing back in Manila when the chaplain came in with a request for a new assistant. The previous assistant had been careless enough to be surprised sorting through the assistant's collection of pornographic photographs at the chaplain's own desk. The chaplain had left his list of requirements with the Battalion S-1. Stokes had learned later the chaplain had a passion for lists. After he went to work for Captain Gautney there was one he liked so much he typed a stencil of it and sent mimeographed copies to his parents, a younger brother, a favorite high school English teacher, a philosophy teacher he liked at Michigan State, the Unitarian minister who lived next door—Stokes did not think the socially ambitious minister of his own church would appreciate the naive dignity and unconscious humor of Captain Gautney's list—his girl friend and several male friends who for one reason or another were not in the service. The title of the list was "Things Not To Do Before Thinking Them Over Carefully." And these things were: 1. Judge a fellow human being. 2. Complain. 3. Lose my temper. 4. Anything else.

The chaplain's list of qualifications for his assistant had been passed around headquarters with much laughter and some ridicule. All he wanted was a college man, sincerely religious (the adjective underlined), a careful driver (again the adjective underlined) who could type and play the organ, had a pleasing singing voice, did not swear, drink or smoke and DID NOT HATE THE ENEMY. At first Stokes had laughed with the others. The chaplain's last specification had captured his imagination. First it had caused him to think about the kind of man who would insist on such a qualification. Naive he might be, dogmatic and humorless, but he had to be a Christian in the purest sense of the word. And that was supported by the fact he did not specify a denomination for his assistant. Then it had caused Stokes to consider whether he himself hated the Japanese as much as he believed he did. There was the rape of Nanking and Pearl Harbor and all that, and he had read of their barbarities and heard the stories told by U.S. combat soldiers and firsthand accounts from Filipino victims of the occupation. But what did he know of them as people? He knew a bit about their history and culture and much of it was admirable. The products of such a history and such a culture could not all be monsters. The atrocities he had read and heard about, and seen a few victims of, had been committed by soldiers. From what he had heard and seen American soldiers were not all exactly saints, either. He had not really thought of any of these things until he read the chaplain's list.

To his own astonishment, and with some embarrassment, Stokes had decided to volunteer for the job. He did not care for his present duty at all. He felt guilty about not being in combat, though not guilty enough to request reassignment as a rifleman, and disliked intensely the unrelieved clerical work. It would certainly be more interesting, and possibly more useful, to work for the kind of man who would draw up such a list. And he had all the qualifications that could be tested in practice and could easily simulate those he lacked. He could type passably and play piano better than passably, promising no difficulty with the simple portable organ used at services. His singing voice was not trained but it was pleasant. He did not smoke because he had swum competitively since junior high school. He liked a drink now and then and had been drunk more than once but did not like it enough that giving up alcohol was any great sacrifice. He swore a good deal, like the others, but that was only something he had picked up since coming into the Army, and profanity was not a part of his normal conversation. He was an excellent driver and, though he liked speed and nipping through traffic, could be as careful as the occasion demanded. Anyone who drove for a woman like his mother had to be. He was not religious, sincerely or otherwise, but was from family habit a regular churchgoer and knew all the motions. The Unitarian minister who lived next door back home and with whom he had enjoyed many stimulating conversations had considered his values morally and ethically sound, so if he professed to be sincerely religious it would not be utterly hypocritical.

Chaplain Gautney had selected him from the handful of volunteers and the three eight balls the personnel officer, Battalion S-1, had slipped onto the list of applicants in hopes of getting rid of one of them. The chaplain had been so pleased with him that in less than a month he had gotten Stokes his third stripe. It had been stimulating working for Captain Gautney, who was a perplexing combination of fundamental beliefs in the literal words of the Scriptures and sympathetic understanding of human frailties except in himself. Stokes had never regretted applying for chaplain's assistant until the foul-up in the equipment had put Captain Gautney's list of "Things Not To Do Before Thinking Them Over Carefully" to its severest test. The wild-goose chases up and down the bay shore in the cold and rain and the smirks of MPs and supply clerks who had come to know him were getting on Stokes's nerves. But he still admired the chaplain and liked working for him. He hoped to God a miracle would happen today and the missing crate would surface for Captain Gautney's sake as well as his own. And if nothing else he would try to turn up a Christian or two.

He hardly knew where to start among the pontoon causeways, T-head piers, quays, landing ships, lighters, piled-up cargo and, back from the bay, supply dumps and warehouses. Though he was hardly in a lyrical mood, Stokes found himself humming. He did not know if it was his subconscious or what, but his choice of song had a certain irony. "I'll be seeing you in all the old familiar places."

It was one of the tunes he had sometimes played for his own amusement on the portable organ back in Manila. He played others for Captain Gautney. The chaplain loved music but his tastes were narrow. His idea of great pop tunes was "Praise the Lord and Pass the Ammunition" and "Coming in on a Wing and a Prayer." His favorite of favorites was "Battle Hymn of the Republic," which Stokes also liked very much, with "God Bless America" the runner-up. The chaplain was also fond of hymns and sang them with unabashed vigor. Stokes had heard a couple of officers joking about hearing the chaplain render a few in the shower facility.

He could start among the LSTs nosed into the shore south of the mile-long quay. From there, with binoculars, you could sometimes see squads of Marines nosing around for Japanese holdouts and blowing up caves. And once he had seen a jeep go by with a jolly-looking Japanese soldier in full uniform in it. The MP on point duty told him the Japanese soldier went up into the hills every day trying to persuade holdouts to give themselves up. So far he hadn't brought any in but he hadn't been shot at, either, the MP said. The weather was too nasty to scrounge among the LSTs, Stokes decided. He'd start at the harbor master's Quonset hut. It was warm there and they always had hot coffee on the stove. And there was a chief petty officer there who had promised to keep an eye out for the chaplain's crate.

The snow turned to muddy slush when it hit the ground. Trucks, half-tracks and amphibs had churned big areas into quagmire but the road itself wasn't too bad, considering the weather and the heavy traffic. The engineers had bulldozers and dump trucks out twenty-four hours a day filling in the bad spots with volcanic rock processed in the big rock crusher that had come on a landing ship, dock. In some stretches they had laid down steel landing mats. Those were the stretches he had to watch. They were as slippery as glaze ice and tractors kept busy pulling out the six-by-sixes that slid off into the quagmire.

The harbor master was almost directly opposite Sakurajima, a mile and a half across Kagoshima Bay. Hundreds of Japanese troops were still holding out over there. Sakurajima was connected to the far shore by a stretch of raw, jagged lava less than half a mile wide, and the Army said it wasn't worth trying to push across as long as the Japanese holed up there didn't do any shooting across the bay. Which they hadn't as long as Stokes had been in Kagoshima. Now and then a big shell landed on the slopes of the twin peaks or the twisted lava beds at their base. When they exploded they made blobs of smoke and fire and the sound boomed across the bay, but Stokes could not hear the guns that fired them. They were too far inland. He'd heard it was replacement gun crews using Sakurajima for target practice. You never saw a Japanese show himself over there. Gray clouds hung in tatters around the two peaks. Brownish smoke belched regularly from the volcano. Minamitake and On-take the twin peaks were called. The taller one was supposed to be thirty-five hundred feet high. It looked higher than that to Stokes. The lava beds glistened with moisture from snow falling on the stone warmed by subterranean fires. Where there was soil Sakurajima was still lush and green despite the freezing weather. The subterranean fires accounted for it.

The first time they had taken a good look at the lava beds on Sakurajima, when they came hunting for the crate of equipment, Captain Gautney had said, "Maurie, do you believe in Hell?"

"Not exactly sir," Stokes had answered truthfully.

"Well, I do," Captain Gautney said. "And that's exactly what it looks like."

Stokes parked the jeep by the harbor master's Quonset hut in the least muddy place he could find. Colored stevedores from the port companies were working down the quay. He had seen a lot of black faces since arriving at Kagoshima City. Stevedores, engineers, truck drivers. It seemed they got all the crap details, just like civilian life. Captain Gautney had noticed it, too. It had pleased Stokes that even though the chaplain took his Scriptures literally he did not go along with some fundamentalists' notion that the sons of Ham were meant to be hewers of wood and drawers of water now and forever more, Amen. Stokes had heard the argument many times that it was that way in the Army because colored troops didn't make good combat soldiers. Although he had never been around any of the colored combat units he could never really accept that, especially after he heard the stories about the DUKW drivers on X-Day and the engineers and truck drivers working right up on the line. It was more than he had done himself. The only time he had ever been shot at was back in Manila by a drunk American soldier. Even that shot hadn't been fired in anger, though it scared him as much as if it had been.

There were Japanese civilian work gangs, too, mostly engaged in hauling away rubble and filling in holes. Stokes felt sorry for them. He thought maybe he would have felt the same way even if he hadn't been exposed to Captain Gautney for three months. They were a sad-looking lot, ragged, with hardly a winter coat among them and with rags or straw sandals on their feet. Captain Gautney had tried to get gloves, shoes and jackets from the salvage dump for those who worked out in the weather but was told that was already in the works and would be done as soon as they could get around to it. There were too many important things to be done and for the time being women, children and the sick had priority.

Chief Petty Officer Zubarik looked up in mock surprise when Stokes approached his desk.

"Jesus," he said. "Not you again?"

"Only a representative of his representative," Stokes replied.

CPO Zubarik groaned.

"So it's a lousy joke," Stokes said. "It's a lousy day."

He took off his helmet and hung it on the peg of a standing coatrack. He stuffed his woolen cap into one pocket of his overcoat and, after transferring Captain Gautney's equipment list to his jacket, thrust his gloves into the other. He hung his overcoat on another peg and draped his muffler over it. He did it deliberately, taking a couple of minutes. Zubarik watched in silence until he was done.

"Why don't you take off your overcoat and stay awhile?" he said then.

"Like to but I'm a very busy man," Stokes replied.

There was a fine lacquer tray, chipped and coffee stained, with thick mugs on it, by Zubarik's desk. Stokes squatted down and looked for a clean mug. One had a wide band of surgical adhesive tape on it. He picked it up and looked at it. Something was printed on the tape with blue-black ink. "St. Sgt. Stokes." There was a halo over the "St." Stokes looked up at Zubarik. The CPO was grinning at him.

"Am I getting another stripe I don't know about?" Stokes said.

"S-t stands for saint, not staff, jackass," Zubarik said. "It's awarded for devoted service to God and Gautney in lieu."

"In lieu of what?"

"Something better."

Stokes went to the stove, poured himself a cup of coffee, added two heaping spoonfuls of sugar and a generous dollop of canned evaporated milk and stirred vigorously. He walked back to Zubarik's desk and sat down, sighing.

"Pour yourself a cup of coffee and sit down," said Zubarik. "Do you a world of good to get off your feet."

"Maybe later," Stokes said, "if I feel as strong as it is. Navy coffee. Ugh."

"Is there any little thing we can do for Your Holiness?" Zubarik said unctuously.

Stokes thought Zubarik sounded different than usual, as if he were just waiting to spring something. Stokes was not going to rush it, though.

That would spoil the game.

"Yes," he said. "Try to think purer thoughts. Oh," he went on, as if it were an afterthought. "There may be a trifling matter."

He took Captain Gautney's much-creased list out of his pocket and unfolded it. Zubarik closed his eyes and pressed the fingers of both hands to his brow.

"Quiet, please," he said urgently. "I'm getting a message."

After a moment he opened his eyes and said gravely, ''Ecclesiastical appointments, wood. Shall I continue? The message is two bits a word."

"That's highway robbery," Stokes said, pretending indignation. "But I'll pay it, if you tell me how you do it."

He knew, of course, that by now Zubarik was as familiar with the chaplain's list as he was.

"I have a direct line to Up There," Zubarik said. "Just like Gautney. Say, Stokes, wouldn't you think They'd tell him where it was if he's really that big Up There?"

"The Lord moves in mysterious ways," Stokes said. "Who are we to question?"

Zubarik was bursting with something. Stokes could feel it. Had he actually located the chaplain's precious crate? It was too good to be true. Stokes tried to hide his interest. Zubarik was just waiting for him to ask. Stokes sipped his coffee, his face as impassive as he could manage.

"Okay, then, you cagey son of a bitch," Zubarik said at last. "Come on."

He got up from his desk and led Stokes outside the Quonset hut were tarpaulin-covered heaps were stacked along the curving side. He took hold of the corner of a stiff tarp, saying "Voila!" There were crates of various sizes in the stack, none of them Captain Gautney's. Stokes did not think it was funny.

"You bastard!" he cried.

"Wait a minute, wait a minute!" Zubarik cried. "Read what's in 'em." Stokes read the stenciled labels. The crates contained chapel equipment and chaplain's field equipment.

"It's all there, jackass," Zubarik said. "All we got to do is bust open a couple and make up Gautney's list."

Stokes was delighted but he wanted to repay Zubarik for holding out on him.

"I don't know," he said thoughtfully. "This equipment might be intended for our boys at the front."

"Screw our boys at the front," Zubarik said. "If Jesus loved 'em that much they'd be here and we'd be there."

The chapel equipment crate they opened contained, in addition to Captain Gautney's requirements, a communion set including nine dozen neatly packed glasses.

"Oh, hell," said Zubarik. "I'm robbing some Catholic chaplain for a lousy Protestant."

He crossed himself.

"You're only robbing Peter to pay Paul," Stokes said soothingly.

"I'll give 'em to Padre Lowery," Zubarik said. "That'll make him an accessory."

Zubarik spread a dry shelter half in the bed of the jeep trailer and after the portable organ and other equipment was loaded covered it all with a tightly lashed tarpaulin.

"Maybe now I can get a little of my own work done," he said. "You and your goddam chaplain have been a real pain in the ass."

"Bless you, my son," Stokes murmured, making the sign of the cross over Zubarik.

They were both damp with melting snow and thoroughly chilled. Stokes went back inside with Zubarik for another cup of coffee. He was anxious to surprise Captain Gautney with the equipment but he wanted to think up a good story to explain how he had come by it. The chaplain was bound to notice it was not in the crate he had stenciled and was all new. Stokes could say the Navy had acknowledged responsibility for losing the equipment and had replaced it but the chaplain might start thanking people and end up getting Zubarik in a mess. What really bothered Stokes was lying to Captain Gautney. The man was so trusting lying to him as indecent. The only drawback to working for the chaplain was the way he made you feel obligated to live up to his standards. Maybe he could dig up a Christian for Gautney and the chaplain would be too excited to notice anything different about the equipment.

"Hey, Zube," he said. "You know if any of those civilian laborers speak English?"

"One of the gang foremen does," Zubarik replied. "Name of Waco. Why?"

"I want to learn Japanese. I promised my mother I wouldn't waste my years in the Army."

Stokes put on his overcoat and helmet and walked to the quay. The Japanese were working diligently and in complete silence. They were all small and scrawny and no self-respecting ragpicker would have taken their clothes as a gift. It made Stokes feel like a clumsy giant, overdressed and overfleshed. He was an intruder here in every sense of the word. He wished one of them would ask what he wanted or even look up and give him an opening.

"Is there somebody here they call Waco?" he asked.

One of the Japanese stopped tamping crushed rock and turned to face him. One of his silver-rimmed spectacle lenses was cracked. He was a good foot shorter than Stokes's six-one. His upper body was lost in a torn U.S. Marine Corps field jacket, which reached almost to his knees. His feet were frozen-looking in sodden straw sandals.

"You Americans are pleased to call me that," he said in a firm, noncommittal voice, his English surprisingly good. "Wakao Kuninori."

Stokes thrust out his hand, not knowing what else to do.

"Pleased to know you, Mr. Kuninori," he said.

The Japanese made no move to take the proffered hand and after an awkward moment Stokes let it drop to his side.

"We Japanese place the patronymic foremost," the little man said ironically. "It is Mr. Wakao. Or, more appropriately, Dr. Wakao."

Stokes felt his jaw dropping.

"You're a doctor?"

The Japanese looked at him coolly. Stokes could see the man was enjoying his discomfiture.

"Not a medical doctor," the man said. "In what manner may I be of assistance to you?"

"Dr. Wakao, are there any Christians here?"

The Japanese looked surprised. Then he smiled sardonically. Who said the Japanese were inscrutable, Stokes thought.

"Yes," said Dr. Wakao. "Very many."

"Gee, that's great!" Stokes said.

"All those with guns," Dr. Wakao said.

The little bastard, Stokes thought.

"You know what I meant," he said angrily.

"There was a small number before the bombings," Dr. Wakao said calmly. "It is possible some of them may have survived."

"I'm a chaplain's assistant," Stokes said. "You know about Army Chaplains?"

"Yes. We Japanese also have had our warrior priests. In feudal times, of course."

"Forget it!" Stokes snapped, whirling to go.

"One moment, please," Dr. Wakao said.

Stokes turned to face him.

"You are offended?" Dr. Wakao asked.

"You're damn right! Wasn't that the idea?"

"Yes. But I am curious. What is it you wish of Christians?"

"Forget it," Stokes said. "I'll ask someone who's not such a turd."

If Dr. Wakao knew the meaning of the word he did not show it. He removed his glasses and wiped them with a scrap of cloth. Holding them up, he looked through the cracked lens and sighed. He put the spectacles back on, adjusted them carefully, and looked into Stokes's face. Stokes returned the look, refusing to be stared down. He was angry with himself for the language he had used and for not just saying the hell with this arrogant and infuriatingly self-possessed little man and getting back to the chapel hut with Captain Gautney's equipment.

"I have been told that were I a captured Japanese soldier new spectacles would be provided," Dr. Wakao said. "But there are none for civilian employees of your government. Now, the question which I find most intriguing is this."

Instead of completing the thought he said, "What is your name, young man?"

Surprised, Stokes said, "Stokes. Sergeant Maurice Stokes."

He was not sure how it had come about but he now felt it somehow proper that Wakao should be questioning him instead of the other way around. And, incongruously, a recollection of his philosophy teacher at Michigan State, as tall as he was and redheaded, popped into his mind.

"The question that intrigues me is this, Sergeant Stokes," Dr. Wakao said, "had I killed Americans in the battle for my city would I be considered a soldier and rewarded with new eyeglasses?"

Stokes laughed. He could not help it.

"It's possible," he said.

Wakao rubbed his chin thoughtfully.

"You Americans are a curious people," he said. "Quite curious."

Stokes knew Wakao was pulling his leg again but it no longer angered him. Instead it amused and stimulated him.

"Yes," he said, speaking as mock-pedantically as Wakao, "sometimes we can be as inconsistent as the Japanese."

The corners of Dr. Wakao's lips twitched.

An American in Navy winter blues, a carbine slung over his shoulder, strolled up to them and said in a surly voice, "Hey, Waco, you ain't being paid to beat your jaw. If you ain't got nothing better to do, soldier, do it on your own time. These Nips are being paid to do a job of work."

"Shove it," Stokes said. "I'm on official business. For the captain."

He had usually found it effective when dealing with the Navy to create the impression the captain he worked for was Navy, not Army. A Navy captain was the equivalent of a bird colonel. It worked better on the telephone, of course, when they could not see you were Army, but enough Navy brass in a mixed situation such as existed at a port establishment had Army personnel under their command to get away with it face to face if you worked it right.

"Oh," the sailor said.

He walked away with studied nonchalance. Wakao's face showed genuine amusement.

"The relationship between your Army and Navy is almost Japanese," he said. "Shall we return to the subject? What is it you wish of Christians?"

"It's the chaplain's idea. He wants to contact some Japanese Christians."

"That also is rather curious," Dr. Wakao said. "It has long been my impression you Americans are more concerned with converting the heathen than in wasting your time on those already enlightened."

He said it with the irony Stokes realized was characteristic of the man and which he now found engaging rather than offensive.

"The chaplain wants to invite them to services and Christmas dinner next week," he said. "Do you know any in Kagoshima?"

"Perhaps," said Wakao. "There were several years of government repression and they made themselves rather inconspicuous."

"Could you tell me where to find them?"

"In the best of times it was difficult for a stranger to find his way about in a Japanese city. And now . . ."

He looked back toward the shattered city.

"Maybe you could take me," Stokes said.

"Why should I desire to?"

Don't get mad at the little bastard again, Stokes told himself. It's what he wants and he's too much for you to handle.

"Because it beats tamping rock out in the cold," he said. "And because you're bored. But mainly because it'll give you a chance to keep sounding off about Americans to me."

Wakao's face did not show whether Stokes's words annoyed or amused him. He can be inscrutable when he wants to, Stokes thought. And he's doing it just to needle me. He won't give me the satisfaction of knowing if I got to him or not.

Wakao nodded toward the silent, dogged civilian laborers.

"We work until dusk," he said. "It is impossible to find one's way about the broken streets in darkness. And of course there is the curfew."

"Maybe I can fix it," said Stokes. "I'll be back in a jiffy."

He went back to the Quonset hut and told CPO Zubarik his problem. Zubarik rummaged through his desk, found a printed form, and typed something on it. He typed expertly, using the touch system.

"You'd make a hell of a chaplain's assistant's assistant," Stokes said. "How about helping me with Captain Gautney's correspondence?"

"Sign here," Zubarik said, holding out a gray Parker 51 fountain pen. "You're not getting my signature on a false official statement."

Stokes had once owned a similar pen which had been lost or stolen in Manila, where they were highly prized on the black market.

The typed name at the bottom of the order was Louis H. Berlioz, Lieutenant Commander, USNR. Stokes wrote the name in neat compact letters unlike his usual loose scrawl.

"Sayonara," he said, turning to go.

"Sayonara, my ass," said Zubarik, holding out his hand. "The fountain pen, Hector."

"A thousand pardons," Stokes said, giving it back.

He went out the door whistling the only passage he remembered from "The Damnation of Faust." He showed the form to the sailor guarding the labor gang.

"I'll take that," the sailor said, reaching for it.

"Not a chance," Stokes said, jerking it back. "The captain wants Waco delivered somewhere in town. I'll need it in case the MPs want to know what I'm doing with a Jap national."

"How come the captain didn't sign the order instead of some lieutenant commander?" the sailor demanded.

"Commander Berlioz takes his orders from the captain just like you and me." He lowered his voice. "He's a real son of a bitch, ain't he?" he said. "That Commander Berlioz."

"Yeah," the sailor said conspiratorially, "a real son of a bitch."

"But the captain, he's a good egg."

"You think so," the sailor said, surprised.

"Yeah," Stokes replied belligerently. "Don't you?"

"Oh, sure," the sailor said quickly.

As Stokes walked away he heard the sailor mutter, "Brownnosin' bastard."

He led Dr. Wakao to the jeep. As he turned to go around to the driver's side he saw Wakao had made no move to get in. I'll be a son of a gun, he thought. Wakao expects me to open the side curtain for him. Stranger yet, Stokes felt a compulsion to do so. He unsnapped the curtain and Wakao got in.

"Are you comfortable, Doctor?" Stokes said, trying to imitate Wakao's ironic shading.

"Quite," said Wakao, unperturbed.

Stokes started the engine and let it warm up. Wakao looked back at the trailer.

"What have you there, Sergeant?" he said. "Bibles?"

"Close," Stokes said. "Chapel equipment."

"Yes," said Wakao. "I rather supposed it was not food and medical supplies for my countrymen."

Stokes let that pass. Wakao must know military government was distributing food, clothing and medicine to the civilian population.

"You may find it difficult negotiating the roads with such a load,"Wakao said. "You have repaired only those useful to your operations."

"Four-wheel drive," Stokes said, putting the jeep into gear.

"Of course," Wakao said. "You have a machine for every purpose."

They had gone but a short distance when Wakao said, "You are of course a Christian?"

"Yes."

"I am a Buddhist. As a matter of fact, we are quite near Kyushu's finest Buddhist temple, the Nishi Hongwanji. Perhaps you wish to view it?"

"I'd like to," Stokes said. "But not today. The chaplain's been waiting for that stuff back there for a week."

"In that case another few moments would be of little importance," Wakao said. "And you will find it most instructive. It is just over there near the ruins of the prefectural office. That extensive walled enclosure."

"Good thing it had a wall around it," Stokes said. "Or there wouldn't be much left."

Wakao chuckled.

"I suppose not," he said.

When they drew closer Stokes saw there was nothing within the walls but an immense charred ruin. Broken tiles and burned wood lay everywhere in heaps. One blackened wooden pillar thrust up from the ruins.

"American bombers," Wakao said.

"That was a pretty low stunt," Stokes said. "Bringing me here like that."

"Is it not instructive, as I promised?"

"It had to be an accident. We don't bomb churches."

"It is quite possible it was accidental," Wakao said. "Your bombing also destroyed the Jo-nan Methodist Church, Saint Xavier Church, the Nippon Fukuin Lutheran Church, the Seventh Day Adventist Church and the former quarters of the Nippon Christian Association. I doubt you would have destroyed Christian churches deliberately."

"Then what's the point?" Stokes demanded.

"You are an intelligent young man," Wakao said. "I believe you are quite aware of the point. Shall we begin our search for Christians?"

"Okay," Stokes said. "Which way?"

"West," Dr. Wakao said. "Beyond that eminence. Shiroyama. Castle Hill."

The hill to which he referred was two or three hundred feet high and wooded with pines and once stately camphors. The hill had been bombarded and fought over. There was enough left of the woods for Stokes to know the hill had once been beautiful. At the base of the hill stone walls rose from a partially filled moat choked with lotus. The ancient stone, like the hillside, bore the scars of battle. The level space girt by the walls was empty. It appeared to be the site of a building but Stokes saw no charred remains as he had at the Nishi Hongwanji.

"Don't try to tell me American bombers did this, too," he said.

"This is the site of the castles of the Shimazu daimyo," Wakao said, amused. "The last structure on it, Tsurumaru-jo, was razed in 1877. After the last rebellion against the Emperor Meiji."

"Oh," said Stokes. "Saigo Takamori."

He was pleased to see Wakao's quickly suppressed reaction to this calculated display of his knowledge of Japanese history. He wondered if Wakao would admit it surprised him. Probably not.

"Takamori committed seppuku in a cave behind the hill," Wakao said matter-of-factly. "Would you care to inspect it?"

"Some other time," Stokes said.

They continued past the hill in silence.

"I'm sorry about that temple," Stokes said after a while. "It's really a crime."

"Precisely."

"I didn't mean that literally," Stokes snapped.

"Mr. Hoshi, an acquaintance of mine, lived on the western outskirts of the city," Dr. Wakao said as they plowed along the narrow muddy street. "I have not seen him since some weeks before the Americans came. But it is possible he has returned."

A number of canals traversed the city. Small bridges of stone spanned them in some places. In others, where they had been destroyed either by Kagoshima's defenders or attackers, they had been replaced by temporary American bridges. Although virtually every wooden structure in the city had burned and none made of masonry had escaped damage, there were no rubble heaps. Civilian laborers had piled everything neatly inside the shells of buildings or in vacant spots where once houses had stood. In many places, fixed to standing walls or fastened in the cleft of sticks thrust into the ground in the sites of vanished homes, were bits of paper or wood with lettering on them. They had been placed there, Dr. Wakao explained, by citizens who had fled and had now returned to search for friends and relatives.

"Were there many suicides?" Stokes asked.

"How did you know of that?" said Wakao.

"It happened all over the Pacific," Stokes said. "Wherever there were Japanese civilians. God knows what they thought we were going to do to them."

"A tragic result of my government's propaganda," Wakao said bitterly. "At the end I went about trying to dissuade those who believed they would be murdered or enslaved. I was not always successful. And once a soldier gave me a beating for my pains. A Japanese soldier. It was then my spectacles were broken."

Stokes was astonished by this admission.

"If you did that," he demanded, "why have you been giving me such a hard time about how terrible we Americans are?"

"It has been reported that in Tokyo alone more than a million innocent persons have perished from bombings, starvation and disease in the past four months," Wakao said grimly.

"It's your own goddam fault!" Stokes blurted, angry now. "We gave you every chance to quit. And who in hell started this war, anyhow?"

For a moment Wakao studied the windshield wiper clearing away the sparse snowflakes on the driver's side, an amused and infuriating smile on his lips.

"Rather unusual weather for this area," he said. "We do not often see snow in Kagoshima City. Is there often snow where you reside in America?"

"Oh, crap!" said Stokes.

Then he wished he had not said it. The sly little bastard knew exactly how to make him behave like an ignorant lout. Probably Wakao's way of getting back at him for the smugly casual way he had mentioned Saigo Takamori.

"I hold Japan's leaders in no greater esteem than America's," Wakao said in the ironic, bantering tone with which Stokes had grown familiar. They were in an area of utter devastation. The earth was cratered and burned over, with here and there a brick fire pit marking the site of a simple home or a chimney and bit of foundation that of a more substantial house. Here were more of the notices left by citizens searching for relatives and friends.

"Mr. Hoshi's house was somewhere hereabout," said Dr. Wakao. "It is difficult to know exactly where. A lovely spectacle, is it not?"

"Yes," Stokes said. "Reminds me of Manila."

"Perhaps he has left a message stating where he may be found," said Wakao, unruffled. "Shall I see?"

"Okay. But hurry up. It's getting late."

It was after one o'clock and he was hungry. He had had an early breakfast. Captain Gautney believed in getting an early start. As he often said, there were not enough hours in the day to do the Lord's work. After Wakao got out of the jeep to read the notices Stokes rummaged around in the back for something to eat. There was a cardboard box of tracts the chaplain's former congregation had sent him to distribute to the troops and which he had not because they contained advertising, a bag of the chaplain's laundry he was supposed to drop off, a Coleman lantern with a broken chimney, an entrenching tool and jack for getting the jeep out of mudholes, a booklet of marriage and baptism certificates, back numbers of the chief of chaplain's monthly circular letter and, what he was looking for, cans of C ration, packages of K ration and Tropical Chocolate bars which Captain Gautney gave to Japanese children he encountered. The military government distributed a special O Ration which included rice, soybeans and canned fish among the local population, but Chaplain Gautney had been unable to get his hands on any of them. When Dr. Wakao returned from reading the notices Stokes had put a can of meat and beans, a package of bacon and egg and a chocolate bar on the seat for him.

"Mr. Hoshi apparently has not returned," he said. "It might be wise to leave a message."

"Let's have lunch first," Stokes said, gesturing toward the rations in the passenger seat.

The look in Dr. Wakao's eyes was ravenous. The tip of his tongue stole out and licked his lips.

"You are most generous," he said, for the first time not completely master of the situation. "But at the moment I am not hungry. With your permission I will have them at a later hour."

Stokes could not understand why a man as uncompromisingly honest as Wakao would lie when he was so obviously famished. It could not be that he was too proud to accept food, because he said he would eat it later. Then he thought he understood.

"Are you married, Dr. Wakao?" he asked.

"Yes."

"Children?"

"Yes. Why do you ask?"

"No reason," said Stokes.

His hunch was right. Wakao had a hungry family. He would load him up with stuff when he dropped him back at the harbor.

"Suit yourself about lunch," he said, tearing open a K ration.

If he hadn't come on what was beginning to look like another wildgoose chase he would be having hot chow in the mess tent and Chaplain Gautney would have his chapel equipment. He tore the top from the carton of tracts and gave the square of cardboard and a pencil to Wakao. While he ate, Wakao wrote a message on the cardboard giving Captain Gautney's name and unit and fastened it to a stick thrust into the muddy ground.

"Don't you know any other Christians?" Stokes asked when Wakao returned to the jeep.

"I fear it would be the same story. Have you inquired at the refugee encampment?"

"The refugee encampment?"

"Yes. Beyond Shiroyama Park. We passed near it on the way here."

"No, we haven't," Stokes said, feeling foolish.

If he and Captain Gautney were organized it should have been one of the first places they tried. They had been too damned busy looking for the chapel equipment.

"I suggest we make inquiries there," Dr. Wakao said without the ironic comments Stokes expected. "If it is agreeable to you."

"Good idea," Stokes said.

He started to tell Wakao to go ahead and eat the food laid out for him, that there would be more to take home to his family, but decided against it. Wakao might get stiff-necked and refuse the food altogether. He gathered up the cans and wrappings from his lunch and, after a moment's hesitation, pushed them through the side curtain where the snap was missing and dropped them on the ground. It was a sure thing he didn't have to worry about spoiling the natural beauty of the countryside here.

When they were back on the road, Wakao seemed to be weighing something in his mind. At last he said, "Have you by any chance a cigarette?"

"I don't smoke," Stokes replied.

Wakao smiled wryly and murmured something in Japanese.

"Freely translated, that means, 'How fortunate for you, how unfortunate for me.' "

"I could get you some."

"Thank you, no. The craving will pass."

"What are you a doctor of, anyway?"

"Letters. My specialty is, was, comparative literature."

"Was?"

"Until two years ago I had a rather good post at a university."

"What happened? It wasn't bombed out, was it? It couldn't have been, not two years ago."

"I was, how shall I put it, considered politically unreliable."

"You shot off your mouth too much, didn't you? Just like you do now?"

Wakao smiled. For the first time his smile was neither unfriendly nor ironic.

"Precisely," he said. "If I understand your idiom correctly. Just as I do now."

"With your background and command of English you could have a good job with military government. Why are you doing manual labor?"

"I do not wish to cooperate with the occupation to that great a degree."

The rear wheels began slipping in the mud. Stokes threw in front wheel drive and shifted into low-low.

"This is a remarkable vehicle," Wakao said. "And you operate it expertly. Ah, here we are. The refugee encampment."

Neat rows of tents were surrounded by high barbed-wire fences. There were searchlights at regular intervals. A large gate made of planks and barbed wire blocked the road leading into the enclosure. At one side was a wooden sentry box. Smoke drifted from a round metal chimney poking out of the roof. Japanese civilians wandered around in the mud among the tents.

"I thought you said this was a refugee encampment," Stokes said. "Not a prisoner of war camp."

"I suspect the American Army fears all Japanese are saboteurs and assassins," said Wakao, his eyes twinkling.

"I suspect they might not be too far wrong," Stokes replied lightly. "Lots of places the civilians have been giving us fits. Or didn't you know?"

Wakao smiled without answering. He appeared to relish being answered in kind.

"I wouldn't be surprised if some of those 'refugees' were GUs and soldiers in civilian clothes," Stokes continued.

Wakao's smile broadened.

"Nor should I," he said.

Stokes stopped the jeep at the gate and climbed out. A soldier came out of the sentry box, looking unhappy at having to leave its warmth.

"Yeah?" he said.

"I want to go through," Stokes said. "Open up."

"You got a vehicle pass?"

"No."

"No dice, then."

"Okay. So I'll leave the jeep here."

"You got a pass?"

"What do you mean, pass? I've got official business here. For the chaplain. Captain Gautney."

"Never heard of him. Don't matter, anyway. Nobody goes in without a pass from the provost marshal."

"Where's the provost marshal?"

"Across the street."

Stokes turned to go.

"Won't do you no good," the soldier said. "Major Smith ain't there. He went to the officer's club to get something for his cold. Old Taylor."

"Then how do I get a pass to get in?"

"You don't, I reckon. Not today. What the hell you want in for, anyway?"

"I'm looking for Christians."

After he said it Stokes realized how stupid it sounded. The soldier gave him an incredulous look.

"Christians?" he said. "There ain't no Christians in there. There ain't nothing but Nips."

"I'm looking for Japanese Christians."

His hands and feet were cold and he was getting damned tired of the pointless conversation.

"You mean there's Jap Christians?" the soldier demanded.

"I'll come back with the chaplain," Stokes said curtly.

"Okay. But he don't get in without no pass, either."

Stokes walked back toward the jeep, boiling.

"Take it easy," the soldier called after him cordially.

Stokes jerked open the side curtain, breaking another snap, and started the engine. He let it race a moment before putting the jeep in gear. Wakao looked at him quizzically.

"You appear displeased," he said. "Was your friend unable to help you?"

"My friend?" Stokes snapped. "That stupid . . ."

Suddenly he was laughing. Here he was, Maurice Stokes, a reasonably intelligent young man, driving around a devastated and historic city thousands of miles from where he belonged, dragging a load of prayer books and religious trappings behind him in the company of a Japanese laborer who was really a college professor and all on an errand that when you really thought about it no man in his right mind could take seriously. What difference did it make if there were Christians in Kagoshima City and whether Captain Gautney found them or not? Hundreds of thousands of men were busy trying to kill each other, people were starving, a whole nation was being smashed into jelly, and he had spent the last week looking for a crate of junk that was probably still sitting somewhere in the Philippines, and the last few minutes working himself into a pointless rage.

"Dr. Wakao," he said gravely, "it's as hard to get in there as it is to get out. Wouldn't that frost you?"

"And you find that so terribly amusing?" Wakao demanded.

Stokes shook his head. It was hard work backing up a jeep with trailer on it when you weren't accustomed to it. The trailer kept jackknifing. He had to give it his full attention.

"What is it you find so amusing, then?" Wakao insisted.

Stokes began laughing again.

"Christians," he said.

15

[Sergeant Rentaro Yoshida/Sergeant George Ebata/Lieutenant Fukujiki]

Miyakanojo fell on December 23, X+41, to XI and I Corps troops converging on the city from the south and east. After the link-up powerful elements of XI Corps drove west to the shores of Kagoshima Bay and then turned north along the coast to Kokubu. By December 30, X+48, they had achieved a link-up with the Marines of V Amphibious Corps, who had reached the west coast of Kagoshima Bay at Shigetomi, north of Kagoshima City and pushed east along the head of the bay. Meanwhile, on the east coast of Kyushu, I Corps had driven north along the Miyazaki plain through the thorny coastal defenses of the remnants of the Japanese 154th "Defense of Route" Infantry Division and the still potent 212th Infantry Division to capture Tsuno. In these operations U.S. Olympic casualties rose to 71,000, of which 17,500 were killed. Japanese military casualties had soared to 194,000, including a growing number of severely wounded receiving treatment of one sort or another (19,000), and for the first time an appreciable number of prisoners, 2,100. The Japanese defense had become more fluid after the fixed coastal positions were smashed and some evacuation of wounded was undertaken. The bulk of the prisoners came from bypassed positions far in the rear near the coasts, either driven to surrender by hunger or persuaded to do so by the intensive psychological warfare campaign. Casualties rose sharply among the quasi-military Volunteer Combat Units as they were thrown into the battle in increasing numbers. By X+48 such casualties had reached 144,000. The GUs did not fight as tenaciously as regular troops. Forty thousand were killed, 51,000 wounded and 53,000 captured. Little attempt was made to evacuate Volunteer Combat wounded and responsibility for the care of the bulk of these thousands fell to the invaders.

There were now three-quarters of a million Americans on Kyushu, including thirteen air groups. Offshore, another quarter-million Americans and British manned the vast fleet supporting land operations. From Okinawa and other islands in the Ryukyus fifty air groups provided continuous massive air support. They were soon to be joined by ten squadrons of British bombers from Europe. In the face of such overwhelming strength the Japanese in southern Kyushu began withdrawing toward the Kirishima Mountains in south-central Kyushu, where strong forces from the north had already assembled. There, new headquarters for the 57th Army was established after Takarabe, west of Miyakanojo, became untenable. The three American corps pushed relentlessly through the valleys from the west, south and east toward the mountain stronghold.

The landing craft, infantry, loafed back and forth along the seven hundred-yard breadth of Aka Point five miles east of Shibushi Harbor. It had been doing so for several afternoons, drawing closer every day until it was now only a hundred yards offshore. The first day it had met with rifle fire from the Japanese positions dug into the rocky shoreline. The LCI had not returned the fire and opposition had slackened daily as the defenders grew accustomed to its unaggressiveness. This afternoon not even a single rifle shot had come its way. As it cruised off the point a loudspeaker blared recordings of popular Japanese music. From time to time the music would stop and a warmly dressed Japanese soldier standing amidships would pick up a bullhorn and exhort his invisible comrades to join him in honorable captivity.

The defenders of Aka Point were among the thousands of Japanese troops whose fortifications lay outside the path of the invaders. After the battle zones had become defined, some of the coast defenses had been abandoned and their troops transferred to combat areas, but the two infantry squads on Aka Point and the two platoons dug in behind them at Takamatsu Village astride the road and railroad had been left there to block an anticipated enemy drive out of Shibushi toward the Fukushima River, to the east. The Americans, however, had not tried to force the narrow coastal passage and had halted two miles to the west after taking the troublesome fortifications at Cape Daguri interfering with their activities in Shibushi Harbor. At first Aka Point and Takamatsu Village had been bombed and shelled regularly, then the high explosives had been replaced with shells strewing leaflets urging the defenders to give themselves up. The leaflets were of two kinds and inspired only rage or amusement, depending upon the temperament of the reader. One of the leaflets bore a photomontage of Sakurajima, a cluster of Japanese soldiers in various grotesque attitudes of death and a Japanese woman holding a baby. The text on the reverse side said, among other things, "Just what is the meaning of this war which continues to destroy your homeland? To die in battle for the cause of prolonging the suffering of your people is obstinate and foolish. Now is the time to bring strong reason into play. Deliver your homeland, deliver your comrades who unwittingly seek the path of annihilation, deliver yourself. Think profoundly of saving yourself and your comrades who uselessly are wasting lives better employed in rebuilding your homeland." The photograph on the other leaflet showed an American soldier squatting to talk with two placid Japanese children. The text said, in part, "An orphanage has recently been set up at the American Army billeting area at Shibushi and two hundred ninety children, some as young as nine months, are being looked after by American doctors and kind-hearted, patriotic Japanese women. But think of the many thousands of helpless children not just at Shibushi but everywhere in Japan, waiting for parents who may never come. Perhaps one of them is yours. Picture to yourself the face of your beloved child when he first sees you in the midst of the ruins. Try to see him clinging tightly to you as if he would never let go again. Surely you cannot but feel it is your duty as a parent to save your life and strength for the sake of your child."

When the leaflets failed to achieve tangible results an unarmed American transport plane flew over Aka Point and dropped small inflatable rubber boats with instructions for their use. "Perhaps you have not listened to the voice of reason, honor and conscience because you mistakenly believe the American soldiers will kill you when you approach them in friendship. Or perhaps you believe some of your comrades may be so deceived by the false words of self-serving militarists that they will try to prevent you from approaching the American lines. If that is so, wait until dark and set out to sea. In the near distance you will see a light. That is the rescue ship. Even though the waves may be rough, keep your courage and go on, humming the song, 'If you are of an ocean land and if you are a man.' You can be sure the rubber boat will not sink and honorable treatment awaits you."

Among many of the cold, weary and hungry defenders, rage or amusement turned to hopelessness. How could one possibly defeat an enemy so strong he could divert guns and aircraft from battle to deliver messages, however false, to a handful of troops which posed no threat? And so rich he could scatter precious paper of excellent quality so prodigally and supply boats of fine thick rubber as if his supply were inexhaustible? But still none surrendered. Those whose foot cloths had rotted lined their boots with the leaflets. They were also useful for starting fires, and insulated the stomach against the damp cold when stuffed into the waistband of breeches. The rubber of the rafts made excellent ponchos and ground sheets.

The detachment's only working radio reported the entire southeastern tip of Kyushu had been isolated by American forces driving north out of Shibushi and southwest out of Miyazaki City. The commander, the senior of the two platoon leaders, said it was but an enemy ruse to confuse and discourage them, but the signals corporal told his comrades privately that the voice giving the report was unmistakably Japanese. The two platoon leaders considered taking their men into the hills under cover of darkness, making their way west, and infiltrating the American rear to destroy the enemy's supply dumps. The plan was abandoned when a patrol sent out to reconnoiter the American lines failed to return.

Then the LCI came. At first the defenders of Aka Point had believed the Americans meant to take by storm what they could not take with lies and trickery. The troops took heart, welcoming the opportunity to die at last like soldiers. But when the intruder's rockets remained silent and its loudspeaker broadcast music reminding them of home and messages from a Japanese claiming to be a soldier like themselves, they saw the American vessel served the same purpose as the leaflets and the rubber boats. They cursed the Americans and the traitor, but when familiar songs emerged from the loudspeaker they sang what words they remembered in low voices and felt sorry for themselves.

The soldier speaking through the bullhorn was Sergeant Rentaro Yoshida, lately of the 37th Tank Regiment. Before the invasion the regiment had been positioned north of 57th Army Headquarters at Takarabe. After the Americans came ashore at Ariake Bay the regiment had been thrown into the counterattack with the 25th Infantry Division. Sergeant Yoshida's Model-1 medium tank never had an opportunity to engage the enemy. With several other vehicles making a night movement it was held up at a bombed bridge spanning the upper Hishida River and knocked out by American fighter bombers shortly after first light. Yoshida continued toward the battle on foot and eventually found himself fighting as an infantryman at Matsuyama Village between Shibushi and Miyakonojo. The 86th Division Headquarters was atop a commanding rise overlooking the village and the hill-girt Hishida. The cave in which Yoshida found himself was at the foot of the rise. From its entrance one could almost reach out and touch the sodden ashes of the wooden houses that had once been Matsuyama.

When the Americans broke into the level place where the village had been and stormed up the dirt path toward division headquarters, Yoshida had joined the others in a final charge. There had been an explosion and then blackness.

When Yoshida regained consciousness he was bound hand and foot, being lowered roughly into the turret hatch of an American Sherman tank. The calamity that had befallen him was so enormous and unexpected he did not grasp it until he lay curled on the steel floor of the turret at the feet of the tank commander and the gunner. He had permitted the enemy to take him alive. The shame and horror of it made him ill. He began retching. There had been so little food in the cave in recent days that nothing came up but bitter, viscous bile. He would not endure the intolerable disgrace of captivity a moment longer. He must kill himself. He strove frantically to break the bonds that held his wrists behind him. Failing, he began dashing his head against the steel plating on which he lay. Voices cried out in anger, a hand reached down and jerked him into a sitting position between two thick legs, which clamped him between them. Then, outrageous beyond belief, there was laughter. Americans were even worse barbarians than he thought. Without honor themselves, they did not have the decency to respect it in others.

He had been told the Americans tortured and murdered anyone unfortunate enough to fall into their hands alive. He hoped it would be soon. There could be no torture more cruel than to keep him alive and a prisoner. Perhaps he could anger them into killing him at once. He turned his head and bit one of the legs holding him. The taste of wool was harsh in his dry mouth. A heavy fist smashed against his temple and, in the moment before blackness descended for the second time that day, he felt elated. They would surely kill him now and end this odious captivity. Instead, when he recovered his senses, he found himself gagged as well as bound. Never in all his twenty-five years had he known such helpless despair. His head ached, it was difficult breathing through his swollen nose, he was parched, and the taste of bile was bitter in his mouth.

Cool air rushed in when the tank commander opened the turret hatch and stood erect in it, his legs inches from Yoshida's eyes. Yoshida had not yet seen the faces of his captors, only their arrogant legs. He could imagine those faces, hard, cruel and odd. He had other thoughts as well, and the fact that he could entertain them in the depth of his disgrace increased his sense of guilt at having been taken alive. For Yoshida could not stop himself from admiring the American tank. How powerful and well-made it was, with its thick armor and mighty cannon, its splendid radio and instruments. How much larger both inside and out than his own Chi-He. Possessing such tanks it was no wonder the Americans had proved invincible. How could they hope to stop them from devouring all of Japan with only flesh and blood to resist them even if the flesh and blood were Japanese? He must crush such thoughts. Japanese spirit must and would find ways to deal with American tanks.

The tank stopped and shouts were exchanged with someone outside. Hands thrust themselves into Yoshida's armpits and lifted him to the hatch. Other hands reached down and took him. Yoshida looked into the face of the tank gunner who had picked him up. He was startled by what he saw. The grimy face beneath the tanker's helmet was scarcely older than a boy's and it was smiling. It was a face totally unrelated to cruel laughter and blows. The soldier who pulled him from the hatch was also young, though not as young as the gunner. There was no cruelty in his face, either, only an expression of great curiosity. It is as if I am some strange animal, Yoshida thought. The soldier handed him down carefully to yet another man on the ground. The third soldier's face was hard and cruel and its expression was frankly hostile. It was a most welcome sight. Men like the other two were too soft to kill a bound foe. But not this one. He could do so easily, even happily. Perhaps he was the one who would torture and kill him and bring an end to his shame. Yoshida prayed it was so.

Yoshida was frightened despite his craving for death when the cruel American drew a gleaming knife from its sheath at his side. And he was mildly surprised. He had not expected death to come so unceremoniously, and by steel. The Americans had no tradition of the sword. Yoshida was disappointed when the American bent to cut the cords binding his ankles and returned the knife to its sheath. The two soldiers half-carried him to a nearby jeep, another plentiful and excellent American vehicle. Did American soldiers ever walk anywhere, he wondered. There was a fine machine gun mounted between the front and rear seats. If he and his comrades had possessed only a few such machine guns, the Americans would not have come running up the path to division headquarters so impudently.

The friendly soldier sat beside him in the rear seat, the other in front beside the driver. The friendly soldier had a canteen hanging at his hip. Yoshida looked at it and licked his parched lips. The soldier unscrewed the cap and held the canteen to Yoshida's mouth. Yoshida jerked his head away. He would accept nothing but death from these enemies of his country. The soldier took a drink himself and smiled reassuringly. Again he held the canteen to Yoshida's lips and again Yoshida refused it. The American shrugged, replaced the cap on the canteen, and covered Yoshida's eyes with a blindfold. The jeep turned around and drove over uneven ground. Yoshida heard the scratch of a match and smelled the maddening aroma of tobacco smoke. After the siege of Matsuyama began he had not even had a cigarette of itadori. There had been no paper in which to roll it. Something was placed between his lips. It was a cigarette. Some of its delicious smoke entered his mouth before he recovered from his surprise and spat it out. When the time came to die perhaps he would accept an American cigarette if one were offered. He would like to smoke a cigarette again before he died. And have a bottle of good Kirin beer. And enjoy a woman and hear the music of a samisen, skillfully played, and eat sliced tuna, fresh from the sea. He was suddenly overwhelmed by self-revulsion. What was he thinking? These things meant life. He was thinking of living, who had lost all right to live and all honor by permitting himself to be taken alive. He must cast away all such thoughts. Even if a cigarette were offered him with the knife already at his throat he would spurn it.

After a while the jeep stopped and he was led, stumbling, along a rutted path and into a warm place filled with voices. The voices stopped when he entered and immediately rose again louder than before. The blindfold was removed. He blinked his eyes. He was in a large tent. There were tall American soldiers in the tent and heaps of equipment and a table with papers on it and folding chairs. The hard-faced soldier pushed him down in one of the chairs and freed his wrists with a slash of the gleaming knife. How he yearned to get his hands on that knife. The Americans would see how a Japanese soldier died. A grenade would be better still. American grenades were strong. He could take many of the enemy with him in death. The Americans crowded around him. They were all like the friendly soldier, displaying no hatred, only curiosity. Again Yoshida felt like a creature in a zoo. Some of the Americans standing within reach had grenades dangling from the harness they wore over their fine jackets. American grenades were activated in a different manner than Japanese but he knew their secrets. He had used captured grenades against the Americans on more than one occasion. Head bent, he studied the grenades from beneath half-closed lids to see how best to snatch one from a harness

A commotion at the tent entrance attracted everyone's attention. Yoshida grew tense and prepared to act. It would be unnecessary to take the hand grenade from its harness. If he moved very quickly he could remove the safety device, release the arming mechanism, and clasp his arms around the grenade's wearer. It would of course be less satisfactory than if the grenade were permitted to explode freely. With the grenade smothered between two bodies he could not be sure of taking more than one of the enemy with him in death. While he was pondering the alternatives the newcomer whose arrival had caused the commotion shouted angrily and the soldiers surrounding Yoshida drew back hastily and sprang to attention. Yoshida was filled with chagrin. His indecision had caused him to miss a great opportunity. But there would be other chances and next time he would act more swiftly.

The newcomer continued to shout at the soldiers, his face swollen with rage. His insignia indicated he was a taisa, a colonel, but his dress and the manner in which he shouted at the soldiers were more those of a sergeant, Yoshida thought. Perhaps he was not as angry as he seemed to be. It had been Yoshida's experience that when an officer was truly angry and most to be feared he spoke quietly, with ice in his voice, not fire. When the taisa finished shouting all but a few of the soldiers left the tent. Those remaining busied themselves with tasks which Yoshida's arrival had evidently interrupted. The soldiers who had brought him left with the others. The taisa now approached him, smiling. He seemed quite a different person from the man who had raged at the soldiers. Though Yoshida was wary of the smile he was not puzzled by the abrupt change. Officers were like that.

The taisa spoke to him, his voice pleasant, and made gestures indicating food, drink and cigarettes. Yoshida did not respond in any way and the taisa's voice grew increasingly angry. It did not matter to Yoshida if the taisa cajoled or threatened. It was all one to a man who had been dead from the moment he permitted himself to be taken alive. Only one thing about the American officer interested him. The holster hanging from his hip. If he could lure the taisa closer he could snatch the pistol from it and kill himself. Yoshida raised his head and pointed to his mouth, then made a drinking motion. The anger quickly vanished from the taisa's face. He spoke to a soldier, who brought a canteen. What a fool he was, Yoshida thought, to have supposed a taisa, and an American taisa at that, would give water to a sergeant with his own hands. But heaven was on his side. The taisa was taking the canteen from the soldier and unscrewing the cap. He drew quite close and, with a smile, held out the canteen. Yoshida took it. He would not drink. He would only pretend to long enough to deceive the taisa. He would die without having accepted even a mouthful of water from the enemy. The cool metal of the canteen felt good to his cracked lips. The water within it bathed the tongue blocking the opening so none might enter his mouth. Just one sallow before dying, Yoshida thought. Was it too much to ask? Yes, he decided, for a man who had forfeited every claim on life. He could not understand this unbearable craving for water. He had gone as long without it many times with his own filled water bottle dangling from his belt.

His intolerable thirst betrayed him. Before he could prevent it his tongue moved back from the opening, his mouth filled with cool water and his parched throat received it. With an anguished groan for his weakness Yoshida dashed the canteen to the ground and lunged at the American officer. His hands found the holster, lifted the flap and seized the pistol butt. But the taisa was quick and not as unwary as he had appeared. With one hand he knocked the pistol from Yoshida's grasp and with the other sent him sprawling. Yoshida lay still, looking up at him. The soldiers in the tent came running. The taisa waved them back. The pistol was in his hand now, pointed down at Yoshida's head. The hand holding the pistol was very steady, the eyes above it bleak. He had not failed after all, Yoshida thought. The taisa would kill him now. Again he knew fear, as he had when the jeep soldier drew the knife to free his ankles, but he composed himself. He wondered if he would be denied a place at Yasukuni. He had been taken by the enemy but he had not given in to them.

The taisa shoved the pistol into its holster, spoke curtly to the soldiers and left the tent without another look at Yoshida. Two of the soldiers jerked Yoshida to his feet and tied his hands behind him. The rope bit into his wrists. They sat him down in the chair and tied him to it with the other ropes. Then they left him to return to their papers, radio and telephones. It was only then that the dreadful truth grew clear to Yoshida. The Americans did not intend to kill him.

He fell into a stupor of despair. He did not know how long he had sat without moving even to ease the bite of the ropes when a soldier untied him from the chair and motioned him toward the front of the tent. Three soldiers stood there laughing together. They stopped laughing at his approach and one of them spoke rapidly to the other two, making frequent gestures toward Yoshida as he did so. Yoshida wondered what was being said about him. It did not matter. Nothing mattered. One of the two who had been listening exchanged papers with the one who talked. Then he and his companion blindfolded Yoshida and escorted him from the tent, one on each side. They were very tall, like all Americans, and quite strong. Where the ground was uneven they took his elbows and lifted him over the difficult places. After they had gone a few yards in this manner one of them picked him up bodily and placed him in a vehicle. It felt like a jeep. One soldier sat beside him and, as Yoshida could tell from the voices, two sat in front. The three Americans talked a good deal at first and there was much laughter. American soldiers seemed always carefree and never tried to hide their laughter. Discipline must be very lax in their army. Yoshida wondered how their sergeants and officers forced them to fight so furiously. After a while the Americans fell silent.

Yoshida's buttocks ached from prolonged sitting. His back also ached because, with his hands tied behind him, he was obliged to lean forward. His head throbbed where he had dashed it against the floor of the tank turret and there was a stinging itch in another area of his skull. His cracked lips burned. His tongue was dry as wood and he felt he would suffocate if he did not moisten his throat. He must have water. He had taken some earlier. His disgrace was already complete. Whatever happened now did not matter. The actions of a living corpse were of no importance.

"Water," he croaked in his own language, knowing no English.

The soldier next to him stirred and spoke. The Americans talked among themselves.

"Water," Yoshida said again, making swallowing motions.

In another moment the neck of a canteen was at his lips. Yoshida drank eagerly, letting water dribble down his chin.

"Wahter," the American said. "Wahter."

He took the canteen from Yoshida's mouth and then placed it to his lips again, saying the word a third time. That must be the American word, Yoshida thought. Wah-ra. He felt something soft at his lips and chin. The American was drying his face. Yoshida found that most strange.

"Cigarette?" the American said.

It was a word foreign to Yoshida. He said nothing.

"Cigarette?" the American said again. "Tobacco."

Tabako. Sigaretto was tabako. The thought of strong rich smoke curling down into his lungs was tormenting. Why not have a cigarette? He had no further depths to plumb. He need not even fear the Americans' scorn. They had no sense of honor. It was obvious they did not despise him as any decent person should. It was indeed a confusing world where men without honor were allowed to triumph. That taisa back at the tent, permitting a sergeant to live after assaulting his person. Even their officers had no sense of honor. What was it then that made them fight so furiously?

"Cigarette?" the American said again.

Yoshida nodded his head.

He drew luxuriously on the cigarette placed between his lips. He wished his eyes were not covered so he could see the smoke drifting upward. That was part of the pleasure a cigarette gave. He was immediately overcome with guilt. Such a mean and odious wish when every moment he drew breath added to his shame. It was contemptibly weak of him to have supposed there were limits to dishonor, as to a farmer's paddy. Dishonor, like duty to the Emperor, was limitless. Nevertheless he smoked the cigarette until it burned his cracked lips.

Despite his discomfort Yoshida fell asleep. He could sleep anywhere, even for minutes at a time while marching. He awakened when he slumped over against the American and was pushed upright again. Night had fallen and it had grown cold when they reached their destination. The path over which he was led was even and he felt gravel beneath his feet. There was a smell of disinfectants in the air. When the blindfold was removed he found himself in an office of some sort, screened off from the rest of the building by partitions that did not reach the arched metal roof. There were electric lights. Three men were in the office. Only one of them interested him and this one interested him very much. Interested and upset him. He was a

Japanese wearing the uniform of an American gunso, a sergeant. Was he such an unspeakable traitor that he had changed allegiance or, just as odious, one of those Japanese who dwelt in the enemy's land and called himself an American? Whichever he might be, his presence restored Yoshida's sense of disgrace to its former level. Americans had no sense of honor but this Japanese, even if he called himself American, would know what a detestable creature was Rentaro Yoshida. But the face of the puzzling gunso showed only concern.

"What have they done to you?" he cried. "It is intolerable!"

Then he spoke in American to the gray-haired taisa seated behind the desk, who in turn spoke harshly to the soldiers who had brought him to this place. At the gunso's first words Yoshida felt both relief and heightened shame. Relief because the gunso's accent revealed he was not a comrade who had betrayed his country and shame because Yoshida was again alone in his guilt. He had allowed himself to be captured, the other had not. One of the two soldiers who had brought him spoke rapidly to the taisa. At one point the taisa burst into laughter and the gunso smiled broadly.

When the soldier finished speaking the gunso said, "Is it true that you inflicted one of your wounds on yourself by striking your head against a tank? And that your hands are bound thus because you attacked first a soldier and then an officer?" The smile returned to his lips as he said, "They say you bit the soldier on the leg."

Yoshida did not answer. The gunso's Japanese had a foreign sound but was as precise and elegant as a scholar's. But it was to be expected that in the enemy's army even a scholar would rise no higher than a sergeant if he was of the Japanese race. True, in his own regiment there was a private who had been a teacher in the middle school but it was known that he entertained subversive ideas and was not to be trusted with authority. It was a measure of the Army's desperate need that he had been permitted to serve at all. His proper place was prison, with other traitors and weaklings.

"You must be extremely uncomfortable," the gunso said. "If your hands are freed will you promise on your honor as a soldier you will behave yourself in a dignified manner?"

"I have no honor as a soldier," Yoshida said belligerently. "And if you had any honor you would know that."

"Nonsense," the gunso replied. "I know what they teach you. But it is false. In your case most certainly. You did not surrender. And you continued to resist after you regained your senses. You have much honor."

Yoshida knew the gunso was mistaken but his words indicated Americans did have some sense of honor after all, however misguided and undeveloped. And the gunso's words offered as much solace as he would ever get, certainly more than he deserved. His arms ached and his scalp itched. There was nothing to lose by agreeing not to attack his captors. They had already proved themselves too clever for him.

"That is not so," he said. "But if my hands are freed I will stand quietly."

The two soldiers who had brought him left while his hands were being untied. One of them spoke to him before parting.

"He said, 'Take it easy,'" the gunso said. "That is said commonly in the American Army as an indication of friendship and concern."

Yoshida thought that very odd, both the phrase and the fact that the soldier should pretend friendship and concern. Japanese soldiers said "gokuro-san," "hard work," to each other.

When his hands were free and he moved his arms a fierce pain shot through his shoulders. He moved them gingerly until the pain abated. The third man in the room placed a chair for him to sit in, facing the taisa. He was a gocho, a corporal, and the first truly fat person Yoshida had seen in well over a year. Most Americans were large and fleshy but none so fat as this one. He wore no tunic and his belly bulged above and below his belt like a sumo wrestler's. Yoshida sat in the chair and raised his hands to his itching scalp. His arms were very stiff. He was surprised when his fingers encountered a bandage over the place that itched. He did not recall the bandage being placed there. Perhaps it was while he was unconscious.

"We will tend to your wounds immediately," the gunso said. "Are you in great pain?"

"A Japanese soldier does not feel pain," Yoshida replied.

He felt like an impostor calling himself a Japanese soldier when he had forfeited all right to do so.

"Are you hungry?" the gunso said. "And please do not tell me Japanese soldiers do not feel hunger."

Yoshida had eaten nothing all day but a handful of boiled millet without salt. There was a dull pain in his belly, as if it were stealthily devouring itself.

"I am not hungry," he said with greater dignity than such an impudent statement as the gunso's deserved.

"You are the guest of my colonel," the gunso said with startling severity, more Japanese than American. "You insult him by rejecting his hospitality. I am surprised a sergeant in the Imperial Army should be so ill-mannered."

Yoshida was taken aback. The reprimand was not entirely undeserved. A taisa was a taisa regardless of which army he served. He had been unaware the taisa considered him his guest. Never before had he been the guest of so highly placed a person. Everything having to do with Americans was so odd. Almost as odd as the sensation of being a living corpse.

"I have not informed my colonel of your rudeness," the gunso continued. "Shall food be brought?"

Yoshida nodded.

A man in a white tunic had entered the office while they talked. He wore spectacles with silver rims and smoked a cigar. When he stood over Yoshida to remove the bandage the heavy smoke drifted down chokingly. White Tunic ignored his coughing. He called out something and another White Tunic came with a basin of water. The second White Tunic put the basin on the taisa's desk and shaved the side of Yoshida's head with a safety razor and then cleaned the wound. He was not gentle. Still another American entered the office bearing a metal tray which he placed on the taisa's desk. There were now six Americans in the office with Yoshida, all of whom seemed to be concerned with him in one way or another. So much attention confused and embarrassed him.

"The doctor says your head wound requires several stitches," the gunso said. "It will be painful."

Yoshida did not flinch or change expression when the needle pushed into his scalp. In this respect, at least, he could show he was still a Japanese soldier. He must have received the wound in the final charge from the cave, he thought. That seemed long ago and to have happened to another person. Perhaps it seemed so because the Rentaro Yoshida to whom it had happened no longer existed. The White Tunic with the cigar rebandaged the wound, put something that stung on his lacerated forehead, and smeared his lips with white ointment. Both White Tunics then left the office. The gunso put the metal tray in his lap.

"Please eat," he said.

A dish containing thick slabs of corned beef was on the tray, slices of soft white bread and a large metal cup from which floated the tantalizing aroma of tea. Yoshida seized the cup in both hands. It was hot but his hands were calloused and insensitive. The tea was a shocking disappointment, terribly strong, harsh and bitter. The Americans were such barbarians. But the tea was better than none at all. He drank deeply and was refreshed. He put the cup down and looked at the food. He had seldom eaten bread and never such bread as this. There was nothing about the Americans that was not odd, even the food they ate. It had been months since there was beef in his regiment's rations. Meat gave strength but right now he would truly relish fish, rice and pickle. Still, this was better and far more abundant food than he had seen in some time. If this was what the Americans provided their enemies it was no wonder they were themselves so large and fleshy. Famished though he was, he hesitated. He wondered if he should wait for the taisa's permission to begin eating. He looked at the gunso and then at the taisa. The taisa smiled and nodded reassuringly. Yoshida ate. The bread was sweet and the corned beef had an excellent flavor. He devoured every morsel and finished the tea, awful though it was. The taisa watched, smiling, as if pleased he had partaken. Yoshida wondered, was it possible everyone was mistaken about the Americans? It was true they killed women and children with their bombs and showed no mercy in battle, but in repose they were quite friendly.

"Cigarette?" the taisa asked.

"Yes," Yoshida replied, ducking his head gratefully.

The taisa and the gunso looked at each other. The gunso gave Yoshida a cigarette and lit it for him with a handsome lighter.

"Then you know some English?" he asked casually.

Yoshida nodded.

"Sigaretto," he said. "Wah-ra. Roosbelt."

The taisa laughed. It was infectious. Yoshida smiled despite himself.

"Now," said the gunso, "we will chat."

He lit a cigarette and blew smoke from his nose. The manner in which he smoked was as American as the manner in which he spoke Japanese. The fat soldier had taken a seat nearby. He had a notebook in his lap, well forward so he could see it over the bulge of his vast stomach, and a pencil in his hand.

"I am Sergeant George Ebata," the gunso said. "How are you called, Sergeant?"

"Rentaro Yoshida."

"Ah," said Sergeant Ebata happily, "Yoshida. In America I have a friend called Yoshida. His parents came from Chiba. Could you be of the same family?"

"I think not," Yoshida replied. "I am from Gifu."

Nevertheless he thought it interesting that Sergeant Ebata knew someone of his name in America. Sergeant Ebata spoke to the taisa, who nodded, and the fat gocho's pencil flew over the notebook.

"You seem very young to be already a sergeant," Sergeant Ebata said "What is the year of your birth?"

"Nineteen twenty," said Yoshida.

"And when did you enter the Army?"

"Nineteen thirty-eight."

Sergeant Ebata was impressed.

"A sergeant after only seven years?" he said. "You are quite an exceptional man."

Yoshida bowed his head modestly. It was true. He knew of few seven-year men who had achieved such rank.

"You were fighting with infantry," Sergeant Ebata said. "The 86th Division. Yet your insignia is that of armor. How can that be?"

Yoshida explained in considerable detail. It was flattering that anyone should show such interest in an ordinary person like himself and it was good to be able to talk of the soldier he had been before he became a living corpse. Sergeant Ebata asked him many questions, pausing only to address the taisa and once to send for more of the dreadful tea. All drank but the fat gocho, who filled page after page of his notebook. Yoshida answered the questions freely, apologizing when he could not supply the information requested. Nothing in his experience or training dictated otherwise. Japanese soldiers were never taken prisoner and therefore he had never been instructed how to conduct himself if captured. When the conversation ended the fat gocho went out and returned with two soldiers wearing white helmets and armbands. Both wore pistols at their belts and one carried a carbine.

"You will sleep now," Sergeant Ebata said. "You must be very tired."

The taisa walked over from his desk and extended his hand. Yoshida bowed in great confusion. He had not expected an officer of high rank to show such familiarity and courtesy to a sergeant. He thought it unusual that the taisa did not also take the hand of Sergeant Ebata. One of the White Helmets placed a blindfold over his eyes.

"It must be done," Sergeant Ebata said apologetically. "It is an established policy."

It was cold outside and Yoshida shivered. It was warmer in the vehicle. They drove for several minutes, sometimes fast and sometimes creeping along. Once they stopped and words were exchanged. At the end of the ride Yoshida was led into a building and the blindfold removed. Sergeant Ebata spoke to a balding, red-faced soldier sitting behind a large desk with many papers on it. He had a cigar in his mouth, like White Tunic, but it was unlit. His mouth pursed and unpursed around the cigar as if he were trying to disgorge it. He wrote something in a large book and gave Sergeant Ebata a piece of paper. There was a rack with rifles and Thompson guns against the wall. Men came and went continuously. When they did not shut the door behind them the soldier with the cigar would shout angrily. Sergeant Ebata and one of the White Helmets took Yoshida outside again but without the blindfold.

"You will have a bath," Sergeant Ebata said.

Yoshida could not believe his ears. A bath. The Americans had a bathhouse. They denied themselves nothing, these Americans. They walked a few yards to a long, narrow tent. To Yoshida's great disappointment it was not a bathhouse at all. There were only showers. The water was hot, however, and he was permitted to enjoy it for several minutes after he washed himself with a large cube of yellow soap. It had been six weeks since Yoshida had enjoyed the luxury of hot water. After the shower a soldier wearing a white armband with a red cross on it sprayed him with powder from a long tube.

"It is for purposes of sanitation," Sergeant Ebata explained. "It prevents the spread of infectious disease."

Instead of his own uniform he was given American clothing, many sizes too large, with American writing on the back of the tunic. They returned to the building where the soldier without hair on the top of his head was still trying to disgorge the cigar. Yoshida was placed in a small room containing only a cot. The door to the room had a small square hole in it, covered with steel mesh. A coat of heavy canvas was slipped over Yoshida's head. The arms ended in long tapes which were tied together behind Yoshida's back.

"It must be done," Sergeant Ebata said. "It is a matter of established policy."

Yoshida nodded understandingly. He did not know why he should be bound in such a manner but if it was a matter of established policy of course it must be done. The coat was not nearly as uncomfortable as the ropes which had bound his wrists behind him. The bandage on his head, which had become soaked in the shower, was replaced with a new one. Americans were wasteful. This was the third time they had dressed the wound in a single day.

"I must leave you now," Sergeant Ebata said. "Tomorrow you will be transferred to more comfortable quarters for a period of quarantine. You have been treated with all courtesies due a brave soldier. Think on this."

Yoshida sat down on the cot. He was very tired now and growing confused again.

"I have left cigarettes for you with the guard," Sergeant Ebata said. "It is unlikely I will see you again."

Yoshida felt lonely after Sergeant Ebata left him. It was only now that he realized he had come to regard the American Japanese as a friend. Sergeant Ebata had been solicitous and they had enjoyed a splendid chat. Yoshida could not sleep. The canvas jacket restricted his movements, the light overhead was bright, and the guard looked in at him through the hole in the door at regular intervals. It was not these things that kept Yoshida awake. It was renewed awareness of his degradation. It was true, but without significance, that the Americans had treated him as if he were a brave soldier instead of a totally worthless creature. What they believed was unimportant. What was important was the dead comrades whose memory he had betrayed, and the Emperor's trust in every Japanese soldier. Should he live it was he and not Sergeant Ebata and the others who would face the scorn of the Japanese nation. He was an inept weakling, for he had failed in every attempt to end his miserable life and had permitted himself the enjoyment of bodily pleasures. He squirmed in an agony of self-torture, recalling how he had relished the first taste of water, the cigarettes, the tinned meat, the hot shower, even the clean softness of the American clothing he wore. The catastrophe which should have cut him off from all human desires instead seemed to have heightened his awareness of them. This was perhaps as great a calamity as capture. When at last he slept it was deeply.

He was awakened in the morning by a different guard. The canvas jacket was removed and he was led to a latrine to relieve himself. The smell of disinfectants almost covered the odor of human wastes. In the Imperial Army even field hospitals had nothing except bandages for the wounded and here the Americans were putting medicines in a latrine.

He felt refreshed, ravenous, and determined that henceforth he would permit neither food nor water to pass his lips. When a large, bizarre breakfast was brought to him on a tray he could not resist it. Fried meat, fried eggs, scorched bread, bitter coffee and purple jelly of delectable sweetness. He could not remember the last time he had anything sweet except the bread the night before, which was an entirely different order of sweetness. He ate awkwardly with the spoon brought in on the tray. He tasted the contents of a tin with a hole punched in the top. Finding it milk of unusual richness and sweetness, he drank it. After breakfast he was given the cigarettes left for him by Sergeant Ebata and an overcoat and gloves and placed in a jeep. The road on which they drove was as clogged with traffic as Tokyo on a busy day. There were trucks, jeeps, sedans and vehicles Yoshida had not seen before. There were great heaps of supplies everywhere and fields of brown tents and many metal buildings with arched roofs. The smell of the sea was in the air. The bay, it must be Ariake, was filled with great ships riding at anchor. Smaller vessels plied between them and the shore. Aircraft passed frequently overhead. It was as if the Americans had always been there. Yoshida was appalled by the sheer weight of their presence. The enemy's tanks and soldiers had come to Matsuyama in overwhelming numbers. He had not dreamed they were but a part of a much greater force. The Americans were like locusts devouring the land.

The jeep drove out into the bay on a broad wooden road that rose and fell gently with the waves. Yoshida was handcuffed and transferred to an open boat with a high, flat bow and an engine that made a great roaring noise. Yoshida sat in the middle of the boxlike boat, its wooden sides rising higher than his head. There were four Americans in the boat with him, one of them a soldier with a carbine. The other three wore uniforms of a different sort. One of them steered the boat, and his two companions busied themselves in other ways. They were no doubt of the American Navy, Yoshida thought. The identification sketches he had studied were of soldiers only.

The boat stopped alongside a large ship, a cargo vessel or transport judging from its lack of armor plate. Two of the sailors held the boat in place with hooks thrust into hanging netting while Yoshida was hauled aboard in a sling. A number of sailors stood about the decks at a little distance, regarding him with curiosity, though not as much as the soldiers had shown the day before. Again Yoshida was surprised to find none of them regarding him with hate or scorn. Two men were waiting for him when the winch deposited him on the deck. One was a soldier with a Thompson gun slung over his shoulder. The other was a Japanese with the silver bar of an American chui on the collar of his American uniform. Another American Japanese, Yoshida thought, and this one an officer. How many of them were serving the Americans, he wondered. Neither was smiling. The soldier with the Thompson gun, in fact, appeared quite bored. A metal ring, shining in the sunlight, came sailing over the rail. The soldier caught it with careless ease. He unlocked Yoshida's handcuffs with a key on the ring and then dropped ring and handcuffs to the boat below. The Japanese in the American officer's uniform pointed to the silver bar on his collar.

"Sergeant Yoshida," he said sternly. "Do you know what this means?" Yoshida was surprised that the chui should know his name.

"Yes, Honorable Lieutenant," he said quickly.

"Then why have you not saluted? Is there no discipline left in your Army?"

Yoshida was stunned. He bowed and saluted. The lieutenant's accent, though not as elegant as Sergeant Ebata's, was just as American. Yet he was speaking as if he were a Japanese shoi fresh from the Military Academy. He was obviously a Japanese American who had not been corrupted by Yankee slackness. Here, at last, was an American who would recognize him for what he was, a despicable coward. Yoshida felt himself wilting under the stern gaze of this officer who saw him as he was.

"As long as you are in my charge you will conduct yourself in a soldierly manner," the lieutenant barked. "Is that clear, Sergeant Yoshida?"

"I will do as the honorable lieutenant orders," Yoshida said. "But I am no longer a soldier."

"I will make that decision, Sergeant," the lieutenant said. "I know the rubbish you have been taught. But you are now under American discipline. And under American discipline a soldier never forgets he is a soldier. Even when he has the misfortune to be taken."

The soldier and the lieutenant took Yoshida down steel ladders and along narrow passageways. They reached a passageway guarded by a soldier whose appearance Yoshida found unusual. He did not look like the other American soldiers Yoshida had seen. His coloring was Japanese but he was not Japanese. Yoshida wondered if perhaps he was a red Indian. Red Indians were great warriors. The red Indian came to attention when he saw the lieutenant. The lieutenant spoke to him and he unlocked a door and threw it open. Yoshida started to enter. The lieutenant stopped him with an angry gesture. Yoshida was aware he had been guilty of another breach of discipline. A sergeant did not precede an officer. And he had not been told to enter the room. Inside the room were five Japanese soldiers. When the door opened two of them were playing go on a long narrow table, one knelt on the floor busy with brush and ink block, another was lying sprawled on a bunk and the fifth sat cross-legged facing the wall. One of the go players was first to spy the lieutenant. He leaped to his feet shouting, "Kiwotsuke!"

The man in the bunk tumbled out and in a moment all were at attention except the man facing the wall.

"I see Second Year Soldier Nanami continues to insist he is dead," the lieutenant said.

"Yes, Honorable Lieutenant," one of the other prisoners shouted smartly.

"Dead man," the lieutenant said sarcastically. "Second Year Soldier Nanami. It has been reported you had two bowls of miso soup and three of rice at breakfast this morning. When you were alive your appetite must have been truly extraordinary."

Yoshida was placed in a smaller room several doors away.

"You are a sergeant," the lieutenant explained. "You are not expected to share quarters with ordinary soldiers."

He explained to Yoshida that he was expected to keep his quarters and his person clean at all times, as if he were in barracks. He called Yoshida's attention to a pair of printed notices fixed to the wall. One listed the rules of conduct he was to follow, the other American words with which to address the guard if he had to relieve himself or had other requests.

"Is it permitted to ask the honorable lieutenant a question?" Yoshida asked humbly.

"Of course," the lieutenant said.

"Is the soldier guarding the passageway a red Indian?"

The lieutenant was startled by the question. A smile, quickly erased, touched his lips.

"He is a Mexican-American," the lieutenant said gravely. "There are many Mexican-Americans in the Army. And red Indians as well. In the American Army are many different kinds of American. Even Japanese as you can see."

"Thank you, Honorable Lieutenant," Yoshida said, disappointed.

After he was locked in, Yoshida looked about his cell. The table and chair were fastened to the floor. The mattress on the bunk was thin but soft and there were several fine wool blankets. The electric light in the ceiling was in a cage of steel mesh. The porthole was riveted shut and covered on the outside. In the door of the cell was a square hole of the sort in the door where he had spent the night. This place was more pleasant and they had not strapped him in a canvas jacket. Yoshida took off his shoes and sat cross-legged on the floor. He did not face the wall as Second Year Soldier Nanami did. As much as he wished he might behave as a dead man he knew he could not and he would not pretend to do so. The second year soldier had earned the lieutenant's ridicule for saying one thing and doing another. He pondered the words the lieutenant had spoken to him on deck. The lieutenant was aware of the ignominy of capture to a Japanese yet, like Sergeant Ebata, the lieutenant regarded him as a soldier. Not only regarded him as a soldier but demanded that he conduct himself as such. Though he was not sure why it should be so, the Japanese who had leaped to attention for the lieutenant had impressed him more favorably than the man who had remained staring at the wall. Discipline was, after all, a splendid thing and not so easily put aside. In the American Army, the lieutenant had said, the soldier was expected to maintain discipline even if he were taken prisoner. If one could overlook the Americans' deplorable attitude about surrender, which he found impossible to do but nevertheless must take into consideration because in other ways they were often quite brave, then it was not unreasonable that they should demand that a soldier conduct himself as a soldier whatever the circumstance. Yoshida sighed. Everything was made so easy for American soldiers. They had Shermans, dry quarters, warm uniforms, cigarettes, food of incredible variety and abundance, medicines for their latrines and a discipline which, in the eyes of their comrades, permitted them to retain their honor even if captured.

He gave himself the task of memorizing the rules of conduct fixed to the wall. He would give the lieutenant no cause to reprimand him again. The rules were simple and undemanding. Such things as keeping the bunk tightly made when not occupied, displaying military courtesy to superiors. obeying the orders of the guards, not attempting to converse through the walls with other prisoners. He learned them quickly. Yoshida had a retentive mind and was accustomed to learning by rote.

Lunch, brought to him on a tray by a black American, was an agreeable surprise. Fish, soup with bean curd, pickle, proper tea and a large bowl of the finest polished rice. Yoshida could not tear his gaze from the black man. He had seen black faces in vehicles on the road that morning but this was the first time in his life he had seen a black man at close range. The color of his skin was of extraordinary richness. He smiled at Yoshida, showing large, very white teeth. The soldier who was not a red Indian came inside the room with the black American. He captured Yoshida's attention and, moving his hand rapidly in front of his mouth, uttered a wild, drawn-out cry. He and the black man burst into uncontrollable laughter. Yoshida looked uncertainly from one to the other. Whatever their color might be, Americans were indeed odd.

As soon as he was alone Yoshida attacked the food. The Americans had provided chopsticks instead of the clumsy instruments with which they themselves ate. Devoting himself single-mindedly to enjoyment of the unexpected treat, he fell unconsciously into euphoria. He was clean, warm and vibrantly alive. The rice, though of a quality he had not seen since the early days of the Pacific war, was badly prepared. The grains had been cooked too dry and did not cling together properly. With his chopsticks Yoshida pursued and devoured every grain, including those that had fallen on the table. When he finished he belched comfortably and took a cigarette from the package Sergeant Ebata had given him. He had no means of lighting it. The American phrases on the wall did not tell him how to ask for a light. He went to the door and put his mouth to the hole in it.

"Honorable guard," he called politely.

When the American came, Yoshida held up the cigarette for him to see. The American shook his head and went away. Yoshida was annoyed. Not at the American, who had quite properly refused to be distracted from duty. He was annoyed because he wished to smoke and was unable to do so. When Yoshida realized the source of his displeasure he fell into deep melancholy. How could he have so quickly forgotten the depth of his disgrace and accepted so easily pleasures he did not deserve? He returned the cigarette to the package and put the package on the lunch tray with the empty bowls. When the guard opened the door to admit the black man he held up a cigarette lighter for Yoshida to see and indicated he would now light a cigarette for him. Yoshida bowed and shook his head. He had given up smoking. The lighter was like that of Sergeant Ebata. Perhaps each American soldier received one. Was there no limit to their possessions?

The black man removed the cigarette package from the tray and put it on the table. Yoshida put it back on the tray. He knew how little character he had and thought it wiser to remove temptation than attempt to resist it. The guard said something to the black man and both laughed. The guard picked up the package, shook his head, and tucked it in Yoshida's shirt pocket.

That night Yoshida lay awake thinking about the other prisoners he had seen. Had they, too, been unconscious when they were taken? Except for Nanami, the second year soldier, they seemed to take their plight lightly, yet he could not believe that any of them had surrendered voluntarily. In any case, his disgrace was greater than theirs. They were ordinary soldiers, he was a sergeant. He wondered if they had been told anything of him and knew his name. He hoped not. It was better to simply lose all identity and, in a sense, cease to exist as a person as he had ceased to exist as a Japanese. Since he had no future as a Japanese he could no longer think of the future. If heaven willed him to survive he would accept it, but nothing beyond mere survival. In the past three days he had known moments of great strength in which he had attempted to end his life, and moments of great weakness in which he had surrendered to pleasurable things. Both extremes were behind him now. Having reached this decision, Yoshida felt at peace with himself for the first time since his capture.

Breakfast was American. He scarcely touched it, taking only enough to sustain life. The black American looked sympathetic when he came for the tray. He pointed to the eggs and patted his stomach to indicate they were good. Then he pointed to Yoshida's stomach and said, "Meshi?" It was strange to hear the Japanese word on the lips of an American. Yoshida tried to tell him he had eaten so little not because he preferred rice to boiled eggs but because food no longer interested him. He could not make the black American or the new guard, who was white-skinned and freckled, understand.

Lunchtime brought Japanese food. Again Yoshida ate little. The black American shook his head sympathetically when he saw how little Yoshida had eaten. Yoshida was sitting cross-legged on the floor when the lieutenant came to his cell in the afternoon. He had been sitting thus for several hours without moving, trying to keep his mind as empty of thought as if it were a stone. When thoughts of his family, the calamity that had befallen him and the plague that was devouring Japan tried to enter, he shut them out. He did not acknowledge the lieutenant's presence though the officer looked at him sternly.

"Are you ill, Sergeant Yoshida?" the lieutenant said at last. "It has been reported you did not eat breakfast or lunch."

"No, Honorable Lieutenant," Yoshida said politely.

The lieutenant pointed to his insignia of rank.

"Have you forgotten what this signifies?" he demanded.

"No, Honorable Lieutenant."

"Then why are you not at attention? Did I not make it clear you are to conduct yourself in a soldierly manner?"

"I am not a soldier, Honorable Lieutenant. I am nothing."

The lieutenant looked extremely annoyed.

"I thought you were done with such foolishness," he said witheringly. "You are too intelligent to behave like Second Year Soldier Nanami."

Yoshida bowed his head meekly but said nothing.

"It has been reported you attempted to make a gift to the mess steward," the lieutenant continued.

"I do not understand."

"You offered him a bribe of cigarettes. What did you expect to gain from this?"

"Oh, that. They were not offered as a bribe, Honorable Lieutenant. I had no need of them."

The lieutenant produced a briar pipe, filled it, lit it, and sat astride the chair facing Yoshida. He studied Yoshida in silence for some minutes. Yoshida was not disconcerted. He returned the lieutenant's gaze with quiet dignity.

"You are a brave man, Sergeant Yoshida," the lieutenant said at last. "But you are also a great fool. And a selfish fool. Do you understand why you are a selfish fool, Sergeant Yoshida?"

"No, Honorable Lieutenant."

"Since the battle for Kyushu began, more than a hundred thousand of your comrades have fallen. Millions of your countrymen are dying of hunger and disease. But that does not seem to concern you. You think only of your own loss of honor. Are not the lives of your countrymen of greater importance than the honor of one sergeant?"

"I have no countrymen, Honorable Lieutenant."

"You say that because you are filled with self-pity," the lieutenant said. "You may ascribe other motives to your behavior but I tell you it is only self-pity."

Yoshida considered that carefully. It was true that yesterday he had been filled with self-pity. But it was not true today. He had accepted his fate.

"Tell me, Sergeant Yoshida, have you given one moment's thought to your comrades who are dying without cause? To the Japanese mothers with no food for their babies? To the children who will have no fathers? Of course not. You have thought only of what a terrible catastrophe has befallen Rentaro Yoshida."

There was some truth to the lieutenant's words. He had given only passing thought to his country's plight. But only because he no longer had a country.

"I suggest you think more about your country and less about yourself," the lieutenant said scornfully. "And consider what a splendid opportunity you have to serve it."

How serve his country, Yoshida thought. Was the lieutenant mad? He had lost all right even to consider himself a Japanese. If any of his countrymen thought of him at all it was as a coward and a traitor. How could he serve his country when he was in the hands of the enemy and helpless?

"Honorable Lieutenant," he said, "I do not understand."

The lieutenant rose abruptly.

"Enough of this," he said. "I am weary of your self-pity and your insolence. If I should relent and honor you with another visit I expect you to display proper courtesy."

He went to the door and called the guard to let him out. After he left, Yoshida wondered if perhaps it had not been wrong to remain seated in his presence. Even though he was no longer a soldier himself it was boorish to behave as if the lieutenant was not a soldier. He hoped the lieutenant was not so angry that he would not come again and accept his apology. And perhaps condescend to explain his puzzling words.

Yoshida slept well that night. In the morning the black American brought miso soup with the otherwise American breakfast. Yoshida did not touch it because of all the things on the tray it was what he liked best and the only thing reminding him of his former life. At breakfast and again at lunch he ate sparingly. He spent most of the day sitting motionless on the floor, emulating a stone that saw, felt, and heard nothing. He found he was able to blot out all thoughts and all sounds for long periods although there were moments when his physical senses grew more, rather than less, acute. At such moments he was conscious of the movement of the blood in his veins, of the gentle motion of the anchored ship on which he was a prisoner, of the myriad sounds filtering through the door, walls and ceiling. At such times a faint singing buzz underlay all other sounds. It was, he thought, the sound of his blood inside his head. He dwelt on that. When he listened carefully to the sound it was easy to shut out thought, and if he listened intently enough no other sound could get through. He was listening to the blood singing in his head when the cell door opened and someone entered. He did not look toward the sound.

"Well, Yoshida," the lieutenant's voice said. "I see you are still playing Second Year Soldier Nanami's childish game."

Yoshida stopped listening to his blood and rose quickly to attention. This was the one concession he was willing to make to his former life, and for the lieutenant's sake, not his own. Yoshida regretted that he still retained enough vanity to be hurt that the lieutenant compared him with the pretentious Nanami. He must work to eliminate all vanity.

"Honorable Lieutenant, I apologize for my insolence yesterday," he said.

"I am pleased to accept the apology, Sergeant Yoshida. You may stand at ease."

Since it was not a command, Yoshida remained at attention. He would never again pander to his body. The lieutenant lit a cigarette and smoked half of it, all the while staring somberly at Yoshida.

"For God's sake, Yoshida!" he cried at last. "Relax!"

Was this an order, Yoshida wondered. He decided that it was and permitted his rigid muscles to soften. The lieutenant offered him a cigarette.

"I do not smoke, Honorable Lieutenant."

The lieutenant looked skeptical.

"I thought otherwise," he said. "But please yourself. Tell me, Sergeant Yoshida, have you given any thought to what I said yesterday? About helping your country?"

"No, Honorable Lieutenant."

"When an American soldier is taken prisoner he continues to believe it is his sacred duty to serve his country. Surely Japanese soldiers are no less patriotic than American soldiers."

Yoshida did not answer.

"Have you cut yourself off from patriotism because you think your countrymen despise you in your misfortune? Surely you are too intelligent to believe your family and your comrades would despise anyone who fought as bravely as you?"

Yoshida still made no reply.

"At Sendai a sergeant major was taken prisoner. By the way, were you and your comrades informed when the American Marines advanced to the Sendai River last month?"

"No, Honorable Lieutenant."

"This sergeant major. He was a Sendai man. His family was still in the area when the city fell. They were permitted to see him. They were filled with joy to find him alive and well cared for. You look as if you do not believe my words. You do not think this is so?"

"No, Honorable Lieutenant, I am sorry."

"Would you believe my words if I showed you a photograph of the happy reunion?"

Yoshida took refuge in silence.

"You have a family in Gifu," the lieutenant said. "And many friends. The war will be over soon, Sergeant Yoshida. You will be permitted to return home. When you return to Gifu you will find you are welcomed, not scorned. Like the Sendai socho. If you wished, you could speed the day of your return. Shall I explain to you how you can do this?"

Yoshida remained silent. It was extraordinary that anyone so intelligent as the lieutenant should believe such a thing. Yet he appeared quite sincere. Although the lieutenant was Japanese in appearance he was too American to comprehend the Japanese meaning, the true meaning of duty and honor.

"What a pity," the lieutenant said. "I wonder how many Japanese soldiers must die because of your stubbornness?"

Yoshida wondered what possible connection he could have with the death of Japanese soldiers. Surely the Americans were not killing the men he had seen in the other room because he would not do whatever it was the lieutenant wanted him to do. The lieutenant would have said as much instead of uttering such mysterious nonsense. Even if the prisoners were killed it did not matter. They were already dead. He dismissed the lieutenant and his words from his thoughts as soon as the door closed behind the officer. He sat on the floor and listened to the singing of his blood. That night, realizing his mattress was too comfortable, he removed it and slept on metal. In the morning, deciding that clothing was also an unwarranted luxury, he stripped to his American underdrawers. He welcomed the cold that caused the skin of his legs to rise in little bumps. The guard and the mess attendant were displeased when they found him half naked and tried to persuade him to dress himself. Shortly after they left, while Yoshida was still partaking of the few bites of food he permitted himself, the cell door flew open and the lieutenant entered. Yoshida sprang to attention. The lieutenant looked at him without expression and left without speaking. He returned in the afternoon carrying a large envelope made of brown paper.

"I have some photographs that may interest you, Yoshida," he said. "Do you wish to see them?"

"No, Honorable Lieutenant."

"Please yourself. I'll leave them. You may change your mind."

The lieutenant paused at the cell door as he was leaving.

"Your head wound is to be redressed today," he said. "When you are taken from this room you must be fully clothed. Is that understood?"

"Yes, Honorable Lieutenant."

When he returned from the infirmary he stripped to his underdrawers again. He entered his cell as if it were a sanctuary. He had felt agitated the entire time he was outside it. There had been too many reminders that he was a person and that beyond the cell's narrow walls was a world that despised him. He had had a moment of curiosity when he passed the door behind which he had seen the five Japanese prisoners the day of his arrival. Were they still there? Had they been told his name and rank? Was the one called Nanami still pretending to be dead? Now that he was back in his sanctuary he thought of them no more. He sat down and listened to his blood. It had been silent from the moment his cell door opened until the door closed behind him again.

The brown envelope on the table was an intrusive presence. What was it the lieutenant wished him to see? Did the photographs hold the answer to the riddle of the lieutenant's strange statements? He tried to ignore the envelope but it marred the purity of his sanctuary and drew his eyes to it like a blemish. He would look at the photographs. If nothing else it would please the lieutenant. There were six large photographs in the envelope, each with a strip of paper glued to the bottom identifying the subject in competent Japanese. The first was titled, "Sergeant Major Kurakake Greets His Family." The sergeant major, dressed in American clothing such as had been given Yoshida, knelt in a room facing three Japanese civilians kneeling in a row a few feet away. His arms enclosed three children clinging to him. The civilians were women, one of them old. The faces of all three women glistened with tears. The other photographs were titled, "Shibushi Orphanage, American Doctor Examining War Orphans"; "Shibushi Orphanage, Japanese Women Volunteers Tending War Orphans"; "Civilians Receiving Rice Allowance in Kagoshima City"; "B-29s Drop Leaflets on Tokyo"; and "American Burial Party Honors Japanese War Dead."

The first and the last two photographs interested Yoshida particularly. The family reunion was almost believable. If it had been posed by Japanese Americans, the Americans had been clever enough to make it appear Japanese in every detail. The leaflet raid was shocking. It had been taken from above. A cloud of leaflets floated beneath a giant American bomber. On the earth below, the familiar outlines of the palace grounds were clearly identifiable. It was truly Tokyo, but a Tokyo ravaged beyond recognition. Within the palace grounds there were no bomb craters and all appeared untouched except in one area, where a building or two had burned. Outside the palace grounds there was only utter desolation. The gaunt remains of ferroconcrete buildings protruded from a gray waste. A patchwork of tiny square roofs extended from the palace walls into the wasteland. In the burial photograph the bodies of Japanese soldiers lay in a neat row beside a long trench. In the foreground was an American soldier with a bugle to his lips. Behind the bodies an orderly row of other American soldiers, wearing white gloves and white leggings, extended rifles, as if preparing to fire a salute. Could these be the same Americans who stole gold from the mouths of corpses and sent home the bones of Japanese soldiers for souvenirs? He studied the row of bodies. There was insufficient detail to identify the types of units to which they had belonged. He envied the dead men. Whatever turn the war took, whatever might happen to Japan, they would never know disgrace. Their souls were already at Yasukuni.

Why had the lieutenant wished him to see this photograph? It could only be to shame him by showing how even Americans honored soldiers who died bravely. But why should the lieutenant wish to shame him when he had seemed so anxious that Yoshida believe Americans honored all soldiers who fought bravely, even those who permitted themselves to be taken? Perhaps it was because the lieutenant was still angry with him. Truth was often revealed in anger. And the truth was the lieutenant secretly despised him and only pretended not to because there was something the lieutenant wished of him.

He replaced the photographs in the order in which he found them and returned the brown envelope to its exact place on the table. When he attempted to close his mind and smother his senses the row of bodies kept reappearing, every corpse an accusation. They had died like soldiers. He still lived. It did not matter that a captured sergeant major's family had accepted him, that Americans ministered to children, fed hungry civilians, and had destroyed Tokyo. It mattered that true soldiers died and he lived on. Perhaps if he ran hard enough at the steel wall of his cell he could dash his brains out. But no, he had passed beyond that. His punishment was to live. The sound of his blood was louder in his ears, as if confirming his existence.

The lieutenant came to his cell next morning. He scarcely looked at the table where the brown envelope lay before seating himself in his favorite position astride the chair. He made himself comfortable and filled his pipe.

"I've never told you my name, have I, Yoshida?" he said. "It's Fukujiki. Are there Fukujikis in Gifu?"

"I don't know, Honorable Lieutenant," Yoshida said warily.

It was not the manner in which he had expected the lieutenant to behave. The lieutenant was somehow aware he had looked at the photographs. The guard had no doubt been observing him through the hole in the door. The lieutenant was more Japanese than he had believed.

"Probably not," the lieutenant said. "My family is from Miyazaki Prefecture. My father's father was a small manufacturer of shochu. Which do you prefer, Yoshida, sake or shochu?"

"I have no taste for either, Honorable Lieutenant."

"Really? I don't care for shochu, myself. Awful stuff."

The lieutenant got to his feet, puffing on his pipe.

"Do you wish to say anything before I go, Sergeant Yoshida?" he asked.

"No, Honorable Lieutenant."

"You did not find the photographs interesting?"

Yoshida did not reply. The lieutenant was taunting him. It surprised him a little that the lieutenant was so callous.

"In the aerial photograph of Tokyo did you observe that the Imperial Palace has not been bombed? The damage was done by embers drifting from outside the walls. Do you understand the significance of that? It means we do not wish harm to befall the Emperor. Your superiors told you otherwise, I imagine. You can see for yourself how they have deceived you."

Yoshida remained resolutely silent. But, unless the photograph was falsified, there was some truth to what the lieutenant said.

"Did you observe how graciously the Japanese women assist us in caring for children separated from their parents, Yoshida? Did the women look as if they had been mistreated in any way? Tell me, Yoshida, were their faces not serene and filled with tenderness for the little ones?"

Yoshida had not really noticed. But it had not surprised him that the Americans were solicitous of Japanese children. They had shown themselves to be so odd that nothing they might do could surprise him any more.

"Which of the photographs interested you most?" the lieutenant said. "Will you tell me if I guess correctly? Now let me see."

He spread the photographs on the table in two rows of three each. He selected two but did not show them to Yoshida.

"It is one of these."

He showed one of them to Yoshida, the photograph of Sergeant Major Kurakake.

"This one interested you for two reasons," he said. "One. Is it what it appears to be or not? Two. If it is what it appears to be, how is it possible the family of Sergeant Major Kurakake has not turned from him in disgust? I assure you, Kurakake is truly a prisoner of war and this is truly his family. But I do not believe it is this photograph that most interests you. I believe it is this one."

With a sudden motion of his hand he presented the photograph of the dead soldiers for Yoshida's inspection. The lieutenant is very shrewd, Yoshida thought. He can see into my mind. Many officers had this ability when they condescended to use it. When he was a first year soldier he had thought all officers possessed it. Then he had come to believe no officer could truly understand a soldier because the gulf between them was too great. After he became a sergeant he discovered some officers had this ability and some did not.

"Why this interests you the most is what most interests me, Yoshida. There are two possible reasons, and only two. One. It pleases you that we understand and respect the spirit of the Divine Race. Two. It displeases you that Lieutenant Fukujiki has seen fit to remind you of your personal dishonor. Which of these two reasons caused you to find this the most interesting of all the photographs? I am curious."

"Why did you wish to shame me, Honorable Lieutenant?" Yoshida blurted. "Is it not obvious I already understand how disgusting I am without such a reminder?"

"You disappoint me, Sergeant Yoshida," the lieutenant said sadly. "I had hoped you were ready to begin thinking for yourself. Your attitude proves your thinking is still distorted by the false teachings of men who do not serve the best interests of the Emperor and the Japanese people."

Twice this morning the lieutenant had mentioned the Emperor. Yoshida found it intensely disturbing both times. It was unsettling that the lieutenant had not come to attention. And any reference to the Emperor was another bitter reminder to Yoshida of how he had failed His Imperial Majesty.

"Since your eyes are so blind I will explain to you the true meaning of the photograph," the lieutenant said. "First, had these soldiers surrendered themselves when further resistance could no longer hinder the American advance they would have been no less honored, for they fought gallantly. Have you been treated dishonorably, Sergeant Yoshida?"

"No, Honorable Lieutenant."

"Secondly, they served no useful purpose by dying. On the contrary. The Hagakure states, 'I have discovered that the principle of Bushido is the way to die at the right moment, in the right place and for the right purpose.' They died at the wrong moment in the wrong place and for the wrong purpose. Had they lived they might one day assist in rebuilding a Japan which will again have an honored place among nations."

The lieutenant paused and took a deep breath.

"Thirdly. For each soldier lying dead in the photograph think to yourself of ten thousand, and not only soldiers but innocent women and children in the path of battle, who still live but will surely die if this insane war continues. And finally, Sergeant Yoshida, and listen well for it is the most important point of all, you have it within yourself to do more to prevent this calamity than if you had a brigade of tanks to hurl against us. And not to do so is wicked."

The lieutenant's calm voice rose suddenly and cracked like a whip.

"It is wicked, I tell you!"

Yoshida was confused and shaken. He was worthless and dishonored but he was not wicked. How could he prevent the slaughter of women and children even if he wished?

"I do not understand, Honorable Lieutenant."

"Look into my face, Yoshida!"

The lieutenant's burning eyes caught and held his.

"I am American," he said. "I have never pretended to be Japanese to win your confidence. But still I can grieve for the agony of the former land of my father and my mother. When you look into my face can you believe I speak stomach talk?"

"No, Honorable Lieutenant. It is not stomach talk."

"Then think on what I have said. If you persist in your obstinate wickedness I will not come again. I will seek one with more spirit. But if you wish to know how you may serve your country and my father's instead of wallowing in self-pity while your comrades die uselessly, tell the guard you wish to see me."

The lieutenant took the photographs with him when he left. There was finality in the way he went out the door and did not look back. Yoshida had expected it to be a great relief to be free of the lieutenant's relentless abuse. But he was not relieved. The lieutenant had filled him with doubts that only the lieutenant could resolve. Yoshida felt a need to hear further explanation of the lieutenant's puzzling beliefs. There was no refuge in apathy. The cell was no longer a sanctuary. Try as he would to confine his world to the sound of his own blood, Yoshida could not shut out the photograph of the dead soldiers or the lieutenant's sometimes angry, sometimes sad words. In the morning he called the guard and said, "Lieutenant Fukujiki."

It took the lieutenant most of the morning to convince Yoshida there were times when a soldier's duty to live was greater than his duty to die, and because living was more difficult than dying, the true measure of a man's worth was whether he was resolute enough to survive and serve.

"We, too, believe that duty can be heavier than a mountain and death lighter than a feather," the lieutenant said. "Just as the great Nanko wished to be reborn seven times so that he might give seven lives for Japan, so our noble Hale said at the very hour of his death, 'I only regret that I have but one life to lose for my country.'"

Yoshida let out his breath in audible appreciation. He was pleased that the lieutenant knew the story of Nanko and surprised to learn the Americans also had such a hero.

"But we do not run blindly toward death," the lieutenant said. "It must serve a purpose. Despite the noble wish of such men as Japan's Nanko and America's Hale, men have but one life on earth. It should not be given in vain. Had Rentaro Yoshida died at Matsuyama it would have been in vain."

Yoshida felt a surge of joy.

"Tell me how I may die to serve Japan!" he cried. "I am ready."

The lieutenant groaned. On his face was an expression of great annoyance. Yoshida was dumbfounded. Was there no pleasing the lieutenant?

"You must live for Japan," the lieutenant said. "Not die."

Very carefully he explained to Yoshida that in his opinion Yoshida's survival at Matsuyama was nothing less than an indication that Heaven had spared him for a purpose. Yoshida accepted the explanation though he thought if Heaven really were on his side he would have instead been granted a glorious death.

Resuming the conversation after a break for lunch, the lieutenant told Yoshida there were many ways in which he could fulfill the purpose which fate appeared to have decreed.

"Shall I speak further of these things?" he said.

"If you please, Honorable Lieutenant."

"Well. For example, American forces have forged a band of steel from Shibushi to Miyazaki City. Many thousands of civilians are cut off without food and but little shelter from the elements in the southeastern part of the prefecture. It is our desire to save them from lingering death. You should know, Sergeant Yoshida, that our great fleets of ships have brought not only the means of making war on the selfish militarists but also food for the hungry people of Kyushu. If you doubt this you may request to see the stockpiles with your own eyes."

"I do not doubt the honorable lieutenant." Yoshida scratched his chin uncertainly. "But what has this to do with me?" he continued.

"It may be within your power to open a way to some of these people and save their lives."

"I am only a sergeant," Yoshida protested.

"When Heaven chooses an instrument it makes the instrument sufficient to its needs. Is that not so?"

"I suppose so, Honorable Lieutenant."

"If you accept this grave responsibility you will be given all necessary instruction and assistance. Do you accept?"

"I accept, Honorable Lieutenant."

The lieutenant was asking too much of a mere sergeant, but if it was Heaven's wish, and if he could somehow save the lives of Japanese people, he would try. "Do one's best and leave the rest to Providence," the saying went.

Yoshida had remained standing during the interview. The lieutenant had sat in the chair, rising occasionally to pace the narrow cell. Now he stood and saluted Yoshida.

"You have made a wise and honorable decision, Sergeant Yoshida. One day, when this war is finished, you will recall with pride what you have done."

Yoshida was not at all sure of that. To save the lives of thousands of his countrymen would be a good thing, but it would not absolve the guilt of his capture. Nothing could do that. Despite the lieutenant's fine words he had lost his honor beyond redemption when he permitted himself to be taken alive.

"In the days ahead you must be very strong, Yoshida," the lieutenant said. "You will be working with Americans. Though it will not be so, to some of your countrymen it will appear you are working not for Japan but for the enemy. They will speak evil of you. But should this happen I beg you to recall the Forty-Seven Ronin and the indignities they suffered willingly because they knew their cause was noble. And think on the honor which came to them when their true purpose became known."

"I will try, Honorable Lieutenant."

Next morning, Yoshida's own uniform, washed and mended, was brought to him. He refused to don the uniform he had dishonored until Lieutenant Fukujiki came and explained it was necessary.

"We have need of your assistance sooner than expected, Sergeant

Yoshida," he said. "Do you recall Private Second Class Nanami from the day of your arrival? He is at last truly determined to die. He has stopped eating."

Yoshida was ashamed. This is what he should have done even though the lieutenant said it was only evidence of self-pity.

"Nanami has an aged mother and father and a wife and children. They will need him when the war is over. He must not be permitted to deprive them of their livelihood. It will be a great kindness to them if you will make Private Second Class Nanami mend his ways."

"How am I to accomplish this, Honorable Lieutenant?"

"I had not imagined you would need to be told, Yoshida. You are a sergeant. Order him to eat."

Yoshida put on the uniform. It was strange to be dressed as a soldier again, even stranger than the first time he had donned his country's uniform and changed in a twinkling from a skilled potter to a raw recruit. Private Second Class Nanami was not in the room where Yoshida had glimpsed him the day he arrived on the prison ship. He was in the sick bay with a guard sitting nearby. Nanami appeared to be sleeping when Yoshida entered. In repose his face was weak, not at all what one would expect of a soldier who seemed to be so resolute. In a curious way it made Yoshida less insecure about his own conduct. It seemed to confirm what the lieutenant had said, that it took more strength to live than to die.

"Private Second Class Nanami!" Yoshida barked.

The guard gave a start and Nanami's eyes flew open. He scrambled out of bed and stood at attention, swaying, utterly disconcerted.

"What is this I hear about your behavior?" Yoshida demanded.

It was invigorating to speak with authority again.

"I—I do not understand, Honorable Sergeant," Nanami stammered.

"Is it true that you refuse to eat?"

"A dead man has no need of food, Honorable Sergeant."

Yoshida slapped his face.

"Don't be insolent," he said. "When food is brought to you, you will eat. That's an order."

"Yes, Honorable Sergeant."

"That's better. Now get back in bed until Lieutenant Fukujiki decides what to do with you."

He let the harshness fade from his voice.

"Don't be such a fool, Nanami. Think of your mother. What will happen to her if you die?"

Tears filled Nanami's eyes at the mention of his mother. Yoshida wondered if it were not a fortunate thing that his own mother had died before the Pacific war began. At least she had been spared the bombings and the suffering. As for the rest of his family, who could tell where they were now or what their fate might be. He had no wife or children. That, too, was a fortunate thing.

Lieutenant Fukujiki was waiting for him outside the sick bay. He had witnessed everything.

"Splendid, Sergeant Yoshida," he said. "I was right to place my trust in you."

In the morning when a small boat came for Yoshida, Lieutenant Fukujiki came to the rail to see him off. He shook Yoshida's hand and as the boat pulled away called out, "Hard work." For a moment Yoshida felt as if he were taking leave of one of his own officers.

Yoshida was assigned to a three-man psychological warfare unit commanded by a gray-eyed lieutenant who spoke good Japanese. The lieutenant was friendly with Yoshida from the beginning and Yoshida did not at first like him precisely for that reason. It was not that he did not trust the American's sincerity, for he had come to believe Americans were sincere though bafflingly inconsistent, but because the lieutenant did not appear to understand how to conduct himself as an officer. He and the sergeant and private first class composing the unit called one another by their first names and slept in the same wood-floored tent. He could not be much of an officer. Yoshida wished he had been permitted to remain under Lieutenant Fukujiki's command. There was an officer. He knew how to speak to a soldier properly. Perhaps it was his Japanese blood.

And, paradoxically, the new lieutenant was in some ways too Japanese. Although his bizarre name, Rebentaru, his long legs, his eyes, his curly straw-colored hair, were unmistakably American, he sometimes wore wooden clogs, geta, with his uniform, always removed his boots before entering his tent, changed his combat jacket for a red silk kimono whenever indoors, often spoke Japanese to his two soldiers, who understood but little of it, and took miso soup, rice and pickle for breakfast. He sometimes prepared Japanese food for all with his own hands, eating with chopsticks and insisting they sit together at the same table, even Yoshida. The sergeant and the private first class disliked Lieutenant Leventhal's Japanese food even though, Yoshida was compelled to admit, he was a superb cook, and after each such meal would slip away to dine on cold American rations, which they ate from tins and cardboard containers. Yoshida himself ate but sparingly. The lieutenant was at first distressed by this but got over it when Yoshida explained that though the food was delicious as any he had ever tasted he did not think it proper that a soldier who had permitted himself to be captured should indulge his physical senses. It was for the same reason he would not accept the cigarettes and candy with which the unit was always so abundantly supplied. The lieutenant was pleased and impressed by Yoshida's reasoning. This was when Yoshida first began liking him.

His first few nights with the unit Yoshida was locked in one of the metal buildings with the arched top, where a guard looked in on him regularly. Then he began sleeping in the big square tent with the lieutenant and the two soldiers. Yoshida got no rest the first night in the tent. It was unnerving to share living quarters with an officer. The two soldiers slept on cots under heaps of thick blankets. Rebentaru slept on a futon on the wooden floor. The American sergeant snored. This did not disturb Yoshida. In fact it helped him feel easier living in the same tent with Americans. His good friend in the 37th Tank Regiment, Sergeant Shintani, had snored in just that manner. Shintani had been incinerated in his tank by an American jellied gasoline bomb and was no doubt waiting impatiently for him at Yasukuni. It would be a long wait, Yoshida thought sadly.

Rebentaru did not seem as much concerned about the starving civilians in Miyazaki Prefecture as Lieutenant Fukujiki had been, for he made no effort to explain to Yoshida how he was to assist the Americans in saving them. They were always riding about in a jeep, all four of them, picking up bundles of leaflets printed in Japanese and delivering them to widely scattered units. Rebentaru was fond of reading the leaflets aloud to Yoshida. In one way or another they all appealed to Japanese soldiers to stop fighting for their own sake and the sake of their country. They were well-phrased, Yoshida thought, but utterly useless. Nevertheless he complimented the lieutenant on them, for that was what Rebentaru obviously wished to hear.

One morning Rebentaru left the two soldiers at the tent and took Yoshida for a proper Japanese bath. They poured wooden buckets of water on one another, scrubbed with soap, and then sat for half an hour in a steaming cement tank. Yoshida knew it was wrong to enjoy such pleasure but it was irresistible. He resolved to go without rice for two full days in expiation. Rebentaru's male organ was very large. Yoshida was impressed but not surprised. He had heard many times this was true of Americans. It might very well explain their great energy and restlessness. While they soaked, Lieutenant Leventhal told Yoshida the time had come at last for him to begin working in behalf of his beleaguered countrymen. East of Shibushi untold thousands of civilians were enduring the most dreadful privations in the Fukushima River valley. Some food had been airdropped to them but it had been taken by Japanese military forces still occupying a complex of fortifications guarding against the American landings which had not come.

"Naturally it has been necessary to abandon this program," Rebentaru said. "We wish to save Japanese lives but not at the expense of assisting Japanese soldiers to continue their useless resistance."

Many of the civilians, he was confident, would come to Shibushi of their own will if the narrow approach along the coast of Ariake Bay was not barred by a detachment of infantry dug in at Takamatsu Village. Wasn't it scandalous, he asked, that Japanese soldiers persisted in preventing Japanese women and children from avoiding starvation.

"If we wished we could send a force of tanks and infantry to take the positions," the lieutenant said. "But wouldn't that be rather foolish for us to risk the lives of our boys when there is no military advantage to be gained? In itself, the Takamatsu detachment poses no threat to our operations."

"Yes, Honorable Lieutenant," Yoshida said. "Quite foolish."

He thought it a bit eccentric of Rebentaru to call American soldiers "boys," but he was beyond being surprised by American oddness.

Lieutenant Leventhal explained that the Japanese troops were themselves in a bad way, weakened by hunger and illness. As Yoshida well knew from his own experience, Rebentaru said, the Americans had compassion even for Japanese soldiers when they were helpless. Yoshida's assignment would be to persuade them to accept the inevitable and save not only themselves but thousands of their suffering countrymen as well.

"Why should they die like beasts in holes in the ground when one day soon they will be sorely needed to rebuild Japan?" he said.

Yes, Yoshida thought, yes. That is exactly what Lieutenant Fukujiki had said and Lieutenant Fukujiki was a man of great wisdom.

"You will do this, then, for your comrades?" Rebentaru asked.

"Yes, Honorable Lieutenant!" Yoshida cried. "Only tell me how I may do so."

Yoshida, with the lieutenant's guidance, spent the afternoon preparing a message to be addressed to the troops on Aka Point and the larger contingent at Takamatsu Village eight hundred yards behind them. He was given a new uniform bearing the insignia of the 189th Regiment of the 86th Infantry Division, the unit to which the troops belonged. Every day after lunch Yoshida went to Shibushi Harbor in the jeep with Lieutenant Leventhal and boarded an LCI for a leisurely cruise back and forth off Aka Point. Yoshida found it pleasant to be out of doors and on the water and listening to Japanese records between his regular periods at the loudspeaker. The first day or so he had nothing to do because rifle fire from Aka Point kept the LCI out of amplified voice range. When it became possible to move in closer, Yoshida delivered his message every ten minutes. At first he spoke uncertainly. How those within sound of his voice must despise him for seeming to assist the enemy. He remembered what Lieutenant Fukujiki had told him and thought about the Forty-Seven Ronin. He gained confidence when his delivery grew more practiced and no Japanese soldiers showed themselves to give visible evidence of his audience.

In the beginning the lieutenant thought it best that he use the approach that had worked so well with Private Second Class Nanami. Stating his rank, Yoshida ordered the soldiers to assemble on a rugged ledge of black volcanic rock on the southwest side of the point, where the cliff was least precipitous, and be picked up by small boats from the LCI. During the LCI's second passage off the point a soldier emerged from the burnt-over bamboo on the top of the cliff and picked his way down the steep slope carrying a white banner. Before a boat could be launched he was cut down from behind by machine gun fire and the LCI was forced to retire out into the bay. That night Lieutenant Leventhal worked late preparing a new message for Yoshida.

"There," he said, presenting the text for Yoshida's inspection, "that should do it."

Rebentaru's calligraphy was good, for an American, Yoshida thought, though a bit mechanical. Yoshida complimented him on it and Rebentaru beamed. Once more Yoshida was impressed by how childlike Americans could be.

"We should have taken this tack in the first place," the lieutenant said. "Or made you an officer instead of a sergeant. Apparently there's someone of higher rank than you in the forward positions."

Yoshida began using the new message next day.

"Honorable Comrades. I am Sergeant Rentaro Yoshida, 189th Infantry Regiment. The Americans found me unconscious on the battlefield. Their doctors tended my wounds and nursed me back to health. They have treated me with kindness and respect. As you can see, it is not true they torture and kill soldiers who fall into their hands. In Shibushi I have seen how they care for little children who have lost their families and give food to the hungry and medicines to the sick. This morning at breakfast I was given miso soup, rice, dried fish, seaweed, egg, pickle and tea. For lunch, sea bream and three bowls of white rice without millet. Tonight there will be beef and soup with tofu and vegetables. What have you eaten today? It has been promised that soon I will see my family in Gifu. Wouldn't you also like to see your mothers and wives and children again? Of course you would. You have only to obey instructions. Talk it over tonight, and tomorrow at fourteen hundred hours come down to the shore where our boats will pick you up. Display white banners and wear only your fundoshi. If there is anyone who might try to stop you, disarm him before leaving your positions. Act together. That is the Japanese way. Now we will leave a small sign of our sincerity. Please observe that only two men will approach the shore and both are unarmed."

The LCI's motor launch was lowered with one man at the wheel and another at the bow. It moved slowly through the water and lay to just off the shelf of convoluted black stone below the ridge. The bowman threw two packages containing cigarettes and chocolate bars as far up on the rocky shore as he could. Yoshida had offered to accompany the boatmen but the lieutenant had turned him down, evasively, Yoshida thought. Rebentaru said he was too valuable to be risked in this manner. When the launch returned without incident, Yoshida thought perhaps the lieutenant might acknowledge he had been wrong about the risk involved but he did not. Next day the packages were gone but there were no soldiers waiting at the shoreline. Yoshida spent the afternoon repeating the message of the day before, omitting only the token of sincerity.

"Now that we've reminded them what tobacco and candy taste like, we'll just let their tongues hang out for some more," the lieutenant said.

Yoshida thought that was a rather callous attitude.

Two more days went by with similar lack of response. Not one of the defenders of Aka Point had showed himself since the death of the soldier attempting to surrender. Yoshida became annoyed with them. How could they be so stubborn and unappreciative? It did not seem to matter at all to them that the Americans were taking great pains to help them. Of course it was partly Rebentaru's fault. Yoshida had suggested that if the soldiers on Aka Point could only be made to understand a man's responsibility to his suffering countrymen as Lieutenant Fukujiki had made it clear to him they would be more inclined to heed the voice of reason. But Rebentaru had said the soldiers on Aka Point were not as compassionate and intelligent as he was and it would only confuse them to inject other considerations.

"They can only understand that which affects them personally," the lieutenant said.

Yoshida conceded there was some truth in that. The common soldier could be infuriatingly slow-witted and selfish. But perhaps if he could reason with them personally.

"We do not know how they regard you," Rebentaru said. "There's a good chance they would kill you if they got the opportunity."

It was typically American of the lieutenant to suppose that death was the worst thing that could happen to a soldier. The worst that could happen to a soldier had already happened to him. Also Yoshida suspected Rebentaru was unwilling for him to go ashore because he did not trust him. This hurt Yoshida deeply. Lieutenant Leventhal was not so insensitive that he did not perceive it.

"Very well," he said. "If I can get permission from higher authority."

When permission came Yoshida paddled ashore alone in a rubber boat. He dragged the boat up on the narrow ledge and sat down nonchalantly on a rock. He allowed only his eyes to move as he studied the face of the hill rising steeply above him. He sensed he was being watched though he saw no one. The face of the cliff was scorched and pitted, naked rock showing in many places. There were openings near the top within which he knew men were hiding. It was strange to be among his own people again, away from the Americans, and stranger still that he did not feel more fully that he was among friends and away from an enemy. The soldiers were in a sense his opponents, the Americans his allies. Though the day was cold he took off his cap and wiped his brow, letting his breath out noisily.

"Phew," he said. "Rowing a rubber boat is hard work. I've got to stop overeating this way."

That had been agreed on with Rebentaru.

He took a chocolate bar from his tunic, unwrapped it, and began eating it very deliberately. It was the first sweet he had allowed himself since he listened to his blood on the prison ship. He did so only because that, too, had been agreed on with Rebentaru. When he finished he lit the first cigarette he had had since the same period. His deep sigh of satisfaction was only partly simulated. He was conscious of movement within the openings high up the ridge but devoted his full attention to studied enjoyment of the cigarette. A skeletal figure, tattered and begrimed, emerged from the cliff, slid down it on its buttocks, digging in its heels to check its descent, and edged toward him. Yoshida continued to concentrate on the cigarette as if nothing else existed. The soldier licked his cracked lips and squatted down silently a few feet away. Yoshida ignored him. After a few minutes another scarecrow figure joined the first. In a little while there were four of them around him in a half circle. Yoshida threw the still burning cigarette on the ground and stretched luxuriously. All eyes fastened on the smoldering butt. After a moment the nearest soldier reached out and picked it up.

"Fine weather for this time of year," Yoshida said casually.

All four of the soldiers sucked in their breath and nodded. Seeing them, Yoshida could no longer be angry with them for their obstinacy. They were such wretched-looking objects he felt sorry for them. Their faces were pinched and their eyes dull. He took another candy bar from his tunic and broke it into four equal pieces.

"Forgive the inadequacy of my offering," he said. "Had I not been so thoughtless I would have brought tinned fish and rice cakes from the ship out there."

The soldiers ate the chocolate quickly. Four more came out one at a time to join the circle. Yoshida passed his pack of cigarettes around. When he produced a lighter of the type so popular with American soldiers a sigh of admiration went up.

"Well, then," he said matter-of-factly. "I suppose you'd like to come with me."

No one answered.

"How many of you are there, anyhow?" he said.

"Perhaps a hundred and fifty now, Honorable Sergeant," one of them said deferentially. "Twenty-five here and the rest back at Takamatsu."

"Nothing much to eat these days I suppose," Yoshida said sympathetically.

"It is very bad," the soldier said. "The officers take what little there is for themselves."

The others nodded agreement.

"I wouldn't put up with that," Yoshida said. "Even if they are officers. We are all as good Japanese as they are, aren't we?"

The soldiers were shocked.

"Look," Yoshida said. "I don't like to say anything against an officer myself but just look at what they've done to you."

The soldiers looked at each other and nodded. Two more joined them.

"My rubber boat is small," Yoshida said. "I can only take back six of you with me in safety. The rest will have to wait."

He said it as if they had all agreed to go with him.

"I'll tell you what I'll do," he said. "I'll take as many as I can and the rest of you go fetch as many of your comrades as would like to join me when I return with a larger boat."

He pointed to four of the more docile-looking.

"You, you, you and you," he said. "You'll have to wait your turn, I'm afraid. The rest of you, fall in."

The last sentence was given as an order. The soldiers rose obediently and formed a ragged line.

"Form a column of twos and follow me," he said.

He led them toward the rubber boat without looking to see if his order was being obeyed. He expected at any moment to hear the sound of a machine gun and feel bullets ripping into his back. He was unexpectedly apprehensive. He had not thought he would ever again value his life. But he had an important mission to accomplish. Lieutenant Rebentaru and Lieutenant Fukujiki, too, were depending upon him. He would not fail them.

American sailors lined the sides of the LCI to help the soldiers aboard. Rebentaru hung over the rail, smiling.

"Beautiful, Yoshida," he called. "Beautiful."

The prisoners squatted on the deck, all of them abject, some showing terror.

"Do not be afraid," the lieutenant said. "You are among friends."

He went to the rail and looked toward the point.

"Look, Yoshida!" he cried excitedly. "Look!"

A dozen or more soldiers were scrambling down the slope toward the water.

The lieutenant spoke in American to one of the LCI's officers and the sailors prepared to lower the launch. Yoshida moved to climb aboard.

"No need for you to go this time," the lieutenant said. "Help me get these men below."

"I beg the honorable lieutenant's pardon but if they do not see me in the boat they will be frightened," Yoshida said.

"You're probably right," the lieutenant replied. "I don't expect I'll have any trouble with these poor fellows."

The launch nosed against the rocky shelf, holding its position with its engine at half-throttle. The soldiers were so weak they had to be hauled aboard bodily.

"Are there any more who wish to come?" Yoshida asked a soldier wearing the three stars of a superior private.

"Yes, Honorable Sergeant, many," he said. "But they are afraid."

Yoshida leaped ashore and climbed to the top of the hill. He stood erect with his hands on his hips.

"Honorable comrades," he shouted. "There is room for many more. Come join us before the boat leaves."

He heard the crackle of the machine gun at the same moment he felt its bullets slam into his breast. He fell to the ground still conscious and tumbled down the hill. He rolled out onto the convoluted black stone ledge at the shoreline. Everyone in the launch, Japanese soldiers and American crewmen alike, were staring at him. He could not help being annoyed. Had they never seen a dead man before, he wondered. Yoshida dismissed them and looked back up the hill down which he had fallen. He felt neither pain nor anger. For the first time since leaving Lieutenant Fukujiki and the prison ship he heard the singing of his blood. But now it did not bring serenity. How stupid of them to kill one of their own comrades who had come to save them, he thought. And how useless.

16

[First Lieutenant Robert Vaccarino/Zenji Wada]

First Lieutenant Robert Vaccarino stood erect in the turret of his M24 tank, making a meticulous study of the terrain through his field glasses. Eight hundred yards ahead, the Sendai River and a steep wooded hill pinched the road between them. The other two light tanks of the reconnaissance patrol were drawn off the road behind his. They had come several miles without encountering opposition or any sign of the enemy but, Lieutenant Vaccarino thought, if the Japs decided to make a stand this side of Kyomachi, the spot up ahead was just the place for it. Kyomachi was a village seven miles up the road, where the Sendai swung eastward again. Aerial reconnaissance had revealed enemy forces concentrated in the area with reinforcements arriving on foot from the west and north. The daily A.M. photos airdropped that morning had shown no enemy traffic or major obstacles on the stretch of the road from a point miles beyond the present position of Lieutenant Vaccarino's patrol to a series of tank ditches and barricades before Kyomachi. The patrol was in the van of an American column that in the past week had driven twenty-five miles north from the head of Kagoshima Bay. The column was now strung out for miles along the road. After the regular morning briefing the light tanks had been sent racing ahead of the column to Kurino Village on the Sendai to check it out. The reconnaissance photos indicated Kurino had been abandoned by the enemy. If the ruins of the village proved unoccupied, the patrol was to probe forward until it encountered opposition or made visual contact with the enemy forces believed to have withdrawn ahead of the advancing column. Depending upon the findings of the reconnaissance patrol, the column would either pause at the Sendai to regroup and replenish or press forward to fall upon the enemy at Kyomachi.

The mission of the American column was to drive east along the Sendai from Kyomachi and wheel south to Kobayashi. Two other American columns were pushing toward Kobayashi, one north from Miyakonojo and the other west out of the Miyazaki City area. When the three columns met at Kobayashi, the last surviving enemy forces in the Operation Olympic objective area would be encircled in the Kirishimas, to which they had withdrawn for a final stand. As he studied the hill half a mile up the road Lieutenant Vaccarino was aware of this, as well as of the commanding general's desire to reach Kobayashi before the other two columns. Vaccarino had found Kurino, a mile back, abandoned. If he found the road clear the column would attempt to overwhelm the enemy blocking force at Kyomachi in one ten-mile lunge.

The lieutenant climbed out of his M24 and summoned his two tank commanders to a conference beside the road. They crouched around a map in the shelter of his tank while he explained the manner in which they would approach the bottleneck up ahead.

Lieutenant Vaccarino's tank had a name, Rapid Robert. The name stemmed as much from the lieutenant's penchant for bold, swift action as for the tank's thirty-five-mile-an-hour speed over open country. Robert Vaccarino had found a home in the Army. It was not because he had been unable to succeed in civilian life but because in the Army the pressure was off. For most of his twenty-six years someone had been pushing him. His parents, his coaches, his fiancée. Make high marks, make the baseball and basketball teams, make All-City, make the dean's list, join the best firm, be noticed, get promoted ahead of your peers. He had done these things, and not so much because he wanted them as because he felt he must. Until he was drafted he had not known this about himself. He had been too caught up in the process of getting ahead. All his life it had been drummed into him that this was the obligation of someone with his personality, his natural ability, his intelligence. And it was only after he had been in the Army some months that he realized his personality, his natural ability and his intelligence were not and had never been all that exceptional. He had only worked harder than most, and that only to achieve the things expected of him by those who overrated him and therefore made excessive demands upon him. The Army made demands too, but they were elementary. Any left-footed idiot could fill them, and without even having to think. You were told exactly what to do and how to do it. Though he had left a responsible, well-paying position to be taught how to take a rifle apart and put it together again, turn one way or the other without falling down, and fold his underpants neatly, he did not feel wasted. Instead he felt as if he were being permitted to rest after running all his life.

On the rifle range he qualified as a marksman. On the drill field he never mistook his left foot for his right. At inspections socks and underwear were always properly folded and in exactly the right place. These things, and his degree in business administration from Columbia University, earned him an appointment to Officer Candidate School only a few months after his assignment to an infantry unit. After OCS he was assigned to the finance section of a headquarters in New York City only a fifteen-minute subway ride from his old apartment. The apartment had long since been rented but he found another in the same neighborhood, though more expensive and less comfortable. He had free time to spend with his fiancée. There was dinner once a week with his parents, as before. On an occasional Saturday or evening he dropped by the branch YMCA where he had coached a boys' basketball team to offer the benefit of his experience to its new coach. It was a gesture more appreciated by the boys, who were impressed with his officer's uniform, than by their coach.

Then his parents and his fiancée began asking why he was still only a second lieutenant. His father said an old business associate of his had been called up in his reserve rank of brigadier general and was in a position to put in a word or two where it counted. Vaccarino's fiancée, Hester, suggested she give a small dinner party for him at her Long Island home and invite his section and department heads. Her father could send a car for them if they did not have their own, and had contacts which made it easy for him to get steaks and scotch whiskey.

"Johnny Walker, Black Label," she said, "and nobody, but nobody can find Black Label these days."

Her mother said the boy Hester had broken up with after she met Robert was a captain in public relations in Hollywood and wondered if he had given any thought to transferring into something like that, where advancement might come more quickly than in finance.

"In public relations you *meet people,"* she explained. "In finance you're simply hidden behind all those tiresome bits of *paper."*

They were measuring him for track shoes again, he thought glumly. Without telling any of them he applied for transfer to an operational branch of the Army. He had already been thinking about that anyhow. He had felt increasingly guilty and uncomfortable shuffling papers and living like a civilian when so many of his acquaintances were off somewhere getting shot at. When orders came sending him to Armored School at Fort Knox his father was outraged, his mother and Hester tearful and Hester's father, who had been a major overseas in the AEF in the First World War, spoke to him cordially for the first time since his return to New York City to man a desk in the finance section.

"I know you're going to make us all proud of you," he said. "Son."

It was the first time he had called Robert that.

"I'm only going to Fort Knox, Kentucky," Vaccarino had said.

"That's just the first step," Hester's father replied. "You'll get your chance don't worry about that. Did I ever show you my Croix de Guerre?"

He had, of course.

At Armored School Vaccarino exchanged his finance-department insignia for the cavalry's crossed sabers. He saw his first combat in the Philippines as a replacement platoon commander in a reconnaissance company equipped with M5 light tanks. For the invasion of Kyushu the company was re-equipped with M24s. It was a better tank than the M5, almost as fast, with thicker armor and a 75-mm. gun instead of the M5's 37-mm. popgun. But despite having superior equipment he found he was uneasier fighting in Japan than in the Philippines. It was not the fanaticism of an enemy battling on his own soil that made the lieutenant feel as he did—the Japanese had fought just as tenaciously in the Philippines—it was the fact that after the first weeks, battles had at times become little more than slaughter and often the victims included bands of civilians. GUs, his men called them contemptuously, both because they were not true volunteers, though GU meant volunteer, and because they fought stupidly. The orders were that they were to be regarded as combatants though they had no uniforms, only a patch of cloth worn on the chest for identification, and usually had only improvised weapons. Vaccarino had seen the bodies of women GUs and of boys only a few years older than the children he had taught to play basketball at the branch YMCA in Manhattan.

Once, when a dozen or so GUs had been detected and annihilated attempting to infiltrate a night bivouac position, and he and several other officers unable to go back to sleep had sat around a charcoal brazier drinking coffee in a Japanese dugout they had taken that day, he had spoken of how much this kind of war disturbed him. The company commander had looked at him and frowned.

"A Jap's a Jap," he said disapprovingly. "A woman hiding a grenade between her tits is gonna kill you just as dead as a son of a bitching regular with a machine gun."

"I know," Vaccarino replied, "but it's a lousy way to fight a war."

"A Jap's a Jap," the captain said again, as if expounding profound doctrine. "And the more we kill today the less we got to kill tomorrow. And Lieutenant, don't you forget it."

Until then, Vaccarino had liked his company commander. He could not fault the captain's logic but he resented his self-righteousness.

Now, as he went over the probe of the narrow passage with his two sergeants, Vaccarino wondered if there might be GUs hiding there. Logically, the road should be defended at this point, and by regular troops rather than the less-skilled militia. It was the last significant natural barrier before Kyomachi. But the Japanese had been behaving unexpectedly to throw them off-balance. At times they had made a stand where the terrain was unfavorable for defense and caught the column barreling along as if on a Sunday drive. At other times, as they might be doing now, they pulled back for miles overnight, hoping that the mere threat of an ambush in likely terrain would slow the column down while they consolidated positions farther north. The Japanese had no mines now and few antitank guns, but the place where the road was hemmed in by the river and the hill would be ideal for a suicide attack with hand-carried charges. There was no room for a tank to maneuver. He had considered taking advantage of the M24's speed to race through the bottleneck, but the road curled around the hill and he did not know if he might run headlong into a tank ditch or barricade around the bend. According to the map, after about two hundred and fifty yards the terrain opened out into sloping terraces and paddy fields. Except at the narrowest point, the space between the hill and the river was wide enough for the tanks to proceed in flank position. Despite his preference for swift thrusts, Vaccarino decided to approach the bottleneck cautiously.

He could see nothing indicating a trap except a good-sized boulder poised among the trees forty or fifty yards up the hillside. Rolling rocks down on tanks was a favorite tactic of the enemy, and especially of the GUs. It did not take a hell of a lot of military training to roll a rock down a hill, Vaccarino thought. He would take care of the boulder before they moved up. He instructed Staff Sergeant Goode to move out ahead, staying on the road.

"Keep buttoned up," he said. "Domsky and I'll stay opened up about a hundred yards behind you."

"Gee, thanks, Lieutenant," Goode said, grinning. "My old daddy always said I wasn't good enough to use for bait. I got to write him he was wrong."

"I didn't know your old man could read," said Domsky.

"Domsky, you get off the road to the right," Vaccarino said. "I'll take the left flank along the river. Goodie, the road is your baby. Domsky and I'll cover the sides."

"What about that boulder, Lieutenant?" Goode asked. "It could give a man a headache."

"Take an aspirin," Vaccarino said.

"Seriously, Lieutenant," said Goode.

"Seriously, Sergeant," Vaccarino said, "I'm going to knock the bastard down before we go in. I don't want any dents in one of my Cadillacs."

The M24s had two Cadillac V-8 engines. Vaccarino had told his platoon it had taken a war to get him to trade up from a Buick. And the next car he bought after the war was going to have Hydra-Matic drive like the M24.

"If you run into anything, don't try to bust through," he continued. "Back the hell out as fast as you can. We'll cover."

Back in his tank, he radioed the company commander of his intentions so that the sound of gunfire when he dislodged the boulder would not be taken as an indication that the patrol was in trouble. If he ran into anything he could not handle, Vaccarino's orders were to withdraw. It took only two rounds of 75-mm. to register on the boulder and knock it from its perch. It careened down the hill, hit the road, bounced high into the air, and arched into the Sendai with a great splash. The echoes reverberated back from the hill, drowning out the smooth throbbing of the tank engines. Vaccarino gave a hand signal and Goode's tank moved back on the road, the turret hatch coming down with a thump as it moved deliberately toward the bottleneck. The other two tanks moved behind it on either side of the road, with Vaccarino and Domsky standing in the open turrets scanning the steep side of the hill and the ground between road and river through field glasses.

When the gun fired, Zenji Wada thought surely the tanks had detected his squad. One of his men must have revealed himself. It was intolerable anyone should do so after he had so patiently explained the necessity of absolute concealment until the instant of attack. After the boulder fell and the gun did not fire again, Wada realized the three Yankee tanks were still unaware of the squad's presence. They moved cautiously, however, as if fearing a trap. And well they might, he thought with deep satisfaction. The tanks were approaching so slowly there was time to see how Chosa and Yoshimoto had fared in the brief and puzzling bombardment. He crawled up a shallow fissure toward the spot from which the rock had plunged, stopping several times to cough up phlegm. But no matter. He no longer feared tubercle bacilli would carry him off. He would die another and nobler way and before the day was much older. Then perhaps his soul would be cleansed of that old dishonor. He was obliged to stop and rest before he reached the site. When he breathed normally it felt as if knotted cords were being drawn through his chest. When he exerted himself the knots became dagger points.

Wada at last reached the place where the boulder had lain. It was as he feared. Both Chosa and Yoshimoto were dead. That left but seven men and himself to attack three Yankee tanks. Fortunately they were not the monstrous Shermans, though they looked formidable enough for all that. A shell had landed squarely in the pit at the base of the delicately balanced rock where Chosa and Yoshimoto had lain waiting to give it the push which would have sent it crashing down on the last of the three tanks, if properly timed. The remains of the two men were mingled beyond identification. It was a disgusting sight. He must not think of their fragmented bodies but of the beauty of their spirits.

Well, he thought indecisively, this certainly altered things. The plan had been to dislodge the boulder when the first Yankee vehicle was blown up by the 12-cm. trench mortar shell hidden in the road just beyond where the passage was narrowest. Then whatever lay between the wrecked vehicle and the boulder was to have been attacked with carried charges. His greatest fear had been that Yankees would send infantry ahead of the tanks and detect his squad before they could carry out this plan. When Wada had seen there were but three tanks approaching the ambush, and these small ones without infantry protection, he had been quite optimistic. Three was the perfect number. The mortar shell would destroy the first one, the boulder would disable the last and his entire squad would then be free to attack the middle one. The squad possessed an arsenal of one shaped hand bomb which would pierce armor if properly thrown and seven ten-kilogram packaged charges. Five of the latter were only black powder but the other two contained picric acid and were very powerful. Wada had selected Chosa and Yoshimoto to dislodge the boulder because there were not enough explosives for all. He himself, as squad leader, had taken both the hand bomb and a picric acid satchel.

When the boulder fell, Wada's plan went glimmering. And when one of the tanks moved ahead, with the other two following at a distance instead of all three moving through the narrow place one after the other as he had expected, Wada became thoroughly confused. Wada was not a soldier. He was a schoolmaster. But he was a true volunteer. Because he was tubercular he had not been obliged to register for the National Volunteer Combat Corps but had nevertheless done so. And when he was not called upon to serve he took it upon himself to do so. He had lived for many years under a shadow. There could never be full absolution for what he had done but the nation's desperate strait had at last presented him with the opportunity to make partial atonement.

In 1929, at the age of twenty-seven, Zenji Wada had been a primary school teacher in western Honshu's Hyogo Prefecture. Late one night there had been a fire. Wada was the first teacher to reach the scene, arriving even before the schoolmaster, who had come from a sickbed. The wooden building was already engulfed in flames when Wada ran up. He nevertheless attempted to enter the burning school to rescue the Emperor's portrait from its sanctuary. The flames drove him back, leaving him with permanent scars on hands and face. By the time the schoolmaster arrived the school was utterly consumed and the Emperor's portrait with it. The schoolmaster heaped hysterical abuse on Wada and then, acknowledging the safety of the Emperor's portrait was his responsibility and not that of a subordinate, had apologized. Before another twenty-four hours had passed, the schoolmaster killed himself. With this action the slate was wiped clean as far as everyone was concerned. Everyone except Wada. It was true that the safeguarding of the Emperor's portrait was the responsibility of the schoolmaster. But as a subordinate of the schoolmaster's it had been his responsibility to act for him in the schoolmaster's absence. By the time the schoolmaster arrived the Emperor's portrait was already ashes. Wada and only Wada might have saved it. No one had dragged him back from the flames. He had run out of the burning school because he feared for his life. Those who had witnessed his action said it would have been humanly impossible to get through the flames to the portrait and though its sanctuary was supposed to be fireproof it might already have been consumed. Events had proved the sanctuary was not fireproof, which was a scandal all its own. But Wada remained inconsolable. It had been his duty to attempt rescuing the Emperor's portrait even if he gave his life doing so.

He remained in seclusion for some weeks after his burns healed. He considered suicide and reluctantly decided against it. The schoolmaster had denied him that recourse by atoning with his own life for the school's disgrace. If Wada killed himself now everyone might think it was in atonement for the schoolmaster's death, which was not the case at all. It was the Emperor Wada had failed, not an incompetent schoolmaster. He decided to return to teaching. That would be his punishment, to continue to live exactly as before and thus be always reminded of his cowardice. And he had a wife to support.

He asked to be sent to a school far from Hyogo Prefecture. He did not believe the sincerity of those who assured him he was blameless in the loss of the Emperor's portrait. When the war came he was himself a schoolmaster, though in an obscure village to the north of Kagoshima Bay. In the interim he had contracted tuberculosis, which he accepted as punishment for his misdeed. Although it was arrested, he for a long time wore a gauze mask over his nose and mouth in public. At the outbreak of the war his only child, Takaharu, was seven, and a student in the primary school's second year class.

The war came to the village long before the Americans reached the shores of Kyushu. One by one the seven male teachers of his staff exchanged their black uniforms for the Army's olive drab, to be replaced by women. In August 1945, refugees and evacuees, many of the latter schoolchildren, began arriving in the village from Kagoshima City and smaller towns along the head of the bay. Some of the children were orphans or separated from their parents. Wada and his wife took it upon themselves to care for as many of them as possible. They took three into their own modest home to share a room with Takaharu, now eleven, and bullied some of the villagers into taking others. Food was desperately short and growing shorter. Every day Wada, his wife and the teachers went from door to door in the village and to outlying farm hamlets with bowls, begging for millet, bean curd or anything at all with which to feed the children.

In October a detachment of infantry from a division that had moved down from the north was billeted in the village and took the primary school for troop quarters. Classes were suspended. It was no great loss for little was being taught. Wada and the teachers had been too occupied keeping themselves and the pupils alive. Many of the children had been withdrawn from the school and most of those remaining were the parentless ones dependent upon the school staff. They were half starved and, despite everything the Wadas could do, vermin infested. Most of them itched with scabies, some were covered with sores, and some suffered from chronic diarrhea. There was no medicine with which to treat them. Freed from classes, they roamed the countryside searching for food. They sometimes stole potatoes from the fields. Wada was censored for their lack of discipline but chose to ignore it. There was no rice for them at all and only occasionally millet. They ate snakes, frogs, rodents, crayfish, water lily roots and the leaves of plants.

The October typhoon destroyed Wada's home. His position as schoolmaster, though he no longer had the use of a school in which to conduct classes, was still such that it was the first house in the village to be rebuilt. The new house was smaller than its predecessor and Wada, his wife, their son and the orphans, now grown in number to five, were obliged to share one room. As if this was not enough, the invasion came only a month later and shortly after that calamity Wada began coughing up blood again for the first time in several years. In December the village Volunteer Combat Team was called up and with it Mrs. Wada and all but three of the teachers, two of them physical wrecks and the other a woman with failing eyesight. Wada was left to look after twelve children almost single-handedly. The villagers began leaving for the north shortly after the Volunteer Combat Team was called up. If the war was progressing so badly that the Army required the assistance of their neighbors, it was time to go. Wada found himself virtually alone in the village with his son and eleven homeless children.

Fortunately they were all eleven and twelve years old and able to help themselves a bit. He had managed to find places for the little ones with families leaving the village. There was no food in the village or in the fields around it. The soldiers and the inhabitants had scoured everything clean.

Wada had wanted desperately to go with the volunteer platoon to meet the enemy. To die for his Emperor would to some small degree mitigate the old disgrace which through the years had not ceased to burden him. But, with the reactivation of his sickness, he was not acceptable. And there was no one else to look after the children. When there was no food left anywhere he could not even do that. He took them north in search of food. At night he could hear the sounds of battle behind them. He felt like a coward, running away from the fighting. He was running away from the Americans as he had run from the flames when the Emperor's portrait burned. If only he could give his life for the Emperor now as he had not done before. It was on the road leading north that Wada first began thinking of himself as a defender of the Emperor and of the children as men he was leading into battle. He fell into the habit of speaking to them quite firmly and by their last names, even his son, Takaharu.

"Wada, how dare you complain of being tired. Exercise and strengthen yourself."

"Hungry, Shinozaki? You say you're hungry? Fasting clears the mind. It makes a soldier fight all the harder."

He tried to attach himself and his squad to units moving toward the fighting or into defensive positions and was met with astonished rejections or pitying looks. Sometimes he was given food for the children but they were always shuffled north, away from the fighting. He could not understand why his men were not wanted when soldiers were so badly needed. True, they were small, but they had the spirit of giants.

"Kondo, address the corporal. Tell him what you have learned."

And Kondo would stand at attention and shout, "A samurai lives in such a way that he will always be prepared to die."

"Umekita, what must a soldier always bear in mind?"

"Duty is heavier than a mountain, while death is lighter than a feather."

"Yoshimoto, how does a soldier die?"

"Like a cherry blossom floating to the ground, Schoolmaster."

"Not schoolmaster, dolt! Squad Leader Wada."

They reached the ruins of Kurino as the last of the troops were departing for Kyomachi. Wada, grown cunning, had left his men some distance away where they could not be seen. He approached a lieutenant deferentially but with determination. He was leader of a squad of well-trained volunteers, he said, though he seemed to have lost his armband somewhere along the way. Was there any way in which he and his men might make themselves useful?

"I'm in a hurry," the lieutenant said impatiently. "Can't you see we are moving out?"

"Perhaps my men can protect your rear," Wada said.

The lieutenant laughed with genuine amusement. He laughed until tears rolled down his sunken cheeks.

"Do you have a battalion then, with artillery and antitank guns?" he said when he was able to speak.

"Only a squad of nine men," Wada said gravely.

Two of his men had wandered off and one had died along the way.

"Where is this squad of yours? There's only you."

"I ordered them to get some sleep, much against their will," Wada said. "They have marched thirty-six hours without food or rest."

"Is that so," the lieutenant said. "Tell me, are they trained to attack Shermans?"

"Of course," said Wada.

"Well, I have an idea. Perhaps you can make yourself useful after all."

"We would be most obliged," Wada said eagerly.

"We'd prepared a trap for the Americans two thousand meters up the road but those idiots at headquarters have ordered everyone back to Kyomachi. How many men did you say you had?"

"Nine, sir."

"Only nine? I see. But I suppose if they handled themselves well they might hold for an hour or so. The passage is very narrow and impossible to outflank. My blood boils when I think about it. I could halt the Americans there for half a day if they'd only permit it."

For a moment he seemed to have forgotten Wada's presence so that Wada was taken by surprise when he said, "What arms have you?"

"None," Wada said with unintended candor.

Excitement made him breathe as heavily as if he had been running, and dagger points tore his ruined lungs.

"None! Then how the devil did you . . . I suppose I could find you an antitank charge or two. You should have grenades and a machine gun in case they send their infantry first but that's out of the question."

He bawled out an order and three soldiers brought packaged charges, straining under their weight. There were seven large rectangular packages and one small metal bomb.

"You do know how to employ them?" the lieutenant demanded.

"We have not been trained in these particular types," Wada said cautiously. "I would imagine they're not too different from those we're familiar with."

"I imagine not," the lieutenant said dryly.

He picked up the metal bomb.

"This is to be thrown. Only six hundred grams of picric acid but it will pierce armor. It's the way it's formed, you see. The others must be carried to the target. They're contact fused. Do you understand?"

"Yes, sir."

"You'll all be killed, of course," the lieutenant said matter-of-factly.

"Of course," Wada said.

The lieutenant told Wada about the boulder and the 12-cm. mortar shell. The mortar shell was hidden beside the road. It had not yet been lowered into its hole. That could be done only after the last of the Japanese troops had passed. He told Wada where it was hidden and how to go about preparing it for the American tanks.

"We'll leave your explosive charges at the ambush site," the lieutenant said. "That will tell you where to position your men."

Wada was relieved. He had been afraid the lieutenant might want to distribute the charges himself and would discover how small his men were.

"I'd leave you some rations, too," the lieutenant said, "but we're in a bad way ourselves. And when you think about it, it would only be wasted. The Americans will kill you tomorrow."

"That is true," Wada said.

Wada returned to his squad and told his men they would soon have an opportunity to fight the Yankees. Their reaction was heartwarming. It made Wada proud to be Japanese. Chosa and Yoshimoto disappointed him, however. They seemed more frightened than eager. They were behaving like children, he thought.

American planes flew over all night, attacking the withdrawing soldiers. Wada could see their flares and hear the hammer of their machine guns and the eruption of their bombs. When he had assured himself all Japanese troops had left the area he marched his men to the narrow place between the hill and the river and ordered them to get some sleep. They had to be up at first light to prepare their ambush. Several times during the night Wada thought he heard children crying. It was a sad sound and his heart went out to them. He considered sending some of his men out to find the children but decided against it. Even if they found the children there was no food to give them. And the men needed their rest. They would want to have their wits about them in the morning. Wada rose at the first hint of dawn and awakened his men. Some of them clung stubbornly to sleep and had to be shaken. It was still dark when he took them across the road to bathe in the cold river. This was the manner in which samurai prepared for battle. Wada grew provoked with them because they could not keep their teeth from chattering.

He found the mortar shell and set it in place according to the lieutenant's instructions. It just fit into the hole that had been dug in the road for it. They lowered the shell into the hole nose up and laid two short lengths of bamboo side by side across the mouth of the hole. Wada balanced a heavy stone on the poles and ran a cord from one of them back into a crevice in the hill. When the tank passed over the hole a pull of the cord would dislodge the stone and send it crashing down on the fuse of the mortar shell. Wada thought he would do this himself but decided it could be as easily done by one of his men. He would be needed more in the attack on the tanks that followed. He chose Umekita. Umekita was not as strong as the others but he seemed alert. He gave Umekita one of the explosive packets, as well. If the tank was not totally destroyed by the mortar shell Umekita was to finish it with the package charge. The charge was quite heavy, ten kilograms.

"Are you strong enough to carry it to the tank, Umekita?" Wada demanded.

"I think so, Squad Leader," Umekita replied.

He could pick it up, but just barely.

"Don't worry," Wada said. "Heaven will give you added strength at the proper time."

He was still displeased with Chosa and Yoshimoto. Their behavior was abominable. Tears streamed down their faces and they kept wiping their snotty noses on ragged sleeves. Though he did not like to think so of Japanese men, he doubted if they could be trusted to carry out a determined attack. He took them up the hill to the boulder. They would be out of the way there. He showed them how to put their weight on the pole thrust under the boulder and extending back into the pit at its base.

"Do nothing at all until you hear the mortar shell explode," he said. "It will be your signal."

He went back down the hill and positioned the rest of his squad. It was full daylight now and he had to act quickly. Kondo, young Wada and Fukuwa he placed in holes that had been dug into the side of the hill along the road. The positions were so constructed that they could not be seen by anyone coming up from the south. Yotsuya, Yoshioka and Shinozaki went into holes between the road and the Sendai. Wada covered them with armloads of vegetation. He breathed heavily with exertion. It was painful but he welcomed the pain as a symbol of the purification he was undergoing. He was coughing a good deal. Sometimes bloody mucus came up and sometimes only bright thin blood.

Wada climbed a few meters up the face of the hill and concealed himself where he had a clear view of the road. He was far enough within the ambush position to be out of the path of the boulder when it came crashing down. In his mind he had given the boulder a name, Suteishi, "Sacrifice Stone," after the tactic used by go players to block movement on the board. He wished this had occurred to him sooner so that he might have mentioned it to Chosa and Yoshimoto and thus put heart into them. He was on the verge of going to them when the three Yankee tanks appeared in the distance.

Wada settled down to wait. When the trap was closed he would hurl his bomb on the nearest tank and follow it with the packet of explosives. The signal for everyone was the discharge of the mortar shell.

By the time Sergeant Goode's tank reached the bottleneck, Lieutenant Vaccarino had closed the distance between Goode and the two tanks following him from one hundred to only fifty yards. When Goode's tank reached the point where the hill pressed against the road, Vaccarino called Sergeant Domsky on the radio and told him to hold up, at the same time nudging his own driver with his foot in the signal to stop. He handed his field glasses to his gunner without removing his gaze from the bottleneck. There was no sign of an ambush, but he had his and Domsky's machine guns spray both sides of the road all the way back to where the road curled around behind the hill. If there were concealed suiciders it might flush them out or blow them up with their own explosive charges. Nothing happened. He had not really expected anything. Ambush parties were generally too well dug in, though GUs sometimes could be panicked into attacking prematurely. He had his assistant driver and gunner and Domsky's remain at the machine guns to cover Goode's flanks. The two tanks held their positions on either side of the road.

The machine gun fire startled Wada but he held fast, praying that his men would do the same. When the tanks stopped firing he knew his men had done so. Good soldiers, he thought, and worthy of his trust. He could not risk revealing himself by raising his head. He followed the progress of the tank by its sound. He heard it grinding cautiously below him. It seemed no more than arm's length away. The sound of the other two tanks drew no closer. They had stopped some distance away. It might prove difficult to get at them. This was a development he had not anticipated even after he saw the tanks separate earlier well down the road. It was most disconcerting. And most disappointing. If they had entered the ambush one after the other it would have been child's play to destroy the second tank with his bomb before the Yankees gathered their wits. The first tank would reach the mortar shell any moment now.

Wada trembled with excitement.

It did not prove necessary to pull the cord dropping the stone. The tank had edged closer to the river than to the side of the hill and the righthand track rolled over the stone and caused it to fall into the hole. The explosion tipped the tank so that it seemed to balance on edge for a moment. The broken track made a loud clattering noise as it flapped freely before it was flung from its mountings. The tank gyrated slowly on its still moving lefthand track, then righted itself facing in the direction from which it had come. The track ground uselessly into the dirt of the road and then stopped. The tank's inside machine gun was firing.

When the shell went off Wada hesitated. There was nothing for him to attack. He heard the shouts of his men as they burst from their stations and knew he had blundered. He should have changed the plan of attack when he saw the tanks separate. But who could have foreseen they would not all enter the ambush together? He rose to his feet and screamed at his squad to take cover. It was too late. They were in the open, running clumsily toward the disabled tank with burdens of explosives too heavy for them. Umekita was closest to the tank. He clutched the charge desperately to his breast, his knees buckling with its weight. He fell before reaching the tank and the ensuing explosion spattered the steel hulk with portions of his body. Kondo flung himself against the tank from the other side. A geyser of blood and flesh rose into the air. The tank budged only a trifle and did not catch fire. Yotsuya and Fukuwa fell before the bullets of the tanks firing from outside the ambush. Fukuwa lay in a heap. Yotsuya blew up with his charge. Young Wada ran out of the ambush toward the tanks, followed by Yoshioka and Shinozaki. Wada knew it was a hopeless errand. Even if they reached the tanks their explosives would not breach the armor. Only his bomb could do that. He crawled after them, keeping to the wooded and steeply sloping hillside.

Goode's tank was still careening to the left from the effect of the mortar shell when the sergeant's voice came bursting over Vaccarino's radio.

"Lieutenant, we lost a track! What do you see?"

"Don't bail out!" Vaccarino ordered. "You're not on fire."

His first instinct when the explosion tilted Goode's tank on edge was to slam down the hatch and open fire with the 75-mm. gun. He was in the act of closing the turret when he saw the small figures emerge from the hillside and the ground between road and river.

"Jesus!" he yelled, dumbfounded. "They're midgets!"

"What'd you say?" Goode's voice bellowed in his earphones.

Vaccarino pushed the turret up again and began firing the top-mounted machine gun. The assistant driver had begun firing his machine gun the moment the attackers appeared. Domsky's guns were also engaging the enemy.

"You're under attack!" Vaccarino cried on the radio. "Keep closed up."

Goode's voice was cut off in mid-sentence when a satchel charge blew off the radio's antenna. The midgets were dropping or exploding all around his tank. Three were still on their feet, stumbling down the road carrying satchel charges almost as large as themselves.

"My God!" Vaccarino yelled. "They're little kids!"

His hand fell away from the trigger. The assistant driver and Domsky's crew kept firing. One of the three children blew up, the other two sprawled in the dirt.

"Cease firing!" Vaccarino shouted. "Cease firing!"

The guns fell silent. One of the children lay on his back in the middle of the road, his limbs moving. Goode's turret hatch opened slowly and the sergeant's helmeted head rose cautiously out of the opening.

Wada stole along the side of the hill, finding cover in its folds. He would be obliged to leave its protection to get close enough to hurl his bomb against a tank. He would have to make a dash for it. He put down his explosive packet. He could not hope to reach the tank with such a burden.

A child's voice cried out.

"Father. Father."

Wada thought his ears were deceiving him. It was the voice of Takaharu. What was Takaharu doing here?

Vaccarino heard the voice calling, also. The skin on his arms and the back of his neck prickled. Suddenly, without any warning, he was crying.

Wada looked toward the source of Takaharu's voice. His son's voice was coming from one of his men, lying on the road, face to the sky. It was incredible.

"I'm hurt, Father," the man said, his voice weaker now but still Takaharu's.

It was Takaharu himself.

Forgetting his bomb, forgetting the American tanks, Wada ran toward his son.

"Watch it!" someone yelled in Vaccarino's ear.

Three streams of tracers converged on the running figure, appearing to fling it back and forth between them before it went down at last. There was only silence on the road now.

"Lieutenant?" Goode shouted. "Okay to come out now? Zimmelman's hurt pretty bad."

There was something in Vaccarino's throat. He had to swallow it before he could answer.

"Come on out, Goodie," he called. "I guess that's all of 'em."

17

[Grace Sato]

Grace Sato lay shivering among the reeds, her head lifted only enough to see across the brown river. She had been a week reaching the Mimi, or was it longer? She trembled as much with exhaustion as with cold. Hunger had ceased to be painful and was instead a gnawing void into which her body was slowly collapsing. When the collapse was complete, she wondered giddily, would she simply disappear? That would be disappointing now that she had come so far and with such difficulty. But invisibility would be a valuable asset. The enemy was all around her, hiding. If they could not see her they could not harm her or prevent her from crossing the Mimi River to her friends on the other side. She put the knuckle of a thumb in her mouth and bit down hard to recapture reality. Pain shot through her gums as well as her knuckle but her mind grew lucid again. There was no sign of life on the opposite bank. She did not know what she had expected to see across the Mimi, certainly not a host with banners, but there should be something, just anything, to indicate the presence of her rescuers. They were there, they must be, in concealed bunkers like those she had slipped past to reach the river. Now that she was here at last, the doubts pushed into the background by the perils of her journey assailed her. Would it not have been wiser to await their coming than to go to them? How would she get through the lines? How would she be received if she managed to do so? The last time she had been in their hands the treatment had been humiliating. Perhaps they had changed. Their propaganda leaflets would lead one to believe so. Even if they had not changed, anything would be better than the last two years. She would wait here until dark. Then, somehow, she would get across the river. Once on the other side she would hide until daylight before giving herself up. Sentries were less inclined to shoot in the daytime. And she must be sure she was among friends. The Americans held the coast as far north as Mimitsu, at the mouth of the river, but there might be Japanese troops in the hills on both sides this far inland. It was said the Japanese still held the inland mountains as far south as the southernmost Kirishima. She curled into a ball and slept.

Grace Sato wore patched black trouserlike monpei and a man's suit coat with a tattered lining and holes in each elbow. Her feet, shod in broken straw sandals, were calloused as the hands of a blacksmith. In the past three days she had been almost without food and for months before that had known constant hunger. She was twenty-four but her thin body looked like a child's. The past two years had so changed her that to a superficial glance she might have appeared to be of any age or either sex.

Four years ago she had been a vivacious junior at UCLA in Los Angeles, California.

Her father had emigrated to the United States in 1909 from Tsukumi in Kyushu's Oita Prefecture. After mustering out of the United States Army in 1918 he had sent home for a bride. Grace was the second of two children, both born in Los Angeles. In May 1942 the family was hustled off to the assembly center at Santa Anita Racetrack, leaving behind a comfortable three-bedroom home and once-flourishing cleaning and pressing shop. A few months later they were transferred to Amache Relocation Camp in Colorado. Until Santa Anita, Mr. Sato had been vociferously patriotic. After that he changed completely and applied for repatriation to Japan. The application was accepted and in August 1943 Grace and her parents sailed from New Jersey on the *Gripsholm.* Her brother did not accompany them. He had broken with his father, sadly on his part, bitterly on Mr. Sato's, and volunteered for the Nisei 442nd Regimental Combat Team, which had begun forming earlier in the year. Grace went without reluctance. Brimming with anger, humiliation and disillusionment, she repudiated the country that had repudiated her. Twenty happy years had vanished in twenty months of indignity and injustice. There was so much she believed she would never forgive or forget. The furniture dealers driving their trucks slowly along the streets where Japanese American families lived and buying household goods at panic prices; the Caucasian "friend" who had taken her father's shop off his hands for next to nothing; being called a dirty Jap; living under the watchful eyes of armed guards when she was guilty of no crime; being forced to leave the school where she was on her way to making the dean's list for the third straight year.

She resented what had been done to her father more than that done to her. She was young and resilient, with nothing to lose but laughter. They had taken from her father the accumulation of a lifetime of hard work and more than that, his pride in being a part of his adopted country. When the bus came to take them to the assembly center he had on his World War I uniform, large on him now that he had grown spare in middle age, in mingled pride and defiance. After a week in the whitewashed horse stall which was their apartment he had taken it outside and burned it ceremoniously in view of a watchtower.

They did not reach Yokohama until November, after transferring from the *Gripsholm* to a Japanese vessel in Goa. The family went by train to Oita, in northeastern Kyushu, an interminable journey as uncomfortable as that from Santa Anita to Granada, Colorado, and from Granada to the port of embarkation. The short trip from Oita to Tsukumi was by charcoal-fueled bus. Mr. Sato still had family there, a brother and sister-in-law, cousins, nephews and nieces. For Grace it was a journey into fantasy. The people resembled her but were enormously different, the land exotic and alien. Tsukumi itself and the surrounding countryside were gray with dust from the Onoda Cement Company. Her father's brother had orange groves. They were given a few days to visit with kinsmen Grace had never seen and many of whom were strangers to her father and mother, and then set to work in the orange groves since it was picking time. Japan was not America they were told repeatedly; everyone worked and worked hard.

Grace was totally unprepared for what she found. Before Santa Anita, her father had spoken only infrequently of the country he had left as a teenager. Unlike many of the other Issei, he had put the old life behind him. After Santa Anita he had begun speaking of his homeland with increasing nostalgia. Japan was beautiful beyond imagination, he told Grace, and life there was simple and tranquil. People respected one another, there was no American rudeness and rush, rush, rush. Japan was beautiful, Grace found, and life simple, brutally so. Of tranquillity there was none. On the contrary, there was constant tension. Grace found it necessary to be always on guard in all she said and did, for she quickly discovered that to almost everyone she was American, not Japanese, and regarded with as much suspicion because of it as she had been in the United States for being Japanese. Even something as innocent as her colorful American clothes aroused open hostility. To wear Western clothes, and particularly gay Western clothes, was unpatriotic. Mrs. Sato spent the better part of a day dyeing everything a drab dark brown. Each had brought a pair of fashionable high-heeled shoes to Japan. These they burned. After Grace's brown and white saddle oxfords wore out she became accustomed to geta, the platform clogs, and jikatabi, the rubber-soled slipper sock with a divided big toe. Although she spoke passable Japanese she spoke as little as possible among strangers because of her foreign accent. She read and wrote Japanese with difficulty. Her aunt suggested, not without malice, that she might be wise to attend primary school with the young children and improve herself. She did not like the food at all. Because her uncle was still comfortably fixed at that time, and had a vegetable garden for household use, food was fairly plentiful but monotonous and foreign. In Los Angeles the Satos had regularly eaten Japanese food as well as typically American food, but Grace did not find bean-paste soup and rice at breakfast an adequate substitute for bacon and eggs. She was a long time growing accustomed to eating, sitting and sleeping on the floor. For the first few months her thighs ached constantly. Grace's uncle had a Western-style room with chairs but her family lived as simply as peasants. They cooked on a shichirin, a portable charcoal stove, in a dirt-floored kitchen and brewed their tea—how Grace missed her morning coffee—in the living room over an open fire pit called an irori. When the family sat around the irori Grace never got over the feeling they were camping out.

There was, as her father had promised, no American rush, rush, rush. But work, in and out of doors, tending the mandarin orange trees, the cucumbers, beans and radishes, cooking the rice when it was still available, mending, sweeping, laundering by hand, was interminable, and there was little recreation even had there been time for it. When Grace grumbled, her father reminded her she was fortunate not to be working in the limestone quarries south of town or in the cement factory, breathing dust to poison her lungs. Life was geared to the growing cycle of oranges. The groves of Grace's uncle were on hillside terraces overlooking the bay. The view was lovely but Grace had little time to enjoy it. The terraces were faced with stone retaining walls and rows of cedars formed windbreaks for the orange trees. The trees were pruned in the spring and fertilized with chicken manure dug into the soil by hand. Everything was done by hand. The trees bloomed in August and the bulk of the crop matured and was picked in November and December. When Grace ate an orange she did so surreptitiously. Oranges fetched too good a price to be eaten by a laborer in the groves.

As time went by Grace found herself recalling her life in California with as much yearning and nostalgia as her father had once recalled his life in Oita Prefecture. The good things she had known, friends, leisure, books, movies, hamburgers, milk shakes, the music of dance bands on the radio, parties, gradually began outweighing the bad things that came after the Japanese attack on Pearl Harbor. First she had hated the Japanese for their perfidy and then, when her country first turned against her, for ruining her life and her family's. Then her hate had turned against America. Now she began hating the Japanese again and as her hate for Japan grew her hate for America lessened. Even life at Amache grew increasingly pleasant in retrospect. The four of them had been crowded into a single room, twenty by twenty-four feet. They had been fenced in by barbed wire, and night and day armed soldiers watched them from high towers. In winter they froze and summer they roasted. But there had been camaraderie at Amache and even good times when she was not too bitter to enjoy them. There had been books to read and classrooms where she helped teach the children. For the latter she had been paid sixteen dollars a month. It seemed a pittance then but would be a fortune in Tsukumi, though even if she had pocket money now there would be little to buy with it. Everything was stringently rationed in Japan, and in Tsukumi, when there were rare luxuries in the shops, tabi, sewing cotton, warm sweaters or soap, they went to friends of the shopkeepers, not outsiders, whether the outsiders came from Beppu, Oita and other larger towns or all the way from America.

Of all the things Grace missed from the Amache days, excepting the camaraderie of kindred spirits, she missed most the "Camp Bible," the Sears, Roebuck catalog. She had spent oblivious hours looking through a much-handled copy with her mother or girl friends and more hours deciding how best to spend her carefully apportioned money. At such times she felt like a child again, eager and greedy, and not at all like a college woman. Everyone with a few dollars ordered from the catalog. It was more than a source of material things. It was a link with the outside world and a means of participating, however tenuously, in normal life. Their funds had been frozen, even the savings account opened for Grace's college education when she was still a child, but the Sato family had a monthly income of sixty-three dollars. In addition to Grace's sixteen dollars there was her father's sixteen dollars for work in the tailor shop, her mother's twelve dollars from a job in the mess hall and her brother's nineteen dollars. A certified public accountant, he received the camp's highest scale for assisting with the camp accounts. Much of this income had gone out in the mail to bring necessities and a few simple luxuries—an electric fan, Grace's red wool knee-length stockings, the flower-patterned yard goods in the curtains partitioning their barracks room.

Before experience made her wary, Grace had spoken of the catalog to her new-found Japanese relatives. Few had believed such a thing really existed and only one of them that it was possible to tap such abundance merely by mailing a money order. This was Grace's cousin Naoko. She was sixteen and fascinated by everything about Grace. Whenever she could contrive to be alone with her foreign cousin she begged for stories of

America. She became Grace's only friend in Japan. She loved dressing up in Grace's American clothes and looking at herself in Grace's hand mirror. There was a full-length mirror in her father's house but she did not dare put on American clothes at home. She helped Grace with her Japanese and tried to learn English. Sometimes they laughed like fellow schoolgirls at Grace's awkward Japanese and Naoko's awkward English. Grace seldom found other cause for laughter.

At first Grace was concerned about her appearance. There were no cosmetics and none of the women did anything to their hair but wash it. Even had cosmetics and hair preparations been available she would not have used them. To paint one's face or wave one's hair was considered as unpatriotic as it was frivolous. After a while she stopped thinking about it. What did it matter if a field hand's lips were pale and dry, her face leathery brown, her nails broken? Did she expect a Prince Charming to drive up in his Ford coupe and carry her off to the school formal? She sought refuge in apathy and in time this strange life became routine. Yet there were moments when the appalling incongruity of her presence in this far corner of an alien land asserted itself and she felt locked in a nightmare. She would lower her pruning hook or mattock in the orange grove, oblivious to the sun sparkling on the bay where oysters grew on rows of stakes, and stare at her sinewy brown arms, or awaken in the night in her bare peasant's room and wonder, close to panic, what am I doing here? I am an American.

Her new life had but a single advantage over the ever more attractive life at Amache. Here she had a room of her own. The sliding screens that formed its walls were but slightly more substantial than the hanging print curtain at Amache but once they closed behind her no one entered without calling out, and she had privacy. Here she could cry if she wished, and if she did so quietly her parents could not hear. Tears and secret night thoughts of life before the war were her only indulgence.

In Tsukumi there was little news of America and of the war none she could trust. It added to her sense of isolation. As the months passed it grew obvious even from the heavily censored and propagandized reports that Japan was being forced back across the Pacific. Grace longed desperately for more and accurate news. MacArthur, Nimitz, Halsey, LeMay, anathema to all around her, became her heroes. Their approach was agonizingly slow but they were coming to rescue her. She felt more intensely American than she dared reveal even to her mother. Even if liberation from existence as a Japanese meant only another Amache back home she would welcome it. When she considered the dreadful possibility she might be refused reentry because she had chosen exile she shut it from her mind. She would rather die than live out her days in Tsukumi.

Everything grew scarcer. One by one her uncle's workers were conscripted for military or labor service until only children, women and middle-aged men remained. The orange trees began to show signs of neglect. Her uncle went about with a worried face and said the war was ruining him. He seemed as much concerned about his own affairs as his country's reverses. After the fall of Okinawa it was said Kyushu would be next. Grace found it difficult to hide her elation. As it was, hostility to her family grew with every American success and every fire raid on the big cities. More and more soldiers and sailors were seen in Tsukumi and on the countryside, foraging for food to supplement their rations. The 115th Independent Mixed Brigade had its headquarters at Saeki, eight miles to the south, and it was said the Imperial Navy had established secret bases there for midget submarines and other special attack forces in preparation for the expected invasion. After June nearly everyone was obliged to register for the National Volunteer Combat Corps. The Satos were pointedly ignored. Grace was secretly overjoyed but her father complained bitterly. He was a loyal Japanese subject, he protested, and had as much right as anyone to serve his country. Grace's mother said nothing. She had fallen into Japanese ways, finally, and seldom spoke of their life in the United States except to speculate on her son's whereabouts. Grace thought often of her brother and, though she knew it was unlikely, pictured him among the soldiers coming to liberate her. He might even be an officer by now. He would bear witness that she was American and would protect their parents from reprisals.

That summer American planes came often to attack the airfields along the coast and the Navy base at Oita. Grace felt a fierce joy when she saw them. In November there was great activity at Saeki. It was said that an American invasion fleet had appeared off the island of Shikoku, just across the Bungo Strait from Tsukumi. Many people fled inland, fearing the Oita coast would be next. Grace was relieved that her father elected to remain where they were. Her cousin Naoko came to her fearfully, asking if it were true that when the Americans came they would make all the young girls their mistresses. Grace assured her that she had seen Americans at their worst and even at their worst they would not do such a thing. Naoko was worried, too, that she might have to fight them. She was a member of a Volunteer Combat Unit. At night Grace imagined she could hear the sound of the American fleet bombarding Shikoku. She was downcast two days later when word came the Americans had been driven off with great losses. Her spirits rose when they made successful landings in the south though she was disappointed the attack had come so far from Tsukumi.

In December her uncle told her father he had heard on good authority the Americans were nearing Tsuno, only sixty miles south of Tsukumi. It was then that Grace decided she could no longer wait to be rescued but would go to meet them. She made her preparations carefully and secretly. She told no one of her intentions, not even her mother or Naoko. Her mother would try to stop her and Naoko was too innocent to be burdened with such a secret. Every day she saved a little of her food until she thought she had enough for three or four days. This she kept hidden with the Volunteer Combatant patch she had made. Once she was safely away from Tsukumi she intended sewing it on the old suit coat of her father's which was her warmest garment. That would give her an excuse for being on the road and would contribute to the deception that she was Japanese. She intended speaking as little as possible and if anyone commented on her accent explain that she formerly lived in northern Honshu, where the dialect was different. She hoped that if she were not obliged to speak she might be mistaken for a boy. She did not think it would be difficult to masquerade as a boy. She neither looked or felt like a woman any more.

On January 1 her uncle gave a small New Year's party for the immediate family, saying gloomily he was only doing so in such parlous times because it would be the last time they were all together. The local small farmers celebrated the lunar New Year in February but Grace's uncle prided himself on being modern. There were a few swallows of precious sake, special cakes of pounded rice called mochi and little else. It was an utterly dismal affair. Grace resolved that it would be her going away party. She left in the middle of the night. She went first to her parents' room and looked at them in silence for a while. They were almost invisible in the darkness. Her father snored. Her mother breathed as quietly as a bird. Grace was sorry she could not tell them good-bye but she would apologize if she ever saw them again. She was sorry she could not say good-bye to Naoko, either. She was sure Naoko would cry when she awakened and found her cousin gone.

The road to Saeki was steep and winding in some places and at others ran along the coast. There were soldiers on the road but none of them noticed her in the darkness. Grace had no map but knew that the national road outside of Saeki would eventually take her to Tsuno. The first two-thirds of the way to Tsuno, as far as Nobeoka, was inland, and the final third was along the coast. The part along the coast was said to be especially dangerous because it was often bombarded from the sea. She intended avoiding the coast as much as possible, and towns as well.

Her uncle had said people were being picked up right and left in the towns and conscripted for labor and sent south to the fighting, and he would not even permit Naoko to go into Tsukumi any more. Grace skirted Saeki after daybreak and did not stop to rest until she was a mile beyond it on the national road. Had she not known there were no other roads in the area she would have doubted it was the main highway to the south. It was narrow and in disrepair. There were few people on it and no vehicles except for an occasional horse-drawn cart or charcoal-burning truck. The Americans often strafed the roads even this far north and military traffic moved by night.

Grace walked until mid-morning with only an occasional rest period, wishing to get as far from Tsukumi as she could in case her father fathomed her plan and came after her. When she felt safe enough to stop for a nap she estimated she had already come twelve of the sixty miles to Tsuno. She slept for two hours, twice as long as she had intended. She had had to sell her watch the first year in Japan but had learned to estimate time by the sun. She ate a roasted sweet potato before continuing on her way. She had planned to sew the Volunteer Combatant patch on her coat at the first opportunity but now decided it might make her more vulnerable to being stopped and questioned. She felt free and purposeful for the first time since her arrival in Kyushu. If she had come twelve miles in less than a day she should be able to reach Tsuno in no more than three. And perhaps the Americans by now were even nearer.

In places the road curled through mountains, climbing and falling. Under other circumstances she might have enjoyed the extraordinary beauty of the scenery. Instead, it discouraged her. If the rest of the way was like this she could not hope to reach Tsuno in only three days. There were still few people on the road and none of them, nor anyone in the occasional hamlet through which she passed, gave her a second glance. There was no reason why they should, she realized. In her straw sandals, baggy trousers and hood, the boku-zukin she had sewed herself, she looked like any other peasant. The man's suit coat she wore was not all that unusual, either. It began growing colder as night fell. She had intended sleeping in the fields but it was too cold for that. When she felt she could walk no more she took the first path leading from the road in hopes it would take her to a hamlet where she might find a shed in which to take shelter. The path ended at a farmhouse after a few hundred yards. There was no light in the house but it had a vague feeling of occupancy. She stole through the farmyard to an outbuilding and crept inside. It smelled of horses and manure but there were no animals in it. She found a pile of straw and burrowed into it. Although she was tired to the point of exhaustion she slept poorly. Frightening thoughts filled her mind and there were moments when she wished she were back with her parents in the comparative comfort and safety of their house. Resolutely she forced herself to think of the friendly welcome awaiting her when she reached the American lines. The straw poked into her and she began to itch all over. She hoped it was only the straw and not vermin.

She left the barn while it was still dark, little more refreshed than when she entered it. She stopped in the yard to drink from the well before setting out again.

That day she walked more slowly and stopped more often for rest than the previous day. She ate more of her meager supply of food as well, partly from a desire to prolong her rest periods and partly for the simple reason she was ravenous. The first day excitement had curbed her appetite. For several miles the road skirted mountains on the right and a stream and railway line on the left. No train passed by the entire day. Grace walked part of the way on the rusty tracks because the roadbed was more even than the highway. She welcomed the stream. There was always water to drink and it was refreshing to wash her face and tired feet from time to time. The road was especially steep and difficult at Sotaro, four miles north of Ichitana Village. It so tired her that she could go no farther than the village, twelve miles from the morning's starting point. She reached Ichitana well before dark but a falling-down house looked so inviting she decided to have a good long rest and leave refreshed in the morning.

She did not attempt to conceal her presence in the village. She had encountered pedestrians on the road whose bundles indicated they were wanderers like herself and she did not think she would arouse curiosity. She screwed up enough courage to beg the light of a twig from one of the villagers and built a fire in the hut's irori. If the old woman who lit the twig for her found anything unusual in her accent she did not show it. The abandoned house had a small bathhouse in the yard. Someone had taken the tub in which the water was heated but Grace bathed herself all over with buckets of cold water from the leaf-choked well. Then she ran back to the house and warmed herself at the fire pit. She reheated a potato for her supper and with it ate a handful of cold rice and millet. She slept the night through, awakening only to renew the fire in the irori.

In the morning she was so stiff it hurt to move. She forced herself to take to the road, hoping that activity would loosen her knotted muscles. Though the return of circulation did bring some relief her calves continued to ache. She stopped frequently to knead them. When she reached Kawachimyo Village, only three miles distant, and found the Kumata Bridge out over the Hon River, she burst into tears and gave up in despair. Emboldened by the ease with which she obtained a light for her fire the previous day she went to the first house she saw and asked for shelter for the night. The middle-aged woman and elderly couple occupying the house found nothing unusual in the request. The younger woman, who reminded Grace vaguely of her mother and aroused a stab of homesickness, told her to make herself at home on condition she did not ask for food. Unfortunately they did not have enough for themselves. Grace accepted the condition gladly. The three occupants of the house found her Japanese amusing, the women putting their hands in front of their mouths to hide their teeth when they smiled. None of them had ever heard an American accent and thought only that she was from some mountain village even more backward than their own.

When the Japanese heated their supper of barley gruel in an iron pot suspended over the irori, Grace withdrew to a corner of the room and ate the last of her provisions. Afterwards they invited her to sit with them around the fire. Although they asked no questions they appeared genuinely concerned that a young woman should be wandering the roads alone. For the first time Grace felt sorry for the Japanese as a people. She was ashamed of the thoughts she had nursed about her uncle, who after all had taken her family in and given them food and shelter for two years despite their unpopularity in the community. She pulled up her trouser legs and began massaging her calves. When an involuntary groan escaped her, the old woman crept forward on hands and knees and probed her leg muscles with fingers as thin and strong as talons, shaking her head and making sympathetic noises as she did so. It was very bad, she said. The muscles were all knotted. It would be several days before Grace could walk in comfort. Grace said it was necessary for her to leave in the morning. In that case the old lady said, the only answer was kyu, moxibustion.

"Kyu?" Grace asked.

"Oh, my," the old woman said, "you certainly are backward, aren't you? Moxa cures all aches, and many other things. Even wickedness. If you wish, I'll apply some to your legs."

Grace thought she might as well humor the old woman. She meant well and it might even help. Sometimes peasant remedies were efficacious. The old woman went across the room on her hands and knees and brought back a small cloth bag. If Grace had not seen her walk in a normal upright position she would have supposed the old woman was crippled. She instructed Grace to sit with her legs thrust out straight in front of her. Grace propped herself on her elbows and watched while the old woman placed a pinch of finely shredded leaf on both sides of her kneecap. The old woman took a burning twig from the fire and applied it to the little cones of moxa. Grace felt a searing pain when the moxa burned down to the flesh. She cried out in surprise and pain. The old man looked up from the straw sandal he was weaving and grinned. He was completely toothless.

"Don't be such a baby," the old woman scolded. "Tomorrow you'll be as good as new and there'll be only a little scar to show for it."

Grace dissuaded her from treating the other leg only with great difficulty. The next morning some of the ache was gone but her legs were still stiff as boards. There was an ugly raw place the size of a pea on both sides of her kneecap. The old woman assured her the leg would feel as good as new once she had walked a bit. The younger woman began warming the barley gruel for breakfast and Grace prepared to leave so she would not embarrass them. The younger woman insisted she take a little tea. The concoction tasted only faintly of tea but it was warming.

Someone had a ferry going over the Hon but there was a charge of fifty sen. A shriveled little old man with a white beard like a billy goat's, who was among the group wanting to cross the river, said he knew where there was a fording place just a short way upriver and invited anyone not wishing to pay the outrageous fee to come with him. They crossed without difficulty less than half a mile upstream. The old man, whose eyes were filmy with cataracts, thought Grace was a boy. He asked where the young man might be going. Nobeoka, Grace said.

"There isn't any Nobeoka any more," the old man said. "The Yankees have knocked it all down. If you take my advice you'll go back wherever you came from. There are only soldiers there now and before you know it they'll give you a spear and send you south. I don't know what the world is coming to."

Grace thanked him for his advice and continued on her way. The moxa burns hurt but her legs bothered her hardly at all. She supposed it was the good rest that had done it. It certainly could not have been a pinch of burning leaves. It would be an amusing story to tell when she was among her own people again. The problem now was not her legs but food. Her stomach ached with hunger. After a few miles the road entered a valley and the going was easier. When she neared what remained of Nobeoka, eight miles from the morning's starting place, she left the road and took to the fields and hills. If the old man was right about the presence of soldiers she could not risk going through the ruins of the town. She unearthed a daikon radish in a picked-over field and broke it into pieces. It was thicker than her forearm and a foot long but so dry and fibrous only a small portion was edible. Beyond Nobeoka she found a path leading southwest toward the coast. She passed groups of children and old people going the other way. She reached the coast at Ifukugata Village before dark only to be confronted by a military checkpoint. She left the road to avoid it. There were more children, old people and women with babies on their backs on the national road, all heading north. She was curious about the northward movement but unwilling to risk asking questions. With soldiers everywhere she thought it unwise to be as open as she had been back in the villages. Nightfall found her still wandering the hills. She crawled into a cave and spent a miserable night, cold and hungry.

She walked all day among steepening hills, sometimes carrying her disintegrating sandals in her hand to save wear, and in mid-afternoon discovered she had circled back to Ifukugata. In despair she decided to brazen it out at the checkpoint. The two soldiers on duty did not even bother to ask for papers. The Americans were at Mimitsu, only twenty-five kilometers down the coast, and civilians were not allowed beyond this point unless they were members of the Volunteer Combat Corps. Didn't she see everyone going in the other direction? Grace thought she would faint with excitement. The Americans were only fifteen miles away. A plan began forming in her mind. She was certainly cleverer than the ignorant soldiers. Instead of fearing them she would use them. She reached into her coat pocket and produced her Volunteer Combatant patch. It had come off, she said, and she had not found an opportunity to sew it on again. She had been ill when her unit was called up and they had gone off without her. If they would kindly direct her to the fighting she would be on her way. Also, she had not eaten all day and it as her understanding Volunteer Combatants were to receive rations when on military duty. It was dangerous to talk so much, she knew, but perhaps these soldiers, like the peasants, would not recognize an American accent. The older of the two soldiers did become suspicious.

"Don't tell us what you're supposed to receive," he said surlily. "You sound like a foreigner, anyhow. If you didn't look Japanese I'd swear you were a miserable Korean."

"She's lived on Okinawa," the young soldier said.

"What do you know about Okinawa?" the soldier demanded. "The closest you've ever been to Okinawa is the brothel at Kumamoto City."

"I know an Okinawa accent when I hear it," the younger soldier said doggedly. "Just because you're a few years older . . ."

They argued for a few minutes, ignoring Grace. Apparently they bickered this way all the time.

"In any case you'd better wait until after dark," the older soldier said, turning back to Grace. "Those damnable Yankees fly up and down the road as if they owned it and you never know when one of their gunboats is going to decide to shell the coast. Just this morning they murdered three hundred women and children on the road just outside Kadogawa."

"It was only fifty," the young soldier said. "Not that that isn't horrible enough. Anyhow, it's better to wait here off the road until nightfall. Sometimes supply trucks come through at night on the way to the front and you can get yourself a ride. I'll tell my relief to stop one for you."

"Thank you," Grace said.

It seemed like a marvelous idea. She was so exhausted she felt as if she could not walk another yard and she was dazed from lack of sleep.

"There's an empty bunker just over there," the younger soldier said pointing across the road. "Why don't you rest yourself there? If there is shelling you'll be safe."

Grace turned to go where he had pointed.

"Don't leave just yet," the soldier said.

He stepped off the road and returned with a small tin and a tent sheet.

"This will put strength in you," he said. "It's fish. And just leave the tent sheet. I'll get it in the morning when I come back on duty."

"I suppose you're so generous because she reminds you of your sister," the older soldier said.

"Shut up," the younger man replied. "Don't you ever have a decent thought in your head?"

The bunker was dry and warmer than the outside air. She ate the fish and licked the tin dry. She wrapped herself in the tent sheet and fell asleep immediately. She dreamed someone was fumbling at her clothes and that a weight was pressing on her body. She swam up out of exhausted sleep to discover it was not a dream. She was too tired to resist or cry out. It did not enter her mind to do so. Her body was so wooden it seemed to belong to someone else. It was only when she felt a sharp pain inside her that she became fully conscious of what was happening. Even then it did not seem to matter a great deal. When the weight was removed from her body she fell asleep. When she awakened again she heard someone breathing in the bunker.

"Are you awake, then?" the voice of the younger soldier said in the darkness.

"Yes. Is it time to go?"

"Look," he said. "I'm sorry."

He did not sound as if he really were.

"A soldier who risks his life every day doesn't always behave as he should," he continued pompously.

Despite everything she felt sorry for him. Now was a sad time to be a Japanese soldier. Or a Japanese anything.

"It doesn't matter," she said.

"It doesn't? You're not a prostitute, are you? You seemed quite a decent girl."

"No," Grace said. "I was a virgin."

"Oh dear me!" the soldier exclaimed. "I'm really sorry."

"I said it didn't matter," Grace said. "Please don't be tiresome."

"All right," the soldier said.

She heard him move closer.

"It may be a little while before the truck comes," he said. "Do you suppose we could—"

"No!" Grace said sharply. "Do trucks really pass through or did you only tell me that to keep me here?"

"I wasn't deceiving you," the soldier said. "I may be only an ordinary soldier but I'm very sincere. My relief will get you a ride on the first truck that passes."

"I'm sorry," Grace said, even as she spoke aware of how incongruous it was for her to be apologizing to a man who had casually violated her.

"Never mind," he said. "Tell me something. What's that dialect of yours?"

"Okinawan," Grace said.

"Then I was right after all!" the soldier exclaimed. "Just wait until old Okazaki hears that."

He fell silent after that. After a while someone came to the bunker entrance and said there was an ammunition truck waiting at the checkpoint. The young soldier went out to the checkpoint with her. When the driver told Grace she would have to ride outside on the load the soldier persuaded him to let her sit in the cab. There was another soldier in the cab with the driver. The driver made Grace sit in the middle.

"If we're attacked we'll have to clear out in a hurry," the driver said cheerfully. "But don't worry, we'll leave the door open when we jump. Did you hear that, Morita? Don't slam the door in her face."

"Shut up," the one called Morita said irritably. "You won't think it's so funny when the Yankee patrols fly over."

"Morita's afraid of the planes," the driver said confidentially. "If he weren't such an idiot it's the shelling from the sea he'd be worrying about. The planes always drop flares first and there's time to slip into one of the revetments we've got dug along the way."

The truck drove without lights, creeping along at a slower pace than Grace might have walked. The driver sounded his horn frequently to warn work parties filling in shell and bomb craters.

"Won't the Americans hear us?" Grace asked timidly.

Morita snorted contemptuously.

"Unless they've crossed the Mimi they're no closer than twenty-five kilometers," the driver said. He laughed. "You don't think they can hear us from their airplanes, do you?"

Grace fell asleep. The sound of explosions awakened her.

"Sounds as if Tomitako's getting it again," the driver said. "Maybe they'll leave us alone tonight."

"I hope they've stopped by the time we get there," Morita said.

They heard a plane in the distance. Grace felt Morita and the driver grow tense. She felt trapped between them. The plane roared overhead and a moment later the road was bathed in light. The driver gunned the engine and drove off the road into a narrow revetment dug into the hillside. Morita was shaking. The plane flew over again, the sound of its engine fading in the distance. The driver backed out of the revetment and continued on his way. This happened twice more during the eight-mile, four-hour trip to Tomitako. After one flew over they heard a loud explosion north of them.

"Somebody got it," the driver said comfortably, as if pleased it was not him.

"I hope it wasn't Higurashi," Morita said. "That drunkard owes me three yen."

Fires were still burning at Tomitako and the driver pulled off the road a bit north of town.

"You'll have to walk the rest of the way," he said. "Nothing but foot traffic from here on."

"How far is it to Mimitsu?" Grace asked.

"Ten kilometers by the coast road," the driver said. "But if you want my advice stay off it. The shelling's really abominable."

"Have you eaten today?" Morita asked abruptly.

"No," Grace answered.

"Take this," he growled, shoving something into her hand. It felt like a potato.

"How old are you?" he demanded.

"Twenty-four."

"So old? You're a bit older than my daughter, then."

"You're a queer one, aren't you?" the driver said. "You never let on you had a family."

"Shut up," Morita said.

Grace found a side road and headed inland. Even without the danger of shelling it would not do to approach Mimitsu directly. It lay on the other side of the river and no doubt the coastal area was filled with Japanese troops to prevent the Americans from crossing. She would walk inland before turning south again and try to cross the Mimi some distance upstream. She munched the potato as she walked. She wondered if she would ever understand the Japanese. Sometimes they seemed so callous and fanatical and at other times they were kind and sentimental. She was surprised that what happened in the bunker still seemed of such little consequence. She had been taught that virginity was such a precious thing. Perhaps when her wandering was over and she was safe it would seem more important. But she doubted it.

When she had walked a while she turned south but found the terrain so hilly that she returned to the road. The stars told her she was heading southwest. After she walked two and a half hours the road took a turn toward the south. When dawn came she saw it paralleled a river that must be the Mimi. There were hills on both sides of the river. She began moving more cautiously, staying off the road. There must be Japanese troops stationed along the river though she could see none. She felt they were watching her from underground bunkers. There might be troops in the hills across the river as well, but whether American or Japanese she had no idea. None of them was likely to shoot at a lone peasant as long as she did not attempt to cross the river. Her legs no longer ached. She had no feeling in them at all. She was so weary it required conscious effort to drag one foot after the other. Her stomach, despite the potato she had eaten, was an emptiness wrapped in a void. She wondered if this was what it was like to starve. The small tin of fish and the potato had been her only food for two days, or was it three? The road and the river turned southeast, toward the coast and Mimitsu. She had no idea how far she was from Mimitsu. In places the road followed along the riverbank, in others it was separated from the river by barren fields. Where the hills shouldered down to the road she moved with added caution lest they conceal bunkers. The sound of artillery was clear but not close. She must try to cross the river while she still had the strength to do so. She went into a field between the road and the river and crawled to a spot on the bank where dry reeds grew in profusion.

It was getting on toward dusk when Grace Sato awakened in her nest in the reeds. Her teeth chattered with cold and it was several minutes before she could move without pain. She could not think clearly. She only knew that she must find food and shelter soon and that it must be behind the American lines. She would die before she would permit herself to fall into Japanese hands again. She had not come this far to surrender so meekly to the need for food and rest. When it was dark she crawled along the riverbank, groping for something on which to float across the river. She was too tired and weak to swim. She found a log with one end in the water, the other in the mud. She struggled feebly to free it, crying with frustration. At last she managed to roll it into the river and slipped in after it. The water was cold, driving the breath from her lungs. She clung to the log with only her head above the surface. It floated slowly in the current. Perhaps it would take her all the way to Mimitsu, she thought, if exhaustion and the cold did not loosen her grip on the rough bark. If that happened, she would drown. She was too weary to swim. The log dragged her over shallows and lodged against the bank. She was disoriented from its movements in the current and did not know which side of the river she was on. She must think clearly. Deep water was on her left. If she was facing the coast she had succeeded in crossing the Mimi. How could she be sure which way she floated? The current. Rivers flowed toward the sea. She knelt in the mud and pushed the log out into the current. The river took it from her. It was a moment before the information registered. She had crossed the river. She was on the American side. She climbed to dry ground looking for a path. There was none. She stumbled doggedly over the rough ground, heedless of fatigue, the cold and caution. She did not know how far she had come when the firing started. She threw herself to the ground and lay still. She heard voices. American voices. They sounded strange and wonderful.

"What the hell you shooting at, you dumb son of a bitch?"

"I heard something out there, goddam it! I tell you there's something out there."

"Help," she cried in a weak voice.

"Jesus, did you hear that? It sounded like a woman."

"Keep down and shut up. It's a Jap trick."

"Don't shoot at me, please," Grace cried. "I'm American."

The only answer was ominous silence.

"Please. My name is Grace Sato. I'm an American citizen."

"Then what the hell you doing here?" a voice answered.

"I . . . my family was deported. Please don't shoot."

"Stand up and walk this way. Slow."

Grace rose to her feet and moved cautiously in the direction from which the voice had come. She stumbled and fell several times, and each time it was more difficult to get up. A voice barked from a few feet away.

"Hold it!"

Grace sank to her knees.

"Prove you're American."

"My name is Grace Sato. I live on Sawtelle Street in West Los Angeles. I go—I went to UCLA. UCLA is in Westwood and Bel Air is on the other side of Sunset. The zoo is at Griffith Park. There's an observatory on Mount Wilson."

She knew she was babbling but she could not stop. She must convince them she was American. Why were they being so awful to her?

"What do you think, Grossberg?" a voice said doubtfully.

"How the hell should I know? I never been to L.A. in my life."

"Me, neither."

"Please," Grace whispered. "I'm freezing and I've been walking a week and I'm hungry."

"Well, hell," said the first voice.

A shape came out of the darkness and pulled her into a bunker. Grace began crying uncontrollably. The sobs forming deep in her chest hurt all the way up, as if she were vomiting something solid and sharp-edged. She threw her arms around the American soldier and clung to him, shaking. He seemed enormous. It was only because she had grown accustomed to tiny people, she realized. The soldier's arms went around her, heavy and comforting.

"Hey, there," he said, embarrassed. "Grossberg, she's soaking wet. Hey, there. Cut out the crying. You're okay now. Everything's okay."

18

[Eiji Mikuni]

The buraku, the hamlet, nestled among pinched, wintry terraces and great forests of fir and red pines seven miles south of fallen Kobayashi on the lower slopes of Mount Takachiho, southernmost of the Kirishimas. The barren twin craters of the ancient volcano were mantled in snow. Below the hamlet the forested slopes fell away to the fields of the Kamamuta River valley, from which the guns of the Americans fired night and day at the Japanese troops dug in among the trees. There were no troops in the hamlet, only a single wounded soldier who had dragged himself up the winding path and now lay semiconscious in the house of the nushidori, the hamlet head, Eiji Mikuni. Of the hundred and twenty-four persons in the twenty-one families which once composed the hamlet, less than a quarter remained. The younger men had long since been conscripted into the Army. Many others had marched away late in December to join in the battle against the Americans driving north out of Miyakonojo toward Kobayashi. Others had fled deeper into the Kirishima mountain range. The latter had done so against the advice of Mikuni. All should remain where they were, he had said. There was little food left in the village but none at all in the mountains. And since they were all going to be murdered anyhow, it would be preferable to die together than be hunted down one by one like animals or perish of cold and hunger. The twenty-eight souls remaining in the hamlet were either very old, very young or chronically ill, except for three young women with small children and one who was pregnant.

It was only because of Mikuni's cunning that there was still food in the hamlet. Old Kakizaki, the roof mender, had been the first to see the soldiers struggling up the path in early December and had run through the woods to inform Mikuni. He had been cutting firewood below the hamlet and had spied them when they were still some distance away. There were two of them. One rode a thin horse, the other walked behind, clutching the horse's tail at the steep places.

"What does it mean, Mr. Mikuni?" Kakizaki asked, alarmed.

Soldiers had never come to the hamlet before. It was tucked away in the folds of the mountainside and no road led to it, only the path. Few outsiders visited the hamlet and when one came it was almost always with unpleasant tidings. The fishmonger to say he would not be returning because he had no wares, an announcement of the death in battle of one of the hamlet's sons, a notice of increased taxes.

Mrs. Mikuni was also alarmed. She was getting old. The years had not brought her serenity as they had Mr. Mikuni. Anything out of the ordinary frightened her these days, even a bird seen out of season.

"They're only the first," she whispered. "They'll come by the hundreds and turn our homes into barracks and put us out into the fields and turn the heads of all the young girls."

"Quiet, woman," Mikuni said, sharply for Kakizaki's benefit. When they were alone he was patient with her but it would not do for the entire hamlet to know how he indulged her. "How can one think with all that racket going on?"

They were not coming to set up camp, of that he was sure. They had already prepared positions farther down the mountain. It would be food they were after. Two months earlier, in October, he had walked six miles to Waritsuke Village on the Kamamuta looking for salt, taking mushrooms to exchange for it. The village was in an uproar. Soldiers had been there requisitioning rice and horses. Since then he had known it would be only a matter of time before they reached their greedy hands into the mountains. He called his daughter and with her help and Kakizaki's quickly spread the word to the scattered households that two-thirds of their winter food store was to be taken into the forest and hidden.

"Why only two-thirds?" Kakizaki had complained. "Why not all?"

"Do you think they're stupid enough to suppose we've nothing to eat?" Mikuni answered. "If they find the storerooms empty they'll begin to wonder what happened to our winter provisions."

"I have never regretted speaking up for you for nushidori last year," Kakizaki said admiringly.

When Mikuni returned from spreading the word he found his wife busy at the fire pit, heating water in the iron teakettle.

"What are you up to now?" he asked.

"When the soldiers come I'll be nice to them and give them tea," she said. "Then perhaps they'll leave us in peace."

Mikuni sighed.

"Put the kettle away," he said quietly. "If you're so anxious to let them know we're aware of their coming we'll put out banners to welcome them."

Mrs. Mikuni gave him a blank look.

"It's better that they believe they've taken us unaware," he explained.

"If you say so," Mrs. Mikuni said.

She put the kettle away and returned to her weaving. It had been more than half a year since the representative of the spinning company had come to buy the raw silk from the cocoons and Mikuni, deciding he might never come again, had instructed her to make it into cloth. Good cloth was almost as precious as rice these days, and very negotiable.

When the soldiers reached the charcoal kiln outside the hamlet, Ikemiya, the kiln tender, ran into the hamlet to announce their arrival. He did not do so secretively. As instructed by Mikuni he shouted out his news as if he had been the first to see the visitors. Mikuni came hurrying out of his house to meet them, adjusting his coat as if he had snatched it up hastily. The soldiers had stopped at the buraku do, which like Mikuni's house was near the center of the hamlet. The do was an opensided thatch-roofed wooden structure housing a Kwannon image and the hamlet bulletin board. The man on the horse had gotten down and was reading the bulletin board. He was an officer. The other, a sergeant, held the horse's reins. Mikuni's apprehension increased when he saw the officer. He was not accustomed to dealing with anyone of such high position. An officer would certainly see through his deception and he would no doubt be carted off to prison. He ran up to the officer, bowing profusely as he approached. He resisted an impulse to throw himself at the officer's feet, confess all, and beg for mercy. It would not do for the people of the hamlet to see their nushidori behave in such a fashion. Instead he introduced himself and tremulously invited the visitors to enter his humble house to warm themselves and take tea, which his wife was preparing at that very moment.

The officer was surprisingly civil. He declined Mikuni's invitation with many expressions of regret. There was important business to be got through first. He produced a pair of documents and showed them to Mikuni. One was from the Army, authorizing him to levy on the hamlet for such supplies as he considered appropriate and ordering full cooperation. The other, from the office of the village of which the hamlet was a constituent, was a list of all the households in the hamlet. The officer requested Mikuni to verify the list and conduct him and the sergeant to every household.

"It is as much for your buraku's benefit as for mine," he said. "It will get things over with more quickly. And you'll be in a position to assure yourself all is being done fairly and properly."

The sergeant had shown signs of increasing impatience. It was obvious he considered the exchange of courtesies and the officer's assurances a waste of time. His face, like the officer's, was drawn and worried but there was a hint of smoldering anger in it. The officer's face seemed to reflect an ineffable sadness. Mikuni began to be glad the officer had come. He would not relish dealing with a man such as the sergeant.

They visited every household in the hamlet. The sergeant made a list of all the food in each storeroom, picking up bags and baskets to estimate weight and even counting the onions and radishes. His face grew harder and angrier as the skimpiness of the tally became evident. The officer's face grew sadder. When the inventory was completed, the officer said he would now be pleased to accept Mikuni's kind invitation to drink tea in his house.

The officer and the sergeant warmed their hands at the fire pit before Mikuni conducted them to the zashiki, the best room in the house. The sergeant withdrew to take his tea at a respectful distance from the officer. The honor of entertaining an officer in her house dazzled Mrs. Mikuni. Before Mikuni could stop her she had brought out pears and pickled plums, onions and radish. The officer would think they were rich and had even more than they had hidden in the woods. But the officer understood that Mrs. Mikuni had merely been carried away. Though he seemed quite hungry, he took only enough to be polite. The sergeant gobbled everything put before him. The officer finished his second cup of tea and put the cup down with a sigh.

"Your hamlet is very poor," he said.

"Yes," Mikuni said. "Very poor. Even before the war we were always poor. Life is difficult in the mountains."

"Yes, I know," the officer said. "I was born in the mountains myself. In a hamlet like this one."

Mikuni was surprised. He would not have thought it possible for someone from such a place to become an officer. But it explained the officer's sympathetic manner.

"In the north," the officer said in a reminiscent tone. "It was even more difficult than here. In winter the snow was as high as the roof."

Mikuni shook his head.

"Terrible," he said.

He would have liked to offer the officer shochu and would have done so if the sergeant had not been there. The sergeant was already suspicious and if he learned they had shochu would imagine all sorts of other things. The officer inclined his head imperceptibly toward the sergeant and said in a low voice, "He doesn't understand people like us. He's from the city. Nagoya."

Mikuni was immensely flattered that an officer would put him in his own category.

"That's true," he said. "City folks don't understand mountain people at all. For that matter, neither do the flatland rice farmers. They say we're ignorant and drink too much."

The officer tired abruptly of the exchange of confidences.

"I'm afraid I'll nevertheless have to take some of your provisions," he said, businesslike but still courteous. "The Army's seriously short of rations."

Mikuni looked down at the straw mat on which he was kneeling and said nothing.

"Half, I'm afraid," the officer said.

That was not catastrophic, Mikuni thought. With what they had hidden in the forest and the yams and daikon still in the ground they might be able to get through the winter somehow. But it would be wise to protest. They would grow suspicious if the hamlet accepted the loss of half its scanty food supply with equanimity. He wondered if he had really deceived the officer. The officer was from the mountains and knew the ways of mountain folk. If he did not protest, the officer certainly would insist on investigating further. For all his having been raised in the mountains he was still a soldier with a duty to perform.

"Half!" Mikuni cried, trying to express shock without, however, appearing to question the officer's authority.

"Watch your tongue!" the sergeant said angrily.

Mikuni bowed until his forehead touched the mat. "I apologize humbly," he said. "We have so little as it is. I don't see how we'll get through the long, hard winter."

"Hard, perhaps," the officer said mysteriously. "But not long." He looked at Mikuni as if wondering whether to say more. He looked at the sergeant.

"See if you can find an empty storeroom," he ordered. "Have everyone bring their levies and see that they don't try to hold anything back."

The sergeant saluted and left. The officer held out his cup for more tea.

"The Americans will be here in another month at most," he said. Mikuni was stunned. He had no idea the war was going so badly. He occasionally got news secondhand from other hamlets in the mura where there was electricity and therefore a radio or two. Though the Americans had made great gains in terms of territory it was said to be at such great cost that it was only a question of time before they sued for peace.

"Yes," the officer said, as if to himself, "the war is not going at all well."

"They say if the Americans win they'll kill all the men or make slaves of us," Mikuni said, deeply troubled. "And the women—Tell me, sir, do you think that is so?"

The officer shrugged. "Who can say what Americans will do," he said. "I have heard that in some places they've fed the people and dressed their wounds and in others behaved like savages."

"Then possibly it is so?" Mikuni asked, persisting because he wanted to hear an answer with his own ears from someone in a position of authority.

"I don't know," the officer said, getting to his feet. "I'll see how Teramoto is getting on."

Mikuni ran after him to the barn where the sergeant was checking off on his tally sheet the food being brought from every house in the hamlet. There was rice in straw bags, millet, barley, taro, radish, yams, mushrooms, onions, carrots and potatoes. Everyone looked properly sullen. That pleased Mikuni. They could not have looked more reluctant or resentful if the Army actually was taking half of all they possessed. Three family heads tried to contribute less than their allotment but were undone by the sergeant's inexorable tally sheet. He boxed their ears for their dishonesty and lack of patriotism. The officer made no move to stop him. It did not enter Mikuni's mind that the officer should. He would have liked to box a few ears himself. What the hamlet had done with its food was a simple and acceptable matter of self-preservation. This was blatant dishonesty. Worse, their selfishness, when everything had gone so well, could ruin them all. But when his fear and anger subsided he realized that in the long run it was for the best. This attempt at petty deception, like the general air of sullenness, almost certainly would dispel any lingering suspicion the soldiers might have.

When everything was put away the sergeant shut the barn door and put an already prepared sign on it. "For Military Use." He did not lock or seal the barn in any way. Now that the food stores were officially designated military property it was inconceivable that anyone would touch so much as an onion. The officer had walked up the path and climbed on his horse while the sergeant was putting up the sign. Mikuni walked along beside the horse as far as the last house. The officer reined in and without looking down at him said, "We'll send for the provisions in due time."

Mikuni, who was finding it extremely difficult not to tremble with relief, expected him to ride off then but the officer lingered.

"I'll catch up with you in a moment, Teramoto," he said.

He waited until the sergeant was out of earshot.

"I said things I should not back there," he said. "Perhaps because your hamlet reminded me of home. Don't repeat what I said to anyone. Not even your wife. Understand?"

Mikuni nodded and bowed.

"One other thing," the officer said, looking off into the distance "Someone else will be coming for the provisions. In two or three days at most. I'd leave things hidden for the time being. They might decide to search the houses again."

He rode away without looking back. Mikuni began shaking so violently he thought he would fall to the ground. He had led the hamlet close to disaster. Only the miracle which had sent such a sympathetic officer had saved it. To give himself time to recover he sat down and pretended to remove a pebble from his sandal. As he walked back to his house many people came out to express their thanks and congratulate him on the success of his scheme. Normally, Mikuni drank praise as the desert drank water. Now he was almost indifferent to it. It was not because he knew he did not deserve their praise, that fate had saved the hamlet, not his scheming. Only he in all the hamlet knew that and he would have been willing to accept their compliments as if deserved. What made him indifferent to the praise and not jubilant like the others were the things the officer had said. It no longer seemed so important that they had saved a few bags of rice and a handful of yams. They might not even survive to eat the food they had risked so much to protect. A hard winter but not a long one, the officer had said. The deeper implications struck him. If the Americans won, it was not just the hamlet that would be destroyed. It would be the whole Japanese nation. That was unthinkable.

People were flocking to the path from all over the hamlet. Mikuni's return to his house became a triumphant procession. Now they were praising him to one another for his modesty as well as his cunning. They spoke in tones calculated to reach his ears. He began to cheer up a bit. The officer might be wrong about the way the war was going. He was only a lieutenant and the news on the radio came from generals, and even the premier, who spoke for the Emperor himself. It might even be treasonable to pay any heed to the officer. It put one in the position of questioning the Emperor. And as for his plan succeeding only because the officer had been sympathetic, there was another side to that coin. The officer had been sympathetic because he was a mountain man himself. But he had only seen through the scheme for that very same reason. One stroke of fate canceled out the other. If the officer had been city bred, like the sergeant, and even as callous as the sergeant, the plan would have succeeded just as well. Or so Mikuni convinced himself.

He cleared his throat loudly for attention. Everyone grew respectfully silent. Though he was the nushidori by their own choice they did not always show him such unqualified respect. Yes, Mikuni thought, the officer most certainly had been mistaken. He was rather weak, anyhow, when one thought about it, to have permitted his good nature to interfere with his duty as a lieutenant in the Army.

"It isn't reasonable to expect now they've stolen our food they'll let it sit here," he said. "They'll no doubt be coming for it shortly. Within a day or two at most, I'd say."

Everyone nodded in agreement but appeared to be wondering what he vas getting at. It pleased Mikuni that none of them was wise enough to anticipate his point. That made him appear all the more cunning.

"When they come," he said, as if thinking deeply, "it wouldn't surprise me if they made another search. So let's not be too hasty about bringing things back from the woods."

Everyone expelled breath audibly and exchanged admiring looks. The air was filled with murmured compliments. Mikuni considered prolonging his triumph by inviting a few special cronies into the house to celebrate over shochu. He decided against it reluctantly. It might create jealousy and hard feelings to single out only a few and he could not afford to entertain the head of every household in the hamlet. And drinking might loosen his tongue to the point where he let something slip. Instead he thanked them all for their cooperation and complimented them on the cleverness with which they carried out his plan.

"It would not have succeeded without the help of everyone," he said modestly.

After they left in the gathering dusk he thanked the stone Jizo in the front yard for protecting his house, prayed before the Amida scroll in the butsudan, knelt and clapped his hands at the household Shinto shrine and, for good measure, went into the kitchen and paid his respects to the sooty wooden Daikoku image. It was dark now. The wall screens had been slid closed and a pine root was blazing smokily in its holder in the daidokoro, the living room. Kerosene had grown so dear they almost never lit the lamp any more. Fortunately there were plenty of roots, which were full of resin and burned like flares. It was the only good thing that had come out of the hamlet's unpaid labor of the year before, when the government had set everyone to work digging up pine roots in the forest. The government had set up a new industry to extract shokon oil from them and thus make Japan independent of petroleum, which had to be brought from conquered lands a great distance away. By the time they were permitted to stop digging, the hamlet had piles of the twisted roots. No one came to take them away and after a while the people began using them, sparingly and surreptitiously at first and then as they pleased.

Mikuni had his wife heat water and give him a good scrubbing in the bathhouse. Though it was a cold day he had sweat as much as if he had been felling trees, which was one of his winter occupations. After he had soaked as long as he liked he went back to the house and Mrs. Mikuni had her own bath. Before his daughter took his grandson for their bath he had her fetch a bottle of shochu from its hiding place in the compost heap. After supper he sat up drinking long after the others went to sleep. It was better to celebrate alone than not to celebrate at all. He did not replenish the pine roof holder but drank by the light of the fire pit, dropping in handfuls of twigs from time to time. The bare room was almost cozy beneath the thatch.

Instead of enhancing his mood the shochu drowned it. The officer's words returned to haunt him. A hard winter but not a long one. The war was not going well for Japan. The Americans would be here in another month. And when they came they would rape and kill as everyone said. The officer had not been reassuring on that point. True, he was only a lieutenant, but the generals and Mr. Suzuki, the premier, were in Tokyo. It was rumored nothing remained of Tokyo but a few palace buildings and hovels more miserable than these mountain houses. What a pity. He had never been to Tokyo, nor expected to—he had never been farther from the hamlet than Miyakonojo, thirty kilometers away by the bus that went through Takaharu—but it had been something in which to take pride, sitting there in all its wealth and splendor. The officer was closer to the fighting and perhaps had knowledge of things the government in Tokyo did not. If not, why would he have said such things? Certainly not to frighten a simple mountain peasant. The question was perhaps not whether the Americans would come or not but what was to be done when they came. One could run off into the mountains or stay and fight them. But in the mountains there would be only lingering death from cold and hunger, and resistance might goad them into even worse barbarities than rape and murder. No, when they came it would be better to die swiftly and with as little pain as possible. He would not permit them to lay their bloody hands on his grandson or his wife or his daughter. If the Americans came, when the Americans came, he would know what to do. He went reeling across the room and groped in the darkness until he found the large knife with which his wife sliced the daikon for pickling. He was annoyed to find she had allowed its edge to grow dull. He began to sharpen it, feeling like a samurai.

He slept late the next morning and awakened ashamed of his gloomy drunken thoughts. Heaven would preserve his family, the hamlet and the Emperor, just as it had preserved their winter food. His wife had put the knife away. She thought it odd that he had sharpened it without the usual nagging but thanked him for his thoughtfulness without further comment. Mikuni was relieved when she did not pursue the subject, as she too often did. He was deeply embarrassed when he recalled his pretensions while sharpening the knife. Eiji Mikuni, son and grandson of poor farmers and woodcutters, a samurai, indeed.

The following day, soldiers came for the requisitioned stores. They came quietly, at dawn. As Mikuni predicted, they made another search of houses and storerooms. From the stealth of their arrival and their chagrin at finding the inventory unchanged it was obvious they had expected to find a good deal more. Mikuni enjoyed a second day of triumph. This time, without anyone having to say anything, Mikuni's cronies assembled at his house for a quiet celebration. They came one at a time, after dark, each bringing his own bottle of shochu and a little something to nibble during an evening of drinking. Mikuni and his cronies were donen, men of the same age. They had all been born in the hamlet and grown up together and been in the same class at primary school. They sat up until late, exchanging drinks in the thimble-size choko and, after a while, singing. They made no attempt to keep their voices down. The houses in the hamlet were far apart and even if they were heard, those who had not come to the party could be counted on to pretend they were unaware of it. It was the first party of any kind in the hamlet for some time and everyone was enjoying himself until Ikemiya, the charcoal burner, had the poor taste to mention the war. Ikemiya was like that. He was unlucky in everything he did and in his middle age had been reduced to felling trees and making charcoal for a Kobayashi capitalist. It had made him understandably bitter.

"You'd think soldiers had better things to do with themselves than steal the food of poor men," he grumbled. "Anyhow, if the Army has captured all those stores from the Americans as they say, what does it want with our few potatoes?"

His complaint interrupted a jolly rendition of the bawdy "My Old Lady Is a Woman" and put a damper on the party.

"Be quiet, Ikemiya," Mikuni scolded. "It's not your place to question the Army."

Ikemiya had only said what Mikuni and the others believed but it was Mikuni's obligation as titular host and as nushidori to discourage such talk. And besides, he did not like hearing his own dark thoughts put into words. Seeing that his reprimand had set his old friend to sulking, Mikuni handed his own cup to Ikemiya and filled it with shochu.

"Drink up," he commanded. "Come on, everyone. 'The Country Headman.' "

Everyone exchanged drinks and began singing, clapping their hands in unison, but the glow was gone. They began speaking of the war and wondering if the Americans would admit defeat before it became necessary for the hamlet's volunteers to be called up.

"It will never come to that," Hatayama said firmly. "The Yankees will get no closer than Miyakonojo if they get that far. They're saying in Tokyo that Miyakonojo will be Japan's second Tennozan."

Hatayama had connections in hamlets where there was electricity and always knew, or pretended to, the latest reports that came over the radio. He had been nushidori before Mikuni and was, by hamlet standards, rich. He owned three acres of terraced fields and a charcoal kiln. Until soy beans became scarce his wife had made and sold tofu. He had, ostentatiously, worn a silk kimono to the party. True, it was homespun, but no one else there wore such finery. No one, even Mikuni, who resented Hatayama's airs more than the others because Hatayama sometimes behaved as if he thought he was still nushidori, thought to mention the fact that beginning with the Philippines there had been any number of second Tennozans. And still the Americans kept coming.

Mikuni was tempted to repeat what the officer had told him and reveal Hatayama for the fool he was but he held his tongue. He would not betray the officer's confidence and anyhow he had no intention of airing such defeatist opinions. That was treason and the authorities might have ears even in such a small mountain hamlet. He would not put it past Hatayama himself to inform on him even though they were donen.

"Tell us, Mikuni," Hatayama said, as if reading his thoughts and looking boldly into his face, "what did that snobbish officer have to say on the subject? It was rather obvious how you kept him to yourself the entire time he was here."

"He did not condescend to honor me with his opinions," Mikuni said uneasily.

"I suppose you were so busy talking he never had an opportunity to open his mouth," Hatayama said.

None of the others, though tipsy, was rude enough to laugh at Hatayama's sally. He was not well-liked.

"He spoke quite freely," Mikuni said.

"Of what, then?" Hatayama demanded.

"For one thing," Mikuni replied, "of how well the buraku appeared to be managed. He was most complimentary on that point."

Hatayama looked disconcerted.

"And for another," said Mikuni, pursuing his advantage, "of the excellence of Mrs. Mikuni's plums. He swore they were the best he had eaten this side of Kumamoto City. The officer was an authority on such things. Tokyo bred, you know."

That finished Hatayama. He left soon after although the cold rain was falling in sheets and he had not finished the shochu he had brought. The others finished their bottles and left as soon as the rain moderated.

Mikuni's spirits picked up a bit after his victory over Hatayama and for a while he almost believed the officer had actually said the things he reported to his cronies. When his shochu and his friends were gone and the twigs guttered in the fire pit, his spirits fell again and he was plunged into gloom. What was one to believe, anyhow? The government in Tokyo said one thing and those close to the fighting said another. Hatayama, who was no fool for all his airs, believed the official reports. But Ikemiya, who was wise in the ways of adversity, believed the opposite. If the Americans were so near to collapse why was it necessary for the Army to take food from the mouths of the people? He took what comfort he could from the fact that in whatever direction the truth lay there was nothing he could be expected to do about it. And as for making a decision about what to do if worse came to worst, that could wait until the worst came. If one could lighten one's heart by emptying one's mind it was better to be a poor peasant than a scholar.

Mikuni was so successful at emptying his mind of depressing notions that he thought little of the war for the next two weeks. His mind was occupied with more pressing matters. There were disputes which only the nushidori could settle, the last of the taro and yams to be got in, firewood to be cut and, with the help of Kakizaki, a leaky place in the thatch to be mended. All that changed two days before the official New Year. The hamlet did not celebrate the official New Year, holding to the old ways in which the first month of the lunar year came in February on the new calendar. A detail of soldiers came with the mura headman to muster the hamlet's volunteers and march them away. It was only then that Mikuni learned Miyakonojo had fallen the previous week and the Americans had scarcely paused to catch their breath before pushing north.

After the volunteers departed, the few men left in the hamlet lingered at the buraku do, stamping their feet in the cold and breathing plumes of vapor. Mikuni had established a reputation for wisdom and cunning with his handling of the food crisis and now they turned to him for comfort and advice. All except Hatayama, who was for once at a loss for words and contented himself with looking as if he could tell everyone what they should do if only they had the good sense to ask him instead of Mikuni. Mikuni did not have the faintest notion what to tell them. He was as frightened and confused as anyone. For just a moment he wished Hatayama was still nushidori. Having no advice to give, he grew very angry and told everyone they were behaving like women.

"The Americans will never get this far," he said with more conviction than he felt. "You'll see. And if something should go wrong, I'm not saying it's possible but if it should, I'll have a plan to fit the occasion." Everyone went home feeling better except Hatayama and Mikuni himself. That night he got out the last bottle of shochu, waiting until his wife and daughter had gone to bed and fetching it himself. He drank only half, not wishing to leave himself completely without resources should a serious crisis present itself later on. He tested the edge of his wife's knife and though it was still keen, sharpened it some more. He did not feel like a samurai. He felt like a frightened old man.

In no more than a week's time the guns of the Americans were heard along the Kamamuta River only five miles away, in the valley at the foot of Mount Takachiho. The shells falling in the forest below the hamlet caused it no damage but filled everyone with apprehension. During the night the apprehension turned to naked fear when moans and piteous cries were heard on the path leading into the hamlet. It was thought to be an omen of doom, or at the very least the spirit of a fox trying to lure the more reckless among them out to investigate. Mikuni lay trembling like the others, trying to shut his ears to the dreadful sound. His wife mumbled prayers beside him in feverish horror and his grandson, little more than a baby, wailed in terror. His daughter, whose concern for her child mitigated her own fear, was the first to realize the sounds came from a human throat and not a spirit. Mikuni, forcing himself to listen carefully, was inclined to agree. But what was a man doing on the path in the chilly darkness, filling the night with his cries? He was the nushidori and it was his duty to investigate. He crawled reluctantly from the sleeping quilts and put on his coat.

"What do you think you're doing?" his wife demanded, her teeth chattering so he would not have understood her had he not known her voice so well.

"There's someone out there who needs help," he said, trying to be matter-of-fact.

"Don't you dare go out!" his wife cried, sitting up. "It's an evil spirit. If you value your soul don't you dare go out."

"It's a man," Mikuni said, as much to convince himself as his wife.

"Yes," said his daughter, who was more modern than either of them and who scoffed at some of the old beliefs. "Shall I come with you, Father?"

"What should I want with you?" he said gruffly. "Your place is with my grandson."

All the same, he was proud of her spirit and when he was outside, with the moans and cries louder in his ears, would not have minded if she had come along. There was a man lying in the snowy path just the other side of the do. The night was dark but he was visible against the whiteness. His arms and legs moved as if he were trying to reach the shelter of the do. The moans came with every breath, the cries at measured intervals. Though it was too dark to see details even after Mikuni reached his side, he knew the man was a soldier.

"Are you badly hurt?" he asked.

The soldier stopped moaning at once.

"I think so," he said in a weak but surprisingly calm voice. "I'm sorry I disturbed you."

The realization that someone had heard him moaning seemed to embarrass him.

"I'll just get you in out of the cold," Mikuni said.

The soldier shrieked when Mikuni tried to pick him up. Mikuni let him fall back in the snow.

"It's my belly," the soldier said apologetically. "Where the shrapnel went in it's very tender."

Mikuni put his hands under the soldier's armpits and dragged him backward up the path toward his house. When he stopped once to catch his breath he called out, "Everyone go back to sleep. It's only a wounded soldier."

He said it not so much to reassure those living close enough to hear the cries as to let them know he had not been too frightened to investigate. When he reached his house the wall screen slid back and his daughter came out to help him lift the soldier onto the porch. When they got him into the daidokoro and stretched out beside the fire pit Mikuni's daughter threw a handful of twigs on the fire. The soldiers trousers and shirt front were dark with blood but there was not as much as one might have expected. He wore a sash of a thousand stitches, which was bloody, too. Instead of Army boots he had on jikatabi, one toe of which was torn away. His leggings were still neatly wrapped though the rest of his uniform was torn and rumpled. There were short straggly black whiskers on his chin, upper lip and cheekbones. His eyes shone brightly in deep, dark pits. Mrs. Mikuni came creeping out of the sleeping room. The fear in her face turned to pity.

"He's only a boy," she said.

"Put the kettle on and we'll wash him off," Mikuni said.

"I don't want to be any trouble," the soldier said in a weak voice.

Mikuni's daughter filled the kettle and hung it on the iron hook over the fire pit. Mrs. Mikuni unwound the soldier's sash, commenting on the fineness of the stitches.

"I'll wash it for you in the morning," she said.

With her help Mikuni removed his tunic, shirt, breeches and winter underwear. He seemed embarrassed to be lying before them clad only in fundoshi. Mrs. Mikuni washed the blood off his belly with gentle hands. The hole was a small one, just below the navel. Blood oozed out drop at a time. It was very dark, almost black.

"Would you like water?" Mikuni asked.

"I ate snow," the soldier said. "They say you shouldn't have water with a belly wound."

He propped himself up on his elbows with a half-suppressed groan and looked at himself.

"It's not very big, is it?" he said, surprised. "I thought my whole stomach had been blown away."

"Does it hurt very much?" Mikuni asked.

The soldier shook his head, the pain in his eyes belying his gesture. Mikuni filled a cup with shochu and held it to his lips. The soldier gulped it down and went into a paroxysm of coughing. A gobbet of blood oozed out of the wound with each cough. He lay back exhausted and Mrs. Mikuni wiped the blood away with a wet cloth.

"What place is this?" he asked.

When Mikuni told him it was obvious it meant nothing to the soldier.

"How far is it from Haraigawa?" he asked.

"Three and a half kilometers," Mikuni said.

"So far? They were taking me there but I got away from them. It's just a place to die. No food or medicine, they say."

"You shouldn't waste your strength talking," Mikuni's daughter said.

She covered him with a sleeping quilt. He fell silent a while, then began talking again, as if it eased him to do so.

"We're surrounded, you know," he said. "Two American columns have joined north of us at Kobayashi. One from the south and the other from the west. They say the Americans kill everybody." He looked at Mikuni's daughter. "And worse," he added.

His eyes closed after a while and he began breathing heavily, moaning occasionally. Mikuni did not know if he had lost consciousness or was only sleeping. The wound did not look too serious though one had no way of knowing the state of things inside. He had once seen a horse punctured in such a manner for bloat and within two days the animal was working in the fields again.

In the morning the soldier was much weaker. The wound was more serious than it appeared. Mikuni had not slept all night, thinking of what the soldier had told him. If they were surrounded there was no hope of escape. And what had occurred in Kobayashi confirmed his worst fears. The time was at hand when he must reach a decision. He still had not made up his mind when people began gathering in the snow around his house. They were curious about the events of the previous night. Mikuni came out and told them what he had learned. The crowd was swept by panic, with everyone shouting at once, demanding to know what should be done. Mikuni could think of nothing to tell them. Hatayama said that he and his wife were taking all they could carry and going into the mountains, where the Americans could never find them if they searched a thousand years. He urged everyone to do the same. That made up Mikuni's mind for him.

"It's bitter cold higher up without shelter," he said. "And who has food for a thousand years? Or even a thousand hours? Things could still take a turn for the better. We must remain where we are. We were born here, and our fathers and our fathers' fathers."

He was surprised and impressed by his own eloquence. So was everyone else except Hatayama.

"And if things do not take a turn for the better?" Hatayama demanded. "What will happen to us then?"

"Then we will die like true Japanese," Mikuni shouted, carried away by his newfound determination. "Not like dogs."

Nevertheless, Hatayama left the hamlet that very day, and with him three other families. Only twenty-eight persons remained and these more because they were paralyzed by indecision than inspired by Mikuni's words. Only Ikemiya, the charcoal burner, seemed unperturbed. He was almost cheerful. Things had happened as he had said they would and for once his misfortune was no greater than that of anyone else.

The soldier grew weaker. The hole in his belly stopped bleeding plugged by a hard black crust. He took no food and was often unconscious. Sometimes he moaned or called for his mother or someone named Sachiko. Though it was depressing, Mikuni was grateful for his presence. Tending to the soldier gave his wife something to do and kept her mind off her own troubles.

The day after Hatayama left there was much firing and shouting in the forest below the hamlet and soon afterward soldiers began streaming up the path. They went through the hamlet toward the top of the mountain without stopping. Mikuni ran alongside one group begging for information. They were withdrawing to the crest for a final stand, he was told. The Americans were not far away. Two families followed the soldiers up the mountain. There were only twenty-two souls left in the hamlet, not counting the dying soldier. They waited fearfully in their houses.

Mikuni drank the last of the shochu. His wife drank one cup with him. His daughter did not join them. She sat with his grandson in her lap, telling him stories to amuse him. The firing stopped. Far down the slope, among the trees, voices shouted in a foreign tongue. Mikuni sat up very straight and listened. He felt an almost overpowering urge to gather up his family and run after the soldiers. But he could not do that, not after persuading the others to stay. The shouting revived the soldier. He struggled up on one elbow and listened.

"The Americans are here," he said in a voice so low Mikuni had to place his ear at the soldier's mouth to hear him. "Have you a knife?" Mikuni rose and brought the knife with which his wife sliced the daikon. The soldier took the handle in both hands and put the point against his neck just below the chin. Mikuni sent his wife and daughter to the sleeping room with his grandson. The soldier was so weak he could not force the knife into his throat. He gave Mikuni a pleading look.

"Please," he whispered. "Help me."

Mikuni was reluctant. He had never killed a man or even an animal larger than a hare. The shouting came nearer.

"Please," the soldier whispered desperately.

Mikuni went to the soldier without rising from his knees. He placed his hands over the soldier's and pushed. The knife went in so easily he was taken by surprise. The soldier must have been extremely weak. Blood spurted up along the blade and some of it splashed Mikuni's hands. The soldier did not utter a sound. His head fell back and his eyes stared blankly at the ceiling. It was not that difficult to kill after all, Mikuni thought. And the soldier's determination strengthened his. Only the blood disturbed him. He did not want to see the blood of his grandson or of his wife and daughter. It was necessary for them to die before the Americans reached the hamlet but it would not be by the knife. He unclasped the soldier's hands from the handle and laid the knife on the mat beside the body. He prayed a moment at the butsudan, asking forgiveness. Then he rose and went slowly to the sleeping room to do what he must.

The Imperial Rescript of January 14, 1946

To Our Good and Loyal Subjects:

After pondering deeply the general trends of the world and the actual conditions obtaining in Our Empire today, We have decided to effect a settlement of the present situation by resorting to an extraordinary measure.

We have ordered Our Government to communicate to the Government of the United States, Great Britain, China and the Soviet Union that Our Empire accepts the provisions of their Joint Declaration.

To strive for the common prosperity and happiness of all nations as well as the security and well-being of Our subjects is the solemn obligation which has been handed down by Our Imperial Ancestors, and which We lay close to heart. Indeed, We declared war on America and Britain out of Our sincere desire to ensure Japan's self-preservation and the stabilization of East Asia, it being far from Our thought either to infringe upon the sovereignty of other nations or to embark upon territorial aggrandizement. But now the war has lasted for more than five years. Despite the best that has been done by everyone—the gallant fighting of military and naval forces and brave volunteers, the diligence and assiduity of Our servants of the State, and the devoted service of Our hundred million people, the war situation has developed not necessarily to Japan's advantage, while the general trends of the world have all turned against her interest. Moreover, famine and pestilence reach into every corner of Our Sacred Homeland, taking the toll of many innocent lives. The thought of those officers and men who have fallen in the fields of battle, those who have died at their posts of duty, or those who met with an untimely death and all their bereaved families, pains Our heart night and day. The welfare of the wounded and the war sufferers, and of those who have lost their homes and livelihood, are the objects of Our profound solicitude. Should We continue to fight it would not only result in the ultimate collapse and obliteration of the Japanese nation but would also lead to the total extinction of human civilization. Such being the case, how are We to save the millions of Our subjects, or to atone Ourselves before the hallowed spirits of Our Imperial Ancestors? This is the reason why We have ordered the acceptance of the provisions of the Joint Declaration of the Powers.

The hardships and suffering to which Our nation has been subjected have been great and hereafter will certainly be greater. We are keenly aware of the inner feelings of all of ye, Our subjects. However, it is according to the dictate of time and fate that We have resolved to pave the way for a grand peace for all the generations to come by enduring the unendurable and suffering what is insufferable.

Having been able to safeguard and maintain the structure of the Imperial State, We are always with ye, Our good and loyal subjects, relying upon your sincerity and integrity. Beware most strictly of any outbursts of emotion which may engender needless complication, or any fraternal contention and strife which may create confusion, lead astray and cause ye to lose the confidence of the world. Let the entire nation continue as one family from generation to generation, ever firm in its faith in the imperishableness of its divine land, and mindful of its heavy burden of responsibilities, and the long road before it. Unite your total strength to be devoted to the construction of the future. Cultivate the ways of rectitude; foster nobility of spirit; and work with resolution so as ye may enhance the innate glory of the Imperial State and keep pace with the progress of the world.

The 14th day of the 1st month
of the 21st year of Showa

Afterword

John Ray Skates

When I first read David Westheimer's *Lighter than a Feather*, I had just begun writing *The Invasion of Japan: Alternative to the Bomb*, after years of research into the plans to invade Japan in 1945. At the beginning I approached the novel mainly as a curiosity and, I must admit, with an academic historian's condescension toward fiction. I expected to find a "fact-based" story only loosely set in a sensationalized or romanticized invasion of Japan. After finishing *Lighter than a Feather*, I called Mr. Westheimer to compliment him on the novel's historical accuracy. He has the context for his novel exactly right. Recently, after rereading the book, I am even more impressed with its historical accuracy—not only in the broad scheme of the invasion of southern Kyushu but in the subtleties and tactical details of Operation Olympic.

The planned invasion, code named Olympic, provides the context for Westheimer's story and the focus of the historical Prologue, which he advises should be read before the novel. In addition, the Prologue tells the story of the struggle within the Japanese government over ending the war and speculates on the outcome if no atomic bombs had been dropped, if the war had continued, and if the invasion of southern Kyushu, in fact, had been launched. In the Prologue, the description of the American plans for the invasion of Japan is historically accurate; the imaginative scenario for Olympic had the war not ended is plausible; and the assumptions and conclusions are based on real historical assessments and are driven by real probabilities.

In the novel itself Westheimer traces the fortunes of several individuals, both American and Japanese, who are caught up in the greatest invasion of the war. Although Olympic never occurred, plans and preparations were well underway when the war ended. Westheimer's novel realistically captures the complex scheme of the operation and its complicated phasing. The myriad military details, both Japanese and American, of the underwater demolition teams, rocket and mortar-firing LSTs, Japanese weapons and defensive tactics are as accurate as any historian's account. Westheimer also reveals detailed and accurate geographic information about southern Kyushu.

Westheimer has a sophisticated knowledge of Japanese defenses. He gets Japanese defensive strategy and tactics exactly right, and Japanese units are correctly identified and accurately positioned. Had the battle occurred, as American forces approached the landing beaches they would have been set upon by kamikaze planes, manned torpedoes, and suicide boats. After the Americans succeeded in running this gauntlet, they would have faced bunkers on the beaches. On the first high ground behind the beaches, battalion-sized cave defenses were positioned to dominate both the beaches and the beach exits. The description of Lieutenant Colonel Tochizawa's battalion defense position and of the defense of that position on pages 177–218, is more vivid than any historian could make it.

Similarly, Westheimer captures the questionable physical condition of the Japanese defenders. The Homeland Army was raised in three mass conscriptions in the spring of 1945. These drafts enlisted old men, young boys, and others who had been deferred for physical or other disabilities. Westheimer correctly describes the supply and communications problems that afflicted this army. The Japanese soldiers would have fought the battle with whatever was on hand, and they were short of food, weapons, and ammunition, especially heavy anti-tank guns and artillery. Expecting neither resupply nor retreat, they would have died in place, as do Westheimer's fictional Colonel Tochizawa and his entire battalion.

If Westheimer correctly assesses Japanese military strategy, he is equally accurate in his assessment of the larger issues of Japanese national strategy. He understands the basic dilemma faced by Japan's leaders over whether the climactic battle should be fought in southern Kyushu or in the Kanto Plain. If resources were held back from Kyushu to defend the Kanto, Kyushu would undoubtedly fall. If all resources were devoted to Kyushu, Kanto would certainly be doomed. As indicated by the actual influx of troops into southern Kyushu in May, June, and July 1945, the Japanese had chosen to fight the climactic battle in southern Kyushu and to worry about the Kanto Plain later. In reality, the decision meant that if Kyushu fell, Japan would be doomed. Therefore, Westheimer believes, as I do, that

Operation Coronet, the invasion of the Kanto Plain, would never have taken place. In the novel Japan surrenders on January 14, 1946, after the fall of southern Kyushu.

Westheimer correctly depicts a Japan in November 1945 that is far nearer to defeat than America realized. The U.S. Navy had only to breach the Straits of Tsushima to complete the naval blockade. The major cities had been burned out by fire bombing. The U.S. carrier fleet ranged unopposed up and down the east coast, and the country's internal transportation network was near complete collapse. The rail system was failing under allied bombing and fuel shortages; intercoastal shipping was immobilized by mines; Japan's cities faced imminent starvation. Nonetheless, Japan's military leadership chose to fight on, counting on Japanese "spirit" to deal the Americans such a blow that unconditional surrender would be softened. Westheimer captures precisely this delusion among Japanese military leaders. "Japanese spirit," they predicted, would overcome scarcities of weapons, ammunition, food, fuel, transport, communications, lack of a navy and of trained soldiers and airmen. Japanese "spirit" would overwhelm the "mere abundance and technology" of the "faint hearted" Americans.

If the great weight of U.S. combat power and nearly limitless resources had been pitted against the dug-in Japanese defenses and meager Japanese resources in Operation Olympic, there can be little doubt of the outcome. In fact, the Japanese leaders themselves had no doubts about the outcome; they hoped only to kill enough Americans to gain more favorable surrender terms. For their part, the Americans—having recently experienced the worst casualties of the Pacific war at Luzon, Iwo Jima, and Okinawa—were clearly worried about casualties. After the war, principally to justify the use of the atomic bomb against Japan, Truman, Churchill, and Stimson all argued that an invasion of Japan would have cost 500,000 to 1,000,000 casualties.

In his fictional description of the progress of Operation Olympic, Westheimer refuses to repeat that largely discredited myth of an all-consuming cataclysmic struggle producing unprecedented casualties. His picture of the progress and costs of Olympic roughly parallels my own study of the invasion (or, perhaps, my study parallels his). U.S. military estimates for Olympic casualties would have compared roughly with losses in D-Day and the Normandy campaign.

The target date for Operation Olympic was 1 November 1945, but on 9 October a vicious typhoon swept over Okinawa and southern Kyushu and forced delay of the operation. Historians have argued about the length of that delay. Westheimer puts the delay at only twelve days. A similar conclusion was reached in a postwar Pentagon staff study. In Westheimer's novel, Olympic is launched on 12 November with successful beach assaults on all three target beaches—Ariake Wan, Miyazaki, and Kushikino.

Over the next thirty days, progress is slow and costly as U.S. infantrymen and tanks breach the beach defenses and laboriously reduce the Japanese cave defenses in the high ground behind the beaches. Westheimer's description of operations and combat in the first thirty days of Olympic is historically sophisticated, plausible, and based solidly in U.S. plans. On X+30, U.S. forces have achieved their initial objectives. Casualties are high but not unprecedented. Battle casualties total 53,000 with 14,000 of those killed or missing. By X+48 the three separate beachheads have been linked up, and U.S. casualties have risen to 71,000 with 17,500 of those killed. These numbers of casualties parallel the first forty-eight days after D-Day, when General Omar Bradley's First U.S. Army suffered 63,360 casualties, 16,129 of whom were killed. By X+48, organized Japanese resistance is limited to a final bastion in the Kirishima Mountains of central Kyushu. U.S. occupation and base building in southern Kyushu are already well underway.

David Westheimer published *Lighter than a Feather* in 1971 at a time when many young revisionist historians were questioning much about the end of the war with Japan, especially the necessity for using the atomic bomb. Furthermore, many of the sources that have been available to me, like Ultra materials, were still classified in 1971. Nonetheless, Westheimer's history of Operation Olympic and the end of the Japanese-American war rings true. The tenacity and "spirit" of Japanese defenders personified by characters like Colonel Tochizawa would have been pitted against the irresistible weight and power of American resources. Westheimer correctly puts Japanese casualties in Olympic far higher than American losses.

Had Olympic taken place, the campaign would probably have progressed much as it does in Westheimer's novel. From my study of the invasion of Japan, I can assure readers of this new edition, titled *Death Is Lighter than a Feather*, that while Operation Olympic never occurred and the characters in the novel are fictional, the events in the novel parallel the American plans for Olympic and the Japanese plans for Ketsu-Go. *Death Is Lighter than a Feather* is a good novel; it is also very good history.

John Ray Skates is author of *The Invasion of Japan: Alternative to the Bomb*, professor of history and past chair of the History Department at the University of Southern Mississippi, and has also served as a Visiting Professor at the Air War College.

Shelters in cliff at Yunomoto, northeast of Akasaki,
mentioned in Lester Waddell episode.
(Photos courtesy of author)

Cleft in ridge south of Kushikino near Akasaki, locale of Miho Naito episode, with seaward observation post and firing positions; overlooks Beach Studebaker.

Interior of cleft.

Bunker at Kanoya Naval Air Base.

Rear view of revetment at Kanoya Naval Air Base.

Entrance to civilian shelter at Shibushi showing side tunnel.

Firing positions, western base of Shibushi hill.

Aka Point, east of Shibushi, locale of Rentaro Yoshida episode.

Beach Cord, south of Miyazaki City, locale of Aaron Bibb episode.

Sendai River looking north, north of Kurino, locale of
Zenji Wada/Robert Vaccarino episode.

Typical southern Kyushu farm hamlet.

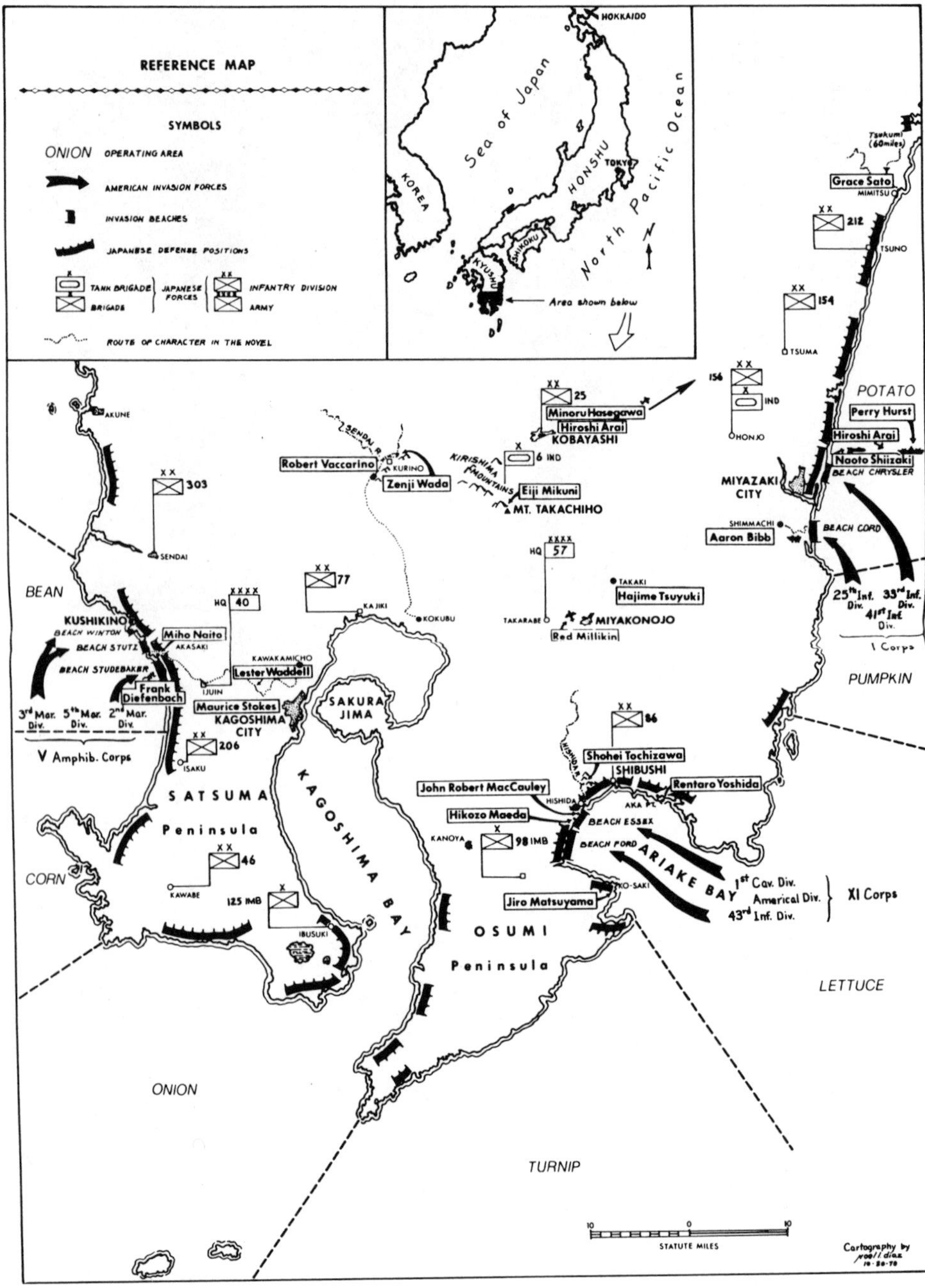
REFERENCE MAP
SYMBOLS
ONION OPERATING AREA
AMERICAN INVASION FORCES
INVASION BEACHES
JAPANESE DEFENSE POSITIONS
TANK BRIGADE
BRIGADE
JAPANESE FORCES
INFANTRY DIVISION
ARMY
ROUTE OF CHARACTER IN THE NOVEL
HOKKAIDO
Sea of Japan
KOREA
HONSHU
TOKYO
SHIKOKU
KYUSHU
North Pacific Ocean
Area shown below
Tsukumi (60 miles)
Grace Sato
MIMITSU
212
TSUNO
154
TSUMA
156
IND
HONJO
POTATO
Perry Hurst
Hiroshi Arai
Naoto Shiizaki
BEACH CHRYSLER
MIYAZAKI CITY
SHIMMACHI
Aaron Bibb
BEACH CORD
25th Inf. Div.
33rd Inf. Div.
41st Inf. Div.
I Corps
PUMPKIN
25
Minoru Hasegawa
Hiroshi Arai
KOBAYASHI
6 IND
KIRISHIMA MOUNTAINS
Eiji Mikuni
MT. TAKACHIHO
HQ 57
TAKAKI
Hajime Tsuyuki
TAKARABE
MIYAKONOJO
Red Millikin
SENDAI R.
KURINO
Robert Vaccarino
Zenji Wada
KOKUBU
AKUNE
303
SENDAI
BEAN
77
KAJIKI
HQ 40
KUSHIKINO
BEACH WINTON
BEACH STUTZ
BEACH STUDEBAKER
Miho Naito
AKASAKI
KAWAKAMICHO
Lester Waddell
Frank Diefenbach
IJUIN
Maurice Stokes
KAGOSHIMA CITY
SAKURA JIMA
3rd Mar. Div.
5th Mar. Div.
2nd Mar. Div.
V Amphib. Corps
206
ISAKU
SATSUMA Peninsula
KAGOSHIMA BAY
86
Shohei Tochizawa
SHIBUSHI
John Robert MacCauley
HISHIDA
Rentaro Yoshida
AKA PT.
Hikozo Maeda
BEACH ESSEX
BEACH FORD
KANOYA
98 IMB
ARIAKE BAY
1st Cav. Div.
Americal Div.
43rd Inf. Div.
XI Corps
KO-SAKI
Jiro Matsuyama
CORN
46
KAWABE
125 IMB
IBUSUKI
OSUMI Peninsula
LETTUCE
ONION
TURNIP
STATUTE MILES
Cartography by noel l. diaz